AN EXEGETICAL SUMMARY OF
MALACHI

To my wife Annie in grateful thanks
for her unflagging support and encouragement for me in
this project, and to our four children,
Sarah, Adam, Helen Marie, and Charlotte,
with the prayer that they, like the sons of Levi,
"will become for YHWH bringers of offerings in
righteousness" (Mal. 3:3).

AN EXEGETICAL SUMMARY OF
MALACHI

James N. Pohlig

Summer Institute of Linguistics

© 1998 by the Summer Institute of Linguistics, Inc.
ISBN: 1-55671-079-8
Library of Congress Catalog Card Number: 98-61751
Printed in the United States of America

Summer Institute of Linguistics, Inc.
7500 West Camp Wisdom Road
Dallas, TX 75236

INTRODUCTION TO PERSPECTIVES ON THE BOOK OF MALACHI AND TO THIS EXEGETICAL SUMMARY

1. Exegetical perspectives on Malachi

The aim of this section is to allow the reader to roughly situate in their various theoretical orientations the authors of the sources which are used in this exegetical summary. To this end, there are here presented perspectives which have dominated O.T. interpretation, with emphasis upon their aspects which are most relevant to the book of Malachi.

1.1 The traditional perspective

This view holds essentially that Israel's priesthood was established by Moses and persisted without much change throughout her history. This priesthood was held by Aaron's descendants, with the rest of the tribe of Levi serving as assistants in the rituals of Israel's worship of YHWH. The relevant OT terminology, however, is variable: 'priest' is limited to Aaron's line; 'Levite' may refer either in general to any member of the tribe or to the non-priestly element of the tribe. When Ezekiel writes of the 'sons of Zadok', he might be trying to limit the priesthood to this particular branch of Aaron's descendants, condemning the other branches for their unfaithfulness to YHWH's covenant. There is certainly no idea that Zadok himself might have actually been non-Israelite, as Julius Wellhausen supposed (see below) [O'Brien]. The traditional perspective views Malachi as a unity composed at one time, or, if consisting of various parts written over a period of time, at least the work of the same author.

Much cited in this exegetical summary is Carl Friedrich Keil's commentary on Malachi in *The Twelve Minor Prophets*, which stands squarely in the traditional perspective. A conservative Jewish voice is heard in *The Twelve Prophets*, edited by A. Cohen.

There is no doubt that much scholarship which emanates from the traditional perspective or which supports elements of it has arisen as reaction to the Graf-Wellhausen Documentary Hypothesis (see below) and has been honed by its opposition toward it. In this category stand Joyce G. Baldwin's *Haggai, Zechariah, Malachi: An Introduction and Commentary*, Pieter A. Verhoef's *The Books of Haggai and Malachi*, and Eugene H. Merrill's *An Exegetical Summary: Haggai, Zechariah, Malachi*.

1.2 The Graf-Wellhausen hypothesis and the historical-critical perspective

In the Graf-Wellhausen-inspired historical-critical model, the effort to identify various strands of OT textual material is carried out, not only to discover the stages of the OT's presumed redaction, but also in order to deduce the presumed development of Israel's institutions, e.g., the prophetic office, the monarchy, and the priesthood. Studies of Malachi within this model have therefore naturally centered both on the documentary traditions represented in the book, and on the question of how Malachi views Israel's priesthood.

Because the historical-critical perspective still dominates the scholarly field, one needs to understand it in order to read even moderately in OT studies, as much as to appreciate its opponents' arguments as those of its proponents. Those knowledgeable of historical-critical claims and concerns may well opt to skip this part of the introduction; the less experienced, are on the other hand, are invited to read on.

The effort to identify various strands of textual material in the Pentateuch was first made in the 17th century in the thinking of one Campegius Vitringa. Jean Astruc of the 18th century adopted as one of his source-identifying criteria the variation in divine names between *Yahweh* and *Elohim*. Astruc also was struck by the apparent duplication of Creation accounts and Flood accounts. He posited that Moses himself had synthesized his sources in writing the Pentateuch.

Many further efforts to identify Biblical sources were made during the later 18th century and early 19th century, under the influence of positivism. For example, W.M.L. De Wette in 1807 posited that the D document was the "book of the law" discovered by Josiah and which became the driving force of the ensuing reform of Israel's worship [Harr].

It fell, however, to Julius Wellhausen of the late 19th and early 20th centuries to systematize an enormous body of theory around what is called today the Documentary Hypothesis. Wellhausen presented an elegant and comprehensive theory which embraced a vision of disparate oral traditions becoming gradually codified and then coalescing into the OT which we know today, together with a far-reaching account of the development of Israel's institutions. Wellhausen's *Prolegomena to the History of Israel*, published in 1878 and coinciding with theories of evolution in the realms of natural history and socio-economy, presented a developmental or evolutionary model of the OT and of Israel's institutions, which proved very attractive to much of the scholarly world. In a sense, Wellhausen's model defined the parameters of OT scholarship for the next century: exegetes either supported it, wished to modify it, or opposed it [O'Brien].

Wellhausen combined De Wette's developmental viewpoint with the thinking of Wilhelm Vatke, who posited a post-exilic finalization of the Pentateuch. Adopting K.H. Graf's hypothesis that Israel's ceremonial laws had developed over a great span of time and that the priestly interests which appeared to be promoted in the Pentateuch came in fact from documents of very late origin in Israel's history [Harr], Wellhausen posited four separate traditions as the sources of four documents or "codes"—the Yahwistic (J) (placed in the 9th century B.C.), the Elohistic (E) (placed in the 8th century B.C.), the Deuteronomist (D) (dated at Josiah's time, c. 640-609 B.C.), and the Priestly (P) (placed around the 5th century B.C.) [Harr]. Thus J was held to be the earliest document and the one which underlay the early history of Israel, that which described the lives of the patriarchs, etc. E was subsumed into the J document by a redactor. D was held to be the essential document arising from King Josiah's reform of Temple worship. P was added to the other documents after the Exile, bringing more precision to the ritual requirements of Israel's worship [O'Brien]. Thus the Pentateuch (or, more precisely, the Hexateuch—for the book of Joshua was seen as having arisen from the same process) became considered a product of the late nation of Israel, and in no way Israel's foundational documents [Harr]. Similarly, Wellhausen dismissed completely any patriarchal antecedents of the nation of Israel, including, of course, the effect of any patriarchal monotheism or monotheistic tendency. He held instead that Israel's monotheism was the result of a long development from crude polytheism of the Canaanite sort, and that the stimulus for this development had been the work of the OT prophets. Likewise, Wellhausen denied any central worship place in Israel before Josiah's reform [Harr].

Because comment on Malachi within the historical-critical perspective has been very concerned to discover Malachi's view of the priesthood, it is desirable to sketch here the development of the priesthood as seen by Wellhausen. He posited that Israel had no true priesthood, charged with performing sacrifices, before the reign of King Josiah. Instead, one performed sacrifices for himself, such as Samuel, Elijah, and the kings did. The so-called priests, whose function began with the creation of places of sacrifice and worship in Israel, took care of bringing oracular word of YHWH to inquirers. They assumed the title of Levites and gave themselves legitimacy by claiming descent from the patriarch Levi, whose line in reality was almost defunct [O'Brien].

In Wellhausen's view, the priesthood became enormously more organized and powerful with the creation of the monarchy. The 'levitical' priesthood, however, suffered a great setback when David dismissed Abiathar from the high priesthood and substituted Zadok, who was probably Jebusite. In this way, Zadok's line came to hold the real priestly power, with the 'levitical' priesthood relegated to rural shrines [O'Brien].

The 'levitical' priesthood gained a theoretical triumph some centuries later when Josiah, in reforming Temple worship, decreed through the D document that the 'levitical' priests would henceforth be equal to the Zadokite priests. The rural shrines were, however, done away with [O'Brien].

But in fact, a practical equalization did not occur. The Zadokites retained their power at the expense of the 'levitical' priests, who became unemployed. No longer able to work in the rural areas, they were kept out of the central sanctuary in Jerusalem. Wellhausen held that Ezekiel sanctioned this condition, saying that such was the punishment of God against the unfaithful 'levitical' priesthood. Ezekiel in effect grafted the Zadokites into the line of Levi in order to legitimatize them [O'Brien].

After the Exile, the Zadokite priesthood became even more secure and less answerable than ever to the people. During this time, the P document was superimposed on J and D, seeking to add legitimacy to the Zadokite priesthood by calling these priests the 'sons of Aaron'. I and II Chronicles retell the history of Israel's monarchy from this point of view [O'Brien].

In the century following the publication of Wellhausen's *Prolegomena*, other theories have transformed his model, often in radical ways. O'Brien lists, however, five cardinal points which the majority of scholars in the historical-critical perspective hold. (1) The priesthood did indeed develop over the centuries. (2) P reflects a later development of the priesthood than does J— although the date of J is disputed. (3) At an early stage of the priesthood, all the Levites were considered members of the priesthood. (4) The Jerusalem monarchy was the occasion for the centralization and the empowerment of the priesthood--although the exact way in which this took place is disputed. (5) P provides for a more restricted group to serve as priests than the entire tribe of Levi—although the identity of this group is disputed [O'Brien].

It has become traditional within the historical-critical perspective to consider that Malachi reflects fairly exclusively the D documentary tradition— a view shared by Smith of the Word Biblical Commentary—because much of Malachi's vocabulary is consistent with that of the D elements in the Pentateuch. It is then inferred that Malachi did not know of P, an ignorance which would then date P as having been developed after Malachi, i.e., after c. 450 B.C. [O'Brien].

Does Malachi equate "priests" with "the sons of Levi"? Some who answer "yes" to this question then infer that Malachi did not know P, which is said to make the sons of Aaron superior to the other Levites. Others, including Glazier-McDonald, answer "yes" also, but posit that Malachi did indeed know of P and that by this time the Aaronide priestly line had become completely and exclusively identified with the Levitical priesthood. Still other scholars, including O'Brien, also hold that Malachi equates the priests with the sons of Levi, and have pointed out that Malachi has some vocabulary reminiscent of P. For this and other reasons, O'Brien concludes that, far from falling within any one documentary tradition, Malachi not only knew of P, but also had access to some kind of D-P integration, perhaps an early version of the Pentateuch, or perhaps the Pentateuch in its final form; she also concludes that no development of the priesthood can be discerned in Malachi [O'Brien].

In the course of its development, the Documentary Hypothesis came under heavy attack. In 1823, H. Ewald, for example, defended the unity of Genesis, although he did posit that Moses employed various sources in writing the book. Franz Delitzsch defended the Mosaic authorship of the all portions of the Pentateuch which are explicitly attributed to him in the text. Reference must also be made to the work of C.H. Gordon, who in the early 1960's criticized the Graf-Wellhausen Hypothesis as being out of touch with ancient Near Eastern cultural reality. Gordon concluded that in their cultural milieu, the ancient Hebrews were able to rely much more on written texts for the long-term transmission of knowledge than had been thought possible by historical-critics, who stressed the primacy of oral traditions. Gordon also took the important step of associating the characteristics of an Hebrew "heroic age" with those of the ancient Greek Heroic Age as reflected in Homer and other texts. Gordon concluded that the Pentateuch was based on many written sources [Harr].

Important inferences arising from the Graf-Wellhausen Hypothesis, many of which play a large part in the resulting evolutionary view of Israel's institutions, have also come under attack. For example, W.F. Albright opposed the theory that the office of the High Priest in Israel developed only as the centralized monarchy grew in power. Albright pointed out the existence of high priests both in Egypt at Karnak and elsewhere, and at Ugarit, a Canaanite city-state. The latter's title, *rabbu kahinima* 'chief of the priests', affords so excellent a cognate to the Hebrew כֹּהֵן *kōhēn* 'priest', that Wellhausen's attempt to derive *kōhēn* from Arabic seems entirely superfluous [Harr].

Frequently, scholars have opposed important inferences arising from the Graf-Wellhausen Hypothesis without calling into question the documentary core of the Hypothesis itself. Standing prominently among exegetes in this category is the Jewish Yehezkel Kaufmann, who accepted the Hypothesis in general, but who posited as fundamental to the Hebrew nation and her culture a monotheistic worldview arising from a very early date [Harr]. Another example is that of A. van Hoonacker, who endorsed a theory of documentary origins of the Pentateuch, but who at the same time espoused Mosaic authorship of it [Harr].

In short, many scholars consider the Graf-Wellhausen Hypothesis and its classic corollaries to be in shreds, but feel frustrated by the large mainstream of scholarship which still holds to it, perhaps more out of the lack of a theory worthy to replace it than out of enthusiasm for it. Kaufmann wrote:

> Both the evidence and the arguments supporting the structure [of biblical criticism] have been called into question and, to some extent, even rejected. Yet biblical scholarship, while admitting that the grounds have crumbled away, nevertheless continues to adhere to the conclusions. The critique of Wellhausen's theory which began some forty years ago has not been consistently carried through to its end. Equally unable to accept the theory in

its classical formulation and to return to the precritical views of tradition, biblical scholarship has entered upon a period of search for new foundations. (Y. Kaufmann, *The Religion of Israel*, translated by Moshe Greenberg. 1960, p. 1; cited in Harr)

Cited regularly in this exegetical summary are studies of Beth Glazier-McDonald and Julia O'Brien, both of whom work within a historical-critical framework. Unlike Glazier-McDonald's *Malachi: The Divine Messenger*, O'Brien's *Priest and Levite in Malachi* is not a commentary; rather, this work seeks to discover whether Malachi can be placed within the historical-critical debate concerning the development of Israel's priesthood, and concludes that it cannot so be placed. Another much cited source is *Micah-Malachi* of Ralph L. Smith, who appears to give some credence to historical-critical findings.

Frequently cited as a secondary source is J.M.P. Smith's *Malachi* of the International Critical Commentary. Smith is a good example of a turn-of-the-century American commentator who is much steeped in historical-criticism.

1.3 The discourse or textlinguistic perspective

Discourse analysis, which has recently developed in the field of linguistics and is now beginning to make its presence felt in Biblical studies as well, constitutes the third perspective represented in this volume. One effect of its application to OT studies has been to challenge the historical-critic's methodology, objecting perhaps most urgently as follows: if the historical-critic insists on dismantling the very Biblical texts which the discourse linguist wishes to analyze, then discourse analysis has no further object of study [personal communication from Robert E. Longacre; see also his "The Flood Narrative: The Discourse Structure of the Flood Story" and "Interpreting Biblical Stories", both in *The Journal of the American Academy of Religion*, xlvii.1 (Supplement, March 1979, 89-133). In the former article, Longacre's analysis of the discourse-level organization of the Hebrew text of the Flood Narrative excludes the hypothesis of documentary strands in the narrative].

Within the realm of Malachi studies, the discourse perspective challenges certain long-held historical-critical conclusions regarding the document's unity. More dramatically, it calls into question the entire historical-critical enterprise of tracing the development of Israel's priesthood, since this enterprise is based on inferences arising from the application of historical-critical methodology to the Pentateuch and to the historical books. For if discourse analysis questions the methodology, then it also must cast doubt upon the validity of the historical-critic's main concerns in the book of Malachi.

The discourse or textlinguistic perspective seeks to understand Biblical Hebrew grammar by taking into account whole "texts", transcending the limit of the sentence, which had traditionally defined the boundaries of Biblical Hebrew grammatical studies. The discourse perspective includes the identification and analysis of discourse genres and their features, the characteristics of the various parts of each genre (e.g., episodes and peaks in narration), as well as the analysis of discourse-determined roles played by various verb forms, word orders, and particles; it also treats the identification of the conventions of participant reference. In addition, thematic phenomena of the discourse and of its paragraphs are treated, as well as principal and subsidiary development (Christo H.J. van der Merwe, "Discourse Linguistics and Biblical Hebrew Grammar", in *Biblical Hebrew and Discourse Linguistics*, ed. by Robert D. Bergen; Dallas, Texas: Summer Institute of Linguistics, 1994; also Robert E. Longacre, "The Structure of the Flood Narrative", in *The Journal of the American Academy of Religion*, 1979 (?)).

Discourse studies of Biblical Hebrew hold forth the promise of explaining many apparent discontinuities in the texts, not as the products of different source texts brought together by a redactor, but as legitimate devices belonging to their Hebrew genres (see Randall Buth, "Methodological Collision Between Source Criticism and Discourse Analysis: The Problem of 'Unmarked Temporal Overlay' and the Pluperfect/Nonsequential *wayyiqtol*", in *Biblical Hebrew and Discourse Linguistics*, ed. by Robert D. Bergen; Dallas, Texas: Summer Institute of Linguistics, 1994).

Representative of the discourse perspective in this exegetical summary is Ewell Ray Clendenen's *The Interpretation of Biblical Hebrew Hortatory Texts: A Textlinguistic Approach to the Book of Malachi*, in which the author applies the features of R.E. Longacre's hortatory genre to Malachi. These features include the crucial "notional structure" or "deep structure" of hortatory discourse, which Longacre characterizes as the *situation*, that which needs changing, or the problem which needs a solution; the demanded or encouraged *change*, which is encoded by commands or exhortations; and the *motivation*, the impetus for change, which is addressed to the audience of the discourse. Among these three elements, it is the change element which is naturally the most prominent in hortatory discourse [Clen].

This approach is liable to identify textual units which are rather novel in comparison with the units adduced by other commentators, and Clendenen does not disappoint in this regard. Equally important is his analysis that the so-called appendix or appendices to Malachi (Mal. 4:4-6 (3:22-24)) in fact comprises the final change element in his "third movement" in the structure of Malachi. The reader is allowed to infer, then, that the many arguments marshaled by others in favor of these verses' identity as appendices are moot.

From Clendenen's analysis of the textual chunking of Malachi, as well as from his view of the structure of the thematically prominent features of the book, the observer is led to a principal theme emerging from O.T. discourse studies, hinted at above by Buth but here made perhaps more explicit: it is no good for the discourse linguist to try to analyze only the shreds of dismembered text left behind by historical-critics, after they have sundered apart the MT by their documentary strand theories. In many cases, the text which has been thus destroyed would have been capable of demonstrating elegant organization under the careful application of discourse analysis (see R.E. Longacre, *Interpreting Biblical Stories*, in Teun A. van Dijk (ed.), *Discourse and Literature: New Approaches to the Analysis of Literary Genres*. John Benjamins Publishing Co., Philadelphia, 1985).

It is also pertinent in this section to mention Julia O'Brien's *Priest and Levite in Malachi*, not because O'Brien works within a discourse perspective, but because she applies the concept of the ancient covenant lawsuit (the ריב *rîḇ*) to the entire book of Malachi.

2. Literary characterization of Malachi

2.1 Identification of the literary genre of Malachi

There is a variety of views as to the best way to characterize the literary genre of Malachi.

(1) Malachi has the form of a speech to an audience, with occasional, 'rhetorical' responses from the audience. The result is sometimes called 'pseudo-dialogue' [M.L. Larson, *The Functions of Reported Speech in Discourse*. 1978. Dallas: Summer Institute of Linguistics; and R.E. Longacre, *The Grammar of Discourse. Topics in Language and Linguistics*. 1983. New York: Plenum Press; cited in Clen].

(2) Malachi's style is that of teaching by conversing with his audience, a style informed by Ezra, who introduced this method of teaching the law [KD].

(3) Malachi's style is that of a series of disputes, certainly more stylized than the disputes which are found in Jeremiah 2:23-25, 29-32 or Micah 2:6-11 [MDM, NICOT, WBC; Wen], and which, unlike the writings of his predecessors, form the backbone of the book's structure [TOTC]. This style became common in Jewish literature of a later period [NICOT].

(4) Malachi has the form of a ריב *rîḇ*, an ancient near-Eastern lawsuit against covenant breakers [O'Brien]. This genre in ancient Near Eastern literature usually has the following form:
1. Preliminary matters.
2. The judge interrogates the prisoner, hurling at him damning questions which are unanswerable.
3. The judge delivers the indictment of covenant breaking.
4. The judge declares the prisoner guilty, usually reminding him that his crimes will not be atoned for by ritual acts.
5. The judge pronounces the curses which were originally invoked as a threat against covenant breaking when the covenant relationship was assumed in the past.

6. The judge gives a final ultimatum to induce the prisoner to remedy his covenant breaking.

[J. Harvey, *Le plaidoyer prophétique contre Israël après la rupture de l'alliance. Etude d'une formule littéraire de l'Ancien Testament.* Scholasticat de l'Immaculée Conception. Paris: Desclée de Brouwer, 1967; cited in O'Brien.]

2.2 Viewpoints on the dialogues between God or his prophet and the audience in Malachi

1. Probably the dialogues never actually occurred; instead, the prophet almost certainly put into words the thoughts which he saw reflected in the people's attitudes and actions [NICOT, TOTC].
2. Many of the dialogues could very well have occurred as various incidents in the prophet's ministry. Later they would have been written down and edited, thus acquiring a literary polish [Gla].

2.3 The prose/poetry debate of Malachi

1. Malachi is poetry [Gla], often of a lower quality than some of the preceding prophets, altough many of Malachi's lines possess rhythm and parallelism [WBC].
2. Malachi is prose which occasionally features poetic effects [J.M.P. Smith, *A Critical and Exegetical Commentary on the Book of Malachi.* International Critical Commentares. 1912. Edinburgh: T.& T. Clark; cited in Clen, NICOT].
3. Malachi is prose of an elevated style, possessing many poetic characteristics [Clen], and often creating a poetic effect [Mer].

3. The format of this exegetical summary

3.1 Discourse units

Discourse units of the text of Malachi are noted according to the viewpoints of various commentators and versions. As a general rule, this exegetical summary notes only those discourse units to which the commentators and versions have applied section headings. This policy is meant to provide an easy guideline to selecting only the major discourse units to be noted down. An exception to this rule has been in made in that the summary has noted also the major discourse units suggested by Ewell Ray Clendenen in his *The Interpretation of Biblical Hebrew Hortatory Texts: A Textlinguistic Approach to the Book of Malachi*, as well as by Beth Glazier-McDonald in her *Malachi: The Divine Messenger*. Neither of these works provides section headings; yet, it has been judged worthwhile to note their discourse units, particularly in the case of Clendenen, since much of the impact of his discourse perspective lies precisely in his suggested discourse units and the consequent phenomena of prominence and subordination in the text.

3.2 The semi-literal English translation

The semi-literal English translation of each verse will be found to be sometimes presented in a double or even triple manner. This is to enable a clear presentation of various textual readings and, more commonly, of various interpretations of the Hebrew syntax.

3.2.1 The presentation of preterite verb forms in the semi-literal translation

The form of Hebrew verb which traditionally has been called *waw conversive* or *waw consecutive* constitutes, in its "imperfect" form, the normal "event-line" verb form in Hebrew narrative texts. Today some circles refer to it as *preterite*, a practice which we follow in this Exegetical Summary for the reason given below.

Older viewpoints regarded the "imperfect" *waw* conversive as the "imperfect" converted into a functional "perfect" form by the prefixed *waw*; hence the term *waw conversive*. Such verb forms typically (but not exclusively) occur in sequences in narrative texts; hence the term *waw consecutive* for the same form.

A more contemporary viewpoint regards this verb form as having been historically distinct from the "imperfect" form. It subsequently became conflated morphologically with the "imperfect", with the further "frozen" addition of a *waw* prefix. This historically distinct form is termed *preterite*.

As has been stated, there is also a perfect verb form with a *waw* prefix, standing in a corresponding relationship with the preterite. This form functions as the principal verb form of predictive texts and is referred to in this volume as perfect *waw* consecutive. We meet both this form and the preterite in the book of Malachi.

In this volume's semi-literal English display of the text, often the *waw* prefix is tagged with a superscripted letter, so that this morpheme may be treated in the Lexicon below. For convenience, we also follow this practice with the occurrences of *waw* in preterite forms and in the perfect *waw* consecutives, e.g.,

וָאֹהַב אֶת־יַעֲקֹב *wā'ōhaḇ 'eṯ yaʿăqōḇ*
And[a]-I-have-loved Jacob (Mal. 1:2)

Although the term preterite implies that such occurrences of *waw* are morphologically different than the other occurrences of *waw*, yet the preterite forms are susceptible to many varieties of linkage and conjunctions in translation, and the translator will therefore be interested in such notes in the Lexicon.

3.2.2 The use of the hyphen in the semi-literal translation

Hyphens are used in the semi-literal presentation to separate various Hebrew morphemes which are bound in the same word, e.g.,

מידכם *miyyedkem*
from-your-hand (Mal. 2:13)

Hyphens are also used to separate semantic values in Hebrew words which are at least partially reflected in the English morphemes appearing in the translation, even though there may be no one-to-one correspondence between the English and Hebrew morphemes, e.g.,

נוכל *nôkēl*
one-cheating (Mal. 1:14)

where the semi-literal translation represents a Hebrew participle.

In cases where even stilted English word order requires the representation of a single Hebrew word to be broken up, a discontinuous hyphenated sequence of English words appears in the presentation, e.g.,

לא־ארצה *lō³ ³erṣeh*
I-will- not -accept   (Mal. 1:10),

where the verb *³erṣeh* would otherwise be represented by 'I-will-accept'.

3.2.3 The use of parentheses and the slashe in the semi-literal translation

Parentheses are employed to signal English words whose semantic values are judged to be implied in the Hebrew text, e.g., **(the-)table(-of) (the-)Lord** (Mal. 1:7), where the definite article is implied twice in English, and where the genitive relationship between *table* and *Lord* is signaled by (-*of*), here a reflection of the so-called construct state of the Hebrew noun *table*.

The slash (/) is employed to indicate two viable literal translations of a Hebrew word or of two different Hebrew textual readings, e.g., **how have-we-defiled-you/it** (Mal. 1:7).

3.3 The presentation of lexical items

Verbs are presented with the sense carried by a particular verb stem (Qal, Niphal, etc.). Thus, for example, under Mal. 3:1 is offered the following presentation:

j. 3rd mas. sg. Qal imperf. of בוא *bô³* [BDB p. 97], [Hol p. 34], [TWOT 212]: 'to come' [BDB; all commentators and versions save the following], 'to appear' [CEV], 'to arrive' [Hol].

In contrast, under Mal. 3:10 is found the following:

a. mas. pl. Hiphil imv. of בוא *bô'* [BDB p. 97], [Hol p. 34], [TWOT 212]: 'to bring' [all lexica, commentators and versions].

Two widely occurring Hebrew particles are presented in very neutral terms, with no effort to supply lexicon glosses. These particles are

    -ו *w'-*, presented as *waw* connective

and

    כי *kî*, presented as *kî* connective.

TRANSLITERATION KEY

Consonants

Letter	Heb	Tlit.	Pronunciation
Aleph	א	ʾ	glottal stop as in *uh'oh* or Cockney *bottle* [ʔ] (silent when word final)
Beth	ב	b̲	v as in *van* [v]
with dagesh lene	בּ	b	b as in *bell* [b]
with dagesh forte	בּ	bb	bb as in *job bill* [b·] (geminate)
Gimel	ג	ḡ	g as in *gate* (no distinction with g) [g]
with dagesh lene	גּ	g	g as in *gate* [g]
with dagesh forte	גּ	gg	gg as in *big gate* [g·] (geminate)
Daleth	ד	d̲	th as in *the* [ð] (voicedinterdental fricative)
with dagesh lene	דּ	d	d as in *door* [d]
with dagesh forte	דּ	dd	dd as in *sad dog* [d·] (geminate)
He	ה	h	h as in *heave* (silent when last letter in a word)
with dagesh, word final form	הּ	h̲	normally not pronounced (mappiq—a graphic distinction)
Waw	ו	w	w as in *well* (though quite possibly [β]) (voiced bilabial fricative)
Zayin	ז	z	z as in *zeal* [z]
with dagesh forte	זּ	zz	zz as in *whiz zoom* [z·] (geminate)
Heth	ח	ḥ	ch as in *loch* (a deep h back in throat) [ħ] (voiceless pharyngeal fricative)
Teth	ט	ṭ	t as in *tip* [t̩] (though possibly [tˤ] (voiceless pharyngealized stop)
Yodh	י	y	y as in *yellow* [y]
Kaph	כ	k̲	ch as in German *Bach* [x] (velar fricative)
word final form	ך	k̲	
with dagesh lene	כּ	k	k as in *king* [k]
with dagesh forte	כּ	kk	kk as in *track car* [k·] (geminate)
Lamedh	ל	l	l as in *liner* [l]
Mem	מ	m	m as in *mail* [m]
word final form	ם		
Nun	נ	n	n as in *noose* [n]
word final form	ן	n	
Samekh	ס	s	s as in *sell* [s]
Ayin	ע	ʿ	as in *aah* said for a doctor, but with h sound [ʕ] (voiced pharyngeal fricative) (silent word final)
Pe	פ	p̄	f as in *face* (though possibly [φ] voiceless bilabial fricative)
word final form	ף	p̄	
with dagesh lene	פּ	p	p as in *pet* [p]
with dagesh forte	פּ	pp	pp as in *scrap paper* [p·] (geminate)
Tsadhe	צ	ṣ	ts as in *cats* [ts] (though possibly [sˤ] voiceless pharyngealized velar fricative)
word final form	ץ	ṣ	

Qoph	ק	q	k as in German *kohl* [q] (uvular stop)
Resh	ר	r	r as in *rain* [r]
Sin (dotless)	שׁ	s̄	(graphic symbol) not pronounced
Sin	שׂ	ś	s as in *sell* [s]
Shin	שׁ	š	sh as in *shell* [ʃ]
Taw	ת	t̠	th as in *myth* [θ] (voiceless inderdental fricative)
with dagesh lene	ת	t	t as in *tall* [t]
with dagesh forte	ת	tt	tt as in *great teacher* [t·] (geminate)

Vowels

Letter	Heb.	Tlit.	Pronunciation
Pathah	-	a	a as in *bat* [æ] (or sometimes [a] as in *father*)
Pathah Hateph (reduced)	-:	ă	a said quickly as in *above* [ə]
Qamets	ָ	ā	a as the first a in *father* [a]
Qamets He	ָה	â	(consonant used with vowel) a as in *father*
Qamets Hatuph	ָ	o	o as in *bought* [ɔ]
Qamets Hateph (reduced)	ָ:	ŏ	a said quickly as in *above* [ə]
Shewa	:	ə	a said quickly as in *above* [ə]
Hireq	ִ	i	i as in *pit* [ɪ]
Hireq Yodh	ִי	î	(consonant used with a vowel) i as in *machine* [i]
Tsere	ֵ	ē	e as in *they* [e]
Tsere Yodh	ֵי	ê	(consonant used with a vowel) e as in *they* [e]
Tsere He	ֵה	ēh	(consonant used with a vowel) e as in *they* [e]
Seghol	ֶ	e	e as in *pet* [ɛ]
Seghol Yodh	ֶי	ệ	(consonant used with a vowel) e as in *they* [e]
Seghol He	ֶה	eh	(consonant used with a vowel) e as in *pet* [ɛ]
Seghol Hateph (reduced)	ֱ	ě	a said quickly as in *above* [ə]
Holem	ֹ	ō	o as in *bowl* [o]
Holem Waw	וֹ	ô	(consonant used with a vowel) o as in *bowl* [o]
Holem He	הֹ	ōh	(consonant used as a vowel) o as in *bowl* [o]
Qibbuts	ֻ	u	u as in *book* [ʊ]
Sureq	וּ	û	u as in *mood* [u]

ABBREVIATIONS AND REFERENCES USED IN THIS WORK

1. Commentaries

Mer   Merrill, Eugene H. *An Exegetical Summary: Haggai, Zechariah, Malachi*. Chicago: Moody Press, 1994.

Keil   Keil, Carl Friedrich. *The Twelve Minor Prophets*. Vol. 2. Translated from the German by the Rev. James Martin. Grand Rapids, Mich.: Eerdmans, 1969.

Ksr   Kaiser, Walter C., Jr. *Malachi: God's Unchanging Love*. Grand Rapids, Mich.: Baker, 1988.

TOTC   Baldwin. Joyce G. *Haggai, Zechariah, Malachi: An Introduction and Commentary*. London: Tyndale Press, 1972.

Coh   Cohen, A. *The Twelve Prophets*. New York: Soncino Press, 1985.

Gla   Glazier-McDonald, Beth. *Malachi: The Divine Messenger*. SBL Dissertation Series 98. Atlanta, Georgia: Scholars Press, 1987.

WBC   Smith, Ralph L. *Micah-Malachi*. (Word Biblical Commentary). Waco, Texas: Word Books, 1984.

NICOT   Verhoef, Pieter A. *The Books of Haggai and Malachi*. New International Commentary on the Old Testament. Grand Rapids, Mich.: Eerdmans, 1987.

II. Journal articles

Dddeuel   Deuel, David C. "'Book of Remembrance' or Royal Memorandum? An Exegetical Note." *The Master's Seminary Journal* 7 (1996), pp. 107–111.

Fischer   Fischer, James. A. "Notes on the Literary Form and Message of Malachi." *The Catholic Biblical Quarterly* (1972), pp. 315–320.

Fuller   Fuller, Russell. "Text-Critical Problems in Malachi 2:10–16." *Journal of Biblical Literature* 110/1 (1991), pp. 45–57.

Glazier-McDonald 2   Glazier-McDonald, Beth. "Malachi 2:12: 'er we'oneh—Another Look." *Journal of Biblical Literature* (1986), pp. 295–298.

Glazier-McDonald 1   Glazier-McDonald, Beth. "Intermarriage, Divorce, and the bat-'el nekAr: Insights into Mal. 2:10–16." *Journal of Biblical Literature* 106/4 (1987), pp. 603–611.

Jones   Jones, David Clyde. "A Note on the LXX of Malachi 2:16." *Journal of Biblical Literature* (1990), pp. 683–484.

Malchow   Malchow, Bruce V. "The Messenger of the Covenant in Mal. 3:1." *Journal of Biblical Literature* (1984), pp. 252–255.

Mckenzie   McKenzie, Steven L., and Howard N. Wallace. "Covenant Themes in Malachi." *The Catholic Biblical Quarterly*, 45 (1983), pp. 549–563.

Redditt   Redditt, Paul. L. "The Book of Malachi in its Social Setting." *The Catholic Biblical Quarterly*, 56 (1994), pp. 240–255.

Waldman   Waldman, Nahum M. "Some Notes on Malachi 3:6; 3:13; and Psalm 42:11." *Journal of Biblical Literature* (1974), pp. 543–549.

Wendland   Wendland, Ernst. "Linear and Concentric Patterns in Malachi." *The Bible Translator* 36 (1985) pp. 108–21.

III. English Versions

CEV	Contemporary English Version
KJV	Authorized Version
JPS	Ténékh (Jewish Publication Society)
NASB	New American Standard Bible
NIV	New International Version
NJB	New Jerusalem Bible
NLT	New Living Translation
NRSV	New Revised Standard Version
REB	Revised English Bible
TEV	Today's English Version

IV. Dictionaries and other resources

Hol	Holladay, William L., ed. *A Concise Hebrew and Aramaic Lexicon of the Old Testament*. Grand Rapids, Mich.: Eerdmans, 1988.
BDB	Brown, Francis. *The New Brown-Driver-Briggs-Gesenius Hebrew and English Lexicon*. Peabody, MA: Hendrickson, 1979.
Gesenius	Kautzsch, E., and A. E. Cowler. *Gesenius' Hebrew Grammar*. Oxford: Clarenden Press, 1910.
Harr	Harrison, Roland Kenneth. *Introduction to the Old Testament*. Grand Rapids, Mich.: Eerdmans, 1974.
O'Brien	O'Brien, Julia. *Priest and Levite in Malachi*. Society of Biblical Literature Series 121 (Dissertation Series). Atlanta, Georgia: Scholars Press, 1990.
Clen	Clendenen, Ewell Ray. *The Interpretation of Biblical Hebrew Hortatory Texts: A Textlinguistic Approach to the Book of Malachi*. Unpublished doctoral dissertation, 1989.

V. Other abbreviations

BH	Biblical Hebrew
BHS	Biblia Hebraica Stuttgartensia
constr.	construct relationship in BH
fem.	feminine
imperf.	the so-called imperfect tense in BH
imv.	imperative
inf.	infinitive
LXX	The Septuagint
mas.	masculine
MT	Masoretic text, including the vowel pointing
part.	participle
pass.	passive
perf.	the so-called perfect tense in BH
pl.	plural
prn.	pronoun
QUES	the Hebrew interrogative particle, which appears as a proclitic on the first Hebrew word in a yes-no question
sg.	singular

EXEGETICAL SUMMARY OF MALACHI

DISCOURSE UNIT: 1:1–5 [Ksr; NASB]. The topic is "a call to respond to God's love" [Ksr], "God's love for Jacob" [NASB].

DISCOURSE UNIT: 1:1 [Clen, Gla, Mer, NICOT, O'Brien, TOTC, WBC; CEV, NAB, NIV, NJB, NLT, NRSV, REB, TEV]. The topic is an introduction [Mer], the content, address, and instrument of the prophecy [NICOT], a heading [TOTC], the superscription, an identification of the source of this book [WBC].

1:1

(a) Oracle.[a] Word[b](-of) YHWH[c] to[d]-Israel[e] by[f]-(the-)hand(-of)[g] Malachi.[h]

(b) Oracle(-of)[a] (the-)word(-of)[b] YHWH[c] to[d]-Israel[e] by[f]-(the-)hand(-of)[g] Malachi.[h]

SYNTAX—Some consider that מַשָּׂא *maśśāʾ* 'oracle' stands in the Hebrew construct relationship with 'the word of YHWH', thus reading 'the oracle of the word of YHWH' (as in (b) above). Others see דְּבַר־יהוה *dᵉbar yhwh* 'the word of YHWH' as a specific restatement of the generic *maśśāʾ* 'oracle'.

LEXICON—a. מַשָּׂא *maśśāʾ* (BDB p. 672), (Hol p. 217), (TWOT 1421e): 'oracle' [BDB; NICOT; NASB, NIV, NRSV, REB], 'message' [NJB, TEV], 'pronouncement' [Hol; JPS], 'burden' [Coh, Keil, Gla, WBC; KJV], 'utterance' [BDB]. *Maśśāʾ* 'oracle' and דָּבָר *dābār* 'word' are conflated and translated 'message' [CEV, NLT, TEV]. *Maśśāʾ* denotes an extremely serious and important pronouncement [Keil, Gla, NICOT]. When applied to prophecy, it denotes an obligation which God has placed upon the prophet to prophesy [TOTC] and often connotes doom upon the objects of the prophecy [Ksr, Keil, Gla, TOTC].

b. constr. of דָּבָר *dābār* (BDB p. 182), (Hol p. 67), (TWOT 399a): 'word' [BDB, Hol; all commentators and versions except the following], 'message' [CEV, TEV], 'speech' [BDB].

c. יהוה *yhwh* (semi-transliterated as 'YHWH' in this volume) (BDB p. 217), (Hol p. 130), (TWOT 484a): 'Yahweh' (Gla; NJB], 'LORD' (TOTC; CEV, KJV, JPS, NASB, NIV, NRSV, TEV]. YHWH is the name of God [Hol]. The construct relationship between 'word' and YWHW is expressed as a phrase: 'the message that the LORD gave' [CEV, TEV]. This expression denotes a revelation of God [NICOT].

d. אֶל *ʾel* (BDB p. 39), (Hol p. 16), (TWOT 91): 'to' [BDB, Hol; all commentators and versions except the following], 'unto' [WBC], 'for' [CEV]. This preposition is also translated by a phrase: 'directed to . . .' [Gla]. The primary function of the preposition 'el is to indicate motion or direction to or towards something [BDB, Hol].

21

e. יִשְׂרָאֵל *yiśrāʾēl* (BDB p. 975), (Hol p. 145): 'Israel' [BDB, Hol; all commentators and versions except the following]. This noun is also translated by a more expanded noun phrase: 'the people of Israel' [TEV]. 'Israel' is the name of the nation as well as a personal name [BDB, Hol].

f. -בְּ *bə-* (BDB p. 88), (Hol p. 32) (TWOT 193): 'by' [WBC], 'with' [BDB]. The proclitic *bə-* denotes here instrument or means [BDB, Hol].

g. constr. of יָד *yād* [BDB p. 388], [Hol p. 127], [TWOT 844]: 'hand' [WBC]. The entire expression *bəyad* is translated 'by' [Coh, Gla; KJV, NRSV], 'through' [Mer, NICOT; JPS, NASB, NIV, NJB, REB]. *Yād* in its concrete sense denotes 'forearm' or 'hand', but here expresses agency; it frequently expresses instrumentality [BDB, Hol].

h. constr. of מַלְאָךְ *malʾāk* (BDB p. 521), (Hol p. 196), (TWOT 1068a): 'Malachi' (a personal name) [all commentators and versions]. The entire verse is translated 'I am Malachi. This is the message that the Lord gave me for Israel' [CEV], 'this is the message that the Lord gave Malachi to tell the people of Israel' [TEV], 'this is the message that the Lord gave to Israel through the prophet Malachi' [NLT]. *Malʾāk* normally denotes 'messenger' or 'angel' [BDB, Hol].

Question—What is the function of Mal. 1:1?

It is to provide a heading for the book [Keil, Gla] in order to introduce its message [all versions].

Question—What relationship does דְּבַר־יְהוָה *dəbar yhwh* 'the word of YHWH' have with מַשָּׂא *maśśāʾ* 'oracle'?

1. *Dəbar yhwh* 'the word of YHWH' is a specific restatement of the generic 'oracle' [TOTC; JPS, NJB, NJB, NIV, NRSV, REB]: 'An oracle: the word of YHWH to Israel.' TOTC argues for this position, saying that to understand the construct state here is to create a tautology with *dābār* 'word.' This position is probably taken also by CEV, NLT, TEV, which conflate *dəbar yhwh* and *maśśāʾ*: 'the message YHWH gave to Israel.'

2. *Maśśāʾ* 'oracle' stands in the Hebrew construct relationship with 'the word of YHWH', thus reading 'the burden of the word of YHWH' [Keil, Gla; KJV].

Question—What is meant by יִשְׂרָאֵל *yiśrāʾēl* 'Israel'?

Here 'Israel' denotes all of God's people, the covenant nation, the exiles and those who remained in the land [NICOT, TOTC, WBC]. Malachi stresses the 'New Israel', living a new cultic and covenantal life [WBC]. The use of 'Israel' here points ahead to the time when there will be but one people [Mer]. This term calls to mind YHWH's covenant dealings with the nation of Israel beginning with the selection of Jacob over Esau [Mer, p. 388].

Question—What is meant by מַלְאָכִי *malʾākî* 'Malachi'?

1. It is the personal name of the prophet Malachi [all commentaries and versions]. Malachi's name means 'my messenger'.

2. Many older and ancient commentators take *malʾākî* as an epithet denoting the prophet's work: 'my messenger' and that the book is anonymous [Coh]. LXX reads ἐν χειρὶ ἀγγέλου αὐτοῦ 'by the hand of his messenger', and the Targum reads 'by the hand of my angel whose name is Ezra the scribe'. The Talmud and some Church fathers follow this view. Some commentators in the past have conjectured that *malʾākî* is short for מלאכיה *malʾākiyyâ* 'Yah is my messenger' or 'messenger of Yah' [Keil].

3. Some commentators have argued that 'Malachi' cannot have been a proper name, for no Jewish father would have called his son that. The prophet, however, could have assumed the name upon receiving the divine call to his task of prophecy [cited in Gla].

4. Some have argued that 'Malachi' was inserted in the superscription by a late redactor of the book, who got it from Mal. 3:1. However, such an identification creates confusion, since the messenger of Mal. 3:1 is clearly indicated as belonging to the future [Gla].

DISCOURSE UNIT: 1:2–2:9 [Clen]. This is the "first movement." The topic is "priests exhorted to honor YHWH."

Comments on this discourse unit. This unit's surface structure and underlying notional structure are analyzed as follows (the change element, regarded as the naturally prominent element of hortatory discourse, is noted within the movement's chiastic structure in bold type):

Surface Structure			*Hortatory Notional Structure*	*Theme*
1st constituent	A	1:2–5	motivation	YHWH's love
2nd constituent	B	1:6–9	situation	failure to honor YHWH
3rd constituent	**C**	**1:10**	**change**	**stop vain offerings**
4th constituent	B'	1:11–14	situation	profaning YHWH's name
5th constituent	A'	2:1–9	motivation	results of disobedience

DISCOURSE UNIT: 1:2–5 [Clen (within the larger discourse unit of Mal. 1:2–2:9), Gla, Mer, NICOT, O'Brien, TOTC, WBC; CEV, NAB, NIV, NJB, NLT, NRSV, TEV]. This paragraph realizes semantic constituent 1A of the "first movement"; its topic is "YHWH's love" [Clen]. The topic is God's election of Israel (Mer). The topic is God's love for Israel [NICOT; CEV, NJB, NLT, TEV]. The topic is the prologue [O'Brien]. The topic is "a privileged people" [TOTC]. The topic is a dispute about God's love [WBC]. The topic is Israel preferred over Edom [NAB, NRSV]. The topic is Jacob the beloved and Esau the hated [NIV]. The topic is Israel as a privileged people [TOTC].

A formal analysis of the discourse unit is:

(A) Yahweh refers to Jacob in blessing: 'you' + 'Jacob' (2)

(B) Yahweh's judgment upon Esau: 'I have wasted his inheritance' (3)

(C) Edom's lack of repentance: 'we will rebuild' (4a)

(B') Yahweh's judgment upon Esau: 'let them build—I will tear down' (4b)

(A') Yahweh refers to Jacob in blessing: 'you' + 'Israel' (5) [Wendland]

DISCOURSE UNIT: 1:2–3:12 [REB]. The topic is "religious decline and hope of recovery."

1:2

I-have-loved[a] you(pl), says[b] YHWH, but[c]-you(pl)-say,[d] in-what-way[e] have-you(sg)-loved-us?

LEXICON—a. 1st sg. Qal perf. of אהב *ʾhḇ* (BDB p. 12), (Hol p. 5), (TWOT 29a): 'to love' [BDB, Hol; Ksr, Keil, Mer, Gla, NICOT, WBC; CEV, KJV, NASB, NIV, NJB, NRSV, TEV], 'to show love' [JPS, REB], 'to love deeply' [NLT].

b. 3rd mas. sg. Qal perf. of אמר *ʾmr* (BDB p. 55), (Hol p. 21), (TWOT 118): 'to say' [all commentators and versions]. Most commentators and versions translate this perfect in the quote formula אמר יהוה *ʾāmar yhwh* 'said YHWH' found throughout Malachi with the English present tense 'says, saith'; it is translated using the English past tense as 'said' by JPS. In this exegetical summary, the semi-literal translation has adopted the convention of the present tense 'says'.

c. -ו *wə-* *waw* connective (BDB p. 251), (Hol p. 84), (TWOT 519): 'but' [Mer, NICOT, WBC; JPS, NASB, NIV, NJB, NLT, NRSV, REB], 'yet' [Gla; KJV], 'and' [Keil], 'and yet' [CEV].

d. 2nd pl. Qal perf. of אמר *ʾmr* (see above): 'to say' [BDB, Hol; Keil, Mer, Gla, NICOT, WBC; KJV, NASB, NRSV], 'to ask' [CEV, JPS, NIV, NJB, REB], 'to reply' [TEV], 'to retort' [NLT]. All commentators and versions employ the English present tense; the semi-literal translation has adopted the same convention.

e. במה *bammâ* (BDB p. 553), (Hol p. 184): 'in what way' [WBC; CEV], 'in what manner' [NICOT], 'how' [Hol; Mer, Gla; JPS, NASB, NIV, NJB, NLT, NRSV, REB, TEV], 'wherein' [KJV], 'whereby' [BDB]. *Bammâ* here expresses skepticism or cynicism [TOTC].

QUESTION—What is meant by אהבתי אתכם *ʾāhaḇtî ʾetkem* 'I have loved you'?

1. This is technical terminology from ancient Near Eastern covenants, used of the lord entering into a covenant relationship with a vassal. Emotional nuances may or may not be present in the term [Mer, WBC; Mckenzie]. *ʾhḇ* 'to love' is the covenantal opposite of שׂנא *śnʾ* 'to hate', where the former is applied to those within the treaty and the latter to those outside the treaty, even in ancient Hittite documents [Mckenzie]. For Malachi, this phrase implies the existence of a covenant between God and Israel [Mckenzie] and denotes that God has preferred to choose one over

another for a special purpose; as in ancient treaties, so also in Mal. 1:3 the phrase stands in contrast with 'hate', whose object is, in effect, the less preferred, the one not chosen for God's purpose [Coh, Ksr, TOTC, WBC].

2. *ʾhḇ* 'to love' here is the true, strong opposite of *śnʾ* 'to hate' in Mal. 1:3; the two words here do not denote merely relative degrees of preference. This love is all-powerful, and the hate of Mal. 1:3 is revulsion to the character of the wicked, although this is not stated in this passage [Keil, NICOT].

QUESTION—What is the significance of the perfect tense of אָהַבְתִּי *ʾāhaḇtî* 'I have loved'?

God has loved Israel since her beginning and still does so, but the emphasis is on God's historic love for the nation [Coh, NICOT].

QUESTION—What is the significance of the people's question to God (אֲהַבְתָּנוּ בַּמָּה) *bammâ ʾăhaḇtānû* 'in what way have you loved us?')?

This question implies that the people feel that God has forsaken his covenant, which implies in turn that they were suffering. Mal. 3:9–11 specifies that they were suffering drought and sickness. Haggai 1:7–11 had said that these punishments were present because the people had neglected the construction of the Temple. Now, in Malachi's time, the Temple is complete, but the sufferings continue—hence the people's accusation in this discourse unit that God was not true to his word. But Malachi will point out that the people's covenant violations were the new cause of their lack of blessings [Mckenzie].

(Was-)not[a] Esau brother[b] of[c]-Jacob? declaration(-of)[d] YHWH, yet[e]-I-have-loved[f] Jacob,

LEXICON—a. -הֲ *hă-* (BDB p. 209), (Hol p. 75), (TWOT 459) + לֹא *lōʾ* (BDB p. 518), (Hol p. 170), (TWOT 1064). *Hă-* is a particle signaling a question, and *lōʾ* marks negation in a declarative sentence [BDB, Hol]. These particles signal a question which expects an affirmative answer, here taken as a rhetorical question, drawing attention to old information. The Hebrew question is translated as a rhetorical question in English [Coh, Keil, Mer, Gla, NICOT, WBC; KJV, NASB, NIV, NJB, NRSV, REB]; it is also translated as a statement, e.g., 'Yet Esau was Jacob's brother' [CEV, JPS, NLT, TEV]. Rhetorical questions are always very prominent in BH; this one is no exception, as it constitutes the point of departure for the rest of the entire discourse unit of Mal. 1:2–5 [Clen].

b. אָח *ʾāḥ* (BDB p. 26), (Hol p. 8), (TWOT 62a): 'brother' [BDB, Hol; all commentators and versions].

c. -לְ *lə-* (BDB p. 510), (Hol p. 167), (TWOT 1063). Most commentators and versions translate 'Jacob's brother' or 'brother of Jacob'; the role relationship is also translated 'to Jacob' [WBC], 'Jacob and Esau were brothers' [TEV]. The proclitic *lə-* here signals "possession" [BDB, Hol].

d. נְאֻם nə²um (BDB p. 610), (Hol p. 223), (TWOT 1272a): 'declaration'
[BDB, Hol], 'oracle' [Gla, WBC], 'utterance' [BDB]. Most commentators and versions translate this as a verb: 'to say' [Coh, Mer, NICOT;
KJV, NIV, NRSV], 'to declare' [JPS, NASB, NJB], 'to answer' [REB,
TEV], 'to reply' [NLT], not explicit [CEV]. This nominalized speech
margin, normally very low in prominence, becomes here more
prominent as it is attached to a rhetorical question and to reported speech
[Clen]. Nə²um is a fixed technical term in prophetic speech and in
combination with other formulas: 'decision, declaration' [Hol].

e. -וְ wə- waw of the attached preterite verb (TWOT 519): 'yet' [Coh, Mer,
Gla, NICOT, TOTC; JPS, KJV, NASB, NIV, NRSV], 'but' [CEV,
TEV], 'even so' [NJB], 'and' [Keil, WBC], not explicit [NLT, REB].

f. 1st s. Qal preterite of אָהַב ²hḇ (BDB p. 12), (Hol p. 5), (TWOT 29a):
'to love' [BDB, Hol; Coh, Keil, Mer, Gla, NICOT, TOTC, WBC;
KJV, NASB, NIV, NJB, NLT, NRSV, REB, TEV], 'to choose' [CEV],
'to accept' [JPS].

QUESTION—What type of question is this?

It is a rhetorical question, used here to begin a new topic [Wendland]. It
means 'Do not forget that . . .' [CEV]. It is also translated in the form of a
statement [JPS, NLT, TEV]: Esau was Jacob's brother.

QUESTION—To whom do Esau and Jacob refer?

1. These names refer to the two sons of Isaac [Ksr, NICOT, TOTC, WBC]
and include the descendants of each [Keil, Mer; TEV]. The covenantal
choice and blessings conferred upon Jacob are seen as extended to his
descendants [Keil, Mer]. The change from sg. to pl. suffixes and
pronouns (from vv. 2–3 to vv. 3–4) show that the referents of these two
passages are different [Mckenzie].

2. These names refer to the nations descended from the two brothers which
were very different in their character and history; Esau stands for Edom
and Jacob stands for Israel [Coh, Gla].

1:3

(a) but[a]-Esau I-have-hated,[b] and[c]-I-transformed[d] his-mountains[e] (into)
wasteland[f] [all commentators and versions]

(b₁) and[g]- (gave) his-inheritance[h] to[i-1]-*jackals(-of)[j-1] (the-)desert.[k] [Coh,
Keil, Mer, Gla, NICOT; JPS,NIV, TEV]

(b₂) and[g]- (transformed) his-inheritance[h] into[i-2]-*dwelling-places(-of)
/pastures(-of)[j-2] (the-)desert.[k] [WBC; NJB, REB]

(b₃) and[g]- (made) his-inheritance[h] *(a-)desert[k] for[i-1] jackals.[j-1] [CEV,
NLT, NRSV]

*TEXT—Gesenius and others follow the LXX and Syriac version (LXX: εἰς
δόματα 'to pastures/dwelling places'), reading לִנְאוֹת lin²ôṯ 'to pastures',
mainly on the grounds that תַּן tan 'jackal' in Hebrew has no known
feminine plural ending. But the -ôṯ ending was not originally unique to the

feminine gender in Hebrew [NICOT]. The reading 'to pastures/dwellings' is followed by WBC, NJB, and REB.

SYNTAX—it is evident that, regardless of the textual reading adopted, the verb שִׂים śîm has two objects [NICOT]. If reading (b) is adopted, then the implied second occurrence of śîm must also be understood as 'transform' as in NJB, and 'desert' qualifies 'dwelling places/pastures'. When reading (b₁) is adopted, then the implied second occurrence of śîm is often understood as carrying a different sense, one approximating 'give', where 'jackals' is seen as being a construct form, as in NICOT; JPS, NIV; and 'desert' qualifies 'jackals'. CEV, NLT, and NRSV, however, treat 'desert' as the second accusative of śîm, reading effectively 'I transformed his heritage into a desert for jackals'.

LEXICON—a. -וְ wə- waw connective (BDB p. 251), (Hol p. 84), (TWOT 519): 'but' [Coh, NICOT, TOTC, WBC; CEV, NASB, NIV, NJB, NRSV, REB], 'and' [Keil; JPS, KJV, TEV], 'yet' [Gla; NLT]. This connective is also interpreted as introducing a subject–focus structure: 'as for' [Mer].

b. 1st sg. Qal perf. of שָׂנֵא śn [BDB p. 971], [Hol p. 353], [TWOT 2272]: 'to hate' [BDB, Hol; Coh, Keil, Mer, Gla, NICOT, TOTC, WBC; JPS, NASB, NIV, NJB, NRSV, REB, TEV], 'to not choose' [CEV], 'to reject' [JPS, NLT]. Like אָהֵב ʾhḇ 'love'. Śn 'hate' is also traditional covenant language in ancient extra-biblical texts [Mckenz)e].

c. -וְ wə- waw of the attached preterite verb (BDB p. 251), (Hol p. 84), (TWOT 519): 'and' [all commentators and versions except the following]. The additive relationship is also signaled by a new clause [JPS, NJB, NRSV, TEV]; 'therefore' [Gla].

d. 1st s. Qal preterite of שִׂים śîm (BDB p. 962), (Hol p. 351), (TWOT 2243): 'to transform into' [BDB], 'to make into' [Hol; Coh, Keil, Mer, WBC; JPS, NRSV], 'to make' [NASB], 'to turn into' [Gla, NICOT; CEV, NIV, NJB]. The phrase 'turn into wasteland' is translated 'to devastate' [NLT, TEV], 'to reduce to a waste' [REB], and 'to lay to waste' [KJV]. The root meaning of śîm is 'to put, set, place', leading to 'to set up, appoint'; when used in the sense of 'to transform into something', it has two accusatives [Hol].

e. constr. of הַר har (BDB p. 249), (Hol p. 83), (TWOT 517a): 'mountain' [BDB, Hol; Coh, Keil, Mer, Gla, NICOT, WBC; KJV, NASB, NIV, NJB], 'hill country' [BDB; CEV, NLT, NRSV, REB, TEV], 'hill' [BDB; JPS].

f. שְׁמָמָה šəmāmâ (BDB p. 1031), (Hol p. 376), (TWOT 2409b): 'wasteland' [NICOT; NIV], 'desolation' [Coh, WBC; JPS, NASB, NRSV], 'waste' [BDB; Keil, Gla; KJV, REB], 'desert' [NJB], 'barren desert' [CEV], 'devastation' [BDB]. This noun is also translated as an adjective: 'desolate' [Mer]; and as a verb: 'to devastate' [NLT]. Šəmāmâ is any deserted area which inspires fear [Hol].

g. -ּו wə- waw connective (BDB p. 251), (Hol p. 84), (TWOT 519): 'and'
   [all commentators and versions except the following]. The additive
   relationship is also expressed by means of a new clause [JPS, NLT].
h. constr.of נחלה naḥălâ (BDB p. 635), (Hol p. 234), (TWOT 1342a):
   'inheritance' [BDB; Keil, Mer, Gla, NICOT, WBC; NASB, NIV,
   NLT], 'heritage' [Hol; Coh; KJV, NJB, NRSV], 'his territory' [JPS],
   'land' [TEV], 'ancestral land' [REB], 'property' [BDB], not explicit
   [CEV]. Naḥălâ refers to inherited property [Hol].
i-1. -ל lə- (BDB p. 510), (Hol p. 167), (TWOT 1063): 'to' [BDB; Coh,
   Mer, Gla; NIV, TEV], 'for' [Keil, NICOT; CEV, JPS, NASB, NLT,
   NRSV]. The proclitic lə- is here introducing a dative of advantage [BDB,
   Hol].
i-2 -ל lə- (see above): 'into' [BDB; WBC; NJB, REB]. The proclitic lə- is
   here expressing change to a different condition [BDB]; it expresses here
   the result of an action [Hol].
j-1. assumed plural constr. of תן tan (BDB p. 1072), (Hol p. 392),
   (TWOT 2528a): 'jackal' [BDB, Hol; Coh, Keil, Mer, Gla, NICOT;
   CEV, NASB, NIV, NLT, NRSV, TEV], 'beast' [JPS], 'dragon'[KJV].
   The construct relationship in (a) between 'jackals' and 'desert' is most
   often translated with 'of', but also with a phrase: 'desert jackals' [NIV].
j-2. constr. pl. of נוה nāwâ (BDB p. 627), (Hol p. 231), (TWOT 1322c):
   'dwelling place' [WBC], 'dwelling' [NJB], 'abode, residence' [Hol],
   'pasture' [REB], 'pasturage' [Hol], 'meadow' [BDB]. Nāwâ in its
   secondary sense refers to a rural place of residence [BDB].
k. מדבר miḏbār (BDB p. 184), (Hol p. 182), (TWOT 399l): 'desert' [Hol;
   Coh, Keil, Mer, NICOT, WBC; JPS, NIV, NLT, NRSV, REB],
   'barren desert' [CEV], 'wilderness' [BDB; Gla; KJV, NASB],
   'wasteland' [NJB], not explicit [TEV]. Miḏbār refers to land uncultiva-
   ted and perhaps inarable, suitable only for pasturage [BDB, Hol].
QUESTION—What is the structure and function of the chiasm in Mal. 1:2b
and 3a?
   The chiastic structure is as follows:

   ואהב את־יעקב wā'ōhab 'et ya'ăqōb . . . yet I have loved Jacob,

   ואת־עשׂו שׂנאתי wə'et 'ēśāw śānē'tî . . . but Esau have I hated.

   It serves to emphasize the statement [NICOT]. The emphasis may be
characterized as follows: although a verb in the waw consecutive form in
narrative text (in this case wā'ōhab 'yet I have loved') ranks naturally
higher in prominence than does a verb in the perfect tense (here śānē'tî 'I
have hated'), in this chiastic structure the second clause achieves as much
prominence as the first by means of object fronting ('ēśāw 'Esau' is placed,
unusually so in Biblical Hebrew, before the verb by which it is governed)
[Clen].

QUESTION—Apart from syntactic considerations, what other factors influence the choice between 'jackals' and 'dwelling places/pastures'?

נָוָה *nāwâ* 'pasture, meadow', is usually seen as a positive word in the OT, connoting prosperity, while 'jackals' is often associated with deserted ruins. For this reason, *nāwâ* does not fit the context so well as תַּנּוֹת *tannôṯ* 'jackals' [Gla].

QUESTION—How does this language of cursing fit into the covenant framework?

The curses of 1: 3-4 are like many curses called down upon treaty breakers in ancient times: may wild animals take over the land, may one's labor result in nothing, etc. [Mckenzie].

QUESTION—To what event does the text refer?

1. It refers to the time when Nabatean Arabs took over Edom, forcing the Edomites to leave and migrate into the Negev [Ksr, NICOT, TOTC, WBC]. This occurred probably in the late sixth or early fifth century B.C. This takeover of the Nabateans must be viewed as gradual; it did not dramatically drive out the Edomites, but rather made their settled, agricultural life impossible in the face of the demands on land and other resources made by the dominant, nomadic Nabateans. It probably took in turn several centuries for the Nabateans (who built the capital city of Petra) to change to a fully settled life themselves [Gla].

2. It refers to the time when the Chaldeans under Nebuchadnezzar conquered and devastated Edom at the same time conquering Judea [Keil].

3. It refers to the time repeated attacks on Edom by the Chaldeans in the first half of the sixth century [Mer].

4. It refers to the conquest of Edom conducted by Nabonidus, the last king of Babylon (559-539 B.C.) [John Lindsay, "The Babylonian Kings and Edom, 605-550 B.C.," *Palestine Exploration Quarterly* 108 (1976), cited in Gla].

QUESTION—What attitude did the Israelites have toward the Edomites, and was their attitude reflected in this passage?

There was a long history of mutual antagonism between Israel and Edom, neighboring countries descended from twin brothers [Gla]. Many OT passages condemn Edom, apparently because Edom had joined the Chaldeans in the destruction of Jerusalem [WBC]. Edomites gloated over the fate of Judah and joined in looting her (Obad. 10-14) [Coh, NICOT]. Some commentators consider that some of these passages generalize Edom as the place of all wickedness and as the type of all of Judah's enemies [WBC]; some see Edom depicted as the archetype of all who reject God's grace [Mer]. The eschatological restoration of Israel is depicted as coordinated with the eschatological judgment of Edom in Isa. 63 and Ezek. 35-36 [NICOT].

1:4
If[a] Edom[b] should-say,[c] We-were-crushed,[d] but[e]-we-will-return,[f] and[g]-we-will-rebuild[h] these ruins,[i] thus says YHWH(-of) hosts:[j] They may-rebuild,[k] but[l]-I will-demolish.[m]

TEXT—The translation of רשׁשׁ *ršš* as 'to be impoverished' originates with older Jewish commentaries and the Targum, which give this sense [Coh], assuming in error that the verb root in question was רושׁ *rûš* 'to be in want, to be poor' [NICOT].

LEXICON—a. כִּי *kî* connective (BDB p. 471), (Hol p. 155), (TWOT 976): 'if' [Keil, NICOT; JPS, NJB, NRSV, TEV], 'when' [WBC; REB], 'yet' [Mer]; 'whereas' [Coh; KJV], 'though' [Gla; NASB], 'and' [NLT], not explicit [CEV, NIV, NLT]. As *kî* introduces a subordinate clause which is preposed to the main clause, it may well mark here a simple condition or circumstantial relation (translated 'if', 'when', etc.), rather than a concessive clause (translated 'even though', etc.) [Clen].

   b. אדום *ʾĕdôm* (BDB p. 10), (Hol p. 3), (TWOT 26e): 'Edom' [all commentators and versions except the following]. Some make explicit the origin of the Edomites: 'Esau's descendants in Edom' [NLT], 'Esau's descendants' [CEV], 'Esau's descendants, the Edomites' [TEV].

   c. 3rd fem. sg. Qal imperf. of אמר *ʾmr* (BDB p. 55), (Hol p. 21), (TWOT 118): 'to say' [all lexica, commentators, and versions except the following], 'to think' [JPS]. Some translations use the English present tense 'says' [Coh, Gla; KJV]; others use a potential expression, e.g., 'may say' [CEV, NIV, NJB, NLT], still others a circumstantial expression, e.g., 'when Edom says' [WBC; REB], and others a condition with 'if' [Keil, NICOT; JPS, NRSV, TEV]. Mer employs the past tense: 'yet Edom said'.

   d. 1st pl. Pual perf. of רשׁשׁ *ršš* (BDB p. 958), (Hol p. 347), (TWOT 2224): 'to be crushed' [NICOT; JPS, NIV], 'to be shattered' [BDB, Hol; NLT, NRSV], 'to be struck down' [NJB], 'to be devastated' [Mer], 'to be in ruins' [CEV], 'to be destroyed' [TEV], 'to be impoverished' [KJV], 'to be beaten down' [BDB; Coh, Gla, WBC; NASB, REB], 'to be dashed to pieces' [Keil].

   e. -ו *wǝ-* *waw* connective (BDB p. 251), (Hol p. 84), (TWOT 519): 'but' [Coh, Gla, WBC; KJV, NASB, NLT, REB].

   f. 1st pl. Qal imperf. of שׁוב *šûḇ* (BDB p. 996), (Hol. p, 362), (TWOT 2340): 'to return' [Coh, WBC; KJV, NASB]. The other commentators and versions omit translating this verb directly, expressing repetition through the following verb, 'to rebuild'. *šûḇ* denotes 'to return, to turn back, but followed by a second verb, it expresses repetition, 'to do again' [BDB; Hol].

   g. -ו *wǝ-* *waw* connective (BDB p. 251), (Hol p. 84), (TWOT 519): 'and' [Coh, WBC; KJV, NASB].

   h. 1st pl. Qal imperf. of בנה *bnh* (BDB p. 124), (Hol p. 42), (TWOT 255): 'to build'; but expressed as 'to rebuild' because of the preceding verb *šûḇ* [all lexica, commentators, and versions except the following], 'to build' [Coh, Mer; KJV], 'to build up' [Keil; NASB]. All the foregoing translations employ the English future tense. JPS translates with the idea of potentiality: 'we can build again'; REB regards the Hebrew verb form as a jussive and translate: 'let us rebuild'.

   i. pl. of חרבה *ḥorbâ* (BDB p. 352), (Hol p. 115), (TWOT 731d): 'ruins' [BDB; JPS, Keil, Gla, NICOT; NASB, NIV, NJB, NLT, NRSV], 'ruined place' [Mer], 'ruined home' [REB], 'waste place' [Coh], 'desolate place' [KJV], 'place of ruins' [Hol], 'desolation' [BDB].

   j. pl. of צבא *ṣāḇāʾ* (BDB p. 838), (Hol p. 302), (TWOT 1865b): 'hosts' [Coh, Keil, Mer, Gla, WBC; JPS, KJV, NASB, NRSV, REB], 'Almighty' [NICOT; NIV, NLT], 'All-Powerful' [CEV], 'Sabaoth' [NJB], not explicit [TEV]. *Ṣāḇāʾ* refers to a soldier or an army, or to military service. The use of the plural in conjunction with YHWH or Elohim first designated God as the Lord of armies or of battle; in later biblical material, this thought was extended to Lord of the angels and stars [BDB].

   k. 3rd mas. pl. Qal imperf. of בנה *bnh* (see above): 'to rebuild' [REB, TEV], 'to build' [Coh, Keil, Mer, Gla, NICOT, WBC; JPS, KJV, NASB, NIV, NJB, NRSV]. NLT introduces a modality: 'to try to rebuild'.

   l. -ו *wə-* *waw* connective (BDB p. 251), (Hol p. 84), (TWOT 519): 'but' [Coh, Keil, Mer, Gla, NICOT, WBC; JPS, KJV, NASB, NIV, NJB, NLT, NRSV], not explicit [CEV, REB, TEV]. The strong contrast between the two clauses linked by this connective is marked in text by the fronting of the two pronouns המה *hēmmâ* 'they' and אני *ʾănî* 'I' in their respective clauses [Clen].

   m. 1st s. Qal imperf. of הרס *hrs* (BDB p. 248), (Hol p. 84), (TWOT 516): 'to demolish' [Hol; NICOT, WBC; NIV, NLT], 'to overthrow' [Mer], 'to pull down' [Coh, Keil; KJV, NJB, REB], 'to tear down' [BDB; Gla, CEV, JPS, NASB, TEV], 'to throw down' [BDB].

QUESTION—What is the significance of ונשוב *wənāšûḇ* 'we will return', and why do many commentators and versions omit this clause?

Šûḇ 'to return' is often used in a modal sense in Hebrew to express the idea of 'again', hence, 'we will build again—rebuild' [NICOT]. This passage may have indicated a determination of the Edomites, driven out of their country into the Negev, to return to Edom [WBC].

And[a]-they-will-call[b] them 'land[c](-of) wickedness'[d] and-'the-people[e] which YHWH has-cursed[f] forever;[g]

LEXICON—a. -ו *wə-* *waw* connective of the attached *waw* consecutive verb [BDB p. 251], [Hol p. 84], [TWOT 519].

   b. 3rd pl. Qal perf. *waw* consecutive of קרא *qrʾ* (BDB p. 894), (Hol p. 323), (TWOT 2063): 'to call' [Keil, WBC; KJV, NASB, TEV], 'to be called' [BDB, Hol; Coh, Gla, NICOT; NIV, NRSV, REB], 'to be known as' [Mer; JPS, NJB, NLT]. This is also translated 'everyone will know' [CEV]. The implied subject is 'men' [Keil]: 'men will call them . . .' $Qr^{\jmath}$ is often, as here, complemented by a phrase introduced with the proclitic -ל *lə-*.

c. constr. of גבול *gəḇûl* (BDB p. 147), (Hol p. 53), (TWOT 307a): 'land' [NIV, NJB], 'country' [NICOT, WBC; NLT, REB, TEV], 'territory' [BDB, Hol; Keil, Mer, Gla; NASB, NRSV], 'region' [JPS], 'border' [BDB; Coh; KJV], 'boundary' [Hol].

d. רשעה *riš'â* (BDB p. 958), (Hol p. 347), (TWOT 2222c): 'wickedness' [BDB; Coh, Keil, Gla; JPS, KJV, NJB, NLT, REB], 'guilt' [Hol]. This noun is also translated as an adjective: 'wicked' [Mer, NICOT, WBC; NASB, NIV, NRSV], 'evil' [TEV]; and as a verb: 'to be sinful' [CEV].

e. עם *'ām* (BDB p. 766), (Hol p. 275), (TWOT 1640a): 'people' (i.e., an ethnic group) [all lexica and commentators; all versions except CEV, NJB, and TEV], 'nation' [BDB; NJB, TEV], not explicit [CEV]. *'ām* refers to an entire people and stresses their ethnic unity [Hol].

f. 3rd sg. Qal perf. of זעם *z'm* (BDB p. 276), (Hol p. 90), (TWOT 568a): 'to curse' [BDB, Hol; Gla], 'to execrate' [Coh], 'to be angry with' [Keil, WBC; CEV, NJB, NLT, NRSV, REB, TEV], 'to have indignation against' [BDB; Mer; KJV], 'to be indignant' [NASB]. This active verb is also translated in the passive: 'to be under the wrath (of the Lord)' [NICOT; NIV], 'to be damned (of the Lord)' [JPS].

g. עד־עולם *'ad̠ 'ôlām* (BDB p. 761), (Hol p. 267), (TWOT 1631a): 'forever' [BDB, Hol; Keil, WBC; all versions except NIV and CEV], 'always' [BDB; NICOT; NIV], 'for all time' [Hol]. This is also translated as an adjective: 'eternal (indignation)' [Mer], as an adverb: 'eternally' [Gla], as a time phrase: 'as long as (they are so sinful)' [CEV].

QUESTION—Was there any national attitude in Israel which would have agreed with this passage?

Although Judah had been devastated by the Chaldeans and sent into exile, she experienced a restoration, whereas Edom never recovered from the enemy invasions and eventual conquest. This fact proved to Judah the reality of YHWH's love for them [Mer].

QUESTION—What does זעם *z'm* mean here?

1. It means 'to be angry with' [Keil, Mer, NICOT, WBC; CEV, KJV, NIV, NJB, NLT, NRSV, REB, TEV].

2. Although it normally means 'to be angry with', here it carries the sense of 'to curse', as in Num. 23:7 and Prov. 24:24 [Gla].

1:5

and[a]-your(pl)-eyes[b] will-see,[c] and[d]-you(pl)-will-say,[e] YHWH he-is-great/ may-he-be magnified[f] beyond/over[g] (the-)border(-of)[h] Israel.

LEXICON—a. -ו *wə- waw* connective (BDB p. 251), (Hol p. 84), (TWOT 519): 'and' [Coh, Keil, WBC; KJV, NASB]. The additive relationship is expressed also by a new clause [Mer, NICOT; JPS, NIV, NJB, NRSV, REB, TEV]; 'then' [Gla]. This conjunction is also translated as introducing a circumstantial clause dependent upon the following clause: 'when' [CEV, NLT].

b. plural constr. of עַיִן ʿayin (BDB p. 744), (Hol p. 271), (TWOT 1612a): 'eye' [BDB, Hol; Coh, Keil, Mer, Gla, NICOT, WBC; JPS, KJV, NASB, NRSV, REB]. The noun 'eyes' is also treated as synecdoche and intensifier and translated on the order of 'you yourselves': 'you (will see) for yourselves' or 'with your own eyes', etc. [CEV, NIV, NJB, NLT]. The fronting of עֵינֵיכֶם ʿênêkem 'your eyes' in the text functions as a means of reintroducing the addressees 'you', referring back to Mal. 1:2 [Clen].

c. 3rd fem. pl. Qal imperf. of רָאָה rʾh (BDB p. 906), (Hol p. 328), (TWOT 2095): 'to see' [all lexica, commentators, and versions except JPS], 'to behold' [JPS].

d. -וְ wǝ- waw connective (BDB p. 251), (Hol p. 84), (TWOT 519): 'and' [Coh, Keil, Gla, NICOT, WBC; JPS, KJV, NASB, NIV, NJB, NRSV, REB, TEV]; 'and then' [Mer]. This conjunction is also translated so as to introduce an independent clause governing the previous clause [CEV, NLT].

e. 2nd mas. pl. Qal imperf. of אָמַר ʾmr (BDB p. 55), (Hol p. 21), (TWOT 118): 'to say' [all lexica, commentators, and versions except the following], 'to shout' [CEV], 'to declare' [JPS].

f. 3rd mas. sg. Qal imperf. of גָּדַל gdl (BDB p. 152), (Hol p. 56), (TWOT 315): 'to be great' [BDB, Hol; Coh, Keil, Gla, NICOT; JPS, NIV, NRSV], 'to be magnified' [BDB; Mer, KJV, NASB], 'to be mighty' [NJB, TEV]. This phrase is also translated 'the Lord's great reputation reaches' [CEV], 'the Lord's great power reaches' [NLT], and 'the Lord's greatness reaches' [REB]. Most versions treat this phrase as a statement; NASB, however, treats it as a wish or prayer: 'The Lord be magnified'.

g. מֵעַל mēʿal (BDB p. 758), (Hol p. 272): 'beyond' [Coh, Mer, Gla, WBC; CEV, JPS, NASB, NIV, NJB, NRSV, REB], 'over' [Keil, NICOT], 'from' [KJV], 'outside' [TEV].

h. constr. of גְּבוּל gǝbûl (BDB p. 147), (Hol p. 53), (TWOT 307a): 'border' [BDB; Coh, Mer, WBC; CEV, JPS, KJV, NASB, NIV, NJB, NLT, NRSV], 'confine' [REB], 'territory' [BDB, Hol; Keil, Gla, NICOT], 'land' [TEV], 'boundary' [BDB, Hol].

QUESTION—Whom is God addressing in this verse?

1. God is addressing Israel [Keil, NICOT, TOTC].
2. God is addressing either Israel or Edom or both [Mer].

QUESTION—What is meant by מֵעַל mēʿal 'beyond/over' in this verse?

1. The word means 'beyond'. This translation is supported by at least some old Jewish commentators, and implies that foreigners will praise the God of Israel. This interpretation is also supported by the Targum and the

Peshitta [Coh]. Analogy with the phrases 'my name' and 'among the nations' in 1:11 and 1:14 favors similar ideas in 1:5, i.e., 'YHWH' and 'beyond the borders of Israel' [Wendland].

2. The word means 'over'. Most biblical occurrences of *mēʿal* appear to demand such a translation, and Malachi's theme here is more on the faithfulness of God's love to Israel than on his deeds abroad. The translation 'above' is supported by the LXX and the Vulgate [NICOT].

DISCOURSE UNIT: 1:6–2:9 [Gla, O'Brien, Mer, TOTC, WBC; NJB, NRSV, TEV]. The topic is "the sacrilege of the priests" [Mer], the first accusation [O'Brien], "a privileged priesthood" [TOTC], "a dispute about God's honor and fear" [WBC], "an indictment of the priests" [NJB], the "corruption of the priesthood" [NRSV], "the Lord reprimands the priests" [TEV].

Comments on this discourse unit: this discourse unit is addressed to the priests [Gla].

A formal analysis of the discourse unit is:

Part 1 (1:6–11)
> (A) Honour is due Yahweh's name: 'my name' (6)
>> (B) The priests' sin: 'my altar' + 'offer' + 'food' + 'sacrifice' defective offerings (7–8a)
>>> (C) Result = no mercy: 'governor' = 'lift up your faces' (8b)
>>> (C) Result = no mercy: 'God' + 'lift up your faces' (9)
>> (B') The priests' sin, defective offerings: 'my altar' + 'food offering' (10)
> (A') Honour is due Yahweh's name: 'my name' (11)

Part 2 (1:12–14)
The three main elements A, B, and C of the first part constitute this part also, but are ordered differently.
>> (B") The priests' sin: 'table of the Lord' + 'food' + 'fruit' + 'meal defective offerings offering' (12–13a)
>>> (C") Result = no mercy: 'I will not accept it from your hand' + 'cursed' (13b–14a)
> (A") Honor is due Yahweh's name: 'my name' (14b)

Part 3 (2:1–9)
> (A) the priests' perversion→curse (1–4)
>> (B) the pure priestly prototype (5–7)
> (A') the priests' perversion→punishment (8–9) [Wendland]

DISCOURSE UNIT: 1:6–1:14 [Ksr, NICOT; CEV, NASB, NIV, NLT]. The topic is "a call to be authentic" [Ksr], God's demand for pure offerings [NICOT], "judgment against priests" [CEV], the priests' sin [NASB], "blemished sacrifices" [NIV], "unworthy sacrifices" [NLT].

Comments on this discourse unit: this unit is addressed both to the priests and to the people at large. In this unit abounds much vocabulary typical of ancient covenants: the father-son theme, the master-servant theme, the theme of the Great King, and the phrase 'cursed be . . .' [McKenzie].

DISCOURSE UNIT: 1:6–1:10 [Clen (within the larger discourse unit of Mal. 1:2–2:9)]. The topic is the "failure to honor YHWH." This paragraph realizes semantic constituent 1B (Mal. 1:6–9), the topic of which is the "failure to honor YHWH", and constituent 1C (Mal. 1:10), the topic of which is "stop vain offerings."

1:6

(A-)son honors[a] (his-)father[b] and-(a-)servant[c] (honors) his-master.[d] Then[e]-if[f] (a-)father I (am), where[g] (is) my-honor,[h] and-if (a-)master I (am), where (is) my-fear[i]? says YHWH of-hosts to-you(pl) the-priests,[j] ones-despising[k] my-name,[l] but[m]-you(pl)-say,[n] how[o] have-we-despised[p] your(sg)-name?

TEXT—WBC follows the Hebrew equivalent of the Syriac and Targum
    readings: אָבִיו ʾābîw 'his father'. NICOT understands *his* as implied in the
    Hebrew text.
LEXICON—a. 3 mas. sg. Piel imperf. [all commentators and versions except
    JPS]—3 mas. sg. jussive [JPS]—of כבד kbd (BDB p. 457), (Hol
    p. 150), (TWOT 943): 'to honor' [all lexica, commentators; all versions
    except CEV], 'to respect' [CEV]. The verb is translated as an indicative
    'honors' by all commentators and versions except JPS; it is translated as
    a jussive 'should honor' by JPS. Against the latter interpretation, it is
    argued that *yəkabbēd* expresses a general truth ('honors') and not a duty
    ('should honor'), which would weaken Malachi's argument [Keil,
    NICOT].
  b. אב ʾāb (BDB p. 3), (Hol p. 1), (TWOT 4a): 'father' [all lexica,
    commentators, and versions.]
  c. עבד ʿebed (BDB p. 713), (Hol p. 262), (TWOT 1553a): 'servant' [BDB,
    Hol; Coh, Keil, Gla, NICOT, WBC; CEV, KJV, NASB, NIV, NLT.
    NRSV, TEV. 'slave' [BDB, Hol; Mer; JPS, NJB, REB].
  d. formal pl. of אדון ʾādôn (BDB p. 10), (Hol p. 4), (TWOT 27b):
    'master' [all lexica, all commentators except WBC; all versions]; 'lord'
    [BDB; WBC]. ʾādôn may refer to a man or to God [BDB, Hol]. The
    formal plural denotes intensity or majesty [NICOT, WBC].
  e. -ו wə- *waw* connective (BDB p. 251), (Hol p. 84), (TWOT 519): 'then'
    [Coh, Mer, WBC; NASB, NRSV, KJV], 'now' [JPS], 'but' [NJB],
    'therefore' [Gla], 'and' [Keil]. If this conjunction begins a sentence
    which is antithetical to the preceding sentence [so Clen], it would appear
    that an English conjunction specifying logical argumentative progression
    (e.g., 'then') is more suitable than 'and'.

f. אִם *ʾim* (BDB p. 49), (Hol p. 19), (TWOT 111): 'if' [all lexica,
commentators, and versions except the following]. The condition is
transformed into a statement 'I am your father' [CEV, NLT, TEV],
apparently on the grounds that this condition has a rhetorical nature; it is
equivalent to a statement. The particle *ʾim* introduces any condition
which is theoretically possible [Hol].

g. אַיֵּה *ʾayyēh* (BDB p. 32), (Hol p. 12), (TWOT 75a): 'where' [all lexica,
commentators, and versions except the following]. The rhetorical
question 'where is my honor?' is also translated 'why don't you respect
me?' [CEV, TEV]. *ʾayyēh* often occurs in poetry or in eloquent
language, introducing a rhetorical question [BEB].

h. constr. of כָּבוֹד *kābôd* (BDB p. 458), (Hol p. 150), (TWOT 943a):
'honor' [BDB; Coh, Keil, Mer, Gla, NICOT, WBC; JPS, KJV, NASB,
NIV, NRSV], 'awe' [NJB], 'respect' [Hol]. The affixed pronoun is
translated 'my' by Coh, Keil, Mer, WBC; KJV. Otherwise, the
objective genitive relationship of the pronoun to the noun, is expressed
as '(the honor) due me' [Gla, NICOT; NIV, NRSV, JPS, REB] and as
'the honor . . . I deserve' [NLT]. This noun is also rendered by a verb
phrase: 'honor me' [CEV], 'respect me' [TEV]. *Kābôd* is both God's
magnificent power and the respect or reverence which is due him
because of it [NICOT].

i. constr. of מוֹרָא *môrāʾ* (BDB p. 432), (Hol p. 187), (TWOT 907c):
'fear' [Hol; Coh, Keil, NICOT, WBC; KJV], 'respect' [Mer; NASB,
NIV], 'awe' [NJB], 'reverence' [BEB; Gla; JPS], 'honor' [NRSV]. The
affixed pronoun is translated 'my' by Coh, Keil, Mer, WBC; KJV.
Otherwise, the objective genitive relationship of the pronoun to the noun,
is expressed as *noun* + 'due (to) me' [Gla, NICOT; JPS, NIV, NJB,
NRSV, REB] and as *noun* + 'I deserve' [NLT]. The noun is also
rendered by a verb phrase: 'to respect me' [TEV].

j. pl. of כֹּהֵן *kōhēn* (BDB p. 463), (Hol p. 152), (TWOT 959): 'priest' [all
lexica, commentators, and versions]. Gla translates 'O priests, to you
who despise my name', thus including 'priests' in the direct speech
which follows.

k. mas. pl. Qal part. of בָּזָה *bzh* (BDB p. 102), (Hol p. 36), (TWOT 224):
'to despise' [all lexica, commentators, and versions except the
following]; 'to scorn' [JPS]; 'to show contempt for' [Hol; NIV]. The
failure to acknowledge the כָּבוֹד *kābôd* 'honor' of God is to treat him as
nothing or as unimportant, the main sense of *bzh* [Mer, NICOT].

l. constr. of שֵׁם *šēm* (BDB p. 1027), (Hol p. 374), (TWOT 2405): 'name'
[all lexica, commentators, and versions except the following]. CEV and
TEV translate 'me', treating *name* as a figure of speech standing for
God himself. The name of God signifies his presence in Deuteronomy;
šēm 'name' occurs frequently in this part of Malachi and thereby
becomes a theme in it [WBC].

m. -ן *wə- waw* connective (BDB p. 251), (Hol p. 84), (TWOT 519): 'but' [Mer, Gla, NICOT, WBC; JPS, NASB, NIV, NLT], 'yet' [Keil], 'and' [Coh; KJV], 'and yet' [TEV], 'and now' [CEV], not explicit [NJB, NRSV, REB].

n. 2nd pl. Qal perf. of אמר *ʾmr* (BDB p. 55), (Hol p. 21), (TWOT 118): 'to say' [BDB, Hol; Coh, Keil, Mer, Gla, WBC; NASB], 'to ask' [NICOT; CEV, JPS, NIV, NJB, NLT, NRSV, REB, TEV].

o. במה *bammeh* (BDB p. 553), (Hol p. 184): 'how' [Hol; all commentators and versions except the following], 'wherein' [BDB; Coh, Keil; KJV], 'in what way' [WBC], 'in what manner' [NICOT].

p. 1st pl. Qal perf. of בזה *bzh*: see above. The BH perfect tense in hortatory discourse commonly describes a situation which needs to be changed; as such, this perfect refers to present circumstances as well as to past action [Clen].

QUESTION—What is the significance of אב *ʾāḇ* 'father'?
God calls himself the Father and Creator of Israel, in the sense that he formed the nation and made it his own [Keil].

QUESTION—What is the significance of מורא *môrāʾ* 'fear"?
1. Although *môrāʾ* generally denotes 'dread', here it should be seen in the context of God's covenant with Israel as denoting reverence, respect, and trust, close to 'honor' [NICOT].
2. *môrāʾ* in the OT does not denote 'dread', but rather 'honor, respect'. However, even more generally, as also in this verse, although parallel with כבוד *kāḇôḏ* 'honor', *môrāʾ* has to do, not so much with inward feelings, as with outward expression, especially with regard to worship and morals [B. J. Bamberger, "Fear and Love of God in the Old Testament." *Hebrew Union College Annual* 6 (1929); cited in WBC].

QUESTION—Who are the referents of לכם *lāḵem* 'to you (pl)'?
1. The priests of Israel are the primary referents, but the whole nation is also addressed through them, for the priests stand for the nation's essence [Keil, NICOT].
2. The priests are the referents [Ksr, Mer, TOTC, WBC].

1:7

You(pl)-offer[a] on my-altar[b] defiled[c] food,[d] but[e]-you(pl)-say,[f] how[g] have-we-defiled[h]-*you[i-1]/it[i-2]? (You have defiled me/it) by[j]-your(pl)-saying,[k] (the-)table(-of)[l] YHWH it-is-contemptible.[m]

*TEXT—The LXX and Targum follow a reading of גאלנוהו *gēʾalnûhû* 'we have defiled it' (referring to the offering) instead of גאלנוך *gēʾalnûḵā* 'we have defiled you' [WBC]; the second reading sounded offensive in Greek and so was changed to the first, but the Syriac and Vulgate support the second reading, which is probably original [NICOT, TOTC]. Since in Jewish law contact with something defiled renders the person defiled, so God would be seen to become defiled by accepting unacceptable sacrifices [Keil]. It is read by NLT and NRSV.

LEXICON—a. mas. pl. Hiphil participle of נגש *ngš* (BDB p. 621), (Hol p. 227), (TWOT 1297): 'to offer' [Hol; Coh, Keil, Mer, Gla, NICOT, WBC; CEV, JPS, KJV, NLT, NRSV, REB, TEV], 'to put' [NJB], 'to place' [NIV], 'to bring up' [Hol], 'to present' [NASB]. The form of the participle denotes habitual action of the priests [NICOT]; as such, the participle helps describe the situation which needs to be changed [Clen].

b. constr. of מזבח *mizbēaḥ* (BDB p. 258), (Hol p. 188), (TWOT 525b): 'altar' [all lexica, commentators, and versions].

c. mas. sg. Piel part. of גאל *gʾl* (BDB p. 146), (Hol p. 53), (TWOT 301): 'to defile' [Hol; Mer, NICOT; NASB, NIV, NLT, REB], 'to pollute' [BDB; Coh, Keil, Gla, WBC; JPS, KJV, NJB, NRSV], 'to desecrate' [BDB]. This participle is also translated as an adjective: 'worthless' [CEV, TEV]. *Gʾl* means to render something unfit to be offered to God or used in his worship [Hol].

d. לחם *leḥem* (BDB p. 536), (Hol p. 175), (TWOT 1105a): 'food' [BDB, Hol; Mer, NICOT; CEV, NASB, NIV, NRSV, WBC; JPS, NJB, REB, TEV], 'bread' [BDB, Hol; Coh, Keil, Gla; KJV], 'sacrifice' [NLT]. *Leḥem* in its primary sense denotes bread; it is then extended to denote food in general [Hol].

e. -ו *wə- waw* connective (BDB p. 251), (Hol p. 84), (TWOT 519): 'but' [JPS, NASB, NIV], 'yet' [Mer, Gla, NICOT], 'and yet' [Keil], 'then' [CEV, NLT, TEV], An additive relationship between this clause and the previous one is expressed: 'and' [WBC; KJV, NRSV], and by a new clause [NJB, REB].

f. 2nd pl. Qal perf. of אמר *ʾmr* (BDB p. 55), (Hol p. 21), (TWOT 118): 'to say' [BDB, Hol; Keil, Mer, Gla, WBC; KJV, NASB, NRSV], 'to ask' [NICOT; CEV, JPS, NIV, NJB, NLT, REB, TEV].

g. במה *bammâ* (BDB p. 553), (Hol p. 184): 'how' [Hol; Mer, Gla, NICOT; CEV, JPS, NASB, NIV, NJB, NLT, NRSV, REB, TEV], 'wherewith' [Keil], 'wherein' [BDB; Coh; KJV], 'in what way' [WBC].

h. 1st pl. Piel perf. of גאל *gʾl* (see above): 'to defile' [Hol; Mer, NICOT; JPS, NASB, NIV], 'to pollute' [BDB; Coh, Keil, Gla, WBC; KJV, NJB, NRSV], 'to failed to respect' [TEV], 'to embarrass' [CEV], 'to desecrate' [BDB].

i-1. 2nd mas. sg. suffix: 'you' [Coh, Keil, Mer, Gla, NICOT, WBC; CEV, JPS, KJV, NIV, NJB, REB, TEV], 'thee' [NASB].

i-2. 3rd mas. sg. suffix: 'it' (referring to 'bread') [NLT, NRSV]; 'him' (referring to YHWH, even if the Hebrew 3rd mas. sg. suffix be read, a reading which is not preferred) [Gla].

j. -ב *bə-* (BDB p. 88), (Hol p. 32) (TWOT 193): 'by' [all lexica, commentators, and versions except the following], 'with' [BDB], 'in that' [Coh, Keil; KJV, NASB]. The proclitic *bə-* denotes here instrument or means [BDB, Hol].

k. inf. constr. of אמר ʾmr (BDB p. 55), (Hol p. 21), (TWOT 118): 'to say'
[all lexica, commentators, and versions except NRSV], 'to think'
[NRSV].
l. constr. of שלחן šulḥān (BDB p. 1020), (Hol p. 372), (TWOT 2395a):
'table' [BDB, Hol; Keil, Mer, Gla, NICOT, WBC; JPS, KJV, NASB,
NIV, NJB, NRSV, REB], 'altar' [Coh; CEV, NLT, TEV]. Šulḥān
denotes a table, whether for personal or cultic use [BDB, Hol].
m. mas. sg. Niphal part. of בזה bzh (BDB p. 102), (Hol p. 36), (TWOT
224): 'to be contemptible' [Coh, Gla, NICOT; KJV, NIV], 'to be
despised' [Hol; Keil, Mer, WBC; NASB, NRSV, REB], 'to deserve no
respect' [NJB, NLT], 'to be treated with scorn' [JPS], 'to be thought
lightly of' [Hol]. Some translations use a potential mode, e.g., 'may be
despised' [JPS, REB NRSV WBC], 'is to be despised' [NASB]. This
verb is also translated as an adjective: 'despicable, contemptible' [BDB].
The verb is also translated idiomatically: 'what's so great (about the
Lord's altar)?' [CEV]. TEV translates the people's words by
summarizing their intent: 'by showing contempt for my altar'. The
following verse then specifies the actions which constitute this contempt.
QUESTION—What is the meaning of שלחן šulḥān?
1. Šulḥān refers, not the table for the showbread, but rather to the tables
referred to in Ezek. 40:39–43, located at the gates of the inner court,
where the sacrificial animals were slaughtered [TOTC].
2. Šulḥān refers to the altar [Coh], for the word is parallel to מזבחי
mizbəḥî 'my altar'. The use of šulḥān concords with the analogy of the
governor's table; also, it reminds one of the common practice of sealing
the formation of covenants with covenantal meals [Mer, NICOT]. In a
similar vein, the construct relationship between šulḥān 'table' and yhwh
'YHWH' may be said to refer to an image of YHWH as the host at a
banquet to which the guests brought food, as in 1 Sam. 20:29, 2 Sam.
9:7–13, etc.; the table then becomes a symbol of hospitality and loyalty
of the host extended toward his guests. To slight the table was to slight
the host [Clen].
QUESTION—To what does לחם leḥem here refer?
1. It refers to sacrifices in general [Coh].
2. It refers to sacrificial meat, thus called in Lev. 21:6,8,17, as were called
also sacrifices in general [Keil, Mer, TOTC] (see C.F. Keil and F.
Delitzsch, Commentary on the Old Testament, vol. 1, Lev. 3:6–16).
There is no thought that Israel shared the common idea of her neighbors
that the sacrifices were actual food for God; rather, the term points
ahead to the analogy of gifts for the governor [Mer].
QUESTION—How should ואמרתם waʾămartem 'but you say' be construed?
1. The clause introduced by this word is the real answer to the question
'How have we despised you?" for a participle (מגישים maggîšîm,
translated 'you offer' in the previous clause) could not supply the answer

to a question. What occurs in this verse before this clause is merely a
commentary on the priests' behavior [Keil].
2. The first part of this verse is the answer to the final question of Mal. 1:6
[most versions]. Gla also takes this position, analyzing the pertinent lines
as:
   1:6e (Question) But you have said, "How have we despised your
        name?"
   1:7a (Answer) "By offering polluted bread on my altar."
   1:7b (Question) Yet you say, "How have we defiled you?"
   1:7c (Answer) By your saying, "The table of YHWH is contemptible."
   In Mal. 1:7b, the priests do not the charge that they have offered
polluted bread on YHWH's altar; rather, they ask how that action has
harmed YHWH himself. They receive the answer that a sin against the
altar is a sin against YHWH, whom it represents [Gla].
QUESTION—What is the meaning of מְגֹאָל *məḡōʾāl* 'defiled'?
1. It means that the sacrificial animals were blemished or otherwise in
imperfect physical condition and thus could not be brought to sacrifice
according to Levitical law [Keil, Mer]. *Məḡōʾāl* is technical cultic
language for something unfit to be sacrificed [Mer].
2. It means that the animals in question were physically unfit for sacrifice,
but more than that, it means that the bad attitude of the priests rendered
the sacrifices unfit [TOTC].
QUESTION—What is the significance of the syntactically extraposed (placed
at the head of the clause, out of normal position) noun phrase at the end of
this verse ((the-)table(-of) YHWH)?
Such a construction often marks the peak of a paragraph in BH; here, it
emphasizes the identification of מִזְבְּחִי *mizbəḥî* 'my altar' with שֻׁלְחַן־יְהוָה
šulḥan yhwh 'the table of YHWH' [Clen].

1:8

(a) And[a]-when[b] you(pl)-bring[c] (a-)blind(animal)[d] to[e]-sacrifice(it),[f] is-it-not[g]
wrong[h]? And-when you(pl)-bring a-crippled(animal)[i] or[j]-one-being-ill,[k] is-
it-not wrong?
(b) Offer[l]-him indeed[m] to-your(pl)-governor.[n] Would-he-be-pleased[o]-with-
you, or[p] would-he-accept[q] you(pl)[r]? says YHWH(-of) hosts.
LEXICON—a. -וְ *wa- waw* connective (BDB p. 251), (Hol p. 84), (TWOT
    519): 'and' [Keil, Gla, WBC; KJV], 'for' [Mer], 'but' [CEV, NASB],
    not explicit [NICOT; JPS, NIV, NJB, NLT, NRSV, TEV]. REB treats
    the clause which this connective introduces as further content of
    בְּאָמָרְכֶם *bəʾĕmorkem* 'by your saying' of the previous verse.
  b. כִּי *kî* connective (BDB p. 471), (Hol p. 155), (TWOT 976): 'when'
    [Mer, Gla, NICOT, WBC; JPS, NASB, NIV, NJB, NLT, NRSV,
    TEV], 'if' [Keil; KJV], 'but' [CEV]. וְכִי *wəkî* denotes a conditional
    sentence [NICOT].

MALACHI 1:8

41

c. 2nd mas. pl. Hiphil imperf. of נגשׁ *n̄ḡš* (BDB p. 621), (Hol p. 227), (TWOT 1297): 'to bring' [BDB; Gla, NICOT; NIV, NJB, TEV], 'to offer' [Keil, Mer, WBC; KJV, NRSV, REB], 'to present' [JPS, NASB], 'to give' [NLT], 'to bring near' [BDB, Hol].

d. עִוֵּר *ʿiwwēr* (BDB p. 734), (Hol p. 268), (TWOT 1586a): 'blind' [all lexica, commentators, and versions except REB], 'blind victim' [REB].

e. -לְ *lə-* (BDB p. 510), (Hol p. 167), (TWOT 1063). The proclitic *lə-* here expresses purpose.

f. Qal inf. of זבח *zḇḥ* (BDB p. 256), (Hol p. 86), (TWOT 525): 'to sacrifice' [Keil, Gla, NICOT; JPS, KJV, NIV, NJB, NRSV, TEV], 'to slaughter' [BDB, Hol]. This verb is also translated as a noun 'sacrifice' in the phrases, such as 'as a sacrifice' [Mer, WBC; NASB, NLT].

g. constr. of אַיִן *ʾayin* (BDB p. 34), (Hol p. 13), (TWOT 81): in its absolute form, *ʾayin* denotes 'nothing, the absence of something'; in the construct state, it functions as a negation, e.g., אֵין־רָע *ʾên rāʿ* 'nothing bad, no evil'. Some translations employ a statement: 'declaring it not bad' [Gla], 'there is nothing wrong' [NICOT; REB], 'it is no wickedness' [Keil]. Other commentators and most versions translate the phrase as a rhetorical question: 'is that not . . . ?' [Mer; NIV, NLT, NRSV], 'is this not . . . ?' [NJB], 'isn't it . . . ?' [CEV], 'is it not . . . ?' [WBC; KJV, NASB]. A rhetorical question is employed by the LXX, Syriac, and Arabic versions. However, NICOT argues that the priests and people had come to sincerely believe that such sacrifices were acceptable to God, because the simple performance of the rites was enough to satisfy him; thus they could say, 'There is nothing wrong.' Keil argues that Malachi is employing irony here, i.e., 'there is nothing wrong' = 'of course it is wrong.''

h. רָע *rāʿ* (BDB p. 948), (Hol p. 341), (TWOT 2191a): 'wrong' [NICOT; CEV, NIV, NJB, NLT, NRSV, REB, TEV], 'evil' [BDB, Hol; Mer, WBC; KJV, NASB], 'bad' [BDB, Hol; Gla], 'of bad quality' [Hol]. This adjective is also translated as a noun: 'wickedness' [Keil] and by a phrase: 'it doesn't matter' [JPS].

i. פִּסֵּחַ *pissēaḥ* (BDB p. 820), (Hol p. 294), (TWOT 1787a): 'crippled' [NICOT; CEV, NIV, NLT], 'lame' [BDB, Hol; Keil, Mer, Gla, WBC; KJV, NASB, NJB, NRSV, JPS, REB, TEV].

j. -וְ *wə-* waw connective (BDB p. 251), (Hol p. 84), (TWOT 519): 'or' [NICOT; CEV, JPS, NIV, NRSV, REB, TEV], 'and' [Coh, Keil, Mer, Gla, WBC; KJV, NASB, NJB, NLT].

k. mas. Qal part. of חלה *ḥlh* (BDB p. 317), (Hol p. 104), (TWOT 655): 'to be ill' [Hol], 'to be weak, sick' [BDB]. This verb is also translated as an adjective: 'sick' [Mer, Gla, WBC; CEV, KJV, JPS, NASB, NRSV, TEV], 'sickly' [REB], 'diseased' [Keil. NICOT; NIV, NJB, NLT].

l. mas. pl. Hiphil imv. of קרב *qrḇ* (BDB p. 897), (Hol p. 324), (TWOT 2065): 'to offer' [Hol; Keil, Mer, NICOT, WBC; JPS, KJV, NASB, NIV, NJB], 'to give' [NLT, NRSV, TEV], 'to present' [BDB; Coh,

Gla; NRSV], 'to bring' [BDB; REB]. This verb is part of the Hebrew technical cultic vocabulary. The reference here could be either to the payment of compulsory taxes or to voluntary gifts, but is probably the latter [NICOT].

m. נָא *nāʾ* (BDB p. 609), (Hol p. 223), (TWOT 1269): 'indeed' [Mer], 'please' [WBC]; 'now' [Keil; KJV]. Various sorts of verbal modalities are employed in some versions at this point, conveying through the means of irony the unacceptable nature of the sacrifices in question: 'try giving' [NLT, TEV], 'if you offer' [NJB], 'just offer it' [JPS], 'try offering' [NIV], 'try presenting that' [NRSV], 'just try giving those' [NRSV], 'do offer them' [NICOT], 'why not offer it' [NASB]. *Nāʾ* is a particle expressing urgency, a plea, or an exhortation [BDB, Hol].

n. constr. of פֶחָה *peḥâ* (BDB p. 808), (Hol p. 291), (TWOT 1257): 'governor' [all lexica, commentators, and versions]. *Peḥâ* is probably a loan word from Akkadian; its use here shows that Samaria and/or Judah were under the rule of a governor who had been placed there by the king of Persia [WBC]. *Peḥ*â denoted in Akkadian 'lord of a district' [BDB], a position lower than 'satrap' for the Persians [NICOT]. This governor's identity and nationality are unknown.

o. 3rd mas. sg. Qal imperf. of רצה *rṣh* (BDB p. 953), (Hol p. 345), (TWOT 2207): 'to be pleased with' [BDB, Hol; Mer, Gla, NICOT, WBC; KJV, NIV, NJB, NRSV, TEV], 'to be pleased' [NASB, `NLT], 'to be gracious to' [Keil], 'to accept' [BDB; JPS], 'to receive' [REB]. This verb is also translated as in the active voice: 'that certainly wouldn't please him' [CEV].

p. אֹ *ʾô* (BDB p. 14), (Hol p. 6), (TWOT 36): 'or' [all lexica, commentators, and versions except the following]. 'or even' [Gla]. The essential additive relationship signaled in this context by 'ô is also expressed by a new clause [JPS, NIV]. *ʾô* is a conjunction expressing choice [Hol].

q. 3rd mas. sg. Qal imperf. of נשׂא *nśʾ* (BDB p. 669), (Hol p. 246), (TWOT 1421). *Nśʾ* in its primary sense denotes 'to lift, to carry, to take'; here, however, it forms with פָנֶיךָ *pānêkā* 'your faces' an idiom (see below).

r. pl. constr. of פנים *pānîm* (BDB p. 815), (Hol p. 293), (TWOT 1782a). The primary sense of *pānîm* is 'face'. *Pānîm* here, however, functions with נשׂא *nśʾ* (see above) as an idiom [Hol p. 246], [BDB p. 670]: 'to accept' [Hol; Keil; KJV, NIV], 'to lift up one's face' [BDB; WBC], 'to show one favor' [NICOT; JPS, NRSV, REB], 'to receive one with favor' [Mer], 'to be favorable to' [Hol], 'to grant one any favors' [TEV], 'to receive one graciously' [NJB], 'to receive one kindly' [NASB], 'to be gracious towards one' [Gla]. The idea of accepting one with favor is also translated 'to make him want to help you out' [CEV] and as 'grant you a cordial reception' [NICOT]. The literal meaning 'to lift up the face of another' probably originated in raising up one who had humbly prostrated himself before his superior [BDB].

QUESTION—Why was the offering of blind, crippled, or sick animals to God condemned?

Because it was contrary to the stipulations of the ceremonial law, which expressly forbade blind and crippled, and implicitly forbade sick animals as well [NICOT].

QUESTION—What relation does part (b) of this verse have to part (a)?

It is the result of part (a) [Clen].

QUESTION—What is the nature of the imperative הקריבהו *haqrîḇēhû* 'offer' and of the following double question?

The imperative is sarcastic, for implicit is the knowledge that no one would ever offer such gifts to the governor. Similarly, the following double question is rhetorical, for a negative answer is understood to both parts. For this reason, the imperative is underlyingly a condition, and the following double question underlying encodes an irreal consequence [Clen].

1:9

And-now[a] **implore,**[b] **please,**[c] **(the-)face(-of)**[d] **God,**[e] **that-he-may-be-gracious**[f]**-to-us.**

LEXICON—a. -ו *wə- waw* connective + עתה *ʿattâ* (BDB p. 774), (Hol p. 287), (TWOT 1650c): 'and now' [BDB, Hol; Keil, Gla, WBC; NRSV, KJV, JPS], 'but now' [Mer; NASB, REB], 'then' [NICOT], 'now' [NIV, TEV], 'now therefore' [BEB], 'in that case' [NJB]. *Wəʿattâ* often introduces a new thought or section [Hol]; *wəʿattâ* often introduces a conclusion drawn from what has been previously states [BEB].

    b. mas. pl. Piel imv. of חלה *ḥlh* (BDB p. 318), (Hol p. 104), (TWOT 656): 'implore' [JPS, NIV, NRSV], 'to entreat' [BDB; WBC (literally 'to appease, to stroke'; NASB], 'to appease' [BDB, Hol; Gla], 'to try to appease' [NICOT], 'to supplicate' [Keil], 'to petition' [Mer], 'to beseech' [KJV], 'to try pleading with' [NJB], 'to try asking' [TEV], 'to placate' [REB], 'to beg' [NLT]. This verb is translated as 2nd mas pl. Piel imperf. in a condition: 'if you placate God' [REB]. It is also translated as a question: 'will you not entreat God's favor . . . ?' [NASB].

    c. נא *nāʾ* (BDB p. 609), (Hol p. 223), (TWOT 1269): 'please' [WBC], 'go ahead' [NLT], not explicit [all other commentators and versions]. *nāʾ* is described as a particle expressing urgency, a plea, or an exhortation [BDB, Hol].

    d. constr. of פנים *pānîm* (BDB p. 815), (Hol p. 293), (TWOT 1782a): 'face' [BDB, Hol; Keil, WBC], 'favor' [NASB], not explicit [all other commentators and versions].

    e. אל *ʾēl* (BDB p. 42), (Hol p. 15), (TWOT 93a): 'God' [all lexica, commentators, and versions].

f. 3rd mas. sg. Qal imperf. of חנן *ḥnn* (BDB p. 335), (Hol p. 110), (TWOT 694): 'to be gracious' [BDB, Hol; NICOT, WBC; KJV, NASB, NIV, NRSV], 'to take pity' [NJB], 'to be good' [TEV], 'to show favor' [BDB; Gla], 'to be merciful' [NLT], 'to show mercy' [REB]. This verb is also translated as a question: 'will he be gracious to us?' [JPS], and as the apodosis to a condition: 'he may show you mercy' [REB].

QUESTION—What is the force of נא *nā°* in this verse?

1. It gives sarcasm or irony to the imperative associated with it [NICOT, TOTC]. This reinforces the theme in the larger passage of the Jews' improper response to authority: they respect the governor more than God [WBC]. Coh and Gla also consider this verse ironic.
2. Although it may give force to the verb, it does not here signal irony [REB].

QUESTION—Why is אל *°ēl* 'God' used in this passage instead of יהוה *YHWH* 'Lord'?

°ēl emphasizes the contrast between God and the governor, who is only human [Keil, NICOT].

QUESTION—Who are the speakers in this passage?

1. The prophet is the speaker, and his words are meant sarcastically, parallel to the irony of the preceding verse [Clen, Coh, Keil, NICOT]. This ironic imperative is perhaps underlying a statement: 'yet you are trying to appease God to gain his favor' [Clen]. Kimchi and Ibn Ezra had interpreted this passage as a genuine call to repentance [cited in Coh], as does REB.
2. The speakers are one group of priests, who are entreating another group to intercede for them; or, perhaps the entire nation entreating the priests to intercede for them (A. van Hoonacker, *Les douze petits prophètes.* Paris: J. Gabalda & Cie., 1908; cited in Gla]. But the effect of such entreaty is still ironic [Gla].
3. The speakers may be both priests and nation. This sentence is, in fact, a common liturgical expression, here employed ironically to bring home the fact that the priests are no more in good standing with God, and thus can no longer fulfill their role as intercessors for themselves or for the nation [Gla].

From^a-your(pl)-hand^b this^c was.

LEXICON—a. מן *min* (BDB p. 577), (Hol p. 200), (TWOT 1212). *Min* introduces a cause, whether agent or source [BDB, Hol].

b. יד *yāḏ* (BDB p. 388), (Hol p. 127), (TWOT 844). In its primary sense, *yāḏ* denotes 'hand, forearm'; here it functions instrumentally: 'by, through'.

c. זאת *zō°ṯ* fem. demonstr. 'this' (BDB p. 260), (Hol p. 86), (TWOT 528). *Zō°ṯ* is the feminine demonstrative pronoun and adjective. It is commonly used to refer in a neutral and anaphoric manner to some thing or some act, etc. [BDB]. See below for examples of the many ways in which this entire phrase has been translated.

QUESTION—How is this phrase understood?

1. It is seen as a circumstantial clause (as long as the priests bring unacceptable sacrifices, God cannot receive them): 'with this kind of thing in your hands' [Mer], 'with such offerings from your hands' [NIV], 'when you bring that kind of offering' [NLT], 'with such an offering on your part' [NASB].

2. It is seen as a parenthesis: 'of your hand has this [the unacceptable sacrifices offered by the priests] occurred' [Keil], 'that is what you have done' [attempted to plead with God] [NJB].

3. It is seen as an assertion from which flows the following phrase: 'you have sinned' [CEV], 'you have done this' [NICOT], 'the fault is yours' [NRSV], 'this hath been by your means' [KJV], 'this is what you have done' [JPS], 'since all this was your doing' [Gla].

4. It is seen as a condition to be fulfilled by the Jews in return for God's favor: 'if you do this [placate God]' [REB, (which does not see this verse as ironic)].

5. It is seen as a comment on the fact that God will refuse to show favor to the Jews: 'it will be your fault' [TEV].

(a_1) **Will-he-receive-with-favor**[a-1] **anyone**[b] **because-of**[c-1]**-you(pl)?**, says **YHWH(-of) hosts.**

(a_2) **Will-he-receive-with-favor**[a-1] **any**[b] **of**[c-2]**-you(pl)?**, says **YHWH(-of) hosts.**

(a_3) **Will-he-withhold-favor**[a-2] **from**[c-3]**-you(pl)?**, says **YHWH(-of) hosts.**

SYNTAX—the two syntactic interpretations given above depend on different understandings of the function of מִן *min* (c-1 and c-2); in interpretation (a_1), min expresses cause, and in (a_2), it is a partitive expression. In interpretation (a_3), followed only by REB, *min* is seen as a complement of 'to withhold'.

LEXICON—a-1. 3rd mas. sg. Qal imperf. of נָשָׂא *nś'* (BDB p. 669), (Hol p. 246), (TWOT 1421). *Nś'* in its primary sense denotes 'to lift, to carry, to take'; here, however, it forms with פָּנִים *pānîm* 'faces' the idiom 'to receive with favor' (see below).

a-2. 3rd mas. sg. Qal imperf. of נָשָׂא *nś'* (see above). *Nś'* in its primary sense denotes 'to lift, to carry, to take'; here, however, it forms with פָּנִים *pānîm* 'faces' the idiom 'to withhold favor' [REB].

b. pl. of פָּנִים *pānîm* (BDB p. 815), (Hol p. 293), (TWOT 1782a). The primary sense of *pānîm* is 'face'. *Pānîm* here, however, functions with נָשָׂא *nś'* (see above) as an idiom [Hol p. 246], [BDB p. 670]: 'to receive with favor' [Mer], 'to receive kindly' [NASB], 'to look upon' [Keil], 'to show favor' [NICOT], 'to lift up faces' [BDB; WBC], 'to accept' [Hol; JPS, NIV], 'to take notice' [NJB], 'to regard persons' [KJV], 'to answer one's prayer' [TEV], 'to have mercy' [CEV]. To translate this rhetorical question, most translations employ a yes-no question here, but Mer

translates 'how . . . ?, and NLT translates 'why . . . ?' TEV uses a
statement: 'he will not answer your prayer'. The literal meaning 'to lift
up the face of another' probably originated in raising up one who had
humbly prostrated himself before his superior [BDB].

c-1. מִן min (BDB p. 577), (Hol p. 200), (TWOT 1212): 'because of'
[NICOT], 'on account of' [Keil]. This interpretation uses the fact that
the priests represented the people in presenting their sacrifices to God,
and that misconduct on the part of the priests would result in God not
accepting the prayers of the people in general. Min introduces here a
cause [BDB, Hol].

c-2. מִן min (see above): 'any of' [JPS, NASB, NRSV]. Some translations
ask the roughly same question but without the partitive idea: 'should he
be gracious to you?' [Gla], 'how can he receive you with favor?' [Mer],
'will he lift up your faces?' [WBC], 'will he accept you?' [NIV], 'will
he take any notice?' [NJB], 'will he regard your persons?' [KJV], 'why
should he show you any favor at all?' [NLT], 'he will not answer your
prayer' [TEV]. CEV renders this same idea as direct speech from God:
'now see if I have mercy on you'. Min introduces here a partitive
expression, expressing part of a whole [BDB, Hol].

c-3. מִן min (see above): 'from' (complement of 'to withhold favor')
[REB].

QUESTION—What is the nature of the question in this passage?
1. It is rhetorical, in keeping with the preceding parts of this verse, and
means to state that God will not extend his favor in the light of the
conditions described earlier [all commentators].
2. It is rhetorical and means to state that God will not fail to extend favor
[REB].

DISCOURSE UNIT: 1:10 [Clen (within the larger discourse unit of Mal. 1:2–
2:9)]. The topic is the command to "stop vain offerings."

1:10
Oh,[a] (would that) one[b] among[c]-you(pl) he-would-shut[d] (the-)doors,[e] so[f]-
you(pl)-would- -not -kindle-fire[g] (on-) my-altar[h] /-light[g] my-altar[h]
uselessly.[i]

LEXICON—a. גַּם gam (BDB p. 168), (Hol p. 61), (TWOT 361a): 'oh, . . .'
[Keil, NICOT, WBC; NASB, NIV, NRSV], not explicit [all other
commentators and versions]. Gam is called an intensifying particle
[Hol], and is said to express addition [BDB].

b. מִי mî (BDB p. 566), (Hol p. 192), (TWOT 1189). Mî is an interrogative
pronoun 'who?'. Here, followed by the imperfect, it functions to express
a wish [BDB, Hol]. See below for translations.

c. -בְּ bə- (BDB p. 88), (Hol p. 32) (TWOT 193). The expression מִי גַם־
מִי גַם בָּכֶם mî gam bākem is translated 'one among you' [Keil, Gla, WBC],
'one of you' [Mer, NICOT; NIV, NJB, REB, TEV], 'someone' [CEV],

'someone among you' [NLT, NRSV]. The proclitic bə- here denotes 'among a group' [BDB, Hol]. The expression 'who among you' idiomatically expresses a wish in Hebrew: 'would that' [Gla], 'that one among/of you would . . .' [Keil, NICOT, WBC; NIV, NRSV], 'if only' [JPS], 'that there were one among you' [NASB], 'I wish' [NLT, TEV], 'better far' [REB]. NJB expresses a similar wish with a question: 'why does one of you not close . . . ?'

d. 3rd mas. sg. Qal imperf. of סגר sḡr (BDB p. 688), (Hol p. 253), (TWOT 1462): 'to shut' [BDB, Hol; Keil, Gla, NICOT, WBC; KJV, NASB, NIV, NLT, NRSV], 'to close' [Hol; Mer; NJB, REB, TEV], 'to lock' [CEV, JPS]. All translations express a desire.

e. dual of דלת delet̲ (BDB p. 195), (Hol p. 71), (TWOT 431e): 'door' [all lexica, commentators, and versions except the following], 'gate' [NASB], 'temple door' [CEV, NIV, NLT, NRSV, TEV], 'great door' [REB].

f. ולא wəlōʾ (BDB p. 520), (Hol p. 170), (TWOT 1064): this particle, although appearing to introduce a coordinate clause, actually introduces a dependent clause [Hol]. It is translated as negative purpose or negative result by all commentators and versions (e.g., 'that you might not enkindle . . .' [Gla], except JPS, which translates this clause as formally coordinate with the preceding clause: 'and not kindle fire'; and KJV, which also translates this clause as formally coordinate: 'neither do ye kindle fire. . . .'

g. 2nd pl. mas. Hiphil imperf. of אור ʾôr (BDB p. 21), (Hol p. 7), (TWOT 52): 'to kindle fire' [Hol; all commentators and versions except the following], 'to build fires' [CEV], 'to light fires' [BDB; NIV, NJB], 'to enkindle' [Gla]. Some make more explicit the relationship of this negative purpose or result clause with the preceding clause by specifying the notion of prevention: 'to keep fire from being lit' [REB], 'so as to prevent you from lighting fires' [TEV]. Others, employing a figure of speech, express the action of which kindling fire is but a means to the end: 'so that these worthless sacrifices could not be offered' [NLT].

h. constr. of מזבח mizbēaḥ (BDB p. 258), (Hol p. 188), (TWOT 525b): 'altar' [all lexica, commentators, and versions]. Only two translations strive to preserve in English the verb—direct object relationship which 'kindle' has to 'altar' in Hebrew: 'to light mine altar' [Keil], 'to enkindle my altar' [Gla]. The other translations use a prepositional phrase: 'on my altar'.

i. חנם ḥinnām (BDB p. 336), (Hol p. 110), (TWOT 694b): 'uselessly' [NASB], 'in vain' [BDB, Hol; Gla, NICOT, WBC; NRSV], 'to no purpose' [Keil; JPS, REB]. This adverbial expression is also translated as an adjective modifying 'fire': 'pointless' [NJB], 'useless' [Mer; NIV, TEV], 'worthless' [NLT], and by an adverbial phrase: 'wasting time' [CEV]. KJV translates 'for nought' (i.e., 'freely, for no pay').

QUESTION—What is the discourse status of this verse?

It is the exhortation based on the reason (inferior sacrifices) given in Mal. 1:6–9 [Clen].

QUESTION—What is the nature of the verb וְיִסְגֹּר *wayisgōr* 'and that he would shut'?

It is ironic, for shutting the Temple doors is not the behavioral change which YHWH is actually seeking. A force of exaggeration is given the phrase by the particle גַּם *gam* [Clen].

QUESTION—What doors are referred to in this verse?

1. Not the entry doors of the Temple itself, but probably the doors between the court of the priests and the great court of the Temple; if these were shut, no sacrifices could be performed [TOTC, WBC], for the tables for slaughtering the sacrificial animals were situated in the court of the priests [TOTC].
2. The doors to the inner court [Keil, Gla].
3. Either the doors to the court of the priests or the doors to the inner court, the location of the burnt offerings [NICOT].

QUESTION—What accounts for the difference between the KJV and more modern versions in translating חִנָּם *ḥinnām*?

The KJV's translation arose from the fact that both LXX and the Vulgate chose to render *ḥinnām* as *gratuito* 'freely' (sometimes a valid translation) instead of *frustra* 'in vain' [NICOT].

QUESTION—What is the significance of kindling fire on the altar?

Preparing the fires on the altar was part of the priests' work in worship [Gla], while the killing of the sacrificial animals was the work those who brought sacrifices to the Temple [TOTC].

QUESTION—What is the significance of this passage?

Malachi here condemns the Jews' worship rituals, as had done Amos, Hosea, Micah, Isaiah, and Jeremiah before him, because the worshippers have rejected all that YHWH stands for [Gla].

(a) There-is-not to-me pleasure[a] in-you,[b] says YHWH(-of) hosts,
(b) and[c]-(an-)offering[d] I-will- not[e] -accept[f] from[g]-your(pl)-hand.[h]

LEXICON—a. חֵפֶץ *ḥēpeṣ* (BDB p. 343), (Hol p. 112), (TWOT 712b): 'pleasure' [BDB, Hol; Keil, NICOT; KJV, NRSV], 'delight' [BDB; Gla, WBC], 'joy' [Hol]. This noun is also translated as a verb: 'to be pleased' [Mer; CEV, NASB, NIV, NJB, NLT, REB, TEV].

b. כֶם- *kem* 2nd mas. pl. prn.: 'you' [all commentators and versions]. CEV makes the pronominal reference explicit: 'you priests'.

c. -ו *wǝ- waw* connective (BDB p. 251), (Hol p. 84), (TWOT 519): 'and' [all commentators and versions except the following]; the negative additive relationship is expressed with 'neither' [KJV], 'nor' [Gla and REB; NASB]. NJB and TEV imply the additive relationship of 'and' without explicitly translating the *waw* connective. Clen analyzes part (b) as a result of part (a) and so would presumably favor a translation of the *waw* connective such as 'so'.

d. מִנְחָה *minḥâ* (BDB p. 585), (Hol p. 202), (TWOT 1214a): 'offering' [all lexica, commentators, and versions], 'sacrifice' [Hol]. *Minḥâ* denotes an offering of any kind [Keil, NICOT]. The position of *minḥâ* 'offering' at the front of its clause indicates that the idea of 'offering' is reestablished as the topic, after its last occurrence in Mal. 1:8 [Clen].

e. לֹא *lō'* (BDB p. 518), (Hol p. 170), (TWOT 1064). Most translations indicate a simple negative: 'to not accept', 'no offering', etc. Some, however, make explicit the notion that God had once accepted the Jews' sacrifices but would no longer do so: 'no longer' [Mer], 'any more' [CEV]. *Lō'* marks negation in a declarative sentence [BDB, Hol].

f. 3rd mas. sg. Qal imperf. of רצה *rṣh* (BDB p. 953), (Hol p. 345), (TWOT 2207): 'to accept' [Mer, Gla, WBC; JPS, KJV, NASB, NIV, NLT, NRSV, REB, TEV], 'to be pleased with' [BDB, Hol; NICOT], 'to refuse to accept' [CEV], 'to find no offerings acceptable' [NJB]. YHWH is made the syntactic object of 'please' in Keil: 'sacrificed offering does not please me'. *Rṣh* is part of the technical cultic vocabulary in Hebrew; it concerns how effective the offerings are with God [NICOT].

g. מִן *min* (BDB p. 577), (Hol p. 200), (TWOT 1212): 'from' [Keil, Mer, Gla, NICOT, WBC; JPS, NASB, NJB, NRSV, REB], 'at' [Coh; KJV]. The preposition *min* here indicates perhaps spatial motion from a starting point, or perhaps logical cause.

h. constr. of יָד *yād* [BDB p. 388], (Hol p. 127), (TWOT 844): 'hand' [Gla, WBC; Keil, KJV, NIV, NJB, NRSV]. The synecdoche of *yād* is recognized and translated concretely as 'you' [Mer, NICOT; JPS, NASB, REB, TEV]. The notion of agency is also conveyed by the pronoun 'your' in the phrase 'your offerings' [CEV]. In its primary sense, *yād* denotes 'hand, forearm'; here it functions instrumentally: 'by, through'.

QUESTION—What is the discourse function of parts (a) and (b)?

They serve together to form the peak of Constituent C, which in turn is the change element, the most naturally prominent element in hortatory discourse and, hence, of the "first movement" of Malachi. The crux of the message, then, is that YHWH wants no more useless sacrifices [Clen].

DISCOURSE UNIT: 1:11–14 [Clen (within the larger discourse unit of Mal. 1:2–2:9)]. This paragraph realizes the first movement's semantic constituent B', the topic of which is "profaning YHWH's name."

1:11

For[a] from-(the-)rising(-of)[b] (the-)sun[c] even[d]-to its-setting,[e] great[f] (is/will be) my-name[g] among-the-nations,[h] and[i]-in-every[j] place,[k] incense/burnt-sacrifice[l] is/will-be-offered[m] to-my-name. And[n]-(a-) pure[o] -offering[p] (is/will-be-brought), because^q great (is/will-be) my-name among-the-nations, says YHWH(-of) hosts.

SYNTAX—This verse, treated as one sentence in many versions, is actually considered by Clen to be two sentences in BH, since it is both begun and ended by clauses introduced by כִּי kî [Clen].

LEXICON—a. כִּי kî connective (BDB p. 471), (Hol p. 155), (TWOT 976): 'for' [Keil, Mer, Gla; JPS, KJV, NASB, NRSV], 'but' [NJB, WBC—where kî is used adversatively], 'verily' [NICOT], 'but' [NJB, NLT], no conjunction used in translation [CEV, NIV, REB, TEV].

b. constr. of מִזְרָח mizrāḥ (BDB p. 280), (Hol p. 189), (TWOT 580c). Mizrāḥ is a noun from זרח zrḥ 'to go forth, to shine' [Hol p. 92], and is used here together with שֶׁמֶשׁ šemeš 'sun' (see below).

c. שֶׁמֶשׁ šemeš (BDB p. 1039), (Hol p. 378), (TWOT 2417a). Šemeš denotes 'sun'. The phrase mizraḥ šemeš is translated locatively by most: 'rising of the sun' [Keil, Mer, Gla, NICOT, WBC; KJV, NASB, NIV, NRSV], 'where the sun rises' [JPS], 'one end of the world (to the other)' [TEV], 'farthest east' [NJB, REB], 'sunrise', i.e., 'the east' [BDB p. 280], [Hol p. 378]. This expression of place (= 'everywhere') is parallel to 'in every place' in Mal. 1:11c [Gla]. Mizraḥ šemeš is also translated temporally: 'dawn' [CEV], 'morning' [NLT].

d. -ו wə- waw connective (BDB p. 251), (Hol p. 84), (TWOT 519). This connective is translated here as an intensive 'even' [WBC; KJV, NASB], but is left untranslated by all other commentators and versions.

e. constr. of מָבוֹא māḇôʾ (BDB p. 99), (Hol p. 181), (TWOT 212b). Māḇôʾ is a noun from בוא bôʾ 'go, come'. The phrase məḇôʾô is translated locatively, e.g., 'its setting' by most: 'setting' [Hol Keil, Mer, Gla, NICOT; NASB, NIV, NRSV], 'going down' [WBC; KJV], 'farthest west' [NJB, REB], 'west' [BDB], 'other end [of the world]' [TEV], 'where it [the sun] sets' [JPS]. Məḇôʾô is also translated temporally: 'dusk' [CEV], 'night' [NLT].

f. גָּדוֹל gāḏôl (BDB p. 152), (Hol p. 55), (TWOT 315d): 'great' [all lexica, commentators, and versions except the following]. This adjective is also translated by verbs: 'to be honored' [JPS, NLT], 'to honor' [TEV], 'to be praised' [CEV]. Gāḏôl here means great in one's position or role [Hol].

g. constr. of שֵׁם šēm (BDB p. 1027), (Hol p. 374), (TWOT 2405): 'name' [all lexica, commentators, and versions except the following]. TEV recognizes the metonymy of 'name' and translates concretely as 'me'. In its primary sense, šēm denotes 'name'; it then refers to one's fame [Hol].

h. pl. of גּוֹי gôy (BDB p. 156), (Hol p. 57), (TWOT 326e): 'nation' [all lexica, commentators, and versions except the following], 'Gentiles' [KJV], 'people' [BDB; TEV], 'people of other nations' [NLT]. The phrase 'the nations' is translated as 'every nation on this earth' [CEV].

Gôy refers to the peoples and ethnic groups around Israel, with emphasis upon their paganness.

i. -ו wə- waw connective (BDB p. 251), (Hol p. 84), (TWOT 519): 'and' [Coh, Keil, Mer, Gla, WBC; JPS, KJV, NASB, NJB, NRSV, REB]. The additive relationship is also expressed by a new clause or sentence [NICOT; NIV, NLT, TEV]. CEV expresses a circumstantial relationship: 'as they burn incense. . . .'

j. constr. of כֹּל kōl (BDB p. 481), (Hol p. 156), (TWOT 985a): 'every' [Hol; Keil, NICOT, WBC; KJV, NASB, NIV, NRSV]. In conjunction with the following entry, some translate 'everywhere' [Mer; JPS, NJB, REB, TEV], 'all around the world' [NLT]. The noun kōl denotes a totality of something [BDB, Hol].

k. מָקוֹם māqôm (BDB p. 879), (Hol p. 212), (TWOT 1999h): 'place' [BDB, Hol; Keil, Gla, NICOT, WBC; KJV, NASB, NIV, NRSV]. In conjunction with the previous entry, some translate 'everywhere' [Mer; JPS, NJB, TEV]. Māqôm very often means 'place' or 'location' [BDB, Hol], whether specified or unspecified; it could mean 'sanctuary' here, i.e., a place of worship, as it does in other passages [TOTC].

l. mas. Huphal part. of קְטַר qtr (BDB p. 883), (Hol p. 317), (TWOT 2011): 'incense' [all commentators and versions except the following], 'sweet incense' [NLT], 'burnt sacrifice' [Gla], 'oblation' [WBC]. This participle of qtr is translated literally as 'to be made to smoke' [BDB], and 'to be made to go up in smoke', referring to a sacrifice [Hol]. The Piel of qtr (the Qal is not attested) means 'to let a sacrifice go up in smoke' [Hol].

m. mas. Huphal part. of נגשׁ ngš (BDB p. 621), (Hol p. 227), (TWOT 1297): 'to be offered' [BDB, Hol; Mer, Gla, NICOT, WBC; JPS, KJV, NASB, NJB, NLT, NRSV], 'to be brought' [NIV], 'to be presented' [REB]. Some versions use the active voice with the indefinite subject 'they': 'to offer' [NLT], 'to burn' [CEV, TEV]. Keil translates this participle, as the previous one, with a complete phrase: 'and sacrifice is offered'. The future tense is employed by Mer, Gla; KJV, and NIV; the near future ('about to be offered') is employed by TOTC. The present tense is employed by Keil, NICOT, WBC; JPS, NJB, NLT, NRSV, and REB. The Qal of ngš means 'to come near, approach' [Hol]. The participles of the two verbs qtr and ngš can be understood as being either in the present or future tense, and the choice of tense has implications for the verse's interpretation (see questions below) [Ksr, Keil].

n. -ו wə- waw connective [BDB p. 251], (Hol p. 84), (TWOT 519). This connective is translated as additive: 'and' [CEV, JPS, KJV, NASB, NIV, NJB, NLT, NRSV, REB, TEV], 'as well as' [Mer]. This connective is also translated as placing מִנְחָה minḥâ 'offering' in apposition with muqtār 'incense/sacrifice', usually with an intensive particle such as 'indeed': 'even pure oblations' [Coh], '—a pure

offering' [NICOT, WBC], 'and indeed, a pure sacrifice' [Keil], 'indeed,
a pure offering' [Gla].

o. fem. sg. of טהור ṭāhôr (BDB p. 373), (Hol p. 121), (TWOT 792d):
'pure' [BDB; Keil, Gla, NICOT, Mer, WBC; JPS, KJV, NASB, NIV,
NJB, NLT, NRSV, REB], 'acceptable' [TEV], 'proper' [CEV], 'clean'
[BDB, Hol]. Ṭāhôr, which can mean 'morally and physically' pure as
well as ceremonially pure, is not usually used to describe acceptable
sacrifices; the normal word is תמים tāmîm 'without blemish' [Ksr,
TOTC].

p. מנחה minḥâ (BDB p. 585), (Hol p. 202), (TWOT 1214a): 'offering'
[BDB, Hol; Mer, Gla, NICOT, WBC; KJV, NIV, NLT, NRSV, REB],
'sacrifice' [Hol; CEV, TEV], 'oblation' [JPS], 'gift' [NJB], 'grain
offering' [NASB].

q. כי kî connective (BDB p. 471), (Hol p. 155), (TWOT 976): 'because'
[WBC; NIV], 'for' [Keil, Mer, Gla, NICOT; JPS, NASB, NLT,
NRSV, REB], 'since' [NJB], no conjunction used in translation [TEV].

QUESTION—What is the meaning of מקטר muqṭār 'something made to go up
in smoke'?

1. Keil translates this participle as a complete phrase ('incense is burned'),
   arguing that the participle refers to the kindling of incense, and so is
   distinct from the following participle of מגש muggāš 'that which is
   offered' ; qtr does not refer to the burning of offerings in general; if it
   did, its participle would stand after the following participle, since a gift
   must be offered before it is burned. There is in any case no explicitly
   stated subject to these participles [Keil].

2. Since qtr can refer to any sacrifice, muqṭār should be translated, 'burnt
   sacrifice will be offered' [Gla].

QUESTION—What are the syntactic difficulties of this verse?

The presence of two Hebrew participles together is unusual and has
occasioned many attempts on the part of scholars to emend the text of this
verse. However, two participles also occur together in Isa. 21:2 as a
subject-verb combination; the two participles in Mal. 1:11 can be
understood in the same way [Gla].

QUESTION—What is the syntactic function of ומנחה טהורה ûminḥâ ṭāhôrâ
'and a pure offering'?

It should be understand in the sense of 'and indeed a pure gift", where the
waw connective has an explanatory role. The phrase thus specifies the
nature of the preceding words 'incense being offered'. The emphasis is on
the idea of 'pure' in contrast to the priests' impure sacrifices [Keil]. Gla
concurs in the explanatory role of this phrase, although she interprets
muqṭār 'that which is made to go up in smoke' differently from Keil.

QUESTION—To what does טהורה ṭāhôrâ 'pure' refer?

1. It indicates the ceremonial acceptability of the sacrifice (cf. Lev. 14:4;
   20:25) [Keil, Gla, NICOT].

2. It indicates a sincere motivation of the worshippers [Kimchi, cited in Coh].

3. It denotes not only physical perfection of the sacrificial animals, but also a moral perfection. In fact, this is the only passage in the OT in which the priestly sacrifices are qualified with *ṭāhôr*. The general adjective associated with sacrifices is תמים *tāmîm* 'without blemish', which does not carry a connotation of moral perfection [TOTC].

4. It may well indicate a pure motivation on the part of the worshippers as well as the physical acceptability of the sacrifices [Gla].

QUESTION—What interpretations have been made of this verse?

1. An early Roman Catholic view considered this to be a prophecy of the Mass, with its doctrine of continual sacrifice [WBC].

2. Some ancient Jews considered this verse as referring to the worship of the Jews of the Diaspora, saying that their study of the Scriptures was held by God to be of value equal to the sacrifices in Jerusalem [WBC]. Or, indeed, that such service in the Diaspora is preferable to the hollow rituals pursued in Jerusalem [G.A. Smith, *The Book of the Twelve Prophets* (2 vols. New York: A.C. Armstrong, 1899; cited in Gla], and that the Jews of the Diaspora in fact brought the true worship of God to the nations [Gla]. There may be some truth to this interpretation, as the Diaspora, even in Malachi's time, was of some considerable extent, and as some of the prophets speak well of the dispersed Jews' piety [NICOT].

3. Jewish proselytes in foreign lands are referred to here. Burnt offerings are understood metaphorically as the proselytes' prayers and worship [C. von Orelli, *The Twelve Minor Prophets* (Edinburgh: T.&T. Clark, 1893; cited in Gla).

4. This verse validates all sincere worship of all religions, saying that God receives it as done to himself [Coh]. Early church fathers espoused this view [Ksr]. This interpretation supplies the present tense 'are brought'. J. Lindblom suggests that, as pagan religions of the time of the Persian empire tended toward monotheism, Malachi is here seizing the opportunity to state that all worship seriously done to the supreme God is in fact received by YHWH [J. Lindblom, *Prophecy in Ancient Israel* (Philadelphia: Fortress, 1962), cited in Gla]. Some scholars assume that only the present tense can be implied in a verbless phrase, and thus that Mal. 1:11 must refer to the prophet's own time, since the surrounding verses do also [Gla]. An objection to this universalistic view argues that, if this interpretation is valid, then Malachi is the only prophet to have expressed this view [TOTC]. Another objection: given that the Levitical sacrifices were never called *ṭāhôr* 'pure', it would be unthinkable that pagan sacrifices should be deemed acceptable [TOTC].

5. Malachi is using hyperbole, saying that even the sacrifices offered by pagans are preferable to—and hence, purer than—those offered by the priests.

6. This verse is (primarily [NICOT]) eschatologically oriented; it looks forward to God's kingdom coming in all the world [Ksr, Keil, Mer, TOTC]. Note that in Mal. 1:14, the implication of the coming kingdom implies further that the Jews will lose the kingdom—this is the basis for the curse in v. 14 [Keil]. Phraseology like *from-rising-of sun and-to its-setting* is used in the OT at least half a dozen times in connection with the coming messianic age, in which the priestly sacrificial system will be summed up and transcended by the sacrifice of Jesus Christ [Gla, TOTC]. Verbless clauses may indeed have a future thrust, if their context warrants it, and participles filling the verb slot of a clause may indeed denote the future [Gla].

1:12

(a) But[a]-you(pl)[b] (are-)profaning[c] me/it* by[d]-your(pl)-saying[e]

(b₁) (the-)table(-of)[f] (the-)Lord[g] is-defiled,[h]
(c₁) it[i] and[j]-its-fruit[k]** are-contemptible.[l] [WBC]

(b₂) (the-)table(-of)[f] (the-)Lord,[g] it[i] is-defiled,[h]
(c₂) and[j]-its-fruit,[k] its-food,[m]*** is-contemptible.[l] [Coh, Keil, Mer, Gla, NICOT; JPS, KJV, NASB, NJB, NLT, REB, TEV]

(b₃) (the-)table(-of)[f] (the-)Lord,[g] it[i] is-defiled,[h]
(c₃) its-food[m]**** is-contemptible.[l] [NIV, NRSV]

*TEXT—some translations read אותו ʾôtô 'it' as the object of *(are-)profaning*, while others read אותי ʾôtî 'me'. This passage was listed by the ancient Rabbis as among the eighteen *Tikkune Sopherim*, alterations where the original Hebrew text appeared to be in danger of blaspheming God [WBC]. Jewish tradition says that the original text read 'me', which scribes later emended to 'it' out of respect for God [WBC; NJB]. ʾôtî 'me' is read by WBC; CEV, REB, and TEV. Among those translations which read ʾôtô 'it', some understand the pronoun to refer to God's name, which itself stands for God [Coh, Mer, Gla, NICOT; NLT]; Keil understands 'it' to refer to the altar of God. JPS, KJV, NIV, NJB, and NRSV also read 'it'.

**TEXT—If וניבו wənîbô 'and its fruit' be kept in the reading of the text, then אכלו ʾoklô 'its food' can be deleted as superfluous [WBC], since the latter seems to have been a scribal addition to explain the rare ניב nîb 'fruit' [Mer].

***TEXT—Retaining both wənîbô 'and its fruit' and ʾoklô 'its food' certainly constitutes the harder reading; since this reading can make sense, it should be retained [Gla].

****TEXT—Since some Hebrew mss. lack wənîbô 'and its fruit', some commentators understand this word to be a dittography of the following word נבזה nibzeh 'is/are contemptible' and so would delete it [NIV, NRSV]. This viewpoint follows S.R. Driver, *The Minor Prophets* (New

York: Oxford University, American Branch, Henry Frowde, 1906); cited in Gla.

SYNTAX—Some understand הוּא *hûʾ* 'it' as belonging to the end of line (b), in which case it stands in the usual position of subject after the verb and refers to 'table', e.g., 'the table of Jehovah, it is despised' [Coh, Keil, Mer, Gla, NICOT; NIV, NJB, TEV].

Other interpreters understand *hûʾ* 'it' to occur at the beginning of line (c). Among these versions, some take 'it' to constitute with 'its fruit' a compound subject [WBC]. NRSV accords to 'it' a kind of destination status for 'food': 'the food for it [the table]', following the Syriac and the Targum. NJB and REB appear to follow this course as well.

SYNTAX—Some take אָכְלוֹ *ʾoklô* 'its food' to be in explanatory apposition with *nîb* 'fruit'. These elements become (in Hebrew, although not always in translation—see below) a complex subject of 'is contemptible' [Coh, Mer, Gla, NICOT; JPS, KJV, NJB, TEV]. Keil also makes 'its food' practically equivalent to 'fruit' by topicalizing 'fruit' and then completing the sentence using 'its food' as subject: '. . . and its fruit—contemptible is its food'. Others take 'its food' to be the simple, sole subject of 'is contemptible' [NIV, NRSV, REB].

LEXICON—a. -וְ *wə- waw* connective (BDB p. 251), (Hol p. 84), (TWOT 519). This connective is here translated adversatively as 'but' [all commentators and versions except the following]; as an adversative plus intensive: 'but even' [CEV]; as an addition: 'and' [Keil].

b. אַתֶּם *ʾattem* 2nd mas. pl. prn.: 'you' [all commentators and versions except CEV]. CEV specifies the pronominal referent: 'you priests'. The Hebrew pronoun expresses emphasis [TOTC], i.e., it reintroduces the topic of the addressees and stresses the topic by its fronted position in the clause [Clen].

c. mas. pl. Piel part. of חלל *ḥll* (BDB p. 320), (Hol p. 105), (TWOT 661): 'to profane' [Hol; Coh, NICOT, Mer, WBC; JPS, KJV, NASB, NIV, NJB, NRSV, REB], 'to desecrate' [Keil], 'to dishonor' [NLT, TEV], 'to insult' [CEV], 'to defile' [BDB; Gla]. The verb is translated in the present progressive tense by Mer, WBC; in the present (probably habitual) tense by Coh, Gla, NICOT; CEV, JPS, NIV, NLT, NRSV, REB, TEV; and in the present perfect tense by KJV, NJB.

d. -בְּ *bə-* (BDB p. 88), (Hol p. 32), (TWOT 193): 'by' [all lexica, commentators, and versions except the following]; 'with' [BDB; Keil; NLT]. Some translations express in what respect the preceding clause is true: 'in that' [Coh; KJV, NASB]; and some express a circumstantial relation: 'when' [JPS, NRSV, TEV]. The proclitic *bə-* denotes here either instrument or accordance with a pattern of behavior, etc., or circumstance with an infinitive construct, e.g., 'when' [BDB, Hol].

e. inf. constr. of אָמַר *ʾmr* (BDB p. 55), (Hol p. 21), (TWOT 118): 'to say' [all lexica, commentators, and versions except REB], 'to think' [REB].

f. constr. of שֻׁלְחָן *šulḥān* [BDB p. 1020], [Hol p. 372], [TWOT 2395a]: 'table' [all lexica, commentators, and versions]; 'altar' [CEV, TEV]. *Šulḥān* denotes a table, whether for personal or cultic use [BDB, Hol].

g. אֲדֹנָי *ʾăḏōnāy* (BDB p. 10), (Hol p. 4), (TWOT 276): 'the Lord' [most commentators and versions], 'Jehovah' [Keil]. Some cast the passage into direct speech attributed to God: 'my altar' [TEV]. *ʾăḏōnāy* is another proper name of God and is parallel to YHWH [BDB].

h. mas. sg. Piel part. of גָּאַל *gʾl* (BDB p. 146), (Hol p. 53), (TWOT 301): 'to be defiled' [Hol; Keil, NICOT; JPS, NASB, NIV, REB], 'to be polluted' [Coh, Mer, WBC; KJV, NJB, NRSV], 'to be despised' [WBC], 'to be worthless [TEV], 'to be polluted' [BDB; Gla]. Some employ the active voice: 'to defile' [NLT]. Some translations employ various modalities or idioms, e.g., 'may be polluted' [REB], 'there's nothing special (about the Lord's altar)' [CEV].

i. הוּא *hûʾ* 3rd mas. sg. prn.

j. -וְ *wǝ-* *waw* connective (BDB p. 251), (Hol p. 84), (TWOT 519). This conjunction is interpreted additively and translated 'and' by most of those who assign הוּא *hûʾ* 'it' to the end of line (b). In this case, the conjunction serves to link line (c) with line (b) in a relation of addition [Coh, Keil, Mer, Gla, NICOT; JPS, KJV, NASB, NIV, TEV, REB]. NJB translates the conjunction as 'hence', making line (c) the result of line (b). NLT reverses the relation between lines (a-b) and (c), saying in effect, 'you bring contemptible food; by this we know that you feel free to defile the Lord's table'.

k. constr. of נִיב *nîḇ* (BDB p. 626), (Hol p. 237), (TWOT 1318b): 'fruit' [BDB, Hol; Coh, Keil, Mer, Gla, WBC; KJV, NASB], 'produce' [NICOT], 'sacrifice' [CEV], 'meat' [JPS], not explicit [NIV, NJB, NRSV]. The possessive suffix 'its' refers to the Lord's table [Keil]. 'Fruit' is interpreted as the gain from man's labor; since some of it is then offered to God, it is translated by some as a verb with 'food' as the object: 'when you offer food' [TEV], 'the food offered' [NJB], 'bringing . . . food' [NLT], 'you can offer . . . food' [REB]. *Nîḇ* appears to be a metaphor, denoting the gain of YHWH's table, what is given YHWH by man [BDB].

l. mas. sg. Niphal part. of בָּזָה *bzh* (BDB p. 102), (Hol p. 36), (TWOT 224): 'to be contemptible' [BDB; Coh, Keil, NICOT; KJV, NIV, NLT], 'to be despicable' [Mer, Gla], 'to deserve no respect' [NJB], 'to be worthless' [CEV], 'to despise' [Hol; TEV], 'to be despised' [NASB, NRSV], 'to hold in no esteem' [REB]. Some translate with a modality: 'can be treated with scorn' [JPS], 'may be despised' [NRSV].

m. אֹכֶל *ʾōḵel* (BDB p. 38), (Hol p. 15), (TWOT 85a): 'food' [all lexica, commentators, and versions except KJV], 'meat' [KJV].

QUESTION—What is the discourse function of this verse?

This verse gives the topic of this discourse unit (Mal. 1:11–14), which is the profanation of YHWH through the slighting of his altar [Clen].

QUESTION—What significance does אֲדֹנָי ʾăḏōnāy have in this passage? This term stresses God's power and rule in comparison with the priests, who were but human [NICOT].

QUESTION—How does the metaphor וְנִיבוֹ wənîḇô 'and its fruit' denote?

1. By comparison with Isa. 42.19, some ancient Jewish commentators understood nîḇô 'its fruit' to mean the priests' words concerning the Lord's table [Coh].

2. It is equivalent to 'food', later in this verse, where 'food' was inserted by scribes to explain the rare nîḇ 'fruit'. 'Fruit' might be seen as the fruit of man's labor, i.e., 'income, produce' [Keil, Mer].

3. Since some Hebrew mss. lack wənîḇô, some commentators understand it to be a dittography of the following word נִבְזֶה niḇzeh 'is/are contemptible' and so would delete it [WBC].

1:13

and[a]-you(pl)-say,[b] behold,[c] what[d]-(a-) hardship[e]! and[f]-you(pl)-sniff[g] (at-)it/me,* says YHWH(-of) hosts. And[h]-you(pl)-bring[i] (a-)stolen/mutilated[j] (animal) or[k]-the-crippled[l] or-the-diseased,[m] and[n]-you(pl)-offer[o] the-sacrifice[p]; shall-I-accept[q] it from[r]-your(pl)-hand[s]? says YHWH.

*TEXT—This passage was listed by the ancient Rabbis as among the eighteen *Tikkune Sopherim*, alterations from the 1st person singular, where the original(Hebrew text appeared to be in danger of blaspheming God [Coh, TOTC]. On the other hand, Keil considers אוֹתוֹ ʾôṯô 'it' as original here, and that the pronoun refers to the table of God: 'it' [Coh, Keil, Mer, Gla, NICOT, WBC; JPS, KJV, NIV, NLT, REB], 'me' [CEV]. TOTC considers the original text to read אוֹתִי ʾôṯî 'me'.

LEXICON—a. וְ- wə- waw connective of the attached waw consecutive verb (BDB p. 251), (Hol p. 84), (TWOT 519): 'and' [all commentators and versions except the following]. The additive relation is expressed by 'also' [Coh, Mer; NASB]. An additive relation is also expressed by a new clause or sentence [JPS, NJB, NRSV, or TEV].

b. 2nd mas. pl. waw consecutive Qal perf. of אָמַר ʾmr (BDB p. 55), (Hol p. 21), (TWOT 118): 'to say' [all lexica, commentators, and versions except the following], 'to exclaim' [REB].

c. הִנֵּה hinnēh (BDB p. 243), (Hol p. 82), (TWOT 510a): 'behold' [BDB, Hol; Coh, Keil, WBC; KJV], 'my' (as an exclamation) [NASB], not explicit [all other commentators and versions]. Hinnēh is a demonstrative interjection or particle [BDB, Hol].

d. מַה mâ (BDB p. 552), (Hol p. 183), (TWOT 1149): attached to תְלָאָה təlāʾâ 'hardship, trouble', it is translated as an exclamation: 'what a . . . !' [Gla; JPS], 'how . . . !' [Mer; NASB, NJB, REB, TEV]. Here mâ is primarily an interrogative particle, e.g., 'what, how'; here, prefixed to the following noun, it produces an exclamation [BDB, Hol].

e. תְלָאָה təlāʾâ (BDB p. 521), (Hol p. 390), (TWOT 1066a): 'hardship' [BDB, Hol], 'burden' [NIV], 'weariness' [BDB; Coh, NICOT; KJV,

NRSV], 'plague' [Keil], 'nuisance' [WBC], 'bother' [JPS], 'pain' [Gla], 'trouble' [Hol]. This noun is also translated as an adjective: 'tiresome' [Mer; NASB, NJB, REB]. Together with מה *mâ* (see above), it is translated as a verb phrase: 'how tired we are of all this!' [TEV].

f. -ו *wǝ- waw* connective of the attached *waw* consecutive verb (BDB p. 251), (Hol p. 84), (TWOT 519): 'and' [all commentators and versions except JPS], 'and so' [JPS].

g. 2nd mas. pl. *waw* consecutive Hiphil perf. of נפח *nph* (BDB p. 655), (Hol p. 241), (TWOT 1390): 'to sniff at' [BDB; Mer, Gla, NICOT; NIV, NRSV,], 'to sniff scornfully at' [REB], 'to snuff at' [Coh; KJV], 'to blow upon' [Keil], 'to puff at' [WBC], 'to turn up one's nose at' [TEV], 'to sniff disdainfully at' [NASB, NJB]. 'to degrade' [JPS]. The verb is translated using the English present tense, i.e., habitual form [all commentators and versions except the following]; the verb is translated using the English past perfect tense [Coh; KJV]. CEV restructures this verse, summarizing it by interpreting the symbolic action of sniffing or blowing: 'You get so disgusted that you even make vulgar signs at me'. NLT translates *nph* 'blow' by expressing an associated action: 'you turn up your noses at. . . .' The primary sense of *nph* in its Qal stem is 'to blow'; in the Hiphil, it can carry a metaphorical meaning 'to enrage' [Hol]. Keil sees the Hiphil as expressing contempt, based on the action of blowing something away.

h. -ו *wǝ- waw* connective of the attached *waw* consecutive verb (BDB p. 251), (Hol p. 84), (TWOT 519): 'and' [Coh, Keil, Mer, WBC; JPS, KJV, NASB]. An additive relationship is also expressed by a new clause or sentence [NICOT; NJB, NLT, NRSV, TEV]. A condition is also expressed: 'if' [REB]; as well as a circumstantial relationship: 'when' [Gla; NIV].

i. 2nd mas. pl. *waw* consecutive Hiphil perf. of בוא *bô* (BDB p. 97), (Hol p. 34), (TWOT 212): 'to bring' [Hol; Coh, Keil, Mer, Gla, NICOT; CEV, JPS, KJV, NASB, NJB, NRSV, REB, TEV], 'to bring in' [BDB; WBC], 'to be presented' [NLT]. This verb is translated using the English present, i.e., habitual form [Keil, Mer, Gla, NICOT, WBC; CEV, JPS, NJB, NRSV, REB, TEV], and using the past perfect tense [Coh; KJV]. Keil understands this first occurrence of *bô* in this verse to mean the bringing of the sacrificial animals to the altar, and the second occurrence below to signify the actual offering of the victims upon the altar.

j. mas. sg. Qal pass. part. of גזל *gzl* (BDB p. 159), (Hol p. 58), (TWOT 337): 'to be stolen' [Mer, NICOT; CEV, JPS, NJB, TEV], 'mutilated' [BDB; Gla; REB], 'to be taken by violence' [Coh, WBC]. This phrase means 'stolen' (Coh), 'to be caught and damaged by wild animals' (TOTC, WBC)], 'to be taken by robbery' [NASB], 'to be robbed' [Keil], 'to be taken by violence' [Hol; NRSV], 'to be torn' [Hol; WBC; KJV], 'to be stolen and mutilated' [NLT]. BDB understands the participle in this context to refer to domesticated animals that have been recovered from predators in a mutilated condition.

k. -וֹ *wə- waw* connective (BDB p. 251), (Hol p. 84), (TWOT 519): 'or' [Mer, NICOT; CEV, NIV, NJB, NRSV, REB, TEV], 'and' [Coh, Keil, WBC; JPS, KJV, NASB, NLT].

l. פִּסֵּחַ *pissēaḥ* (BDB p. 820), (Hol p. 294), (TWOT 1787a): 'crippled' [NICOT; CEV, NLT], 'lame' [BDB; Hol; Coh, Keil, Mer, Gla, WBC; JPS, KJV, NASB, NJB, NRSV, REB, TEV].

m. mas. sg. Qal part. of חלה *ḥlh* (BDB p. 317), (Hol p. 104), (TWOT 655): 'to be diseased' [NICOT; NJB], 'to be sick' [BDB], 'to be ill' [Hol]. This is translated as an adjective: 'sick' [Coh, Keil, Mer, Gla, WBC; CEV, JPS, KJV, NASB, NLT, NRSV, TEV], 'sickly' [REB].

n. -וֹ *wə- waw* connective of the attached *waw* consecutive verb (BDB p. 251), (Hol p. 84), (TWOT 519): 'and' [NICOT; JPS, NIV, NRSV], 'thus' [Coh, Keil, Gla; KJV], 'so' [NASB], not explicit [WBC; REB]. The additive relationship is expressed also by a dash in the punctuation [Mer; NLT] and by a new clause [NJB]. The clause introduced by this connective is also translated as a phrase denoting destination: 'and for an offering . . .' [CEV], 'as your offering to me' [TEV]. The clause introduced by this connective is seen as a circumstantial clause following the preceding clauses: 'when you bring the offering' [Clen].

o. 2nd mas. pl. *waw* consecutive Hiphil perf. of בוא *bôʾ* (see above): 'to offer' [NICOT; JPS], 'to bring' [Coh, Keil, Mer, WBC; KJV, NASB, NJB, NRSV], 'thus ye brought' [KJV]. It means 'having brought such sick, etc. animals to be slaughtered, you then sacrifice them' [Keil]. This verb is also translated as a noun: 'offering' [REB]; and as a verbal adjective: 'presented' [NLT]. The English present tense is employed [all commentators and versions except the following], the past tense is also employed [KJV].

p. מִנְחָה *minḥâ* (BDB p. 585), (Hol p. 202), (TWOT 214a): 'sacrifice' [Hol; NICOT], 'offering' [BDB; Coh, Mer, Gla, WBC; KJV, NASB, NJB, NLT, NRSV, TEV], 'sacrificial gift' [Keil], 'oblation' [JPS]. *Minḥâ* is an offering of any kind [Keil, NICOT].

q. 1st mas. sg. Qal imperf. of רצה *rṣh* (BDB p. 953), (Hol p. 345), (TWOT 2207): 'to accept' [Coh, Mer, Gla, WBC; CEV, JPS, KJV, NJB, NLT, NRSV, REB, TEV], 'to accept with pleasure' [NICOT], 'to receive' [NASB], 'to take pleasure in' [Keil], 'to be pleased with' [BDB, Hol]. This verb is translated using the future tense (e.g., 'shall I accept . . . ?') [WBC; JPS, Keil, NRSV]. It is also translated using the modality 'should' [Coh, Mer, Gla, NICOT; CEV, KJV, NASB, NLT], and an equivalent of 'should': 'am I to accept . . . ?' [NJB, REB]; also with an idiomatic phrase: 'do you think I will accept . . . ?' [TEV]. Clen sees this verb as irreal, e.g., 'would I accept . . . ?' All commentators and versions regard this question as rhetorical, understanding a negative answer.

r. מִן *min* (BDB p. 577), (Hol p. 200), (TWOT 1212): 'from' [Keil, Mer, Gla, NICOT, WBC; JPS, NASB, NJB, NLT, NRSV, REB], 'at' [KJV], 'of' [Coh]. *Min* here indicates perhaps spatial motion from starting point or perhaps logical cause.

s. יָד *yāḏ* (BDB p. 388), (Hol p. 127), (TWOT 844): 'hand' [Coh, Keil, WBC; KJV, NASB, NIV, NJB, NRSV]. The synecdoche of *yāḏ* 'hand' is recognized and translated concretely as 'you' by Mer, Gla, NICOT; JPS, NJB, NLT, REB and TEV. The notion of agency is also conveyed by the pronoun 'your' in the phrase 'your offerings' [CEV]. In its primary sense, *yāḏ* denotes 'hand, forearm'; here it functions instrumentally: 'by, through'.

QUESTION—What is the meaning of גָּזֵל *gzl*?

1. It means 'to steal' [Coh, Gla]. Some have objected to this sense here on the grounds that a priest would not have been able to know whether an animal brought to sacrifice had been stolen or not. On the other hand, since the Jews would not have dreamed of consuming meat which had been mutilated by wild animals, it is unlikely that they would have brought such to the Temple [Gla].

2. It means seized and torn by wild animals [TOTC, WBC]. Such animals were forbidden for sacrifice.

QUESTION—What is the relationship of this verse to the preceding verse?

The derogatory actions listed in this verse constitute the evidence for the accusation of profaning YHWH's altar given in the preceding verse.

QUESTION—What is the nature of the sequence of the four verbs in the *waw* consecutive perfect tense in this verse?

The first three of these verbs (וַאֲמַרְתֶּם *waʾămartem* 'you say', וְהִפַּחְתֶּם *wᵊhippaḥtem* 'you sniff', and וַהֲבֵאתֶם *wahăḇēʾtem* 'you bring') occur in an embedded expository discourse; as such, they do not refer to sequential action—and care should be taken that a translation not read that way; rather, verbs in such a sequence refer to simultaneous or random events. However, the fourth *waw* consecutive perfect verb in the sequence (וַהֲבֵאתֶם *wahăḇēʾtem* 'you offer') belongs to a circumstantial clause: 'when you offer . . . ' [Clen].

1:14

And[a]- (the-)one-cheating[b] -is-cursed/-be-cursed,[c] while[d]-there-is[e] in[f]-his-flock[g] (a-)male-animal[h] and[i]-(he-)-vows[j] and/but[k]-(he-)sacrifices[l] (a-)blem-ished[m](-animal) to-the-Lord, for[n] (a-) great[o] -king[p] I (am), says YHWH(-of) hosts, and[q]-my-name is-feared/will-be-feared[r] among[s]-the-nations.[t]

SYNTAX—Some translations take זָכָר *zākār* '(a-)male' to be the object both of וְיֵשׁ *wᵊyēš* 'and-there-is' and וְנֹדֵר *wᵊnōḏēr* 'and-(he-)-vows' [NICOT; NIV, NASB, NRSV, TEV]. Others, however, take מָשְׁחָת *mošḥāt* '(a-)blemished (animal)' as the object of both *wᵊnōḏēr* 'and-(he-)-vows' and וְזֹבֵחַ *wᵊzōḇēaḥ* 'and/but-(he-)sacrifices' [Coh, Keil, Mer; JPS, KJV, NJB, REB]. In this case, Mer translates the *waw* connective preceding 'and-

(he-)-vows' adversatively as 'but'; the *waw* connective following 'and-(he-)-vows' must be interpreted additively as 'and'. NJB is similar to Mer, but interprets 'and/but-(he-)sacrifices' as expressing the manner of 'and/but-(he-)sacrifices' (i.e., 'paying' one's vow *by* sacrificing').

LEXICON—a. -וְ *wə- waw* connective (BDB p. 251), (Hol p. 84), (TWOT 519): 'and' [Keil], 'but' [Coh; KJV, NASB], not explicit [Mer, Gla, NICOT, WBC; CEV, JPS, NIV, NJB, NLT, NRSV, REB, TEV].

b. mas. sg. Qal part. of נכל *nkl* (BDB p. 647), (Hol p. 238), (TWOT 1366): 'to cheat' [WBC; TEV], 'to deceive' [Keil], 'to deal craftily' [Coh], 'to act deceitfully' [Hol], 'to be crafty' [BDB]. This participle is also translated as a simple noun: 'cheat' [Gla, NICOT; JPS, NIV, NLT, NRSV, REB], 'hypocrite' [Mer], 'rogue' [NJB], 'deceiver' [KJV], 'knave' [BDB], 'swindler' [NASB].

c. mas. sg. Qal pass. part. of ארר *ʾrr* (BDB p. 76), (Hol p. 28), (TWOT 168): 'to be cursed' [BDB; Coh, Keil, Mer, NICOT, WBC; JPS, KJV, NASB, NIV, NJB, NLT, NRSV, TEV], 'to punish' [CEV], 'accursed' [Gla], 'to be inflicted with a curse' [Hol]. This word is translated as a wish or pronouncement of a curse [Mer, WBC; JPS, KJV, NASB, NJB, NRSV, REB, TEV] and as a threat to be carried out in the future [CEV]. All other translations render the word as a statement of fact, e.g., 'cursed is he. . . .' *ʾrr* 'to curse' is part of Hebrew covenant vocabulary, e.g., the ritual curses upon covenant breakers in Deut. 27:15–26 [TOTC].

d. -וְ *wə- waw* connective (BDB p. 251), (Hol p. 84), (TWOT 519): 'while' [NICOT], 'though' [REB], 'when' [TEV], 'who' [NASB], not explicit [most commentators and versions].

e. יֵשׁ *yēš* (BDB p. 441), (Hol p. 145), (TWOT 921): 'to have' (the subject of the verb is the cheat) [all commentators and versions except the following]. NLT conflates the clause וְיֵשׁ בְּעֶדְרוֹ זָכָר *wᵊyēš bᵊʿedrô zākār* 'and-there-is in-his-flock (a-)male' and the following וְנֹדֵר *wᵊnōḏēr* 'and-(he-)vows', translating 'who promises to give a fine ram from his flock'. Formally a noun, *yēš* functions as a particle denoting the existence of something, e.g., 'there is' [BDB, Hol].

f. -בְּ *bə-* (BDB p. 88), (Hol p. 32), (TWOT 193): 'in' [all lexica, commentators, and versions except NLT], 'from' [NLT]. The proclitic *bə-* here denotes locality, 'in' or 'among' [BDB, Hol].

g. constr. of עֵדֶר *ʿēḏer* (BDB p. 727), (Hol p. 266), (TWOT 1572a): 'flock' [all lexica, commentators, and versions], 'herd' [Hol].

h. זָכָר *zākār* (BDB p. 271), (Hol p. 89), (TWOT 551e): 'male' [BDB; all commentators and versions except the following], 'male animal' [Hol], 'an acceptable male' [NIV], 'a good animal' [TEV], 'fine ram' [NLT], 'sound ram' [REB].

i. -וְ *wə- waw* connective (BDB p. 251), (Hol p. 84), (TWOT 519): 'and' [Keil; NASB, NIV, NRSV], 'but then' [NLT], 'but' [Mer, Gla; JPS, NJB].

j. mas. sg. Qal part. of נדר *nḏr* (BDB p. 623), (Hol p. 229), (TWOT 1308): 'to vow' [BDB; all commentators and versions except the following], 'to make a vow' [Hol; Gla], 'to pay a vow' [NJB, REB], 'to vow to give' [NIV, NRSV], 'to promise to give' [NLT], 'to promise' [TEV]. Mer understands the object of the vow to be the unblemished male (*zāḵār*); the vower then substitutes a worthless animal. The situation is where a worshipper has offered a vow, and where Lev. 22:19 requires a male animal to be sacrificed [NICOT].

k. -ו *wə-* waw connective (BDB p. 251), (Hol p. 84), (TWOT 519): 'and' [Coh, Keil, Mer, NICOT, WBC; JPS, KJV], 'but' [NASB], 'but then' [NIV, NLT], 'then' [Gla], 'yet' [NRSV], not explicit [REB].

l. mas. sg. Qal part. of זבח *zḇḥ* (BDB p. 256), (Hol p. 86), (TWOT 525): 'to sacrifice' [all commentators and versions], 'to slaughter for a sacrifice' [BDB, Hol].

m. mas. sg. Huphal part.of שחת *šḥṯ* (BDB p. 1007), (Hol p. 366), (TWOT 2370): 'blemished' [Hol; Coh, Mer, NICOT, WBC; JPS, NASB, NJB, NIV, NRSV], 'corrupt' [Keil], 'corrupt thing' [KJV], 'spoiled thing' [Gla], 'unhealthy' [CEV], 'worthless' [TEV], 'defective' [NLT], 'damaged' [Hol; REB], 'ruined' [BDB]. The participle may also be understood as mutilated or castrated [NICOT], or as having any fault making the animal unfit for sacrifice to God [Keil], thus violating the stricture laid down in Lev. 22:23. In focus is the temptation to give to God an inferior offering in fulfillment of a vow previously offered [NICOT, TOTC, WBC].

n. כי *kî* connective (BDB p. 471), (Hol p. 155), (TWOT 976): 'for' [all commentators and versions except the following], 'because' [CEV], not explicit [WBC; REB].

o. גדול *gāḏôl* (BDB p. 152), (Hol p. 55), (TWOT 315d): 'great' [all lexica, commentators, and versions].

p. מלך *meleḵ* (BDB p. 573), (Hol p. 198), (TWOT 1199a): 'king' [all lexica, commentators, and versions]. The lack of the Hebrew definite article has apparently induced most to translate 'I am a great king'. CEV, however, translates 'I am the great king'—perhaps an implicit acknowledgement that the term 'great king' is drawn from the old Hittite Empire and referred to the Emperor: there could be only one 'great king' at a time!

q. -ו *wə-* waw connective (BDB p. 251), (Hol p. 84), (TWOT 519): 'and' [all commentators and versions].

r. mas. sg. Niphal part. of ירא *yrʾ* (BDB p. 431), (Hol p. 142), (TWOT 907): 'to be feared' [all lexica, commentators, and versions except the following], 'to be awesome' [Mer, Gla], 'to be reverenced' [Hol; NRSV], 'to be revered' [JPS], 'to be worshipped' [CEV], 'to be held in awe' [REB], 'to be dreadful' [KJV]. The active voice is used by some: 'my name inspire awe' [BDB; NJB], 'people fear me' [TEV]. All the translations employ the English present tense. NIV uses a modality of obligation: 'is to be feared'.

s. -בְּ *bə-* (BDB p. 88), (Hol p. 32), (TWOT 193): 'among' [all lexica, commentators, and version]. The procliticbə- here denotes 'among a group' [BDB, Hol].

t. pl. of גּוֹי *gôy* (BDB p. 156), (Hol p. 57), (TWOT 326e): 'nation' [all lexica, commentators, and versions except the following], 'people of all nations' [TEV], 'heathen' [KJV]. *Gôy* refers to the peoples and ethnic groups around Israel, with emphasis upon their paganness [Hol].

QUESTION—To whom is this verse addressed?

It is addressed to all the Jews, for in this passage the prophet expands the curse from the priests to the entire nation. The nation as a whole has been cheating God by offering inferior sacrifices. The priests are clearly indicted as well, having obviously tolerated this abuse [Gla].

QUESTION—Why do some versions add an adjective to qualify זָכָר *zākār* 'male animal', e.g., 'a good animal' [TEV]?

They want to make explicit an idea which is implicitly projected onto *zākār* by the opposite expression, מָשְׁחָת *mošḥāt* 'blemished, corrupted' [Gla].

QUESTION—What kind of implied information is associated with זָכָר *zākār* 'male animal' in this passage?

Various versions which include implicit information with this word add an adjective to make explicit the idea that one has in his flock an acceptable animal to sacrifice: 'acceptable' [CEV, NIV], 'good' [TEV], 'sound' [REB], 'unblemished' [JPS], 'fine' [NLT]. *Zākār* 'male animal' signifies 'the choicest animal, physically whole and well and in its prime' [Mer].

QUESTION— What is the nature of the sequence of the two participles (וְנֹדֵר *wᵊnōḏēr* 'and he vows' and וְזֹבֵחַ *wᵊzōḇēaḥ* 'and he sacrifices')?

These two participles stand in a sequential relationship; one arrives at this interpretation not from overt verbal marking but from implied information on the nature of vows and sacrifices. Furthermore, the complex 'and-there-is in-his-flock (a-)male-animal and-(he-)vows and/but-(he-)sacrifices (a-)blemished(-animal) to-the-Lord' describes the agent for the purpose, not of identifying him or his qualities, but of explaining why he is called a נֹכֵל *nōḵēl* 'cheat' [Clen].

QUESTION—How is 'great king' understood?

This phrase invokes the vocabulary of ancient Hittite covenants, in which the conquering king is called the 'Great King.' The vassal parties to such treaties were obliged under threat of punishment to observe the treaties' conditions [Mer, WBC].

QUESTION—How is the phrase וּשְׁמִי נוֹרָא בַגּוֹיִם *ûšᵊmî nôrāʾ ḇaggôyim* 'my-name is/will-be-feared among-the-nations' understood?

1. The Gentile nations have heard of the renown and power of Israel's God—which, however, is distinct from trusting and serving him [Mer, NICOT].
2. The time is coming when all nations will worship Israel's God [TOTC].

DISCOURSE UNIT: 2:1–16 [Ksr]. The topic is "a call to love God totally."

DISCOURSE UNIT: 2:1–9 [Clen (within the larger discourse unit of Mal. 1:2–2:9), Mer, NICOT; CEV, NASB, NIV, NLT]. This paragraph realizes the first movement's semantic constituent A', the topic of which is the "results of disobedience" [Clen]. The topic is the priests' teaching duties [Mer], "the priesthood in the balance" [NICOT], ultimatum and punishment [O'Brien], "true and false prophets" [CEV], "priests to be disciplined" [NASB], an "admonition for the priests" [NIV], "a warning for the priests" [NLT].
Comments on this discourse unit. Although the priesthood had always born some responsibility for teaching, its role became more important with the decline of the Old Testament prophets [Mer].

A formal analysis of the discourse unit is:
  (A) the priests' perversion→curse (1–4)
    (B) the pure priestly prototype (5–7)
  (A') the priests' perversion→punishment (8–9) [Wendland]

2:1
And-now[a] to-you(pl) this the-command/decree,[b] the-priests.[c]
LEXICON—a. ועתה *wəʿattâ* (BDB p. 774), (Hol p. 287), (TWOT 1650c): 'and now/now' [all lexica, commentators, and versions except the following]. The idea of a new thought is expressed in other ways by some versions: 'I, the Lord . . . , have something else to say . . .' [CEV], 'listen, you priests . . .' [NLT], 'the Lord . . . says to the priests . . .' [TEV]. *Wəʿattâ* often introduces a new thought or section [Hol]; *wəʿattâ* often introduces a conclusion drawn from what has been previously states [BDB], and here it indicates that this discourse unit is the conclusion or result of the previous discourse unit [Clen]; *wəʿattâ* here marks the transition from the subject of the priests' guilt to that of their sentence [Gla].
  b. מצוה *miṣwâ* (BDB p. 846), (Hol p. 210), (TWOT 1887b): 'command' [Hol; NICOT; NLT, NRSV, TEV], 'commandment' [BDB; Coh, Keil, Mer, Gla, WBC; KJV, NASB, NJB], 'charge' [JPS], 'admonition' [NIV], 'decree' [REB]. *Miṣwâ* is part of Hebrew covenantal vocabulary [Mer].
  c. pl. of כהן *kōhēn* (BDB p. 463), (Hol p. 152), (TWOT 959): 'priest' [all lexica, commentators, and versions]. The definite article here signals a vocative relationship, e.g., 'O priests' [all commentators and versions].
QUESTION—What is the form of this sentence and the function of its form?
  Its form is a cleft sentence, and it serves to topicalize the addressees, the priests [Clen].
QUESTION—To what does מצוה *miṣwâ* 'command' refer?
  1. It refers to a warning, and then to the resulting sentence, of punishment which God is passing upon the priests, specified in Mal. 2:2; *miṣwâ* means specifically the command given by God to some earthly agent to

inflict the punishment which he has ordained [Keil—see Mal. 2:4 below, Gla].

2. It refers implicitly to God's requirement that the priests act in a worthy manner [Coh].

3. It refers to the priests' responsibility to warn the people, [Meir Leibush Malbim, cited in Coh], or to teach the people God's Word [Mer].

4. It looks ahead to Mal. 2:4, referring thus to the covenant with Levi, establishing the office of the priesthood. The function of the priesthood is essentially given in Mal. 2:2. Rather than simply introducing this discourse unit, Mal. 2:1 constitutes the unit's entire focus [NICOT].

2:2

If[a] you-do- not[a] -listen[b] and-if you-do- not -lay[c] to-heart[d] to-give[e] honor[f] to-my-name, says YWHW(-of) hosts, then[g]-I-will-send[h] upon[i]-you(pl) the[j]-curse,[k] and[l]-I-will-curse[m] your(pl)-blessings,[n] and-indeed,[o] I-have-cursed[p]-them,[q] because[r] you(pl)-are- not -laying[s] (it) to-heart.

LEXICON—a. אִם ʾim 'if' (BDB p. 49), (Hol p. 19), (TWOT 111) + לֹא lōʾ (BDB p. 49), (Hol p. 170), (TWOT 1064): ordinary declarative negation 'not' [Hol p. 170], [TWOT 1064]; 'if . . . not' [all lexica, commentators, and versions except the following], 'unless' [JPS, REB]. NLT employs 'or': 'honor my name . . . or I will bring. . . .' ʾim is a particle introducing any condition which is theoretically possible [Hol]. Lōʾ expresses negation, e.g., 'not' [Hol].

b. 2nd mas. pl Qal imperf. of שָׁמַע šmᶜ (BDB p. 1033), (Hol p. 376), (TWOT 2412): 'to listen' [all commentators and versions except the following], 'to hearken' [Coh], 'to hear' [BDB, Hol; Keil, WBC; KJV], 'to obey' [Hol; JPS]. 'If you do not listen' is language typical of ancient Hittite treaties [Mckenzie].

c. 2nd mas. pl Qal imperf. of שִׂים śîm with עַל־לֵב ᶜal lēḇ (see below) (BDB p. 525), (Hol p. 351), (TWOT 2243): 'to lay to heart' [BDB; Coh, Keil; JPS, KJV, NRSV], 'to take to heart' [Hol; Mer; NASB, NLT], 'to set one's heart' [NICOT; NIV], 'to set something to heart' [WBC], 'to sincerely resolve' [NJB], 'to take seriously the need' [CEV], 'to direct one's mind' [Gla], 'to pay heed' [REB], 'to pay attention' [Hol], not explicit [TEV]. The primary sense of śîm is 'to put, place' [Hol].

d. לֵב lēḇ 'heart'; with עַל ᶜal 'upon' = 'to heart, to mind' (BDB p. 524), (Hol p. 171), (TWOT 1071a). See the expression with שִׂים śîm above.

e. Qal inf. of נָתַן ntn 'give' (BDB p. 678), (Hol p. 249), (TWOT 1443): 'to give' [BDB, Hol; Coh, Keil, Mer, Gla, WBC; KJV, NASB, NRSV].

f. כָּבוֹד kāḇôḏ (BDB p. 458), (Hol p. 150), (TWOT 943a): 'honor' [BDB; Gla; NASB, NLT], 'glory' [BDB; Coh, Keil, Mer, WBC; KJV, NRSV], 'respect' [Hol]. Many translations render לָתֵת כָּבוֹד lātēt kāḇôḏ 'to give honor' with a verb: 'to honor' [NICOT; CEV, NIV,

REB], 'to do honor to' [JPS], 'to glorify' [NJB]. TEV amplifies by
translating: 'you must honor me by what you do'.

g. -ו wə- waw connective of the attached waw consecutive verb (BDB
p. 251), (Hol p. 84), (TWOT 519): 'then' [Coh, Gla, NICOT, WBC;
NASB, NRSV, TEV], 'even' [KJV], 'certainly' [NJB], 'or' [NLT],
'otherwise' [CEV], 'indeed' [NJB], not explicit [Keil, Mer; JPS, NIV,
REB]

h. 1 sg. Piel perf. waw consecutive of שלח šlḥ (BDB p. 1018), (Hol
p. 371), (TWOT 2394): 'to send' [BDB, Hol; Coh, Keil, Mer, NICOT,
WBC; JPS, KJV, NASB, NIV, NRSV], 'to send out' [Gla], 'to bring'
[NLT, TEV], to lay' [NJB, REB]. All translations employ the English
future tense except Keil, which employs the present [Keil].

i. -ב bə- (BDB p. 88), (Hol p. 32) (TWOT 193): 'upon' [Coh, NICOT;
KJV, NASB, NIV], 'on' [WBC; NJB, NRSV, REB, TEV], 'against'
[Keil, Gla; NLT], not explicit [Mer; CEV, JPS]. The proclitic bə-
denotes here locality, e.g., 'among' [BDB, Hol].

j. -ה ha- (BDB p. 209), (Hol p. 75), (TWOT 459): 'the' [Coh, Keil, Mer,
Gla, WBC; NASB, NRSV], 'a' [NICOT; JPS, KJV, NIV, NJB, NLT,
NRSV, REB, TEV]. The definite article ha- makes its associated noun
signify the entire range of qualities denoted in the word [NICOT].

k. מארה mə'ērâ (BDB p. 76), (Hol p. 181), (TWOT 168a): 'curse' [all
lexica, commentators, and versions except the following], 'malediction'
[Hol]. A phrase is also used to translate this noun: 'terrible curse'
[NLT]. Mə'ērâ, like מצוה miṣwâ 'command' of Mal. 2:1, is a Hebrew
technical term relating to covenants. Covenant breakers were always
threatened with curses, e.g., Lev. 26.14–39, Deut. 27:11–26 [Mer].

l. -ו wə- waw connective of the attached waw consecutive verb (BDB
p. 251), (Hol p. 84), (TWOT 519). This connective is translated here in
an additive manner: 'and' [Coh, Keil, Mer, Gla, NICOT, WBC; JPS,
KJV, NASB, NIV, NJB, NRSV]; as a new sentence, e.g., 'I will
make . . .' [CEV, NLT, REB, TEV]. NLT employs a new sentence
with 'even': 'even the blessings'.

m. 1st sg. Qal perf. waw consecutive of ארר 'rr (BDB p. 76), (Hol p. 28),
(TWOT 168): 'to curse' [BDB, Hol; Coh, Keil, Mer, NICOT, WBC;
KJV, NASB, NIV, NJB, NLT, NRSV], 'to put a curse on something'
[TEV]. God can turn curses into blessings (e.g., Deut. 23:6) or blessings
into curses and acts as part of the covenantal reality [NICOT]. Some
versions focus on the end result of the cursing, which is to produce evil:
'to turn something into curses' [CEV, JPS, REB]. Gla gives as the sense
of 'rr 'to put a ban on something', i.e., to curse the function of
something; this sense is derived from Akkadian arāru 'to ban, block off'
[Herbert Chanan Brichto, The Problem of "Curse" in the Hebrew Bible
(Philadelphia: Society of Biblical Literature and Exegesis, 1963; cited in
Gla]. Here God is prohibiting the proper functioning of the ban's object
[Gla].

n. pl. constr. of בּרכה *bərākâ* (BDB p. 139), (Hol p. 50), (TWOT 285b): 'blessing' [all commentators and versions except the following]. TEV makes explicit its reading of the meaning of *bərākâ* here: 'the things you receive for your support'; similarly, 'your produce' [Gla]. *Bərākâ* can have the sense of 'gift with associated blessing' [Hol], 'prosperity' [BDB].

o. וגם *wəgam* (BDB p. 168), (Hol p. 61), (TWOT 361a): 'indeed' [all commentators and versions except the following], 'yes/yea' [Coh, Keil, NICOT; KJV, NIV, REB], 'in fact' [CEV, TEV]. All of these translations provide some kind of intensifying function. *Wəgam* expresses either addition of an element or emphasis [Hol].

p. 1st sg. Qal perf. of ארר *ʾrr* (see above): 'to curse' [BDB, Hol; Coh, Keil, Mer, NICOT, WBC; KJV, NASB, NIV, NLT, NRSV], 'to put a curse on something' [TEV], 'to turn something into curses' [CEV, JPS], 'to lay a curse' [NJB], 'to ban' [Gla]. Many translations intensify the accomplished nuance of this verb by using 'already' [Keil, Mer, Gla, NICOT, WBC; CEV, KJV, NIV, NLT, NRSV, TEV]. Coh employs the English present tense, and NJB and REB (by ellipsis) employ the future tense.

q. ־ה *hā-* fem. sg. obj. suffix: 'them' [Coh, Keil, NICOT, WBC; JPS, KJV, NASB, NIV, NLT, NRSV, TEV], 'it' [Gla].

r. כּי *kî* connective (BDB p. 471), (Hol p. 155), (TWOT 976): 'because' [all commentators and versions except NJB], 'for' [NJB].

s. mas. pl. Qal part. of שׂים *śîm* with על־לב *ʿal lēb* (see above). The Hebrew phrase implies that there is a complement, which NIV makes explicit: 'to honor me', and which CEV makes explicit: 'your duties as priests'. Mer uses the English present progressive tense; some others use the present (habitual) tense [Coh, WBC; JPS, KJV, NASB, NJB, NRSV, TEV]; still others use the present perfect tense [NICOT; CEV, NIV, NLT]. The Hebrew participle lends the phrase an emphatic air, implying that the priests are not taking their duties seriously [NICOT].

QUESTION—What is the significance of this verse?

There is both command and sentence of punishment which is threatened if the command is not obeyed, but this verse serves notice that the sentence has in fact caught up with the command: the grace period has ended, and the sentence is pronounced, a sentence which actually has already begun to be carried out [Gla].

QUESTION—To what does בּרכותיכם *birkôtêkem* 'your blessings' refer?

1. It refers to the verbal blessings given by the priests to the Israelites in general. God will vitiate the blessings or make them work against the people [Keil, Malbim (cited in Coh)]. A curse upon these blessings would have been considered very powerful because the priestly blessing came to have the greatest solemnity of any element in the Temple worship, finally turning into the only occasion in which God's divine name was pronounced in Israel [NICOT].

2. It refers to the blessings which God bestowed upon Israel after the rebuilding of the Temple [Kimchi (cited in Coh)].
3. It refers to the material sustenance which by right went to the priests in return for their service [Gla, NICOT]. God is blocking the fertility of the fields—this interpretation views זרע *zera͑* of Mal. 2:3 as seed sown in the fields. These blocked blessings are identical to those promised in Mal. 3:10 [Gla].
4. It refers to the existence of the priesthood itself: the priests' status (1 Sam. 2:28), their functions (Num. 6:22–27), and their prerogatives (e.g., benefiting from the tithes) will be struck down by God, as he turns this blessing into a curse [NICOT].
5. Some translations are ambiguous: JPS, KJV, NRSV, REB.

QUESTION—What is the syntactic relationship of וארותי את־ברכותיכם *wa͗ārôtî ͗et birkôtêkem* 'and I will curse your blessings' to the preceding part of the verse?

This phrase begins an amplification of the sense of the threatened curse; this amplication continues to the end of Mal. 2:3 [Clen].

QUESTION—How should וגם ארותיה *wəgam ͗ārôtîhā* 'and-indeed, I-have-cursed-it' be understood?

1. God has already cursed the blessings [Keil, Rashi (cited in Coh)]. Such an interpretation is required by וגם *wəgam*, a particle of emphasis [Keil, NICOT].
2. The cursing is a present activity [Coh].

QUESTION—How should the fem. sg. object suffix of ארותיה *͗ārôtîhā* 'I have cursed it' be understood?

1. It marks distribution: 'each particular blessing' [Keil].
2. It refers to the blessed state of the priesthood in general (ברכה *bərākâ* 'blessing' is feminine in gender), whereas the plural form of 'blessings' (see j. above) refers to the blessings in detail [NICOT].

2:3

Behold[a]-me **about-to-rebuke**[b-1]/**about-to-cut-off**[b-2] to-you(pl)/becauseof[c]-you(pl) *the-seed/the-offspring*[d-1]/the-arm/the-shoulder,[d-2]
and[e]-I-will-spread[f] dung[g] upon-your(pl)-faces,[h]
the-dung(-of) your(pl)-festivals,[i]
and[j]-***he-will-carry-away**[k] you(pl) to[l]-it.[m]

*TEXT—Although the Masoretic text reads הזרע *hazzera͑* 'the seed of the field; offspring', the LXX (reading τὸν ὦμον 'the shoulder') and Vulgate readings suggest the Hebrew הזרע *hazzərôa͑* 'the arm' [Keil]. The latter reading is adopted by Keil and NJB.

**TEXT—Versions which read 'the arm' above also read גדע *gōḏēa͑* 'cutting off' instead of the MT גער *gō͑ēr* 'rebuking'. KJV's 'I will corrupt' is based perhaps upon the LXX's ἀφορίζω 'I will cut off, separate, take away', which in turn appears to be based upon a reading either of גרע *gr͑* 'to diminish, take away' or of גָּדַע *gdᶜ* 'to cut off' [Mer, NICOT]; the LXX translators obviously guessed at the meaning of the Hebrew [NICOT]. REB's 'I will cut off' and NJB's 'I am going to break' (to collocate with 'arm') are based on the variant reading of *gdᶜ* 'to cut off'.

***TEXT—Although many versions follow the MT reading of וְנָשָׂא *wǝnāśā²* 'and he will carry', some appear to favor the reading suggested by the LXX and Syriac readings and proposed by the editors of BHS (וְנָשָׂאתִי אֶתְכֶם מֵעָלַי *wǝnāśā²tî ²etkem mēᶜālay* 'I will carry you away from beside me' [Mer]): 'I will put you out of my presence' [NRSV], 'I shall banish you from my presence' [REB], 'and then be done with you' [CEV], 'I will add you' [NLT].

LEXICON—a. הִנֵּה *hinnēh* (BDB p. 243), (Hol p. 82), (TWOT 510a): 'behold' [Coh, Keil, WBC; KJV, NASB], 'now, . . .' [NJB], 'indeed' [Gla], not explicit [Mer, NICOT; CEV, JPS, NLT, NRSV, REB, TEV]. *Hinnēh* is a demonstrative interjection or particle [BDB, Hol].

b-1. mas. sg. Qal part. of גָּעַר *gᶜr* (BDB p. 172), (Hol p. 63), (TWOT 370): 'to rebuke' [all lexica, commentators, and versions except the following], 'to punish' [CEV, TEV], 'to restrain' [Gla]. Most translations employ the English future tense; Keil employs the present (habitual), Gla and WBC the present progressive, and Mer and NASB a kind of near future expression, e.g., 'I am about to. . . .' In this context, *gᶜr* means 'to threaten with a curse' [NICOT]. *Gᶜr* is part of the vocabulary of cursing in the OT; it denotes the restraining of something so that it will not work as it should, or so that it will be destroyed, cf. Mal. 3:11, where the locusts are restrained by God [Gla]. The phrase . . . הִנְנִי גֹעֵר *hinǝnî gōᶜēr* . . . 'behold me about to rebuke . . .' is parallel to phrases in Mal. 2:2-4 which use the *waw* consecutive perfect, and it does not appear to differ in prominence from them [Clen].

b-2. גָּדַע *gdᶜ* (BDB p. 154), (Hol p. 56), (TWOT 316). This reading is based upon a suggested emendation of the MT: 'to cut off' [REB], 'to break' [NJB], 'to corrupt' [KJV]. NJB employs a kind of English near future tense, e.g., 'I am about to . . .' The primary sense of *gdᶜ* is 'to cut off' [Hol], 'to hew down or off' [BDB]. *Gdᶜ* may also have the sense of 'to break in pieces' [Hol].

c. -לְ *lǝ-* (BDB p. 510), (Hol p. 167), (TWOT 1063): 'your' (modifying 'seed/offspring') [all commentators and versions except the following], 'for your hurt' [Coh], 'because of you' [NIV], 'to your disadvantage' [Gla]. The proclitic *lǝ-* here perhaps introduces a dative of possession, or perhaps expresses disadvantage, or perhaps expresses reason [BDB, Hol].

d-1. זֶרַע *zeraᶜ* (BDB p. 282), (Hol p. 92), (TWOT 582a): 'seed' [BDB, Hol; Coh, Gla, WBC; JPS, KJV], 'offspring' [BDB, Hol; Mer; NASB, NRSV], 'descendant' [Hol; NICOT; CEV, NIV, NLT], 'children' [TEV]. The primary sense of *zeraᶜ* is 'seed of the field' or of any plant, tree, etc.; a secondary sense is the seed of men and of animals; a tertiary sense is 'offspring, descendants' [BDB, Hol].

d-2. זְרוֹעַ zərōaᶜ (BDB p. 283), (Hol p. 92), (TWOT 583a). This reading is not found in any Hebrew ms., but is suggested by the LXX (which reads τὸν ὦμον 'the shoulder') and Vulgate (which reads *brachium* 'arm', [following Wilhelm Rudolph, *Haggai-Sacharja-Maleachi*, Kommentar zum Alten Testament, Band 3, 4. Gütersloher Verlagshaus Gerd Mohn, 1976; cited in Gla. Rudolph's motivation in proposing to emend the MT following the LXX and Vulgate was the argument that a curse on the land's agriculture, signaled by זֶרַע zeraᶜ 'seed of the field', would affect all the nation, not only the guilty priests, and that therefore the original Hebrew text could not have read zeraᶜ 'seed']: 'arm' [BDB, Hol; Keil; NJB, REB], 'shoulder' [BDB (God will withhold from the priests the shoulder of the sacrificial animals, which was set aside in Deut. 18:3 for their consumption)], 'strength' [BDB], 'activity of power' [Hol]. Others hold that the cutting off of the arm is a metaphor for depriving the priests of their priestly role (cf. 1 Sam. 2:31) [this position of Rudolph is cited in Gla].

e. -וְ wə- waw connective of the attached waw consecutive verb (BDB p. 251), (Hol p. 84), (TWOT 519). All commentators and versions translated an additive relation here, most of them by 'and'.

f. 1st sg. Piel perf. waw consecutive of זרה zrh (BDB p. 279), (Hol p. 92), (TWOT 582): 'to spread' [Hol; Coh, Mer, NICOT; KJV, NASB, NIV, NRSV], 'to scatter' [BDB, Hol; Keil], 'to smear' [Gla, WBC], 'to rub' [CEV, TEV], 'to strew' [JPS], 'to throw' [NJB], 'to fling' [REB], 'to splatter' [NLT].

g. פֶּרֶשׁ pereš (BDB p. 831), (Hol p. 299), (TWOT 1835a): 'dung' [Hol; Coh, Keil, Gla, NICOT; JPS, KJV, NLT, NRSV, TEV], 'offal' [Mer, WBC; NIV, NJB, REB], 'manure' [CEV], refuse' [NASB]. The victims' intestines and contents were disposed of before the sacrifice was offered [Gla]. *Pereš* refers to the faeces in the stomach and intestines of slaughtered animals [BDB, Hol].

h. constr. of פָּנִים pānîm [BDB p. 815), (Hol p. 293), (TWOT 1782a): 'face' [all lexica, commentators, and versions].

i. pl. constr. of חַג ḥaḡ (BDB p. 290), (Hol p. 95), (TWOT 602a): 'festival' [Hol; Mer, WBC], 'feast' [BDB; Keil, Gla, NICOT; NASB], 'sacrifice' [Coh], 'offering' [NRSV], 'festal sacrifice' [JPS], 'festival sacrifice' [NIV, NLT], 'pilgrim-feast' [REB], 'animal sacrifice' [CEV], 'solemn feast' [KJV, NJB]. TEV employs a phrase: 'the animals you sacrifice' [TEV]. *Ḥaḡ* here is used as a metonym to refer to the animal offerings at the festivals [Keil]. *Ḥaḡ* often refers to a festival associated with pilgrimages [Hol].

j. -וְ wə- waw connective of the attached waw consecutive verb (BDB p. 251), (Hol p. 84), (TWOT 519): 'and' [all commentators and versions].

k. 3rd mas. sg. Qal perf. *waw* consecutive of נשׂא *nś³* (BDB p. 669), (Hol p. 246), (TWOT 1421): 'to carry away' [Hol; Keil], 'to carry' [BDB; WBC], 'to sweep away' [NJB], 'to take away' [KJV]. Most versions assume an indefinite subject, some supplying 'they' as the subject, and others employing a passive construction: 'to be taken away' [Coh, Mer; NASB], 'to be taken out' [TEV], 'to be carried off' [NICOT; NIV], 'to be carried out' [JPS], 'to be carried away' [Gla]. Other versions employ the 1st person sg. as the subject (based apparently on the LXX and Syriac readings 'I will carry you away from beside me' [Mer]): 'I will put you out of my presence' [NRSV], 'I shall banish you from my presence' [REB], 'and then be done with you' [CEV], 'I will add you' [NLT].

l. אל *³el* (BDB p. 39), (Hol p. 16) (TWOT 91): 'to/unto' [Coh, Keil, NICOT, TEV, WBC; JPS, NLT], 'with' [Mer, Gla; KJV, NASB, NIV, NJB]. The primary function of the preposition *³el* is to indicate motion or direction to or towards something [BDB, Hol].

m. ו- -*w* 3rd mas. sg. obj. suff.: 'it' [all commentators and versions except the following]. Some translations make explicit their understanding of the pronoun's referent: 'its heap' [JPS], 'the dung heap' [NLT, TEV].

QUESTION—What is the significance of הנה *hinnēh* 'behold' at the start of this verse?

Although *hinnēh* is formally a demonstrative interjection or particle, its use here with a participle, signaling imminent future, appears to possess the same amount of prominence, no more and no less, as the clauses using the *waw* consecutive perfect with which its clause is parallel ('and I will spread dung . . .', 'and you will be carried away. . . .') [Clen].

QUESTION—What is the significance of גער *gᶜr* 'to rebuke' in this passage?

1. It is that God will judge and execute sentence upon the priests' descendants, removing them from their priestly role [NICOT]. *Gᶜr* here refers to the curses God sends forth upon the descendants (Mal. 2:2). Such curses are, of course, verbal in origin, but bring concrete results [Mer].

2. It is that God will stop the arm (reading זרוע *zᵊrōaᶜ* 'arm' instead of זרע *zeraᶜ* 'seed of the field; offspring'; see *TEXT above) from functioning—i.e., *zᵊrōaᶜ* 'arm' is metonymy for the ability of the priests' to perform their duties: God will nullify their work [Keil]; or it is metonymy for the priests' hands lifted to bless the Israelites: God will curse the priests' ritual blessing of the people [NICOT].

3. It is that God will curse the crops and harvests of the people. Such cursing—or banning [Gla]—will restrain the land's productivity, ruining its fertility [Coh, Gla].

QUESTION—To what does זרע *zeraᶜ* refer?

1. It refers to the crops of the Israelites; cursed crops will mean that the priests will not receive their due offerings from the people [Coh, Gla].

2. It refers to the crops of the priests [T. Laetsch, *The Minor Prophets. Bible Commentary*. St. Louis: Concordia, 1956, quoted in NICOT, Coh].

3. It refers to the descendants of the priests [NICOT], who are threatened with God's curse as in Deut. 28:32 and Exod. 20:5; the curse would cut off the priests' posterity, thus in effect ending the priesthood [NICOT].

QUESTION—How is לכֶם *lākem* to/because-of-you(pl) translated?

1. It is translated as a dative of possession, 'your' (modifying 'seed/off-spring/arm') [all commentators and versions except the following].

2. It is translated as a dative of disadvantage: 'for your hurt' [Coh], 'to your disadvantage' [Gla].

3. It is translated expressing cause or reason: 'because of you' [NIV]. NIV considers that *lākem* does double duty, expressing both cause and a kind of possession: 'because of you I will rebuke your descendants'.

QUESTION—To what does פֶּרֶשׁ *pereš* 'dung' refer?

It refers to the dung of the animals offered at the annual festivals. Dung cast onto the priests' faces would render them unclean, incapable of fulfilling their religious functions [NICOT]. The priests would end up in the same rubbish dump as the dung [Coh, Mer, Gla]. The reference to the spreading of dung on the priests' faces is a figurative expression, evoking the humiliation which will attend the priests as YHWH removes them from their honored position: they will be removed as the dung of the offerings is removed [Clen].

2:4
and[a]-you(pl)-will-know[b] that I-sent[c] to[d]-you(pl) this command[e]
*to[f-1]-be[g]/from[f-2]-being[g] my-covenant[h] with Levi,[i] says YHWH(-of) hosts.

*TEXT—Most translators read the MT לִהְיוֹת *lihyôt* 'to be', but REB apparently follows a suggested emendation of the MT, either of מֵהְיוֹת *mihyôt* 'from being' = 'cessation' (a possibility noted in BHS), or of לַחֲתֵת *ləḥātēt* 'to break, shatter' [this emendation is mentioned in Gla, also in BHS]. Although NEB and JB both read *mihyôt*, similar to REB [WBC], the majority of versions seem to feel, as does Gla, that a reading signifying the abolition of the Levitical priesthood is inappropriate in the light of Mal. 3:1–5, and that the MT therefore makes more sense. Some have objected to the MT reading, arguing that -לְ *lə-* plus the infinitive of הָיָה *hyh* 'to be' denotes only a future state; however, Helmer Ringgren asserts that it may also be applied to the present, cf. 1 Sam. 19:8 [Helmer Ringgren, "הָיָה hayah", TDOT, 3.37; cited in Gla].

SYNTAX—Many translations regard the verbal expression *lihyôt* 'to be', i.e., 'that it might be' as having 'my covenant with Levi' as its subject. In this case the verb would have no complement and would signify 'to continue to exist' [NICOT, WBC; CEV, JPS, NASB, NIV, NJB, NLT, NRSV, TEV]. Similarly, REB, which reads *mihyôt* 'from being' instead of *lihyôt*, treats 'my covenant with Levi' as the subject.

Other translations regard only 'my covenant' as the subject of *lihyôṯ* 'to be', i.e., 'that it might be'; 'with Levi' is regarded as the complement of the verbal expression [Coh, Mer; KJV].

Keil takes הַמִּצְוָה *hammiṣwâ* 'the commandment', not only as the object of שָׁלַחְתִּי *šillaḥtî* 'I have sent', but also as the subject of *lihyôṯ*; 'my covenant with Levi' is then taken as the complement of *lihyôṯ*: 'that it (the commandment, i.e., the sentence of punishment expressed in Mal. 2:3) may be my covenant with Levi'.

J.M.P. Smith (*A Critical and Exegetical Summary on the Book of Malachi*, ICC, Edinburgh: T. & T. Clark, 1912, repr. 1961; cited in NICOT) takes 'my covenant' as the subject of *lihyôṯ* and 'with Levi' as the complement. He regards the proclitic -לְ *lǝ-* as expressing a circumstantial relationship: '. . . seeing that my covenant is with Levi'.

LEXICON—a. -וְ *wǝ-* *waw* connective of the attached *waw* consecutive verb (BDB p. 251), (Hol p. 84), (TWOT 519). This is translated as a simple additive relation: 'and' [Keil, WBC; KJV, NIV], and as a new sentence or clause with no conjunction [CEV]. Others put this conjunction in a temporal or result relationship with the preceding passage: 'then' [Coh, Mer; JPS, NASB, NJB, NRSV, REB, TEV], 'then at last' [NLT], 'and thereby' [Gla].

b. 2nd mas. pl. Qal perf. *waw* consecutive of יָדַע *yḏᶜ* (BDB p. 393), (Hol p. 128), (TWOT 848): 'to know' [BDB, Hol; Coh, Mer, Gla, NICOT, WBC; JPS, KJV, NASB, NIV, NJB, NLT, NRSV, REB, TEV], 'to perceive' [Keil], 'to come to understand' [Hol]. All of these translations employ the English future tense, except JPS, which employs an imperative: 'know, then . . .' and CEV, which makes explicit a purpose relationship: 'I am telling you this, so I can . . .' [CEV].

c. 1st sg. Qal perf. of שָׁלַח *šlḥ* (BDB p. 1018), (Hol p. 371), (TWOT 2394): 'to send' [all lexica, commentators, and versions except the following], 'to give' [TEV], 'to issue' [REB].

d. אֶל *ʾel* (BDB p. 39), (Hol p. 16) (TWOT 91): 'to/unto' [all commentators and versions except the following], 'against' [REB], not explicit [WBC]. The primary function of the preposition *ʾel* is to indicate motion or direction to or towards something [BDB, Hol].

e. מִצְוָה *miṣwâ* (BDB p. 846), (Hol p. 210), (TWOT 1887b): 'command' [NICOT; NRSV, TEV], 'commandment' [BDB, Hol; Coh, Keil, Mer, Gla, WBC; KJV, NASB, NJB], 'admonition' [NIV], 'warning' [NLT], 'charge' [JPS], 'decree' [REB], not explicit [CEV]. *Miṣwâ* here is identical to that in Mal. 2:1 above [Keil].

f-1. -לְ *lǝ-* (BDB p. 510), (Hol p. 167), (TWOT 1063): most commentators and versions express purpose here. The proclitic *lǝ-* here expresses purpose or perhaps reason [BDB, Hol].

f-2. מִן *min* (BDB p. 577), (Hol p. 200), (TWOT 1212). REB reads *min* instead of -לְ *lǝ-*, using the preposition to express content: 'I have issued this decree against you: my covenant with Levi falls. . . .' The preposition *min* expresses negation when followed by an infinitives such as 'to stop, to hinder, to cease' [BDB, Hol].

g. Qal inf. of היה *hyh* (BDB p. 224), (Hol p. 78), (TWOT 491): 'to continue' [Mer; NASB, NIV], 'to be maintained' [NICOT, WBC], 'to be' [Coh, Keil; KJV], 'to hold' (in the sense of 'to continue') [Gla; NRSV], 'to not be broken' [TEV], 'to continue to keep' [CEV], 'to affirm one's intention to maintain' [NJB], 'to endure' [JPS], 'to be continued' [NLT]. It is clear that some translations focus upon God as the agent of a continuing covenant, as in CEV and NJB. *Hyh*, the principal verb to be in Hebrew, has a large variety of functions; besides that of a copula, it can denote both incipient existence, e.g., 'to become' and continued existence, e.g., 'to continue to be'; it also often carries along narration, e.g., 'to happen' [BDB, Hol].

g. inf. of היה *hyh* (see above): 'to fall' [REB]. This apparently uncommon use is claimed for *hyh* by G.R. Driver, *Journal of Theological Studies* 39 (1938) [WBC].

h. constr. of ברית *bərît* (BDB p. 136), (Hol p. 48), (TWOT 282a): 'covenant' [all lexica, commentators, and versions], 'agreement' [Hol; CEV].

i. לוי *lēwî* (BDB p. 532), (Hol p. 174), (TWOT 1093): 'Levi' [BDB, Hol; Coh, Keil, ,Mer, Gla, NICOT, NJB, WBC; JPS, KJV, NASB, NIV, NRSV, REB], 'the priests, the descendants of Levi' [TEV], 'your ancestor Levi' [CEV], 'the Levites' [NLT].

QUESTION—What is the syntactic position of this verse?

It is parallel to Mal. 2:1 [Gla].

QUESTION—What is the intent of this verse?

1. It is redemptive in nature: God wants to preserve the priesthood ('that my covenant . . . may hold') by leading the priests to repentance, or to purify it by ridding it of the bad priests [NICOT, TOTC]. That is, the verse announces God's penalty upon the priests. Thus the מצוה *miṣwâ* 'commandment' (which is identical to the *miṣwâ* of Mal. 2:2—the command to glorify the name of YHWH [Gla]) is not merely a sentence of punishment pronounced upon the priests who remain unrepentant of their sins, but it also becomes an avenue to renew the priesthood and the entire nation [Gla].

2. This verse merely announces the punishment to come upon the faithless priests. In the phrase להיות בריתי את־לוי *lihyôt bərîtî ʾet lēwî* 'to-be my-covenant with Levi', להיות *lihyôt* 'that it may be' does not mean to continue or be maintained. 'The commandment' must therefore be considered as the subject of 'to-be': 'that this my commandment may be my covenant with Levi', i.e., God, who in the past ordered his relationship with the Levites according to his covenant, now will do so according to the sentence (מצוה *miṣwâ* 'commandment') of punishment which he has declared [Keil]. This interpretation accords with, and is necessitated by, Keil's understanding of *miṣwâ* in Mal. 2:1 above.

QUESTION—To what does 'covenant with Levi' refer?
1. It refers to God's establishment of the office of the priesthood in Israel
(cf. Deut. 33:8–11, Exod. 6:16–20, and Num. 25:10–13). A specific
link between this passage and Num. 25:10–13 is made when Mal. 2:5
employs שלום šālôm 'peace', which is also used in the Numbers
passage, where Phinehas becomes a symbol of the entire priesthood
[Mer].
   Many scholars suppose that Malachi does not differentiate priests
from Levites in general, and that the covenant referred to in this verse
must therefore be that of Deut. 33:10, which neither makes such a
distinction [Gla]. If one assumes that the tribe of Levi became divided
into an upper and a lower order during the monarchy, why does Malachi
not refer to such a division? The answer revolves perhaps around the
Zadokites, whom Wellhausen held to be not originally numbered among
the Levites, but who controlled the priesthood in Jerusalem until its fall.
But as Ezekiel 40–44 enumerates the Zadokites among the Levites, it
would then appear that perhaps during or after the exile they began to be
considered as belonging to the tribe of Levi, where it was felt they
should be, since they were priests. It is concluded that the term
"levitical" began therefore to bear a functional load and not just a
genealogical one [Gla].
2. It refers to the blessing which Moses gave Levi (Deut. 33:8–11), and not
to Num. 25, in which God made a promise only to Phinehas and not to
the Levites as a whole. 'Levi' stands for the entire priesthood [Coh,
Keil, WBC]. Moses' blessing was elevated over time into covenantal
quality [TOTC], for the priesthood had both duties and privileges [Keil].
3. It refers to the relationship of God with the Levites, which at some time
in Israel's early history God must have formalized as a covenant (cf. Jer.
33:20–21) [NICOT].
4. It refers to Numbers 25:10–13, to the "covenant of perpetual
priesthood" (Num. 25:13) with Phineas and his descendants. The
phraseology even of this passage is very similar to Mal. 2:5. This
covenant then became generally applied to all the Levites, and Phineas
became the symbol of the ideal priest. In effect, Malachi pits the ideal of
the ancient Levites against the corrupt priesthood of his day [Gla].

2:5
My-covenant[a] was[b] with[c]-him
the-life[d] and-the-wholeness[e], and[f]-I-gave[g]-them to-him;
reverence,[h] and[i]-he-revered[j]-me,
and[k]-before[l] my-name[m] he-stood-in-awe.[n]
SYNTAX—There are various interpretations of the syntax of colon 1–2a
בריתי היתה אתו החיים והשלום) bərîṯî hāyəṯâ ʾittô haḥayyîm wəhaššālôm
'my-covenant was with-him the-life and-the-peace'):

1. 'The life' (haḥayyîm) and 'the peace' (wəhaššālôm) are in a genitive
   relationship with 'my covenant' (bərîṯî) [Gla, NICOT; NASB]. This
   interpretation is preferable because the contents of the covenant are
   clearly defined [NICOT].
2. 'The life' (haḥayyîm) and 'the peace' (wəhaššālôm) constitute 'my
   covenant', i.e., 'my covenant was life and peace'. Option 1 above
   assumes a syntactic ellipsis which cannot be defended in Biblical
   Hebrew. To be sure, the final significance of the two options is about the
   same [Keil].
3. NJB regards bərîṯî hāyəṯâ ʾittô 'my-covenant was with-him' as the first
   predication. haḥayyîm wəhaššālôm 'the-life and-the-peace' is regarded as
   being in apposition with 'my covenant'. This syntactic interpretation
   focuses upon the very existence of the covenant [NICOT].

SYNTAX—The syntax of colon 2b-3 (וָאֶתְּנֵם־לוֹ מוֹרָא וַיִּירָאֵנִי) wāʾettənēm lô
môrāʾ wayyîrāʾēnî 'and-I-gave-them to-him; reverence, and-he-revered-
me') is interpreted as follows:

1. Môrāʾ 'reverence' is parallel to 'the life and the peace' in colon 2a: the
   covenant is one of reverence as well as of life and peace. Thus
   wayyîrāʾēnî 'and he feared me' is also parallel to wāʾettənēm 'and I gave
   them to him' [Coh, Mer; JPS, NJB].
2. Môrāʾ 'reverence' stands as a kind of goal of the preceding clause, e.g.,
   KJV's translation 'I gave them to him for the fear' [Keil, Mer; most
   versions]. The elipsis featured in this passage is meant to stress the
   reciprocity inherent in the covenant [Clen].

LEXICON—a. בְּרִית bərîṯ (BDB p. 136), (Hol p. 48), (TWOT 282a):
   'covenant' [all lexica, commentators, and versions except the following],
   'agreement' [Hol; CEV].
b. 3rd sg. fem. Qal perf. of היה hyh (BDB p. 224), (Hol p. 78), (TWOT
   491): 'was' [all commentators and versions except the following], 'has
   been' [Gla]. JPS makes more explicit the aspect of God's ownership of
   the covenant: 'I had a covenant'. NLT makes explicit its understanding
   of goal in hyh here: 'the purpose of my covenant with the Levites
   was. . . .'
c. את ʾēṯ (BDB p. 85), (Hol p. 31), (TWOT 187): 'with' [all commentators
   and versions]. ʾēṯ expresses accompaniment or ideas derived from it
   [BDB, Hol].
d. חיים ḥayyîm (BDB p. 313), (Hol p. 101), (TWOT 644f): 'life' [all
   lexica, commentators, and versions except CEV], 'full life' [CEV].
   Ḥayyîm embraces a range of concepts, from the condition of being alive
   to what makes for a happy and prosperous life; often spiritual well-being
   is included [BDB, Hol].
e. שלום šālôm (BDB p. 1022), (Hol p. 371), (TWOT 2401a): 'wholeness'
   [Hol; Mer], 'peace' [BDB, Hol; Coh, Gla, NICOT, WBC; KJV, NASB,
   NIV, NLT, NJB], 'salvation' [Keil], 'well-being' [Hol; JPS, NRSV,
   TEV], 'welfare' [BDB; REB]. Šālôm embraces all factors of life well

lived, from physical comforts and prosperity to health, peace, and right relation with God, especially in terms of Israel's covenant with YHWH [BDB].

f. -ו wə- *waw* connective of the attached preterite verb (BDB p. 251), (Hol p. 84), (TWOT 519): 'and' [all commentators and versions except the following]. A new clause, which also stands in an additive relationship with the preceding clause, much like 'and': [Gla; JPS]. NRSV alters the relationship by subordinating it by means of the relative pronoun 'which'.

g. 1st mas. sg. Qal preterite of נתן *ntn* (BDB p. 678), (Hol p. 249), (TWOT 1443): 'to give' [BDB, Hol; Coh, Mer, Gla, NICOT, WBC; JPS, KJV, NASB, NIV, NJB, NLT, NRSV], 'to lend' [Keil], 'to bestow' [REB], 'to bless' [CEV], 'to lay on' [REB].

h. מורא *môrā⁰* (BDB p. 432), (Hol p. 187), (TWOT 907c): 'reverence' [BDB; Gla, NICOT; JPS, NASB, NLT, REB], 'respect' [NJB], 'fear' [Hol; Coh; KJV, NIV, NRSV]. Some versions employ a phrase expressing God's purpose: 'so that they might respect me' [TEV], 'I gave them to him for the fear' [KJV], and, turning the syntactic subject—object relationship around: 'to fill him with awe' [Mer]. Other versions make explicit their reading of the covenant's requirements: 'this called for reverence' [NIV, NLT, NRSV], also 'I laid on him the duty of reverence' [REB], similarly, Gla. Still other versions employ a genitive relationship, e.g., 'a covenant of reverence' [JPS], also [NJB]. NASB's 'I gave them [life and peace] to him as an object of reverence' is rather unintelligible.

i. -ו wə- *waw* connective of the attached preterite verb (BDB p. 251), (Hol p. 84), (TWOT 519): 'and' [Coh, Keil, Gla, NICOT, WBC; NJB, NLT, NRSV]. Some versions intensify the connective: 'and indeed' [Mer], 'so' [NASB]. Others achieve an additive relationship by beginning a new sentence: [REB]. Still others translate with a subordinate relationship instead of additive: 'wherewith' [KJV], 'which' [JPS].

j. 3rd mas. sg. Qal preterite of ירא *yr⁰* (BDB p. 431), (Hol p. 142), (TWOT 907): 'to revere' [Mer, Gla, NICOT; NASB, NIV, NLT, NRSV, REB], 'to fear' [BDB, Hol; Coh, Keil, WBC; KJV], 'to respect' [CEV, NJB, TEV], 'to show reverence' [JPS].

k. -ו wə- *waw* connective (BDB p. 251), (Hol p. 84), (TWOT 519): 'and' [all commentators and versions except JPS], 'for' [JPS].

l. מפני *mippənê* (BDB p. 815), (Hol p. 293): 'before' [Keil, KJV, Mer, Gla, WBC]. This expression, together with the following noun שמי *šəmî* 'my name', forms the complement in Hebrew of the verb נחת *niḥat* 'he was in awe'. This complement is restructured by other versions: 'of my name' [NICOT; JPS, NASB, NIV, NLT, NRSV, REB]. *Mippənê*, which is a compound preposition, is formally composed of the preposition מן *min* 'away from' plus the construct of פנים *pānîm* 'face'. Its concrete

sense is 'away from, out from' [Hol]; here, however, it carries
figuratively the sense of 'on account of' [Hol], 'because of' [BDB].

m. שֵׁם *šēm* (BDB p. 1027), (Hol p. 374), (TWOT 2405): 'my name' [all
commentators and versions except TEV]. TEV, identifying the
metonymy in the use of *šēm* here, translates concretely as 'me'.

n. 3rd mas. sg. Niphal perf. of חתת *ḥtt* (BDB p. 369), (Hol p. 121),
(TWOT 784): 'to stand in awe' [Gla, NICOT, Mer; JPS, NIV, NLT,
NRSV], 'to be in awe' [BDB; WBC], 'to tremble' [Keil], 'to be afraid'
[Coh; KJV], 'to fear' [TEV], 'to hold in awe' [NJB], 'to respect'
[CEV], 'to live in awe' [REB], 'to be terrified' [Hol].

QUESTION—To whom specifically do the pronouns 'he' and 'him' refer?
They refer to Phineas (Num. 25:10-13; cf. Ps. 106:30-31) [Mer].

QUESTION—What explicit relationship is seen in the clause which centers
around היתה *hāyət̞â* 'was'?

1. Most commentators and versions do not specify any relation in the
translation other than equative or a genitive.

2. Some versions make explicit their understanding of an underlying
relationship. NLT specifies that it is a purpose clause: 'the purpose of
my covenant with the Levites was to bring life and peace'; CEV and
TEV employ the verb 'promise', e.g., 'I promised them life and well-
being' [TEV].

2:6
**Instruction(-of)[a] truth[b] it-was[c] in[d]-his-mouth,[e] and[f]-perversity[g] was- not
-found[h] on[i]-his-lips;[j] in[k]-peace[l] and-in-uprightness[m] he-walked[n] with-me,
and[o]-many[p] he-turned[q] from[r]-sin.[s]**

LEXICON—a. constr. of תורה *tôrâ* (BDB p. 435), (Hol p. 388), (TWOT
910d): 'instruction' [BDB; Hol; Gla; NASB, NIV, NRSV], 'rulings'
[JPS], 'teaching' [Mer, WBC], 'law' [BDB; Coh, Keil, KJV, NJB].
NICOT employs a phrase in order to specify what kind of instruction:
'instruction . . . in the law'. Some versions translate with a verb: 'to
teach' [CEV, TEV], 'to pass on' [NLT], 'to give' [REB]. The primary
sense of *tôrâ* is 'instruction'; 'law' is a derived secondary sense [BDB,
Hol].

b. אמת *ʾĕmet̞* (BDB p. 54), (Hol p. 22), (TWOT 116k): 'truth' [BDB; Coh,
Keil; CEV, KJV, NJB, NLT], 'fidelity' [Hol]. Many versions employ an
adjective instead of a noun in order to translate the construct relationship
between *tôrâ* and *ʾĕmet̞*: 'true' [Mer, Gla, WBC; NASB, NIV, NRSV,
REB], 'proper' [JPS], 'reliable' [NICOT]. TEV employs a clause: 'what
was right'. NLT also employs a clause specifying who it was that gave
the law: 'all the truth they received from me'.

c. 3rd fem. sg. Qal perf. of היה *hyh* (BDB p. 224), (Hol p. 78), (TWOT
491): 'was' [Coh, Keil, Mer, Gla, NICOT, WBC; KJV, NASB, NIV,
NJB, NRSV], 'were' [JPS]. *Hyh* functions as a copula here.

d. -בְּ *bə-* (BDB p. 88), (Hol p. 32), (TWOT 193): 'in' [Coh, Keil, Mer, Gla, NICOT, WBC; JPS, KJV, NASB, NIV, NJB, NRSV]. The proclitic *bə-* denotes here abstract locality, e.g., 'in' [BDB, Hol].

e. constr. of פֶּה *peh* (BDB p. 804), (Hol p. 289), (TWOT 1738): 'mouth' [BDB, Hol; Coh, Keil, Mer, Gla, NICOT, WBC; JPS, KJV, NASB, NIV, NJB, NRSV], 'lips' [REB]. Some versions translate this figure of speech concretely: 'he/they taught' [CEV, TEV].

f. -וְ *wə-* waw connective (BDB p. 251), (Hol p. 84), (TWOT 519): 'and' [all commentators and versions except the following]. The additive relationship is also expressed by a new sentence or clause [Mer; NLT, TEV].

g. עַוְלָה *ʿawlâ* (BDB p. 732), (Hol p. 267), (TWOT 1580b): 'perversity' [Hol; Keil], 'iniquity' [KJV], 'unrighteousness' [BDB; Coh, Mer, Gla; NASB], 'guilt' [NJB], 'wrong' [BDB; WBC; NRSV, TEV], 'lie' [CEV], 'wickedness' [Hol]. Some translate with an adjective: 'perverse' [JPS], 'false' [NIV], 'unjust' [NICOT]. REB translates with a phrase: 'word of injustice'. NLT translates with a compound verb: 'to lie or cheat'.

h. 3rd mas. sg. Niphal perf. of מָצָא *mṣʾ* (BDB p. 592), (Hol p. 209), (TWOT 1231): 'to be found' [BDB; Coh, Mer, Gla, NICOT, WBC; KJV, NASB, NIV, NJB, NRSV], 'to fall' [REB]. Some translate with the verb 'to be' [Keil; JPS]. CEV employs a verb of speech 'to tell'. The anomaly of the mismatch of genders between subject noun and governed verb is well attested [e.g., Gesenius §143, 1, *b*]. The primary sense of the Niphal of *mṣʾ* is 'to be found, to be encountered of discovered' [BDB, Hol].

i. -בְּ *bə-* (see above): 'on/upon' [all lexica, commentators, and versions except the following], 'in' [Coh; KJV]. The proclitic *bə-* denotes here abstract locality [BDB, Hol].

j. constr. of שָׂפָה *śāpâ* (BDB p. 973), (Hol p. 354), (TWOT 2278a): 'lips' [all lexica, commentators, and versions except the following]. Some express this figure of speech with a verb: 'to tell' [CEV], 'to teach' (by ellipsis) [TEV], 'to cheat' [NLT]. The primary sense of *śāpâ* is 'lip'; secondary senses are 'manner of speaking, speech' and 'language' [BDB, Hol].

k. -בְּ *bə-* (see above): 'in' [all commentators and versions except the following], 'with' [WBC; JPS]. The proclitic *bə-* denotes here either character or circumstance [BDB, Hol].

l. שָׁלוֹם *šālôm* (BDB p. 1022), (Hol p. 371), (TWOT 2401a): 'peace' [BDB, Hol; Coh, NICOT, WBC; KJV, NASB, NIV, NJB], 'wholeness' [Hol; Mer], 'salvation' [Keil], 'harmony' [REB, TEV], 'integrity' [Gla]. A verb is also employed: 'to obey' [CEV], and a noun phrase: 'good life' [NLT]. *Šālôm* embraces all factors of life lived well, from physical comforts and prosperity to health, peace, and right relation with God, especially in terms of Israel's covenant with YHWH [BDB].

m. מִישׁוֹר *mîšôr* (BDB p. 449), (Hol p. 193), (TWOT 930f): 'uprightness'
[BDB; Coh, Mer, NICOT, WBC; NASB, NIV, NRSV, REB], 'justice'
[Gla; NJB], 'equity' [KJV], 'integrity' [Keil], 'complete loyalty' [JPS],
'righteousness' [Hol]. NLT translates 'righteous lives', while other
employ a verb phrase: 'they did what was right' [TEV], 'he lived right'
[CEV].

n. 3ʳᵈ mas. sg. Qal perf. of הָלַךְ *hlk* (BDB p. 229), (Hol p. 79), (TWOT
498): 'to walk' [Coh, Keil, Mer, Gla, NICOT, WBC; KJV, NASB,
NIV, NJB, NLT, NRSV, REB]. Other versions translate more
concretely: 'to serve' [JPS], 'to live' [TEV; NLT adds 'to live' with 'to
walk']; translation not explicit [CEV]. This word denotes an intimacy of
relationship to God [NICOT]. The primary sense of *hlk* is 'to go'; a
secondary sense concerns manner of living: 'to conduct oneself' [BDB,
Hol].

o. -וְ *wə-* *waw* connective (BDB p. 251), (Hol p. 84), (TWOT 519): 'and'
[all commentators and versions except TEV]. TEV expresses an additive
relation 'but also' here.

p. pl. of רַב *rab* (BDB p. 912), (Hol p. 330), (TWOT 2099a): 'many'
[BDB; Coh, Keil, Mer, Gla, NICOT, WBC; KJV, NASB, NIV, NJB,
NLT, NRSV, REB], 'the many' [Hol; JPS], 'many others' [TEV], 'a lot
of people' [CEV]. *Rab* can mean 'the rank and file of people' [Hol], 'the
masses'.

q. 3ʳᵈ mas. sg. Hiphil perf. of שׁוּב *šûb* (BDB p. 996), (Hol p. 362),
(TWOT 2340): 'to turn' [Mer, WBC; NIV, NLT, NRSV], 'to lead'
[CEV], 'to lead back' [Hol], 'to turn away' [Coh, Gla, NICOT; KJV],
'to turn back' [NASB, REB], 'to convert' [NJB], 'to hold back' [JPS],
'to bring back' [BDB, Hol; Keil]. TEV attempts to specify the sense of
this verb: 'they . . . helped many others to stop doing evil'.

r. מִן *min* 'from' (BDB p. 577), (Hol p. 200), (TWOT 1212): 'from' [all
commentators and versions except TEV]. TEV rephrases with a clause
'to stop doing evil'. The preposition *min* introduces here a phrasal
complement indicating cessation of an activity [BDB, Hol].

s. עָוֹן *ʿāwōn* (BDB p. 730), (Hol p. 268), (TWOT 1577a): 'sin' [NICOT;
CEV, NIV, REB], 'sinning' [NJB], 'evil' [TEV], 'iniquity' [BDB; Coh,
Mer, Gla, WBC; JPS, KJV, NASB, NRSV], 'guilt' [BDB; Keil]. A
connotation of habitual sin is recognized and translated: 'lives of sin'
[NLT]. *ʿāwōn* can denote wrong actions, guilt, or the punishment of sin
[BDB, Hol]. *ʿāwōn* is deliberate sin and its consequent guilt [NICOT].

QUESTION—What does תּוֹרָה *tôrâ* denote in this passage?

It denotes instruction and here refers to the oral teaching of God's law,
which Malachi insists is one of the priests' main duties [NICOT]. *Tôrâ*
originally denoted instructions in carrying out the requirements of proper
worship of YHWH. Here, however, it also includes moral teaching and is
perhaps parallel to דַּעַת *daʿat* 'knowledge' of Mal. 2:7. Such instruction
not only pertains to problems raised in the past, but also must be able to

MALACHI 2:6

81

respond to new ethical and procedural questions raised by changing conditions [Gla].

QUESTION—What does אמת ʾĕmet denote in this passage?

It denotes truth based upon God's will [Keil]. ʾĕmet is related to אמונה ʾĕmûnâ 'steadiness, reliability; honesty' [Hol p. 19] and is derived from אמן ʾmn 'to confirm, support, uphold' [TWOT 116]. ʾĕmet characterized the early priests' teaching of God's will [NICOT].

QUESTION—What is the syntax of ועולה לא־נמצא waʿawlâ lōʾ nimṣāʾ 'and perversity was not found'?

As ʿawlâ 'perversity' is feminine, the verb nimṣāʾ 'was found' does not agree in gender with it, but is rather impersonal, and 'perversity' is the object: 'he (i.e., they) did not find perversity' (cf. Gesenius §143, 1, b) [Keil].

QUESTION—What does עולה ʿawlâ denote in this passage?

It is the opposite of אמת ʾĕmet and thus denotes conduct which is not conformed to God's will [Keil, NICOT].

QUESTION—To what does שלום šālôm 'peace' refer in this passage?

1. It refers to complete harmony with God [NICOT].
2. It refers to the salvation given by God [Keil].
3. It refers to perfection of one's life with God and of one's service to him. Šālôm corresponds to the Akkadian šalmēš, which denotes in one ancient text perfection of a priest's service in rituals. The Hebrew root can denote the same, and moral integrity as well [Moshe Weinfeld, *Deuteronomy and the Deuteronomic School* (Oxford: Clarendon, 1972); cited in Gla].

QUESTION—What does מישור mîšôr 'uprightness' denote?

It denotes conduct characterized by moral integrity [Keil, NICOT].

QUESTION—What does השיב hēšîb 'he turned' denote?

It denotes the action of turning someone away from sin and back to keeping God's covenant [NICOT].

2:7

For[a] (the)-lips(-of)[b] (a)-priest[c] should-guard[d] knowledge,[e] and[f]-instruction[g] they-should-seek[h] from[i]-his-mouth,[j] because[k] (a)-messenger(-of)[l] YWHW(-of) hosts (is) he.

SYNTAX—This verse is syntactically subordinate to the preceding verse, as it expounds the reason for the ancient priests' correct behavior [Clen].

LEXICON—a. כי kî connective (BDB p. 471), (Hol p. 155), (TWOT 976): 'for' [Coh, Keil, Mer, Gla; JPS, KJV, NASB, NIV, NRSV, REB], 'because' [WBC], 'verily' [NICOT], not explicit [CEV, NJB, NLT, TEV].

b. dual constr. of שפה śāpâ (BDB p. 973), (Hol p. 354), (TWOT 2278a): 'lips' [all lexica, commentators, and versions except the following], 'manner of speaking' [Hol], 'speech' [BDB]. Some versions translate concretely the synecdoche as 'priest' [CEV, TEV]. REB translates 'words'.

c. כֹּהֵן *kōhēn* (BDB p. 463), (Hol p. 152), (TWOT 959): 'priest' [all lexica, commentators, and versions].

d. 3rd mas. pl. Qal imperf. of שָׁמַר *šmr* (BDB p. 1036), (Hol p. 377), (TWOT 2414): 'to guard' [Gla, WBC; JPS, NLT, NRSV], 'to preserve' [Mer, NICOT; NASB, NIV], 'to keep' [BDB; Coh, Keil; KJV], 'to teach' [TEV], 'to safeguard' [NJB], 'to spread' [CEV], 'to be careful about, protect' [Hol]. Most translations indicate obligation, e.g., 'should preserve' [Mer]; CEV combines obligation with attitude: 'should be eager to spread'. Of the only versions which indicate customary action instead of obligation, REB translates with an English idiom: 'for men hang on the words of the priest', and NICOT translates 'the lips of a priest preserve knowledge'. Priests are represented as storehouses of knowledge which they can dispense as they choose [NICOT]. יִשְׁמְרוּ *yišmᵉrû* 'they should guard' and יְבַקְשׁוּ *yᵉḇaqšû* 'they should seek' below are directive expressions, but possess little prominence in comparison to the crucial narrative sequence of Mal. 2:5 [Clen].

e. דַּעַת *daᶜat* (BDB p. 395), (Hol p. 73), (TWOT 848c): 'knowledge' [Hol; Coh, Keil, Mer, Gla, NASB, NICOT, WBC; CEV, JPS, KJV, NIV, NJB, NLT, NRSV, REB], 'discernment, understanding, wisdom' [BDB]. TEV translates with a phrase specifying the kind of knowledge in focus: 'the true knowledge of God'. *Daᶜat* refers to knowing the Lord and what he desires [Keil], to knowing the difference between good and evil [Gla].

f. -ו *wᵉ-* *waw* connective (BDB p. 251), (Hol p. 84), (TWOT 519): all commentators and versions express an additive relation here, most of them translating 'and'. NJB and TEV expresses the same relation by beginning a new sentence, or clause.

g. תּוֹרָה *tôrâ* (BDB p. 435), (Hol p. 388), (TWOT 910d): 'instruction' [BDB, Hol; Mer, Gla, WBC; CEV, NASB, NIV, NLT, NRSV, REB], 'the law' [BDB; Coh, Keil; KJV, NJB], 'will' [TEV], 'ruling' [JPS]. NICOT specifies the content of the instruction: 'instruction in the law'. The primary sense of *tôrâ* is 'instruction'; 'law' is a derived secondary sense [BDB, Hol].

h. 3rd mas. pl. Piel imperf. of בקשׁ *bqš* (BDB p. 134), (Hol p. 47), (TWOT 276): 'to seek' [BDB, Hol; Coh, Keil, Mer, Gla, NICOT, WBC; JPS, KJV, NASB, NIV, NJB, NRSV], 'to try to get' [Hol]. Some translate with a phrase: 'should come . . . for instruction' [CEV], 'should go to them to learn' [TEV], also NLT. Most translations express obligation, e.g., 'should seek'; some, however, express habitude, e.g., 'people are seeking' [NICOT, also Keil; JPS, REB]. *Bqš* denotes successful seeking; the people will find what they are looking for [NICOT].

i. מִן *min* (BDB p. 577), (Hol p. 200), (TWOT 1212): 'from' [all mentators and versions except the following], 'at' [Coh; KJV]. The preposition *min* expresses here metaphorical direction of movement or source.

j. constr. of פֶּה *peh* (BDB p. 804), (Hol p. 289), (TWOT 1738): 'mouth' [BDB, Hol; Coh, Keil, Mer, Gla, NICOT, WBC; JPS, KJV, NASB, NIV, NJB, NRSV]. Some translate concretely the synecdoche introduced by 'mouth', translating 'him', 'them', or 'you', i.e., the priest [CEV, NLT, REB, TEV].

k. כִּי *kî* connective (see above): 'because' [Keil, Gla, NICOT, WBC; CEV, NIV, REB, TEV], 'for' [Coh, Mer; JPS, KJV, NASB, NLT, NRSV], 'since' [NJB].

l. מַלְאָךְ *malʾāk* (BDB p. 521), (Hol p. 196), (TWOT 1068a): 'messenger' [all lexica, commentators, and versions except the following]. CEV translates with a clause: 'you speak for me'.

QUESTION—How is כִּי *kî* at the start of this verse interpreted?

1. As a marker of emphasis: 'yes', 'verily', to go with the first interpretation of יִשְׁמְרוּ *yišmərû* 'they guard' below [NICOT].

2. As a particle marking the reason for the preceding statements of Mal. 2:6—generally 'for' or 'because' [most versions].

QUESTION—How is יִשְׁמְרוּ *yišmərû* 'they guard, they should guard' understood?

1. It is understood as habitual: good priests, like those of the early priesthood, preserve knowledge [NICOT].

2. It is understood as denoting an obligation [most translations].

QUESTION—What is the significance of the expression מַלְךְ יהוה־צְבָאוֹת *malʾak yhwh ṣəḇāʾôt* 'messenger of the Lord of hosts'?

This expression implies here that the ideal priests are God's messengers to apply his instruction to the people [NICOT]. Although this same expression is applied also to Haggai and the other prophets (Hag. 1:13) [Keil, Gla, NICOT], a strong distinction was maintained in that the priests were keepers of the instruction (תּוֹרָה *tôrâ*), whereas the prophets were keepers of the messages (דָּבָר *dāḇār*) of God [NICOT]. Gla sees in this expression the post-exilic reality, reflected by Malachi, of the priests becoming God's principal spokesmen, replacing the prophets of old. The loss of the monarchy, around which the prophets had clustered, and the realities of the Persian rule meant that the prophets wielded diminishing influence among the Jews. The prophets' decline was aggravated by their loss of credibility with the people, documented by many of the literary prophets. The Jews turned instead to the priests, whose thought was at least founded upon externally-recognized sources [Gla].

2:8

But[a]-you(pl)[b] have-turned[c] from[d]-the-way,[e] you-have-caused-to-stumble[f] many[g] by[h]-the-(your)-instruction[i]/in[h]-the-law,[i] you(pl)-have-violated[j] (the)-covenant(-of)[k] the-Levi,[l] says YHWH(-of) hosts.

LEXICON—a. וְ *wə-* *waw* connective (BDB p. 251), (Hol p. 84), (TWOT 519): 'but' [all commentators and versions except the following], 'however' [Mer.].

b. אתם *ʾattem* 2nd mas. pl. prn.: 'you' [all commentators and versions]. This is an emphatic pronoun to drive home the difference between what the priests should be like and what they actually are; one should translate 'as for you' [Gla; NASB]. *ʾattem* is the 2nd mas. pl. pronoun 'you'.

c. 2nd mas. pl. Qal perf. of סור *sûr* (BDB p. 693), (Hol p. 254), (TWOT 1480): 'to turn' [Mer, WBC; NIV], 'to turn away' [JPS, TEV], 'to turn aside' [BDB, Hol; Coh, Gla; NASB, NJB, NRSV, REB], 'to desert' [NICOT], 'to depart' [Keil; KJV], 'to turn the back on' [CEV], 'to leave' [NLT].

d. מן *min* (BDB p. 577), (Hol p. 200), (TWOT 1212): 'from' [all commentators and versions except the following], 'out of' [Coh, KJV]. The preposition *min* expresses here direction of movement from.

e. דרך *derek* (BDB p. 202), (Hol p. 74), (TWOT 453a): 'way' [BDB; all commentators and versions except the following], 'right path' [TEV], 'course' [JPS, REB], 'God's paths' [NLT]. CEV, considering that *derek* here stands for God, translates 'me'. *Derek* denotes in its primary sense 'way, path'; a secondary sense carries the meaning of conduct or habitual pattern of living which is required by God [Hol].

f. 2nd mas. pl. Hiphil perf. of כשל *kšl* (BDB p. 505), (Hol p. 166), (TWOT 1050): 'to cause to stumble' [BDB, Hol; Coh, Mer, Gla, NICOT, WBC; KJV, NASB, NIV, NLT, NRSV, REB], 'to make stumble' [Keil; JPS], 'to lead to do wrong' [TEV], 'to cause to lapse' [NJB], 'to lead to do sinful things' [CEV]. The priests have led many people to misunderstand what the Law requires and thus to fail to keep it [Mer].

g. pl. of רב *rab* (BDB p. 912), (Hol p. 330), (TWOT 2099a): 'many' [BDB, Hol; all commentators and versions except the following], 'others' [CEV]. JPS translates 'the many', giving the idea of 'the masses'. *Rab* can indeed mean 'the rank and file of people' [Hol].

h. -ב *bə-* (BDB p. 88), (Hol p. 32), (TWOT 193). Most commentators and versions understand this proclitic to express instrument here: 'by' [most commentators and versions], 'through' [Gla; JPS]. Some translations express the instrument as the subject of the verb, e.g., 'your teaching has led . . .' [CEV, TEV, also NLT]. A minority of translations take the proclitic to express reference, i.e., many have been made to stumble in regard to the law, etc.: 'at the law' [Keil; KJV], 'in the law' [Coh, Mer]. The proclitic *bə-* denotes here either instrument or abstract locality [BDB, Hol].

i. תורה *tôrâ* (BDB p. 435), (Hol p. 388), (TWOT 910d): 'instruction' [BDB, Hol; Gla; NASB, NRSV], 'law' [BDB, Hol; Coh, Keil, Mer; KJV], 'teaching' [NICOT, WBC; CEV, NIV, NJB, REB, TEV], 'rulings' [JPS], 'guidance' [NLT], 'direction' [BDB]. Most translations which translate 'instruction', 'teaching', 'rulings', or 'guidance' add the possessive 'your' to the noun: Gla, NICOT, WBC; CEV, JPS, NIV, NJB, NLT, NRSV, REB, TEV; NASB translates 'the instruction'.

These same translations take the proclitic -בְ bə- above to indicate
instrument, while those translating tôrâ as 'law' take the proclitic to
indicate abstract locality, i.e., reference (see the questions below). The
primary sense of tôrâ is 'instruction'; 'law' is a derived secondary sense
[BDB, Hol].

j. 2nd mas. pl. Piel perf. of שִׁחֵת šḥt (BDB p. 1007), (Hol p. 366),
    (TWOT 2370): 'to violate' [NIV], 'to destroy' [NJB], 'to annul'
    [NICOT], 'to break'[CEV, TEV], 'to corrupt' [Coh, Keil, Mer, Gla,
    WBC; JPS, KJV, NASB, NLT, NRSV], 'to set at naught' [REB], 'to
    spoil' [BDB, Hol], 'to ruin' [BDB, Hol]. This verb here means to
    morally corrupt the covenant [TOTC]. This passage must be understood
    to say that the covenant will continue because God is committed to it,
    but that these particular priests have lost their part in it [Mer, NICOT,
    TOTC].

k. בְּרִית bərît (BDB p. 136), (Hol p. 48), (TWOT 282a): 'covenant' [all
    lexica, commentators, and versions except the following], 'promise'
    [CEV].

l. לֵוִי lēwî 'Levi' (BDB p. 532), (Hol p. 174), (TWOT 1093): 'Levi' [all
    commentators and versions except the following], 'Levites' [JPS, NLT,
    REB]. CEV translates 'your ancestor Levi', making explicit the identity
    of Levi. TEV translates 'you', taking the present generation of priests to
    be the sense of 'Levi' here. Gla translates hallēwî 'the-Levi' as an
    adjective: 'Levitical'. The construct relationship between 'covenant' and
    'Levi' is expressed by most with 'of', but it is also translated as 'the
    covenant I made with the Levites' [NLT] and 'the promise I made with
    your ancestor Levi' [CEV].

QUESTION—How does this verse's structure relate to what precedes it?
    This verse's first two parts, describing the current priesthood (But-you
    have-turned from-the-path, you-have-caused-to-stumble many by-the-
    (your)-instruction/in-the-law) are in antithesis to the last two parts of Mal.
    2:6, in which the early priests are described (In-peace and-in-uprightness
    he-walked with-me, and-many-ones he-turned from-sin). In addition, Mal.
    2:8c (you-have-violated (the)-covenant-of the-Levi) is the antithesis of Mal.
    2:4 (I-sent to-you this commandment to-be my-covenant with Levi)
    [NICOT]. Similarly, Clen sees all of this verse as antithetical to Mal. 2:5–
    7, which is an embedded paragraph describing the praiseworthy conduct of
    the early priests.

QUESTION—In what way should one understand the proclitic -בְ bə- in
בַּתּוֹרָה battôrâ in-the-law?

1. Tôrâ signifies here the law of God, which cannot be the means of
    stumbling; bə- therefore cannot express instrument. Also, battôrâ is
    analogous to the noun מִכְשׁוֹל mikšôl (derived from the verb כָּשַׁל kšl 'to
    stumble') 'something stumbled over, offense, obstacle' [Hol p. 195], and
    thus signifies that the law of God is made into an obstacle over which
    one stumbles and falls [Keil, Mer, TOTC]. The definite article 'in-the-

law' suggests that God's Law is meant here [Mer]. The priests are charged with having kept the people from understanding the Law correctly [Mer]. This interpretation is followed also by the Peshitta [WBC].

2. The vast majority of translations take the proclitic -בְּ *bǝ-* to indicate instrument, but only Gla attempts to justify the translation 'instruction', noting that *tôrâ*'s root meaning is instruction given to worshippers and followers of YHWH. Originally concerned, both in Leviticus and in several of the literary prophets, with distinguishing the sacred from the profane, what was acceptable to God from what was not, *tôrâ* in Malachi is generalized to include instruction on life-styles acceptable to God. Thus *tôrâ* might be seen as parallel to דַּעַת *daʿat* 'knowledge', i.e., moral knowledge [Gla] of Mal. 2:7.

QUESTION—How is the construct relationship between בְּרִית *bǝrît* 'covenant' and הַלֵּוִי *hallēwî* 'the Levi' expressed?

1. It is translated using 'with'—('with Levi' [Mer, NICOT; NIV—this is also the intent of Keil], 'with you' [TEV], 'with your ancestor Levi' [CEV], also NLT, REB).
2. It is translated 'of'—('of the Levites' [JPS], also KJV, NJB, NRSV).
3. Although NICOT translates 'with', he views the construct relationship as expressing an objective genitive: the covenant is one which *concerns* Levi, as in Mal. 2:4–5.

QUESTION—What is the sense of הַלֵּוִי *hallēwî* 'the Levi'?

'The-Levi' here stands for Levi's priestly descendants, the entire priestly institution, the definite article indicating something other than a mere person [Keil, NICOT, WBC; NIV].

2:9

And[a]-so[b] I,[c] I-made[d] you(pl) despised[e] and[f]-abased[g] before[h]-all-(of)[i] the-people[j] inasmuch-as[k] you(pl)-(are)-*not[l] keeping[m] my-ways[n] and[o]-(*are/are-not-)lifting[p] faces[q] in/with-regard-to[r]-the-instruction.[s]

*SYNTAX—the negation אֵינְכֶם *ʾênǝkem* 'you are not' (see (l) below) is viewed by most commentators and versions as applying only to 'keeping my-ways' [Coh, Keil, Mer, NICOT, WBC; CEV, JPS, KJV, NASB, NIV, NJB, NLT, NRSV, REB, TEV], while it is viewed by Gla as applying also to 'lifting faces in-the-instruction', making this latter phrase into a negative construction as well [Gla]. Because of the demands of the context, the sense of the idiom 'lifting faces in-the-instruction' depends upon whether its syntax is positive or negative (see below).

LEXICON—a. -וְ *wǝ-* *waw* connective (BDB p. 251), (Hol p. 84), (TWOT 519): 'and' [Gla; JPS, NRSV]. Most translations treat וְגַם *wǝgam* as one functional particle (see below), which is used, like *gam*, to add elements or to emphasize them [Hol p. 62] (see below).

b. גַם *gam* (BDB p. 168), (Hol p. 61), (TWOT 361a): 'therefore' [Coh, Mer; KJV], 'thus' [Keil], 'so' [NICOT, WBC; CEV, NASB, NIV, NJB, NLT, REB, TEV], 'and so' [NRSV], 'and' [JPS]. Unlike the

MALACHI 2:9 87

translations above, most of which indicate consequence of some sort,
Gla translates 'indeed'. *Gam* is employed to emphasize or to associate
elements together [BDB, Hol]. *Gam* can mark the peak of an expository
discourse [B.K. Waltke and M. O'Conner, *An Introduction to Biblical
Hebrew Syntax*. Winona Lake, IN: Eisenbrauns, 1990; cited in Clen].

c. אֲנִי *ʾănî* 1st sg. prn.. Most translations render the first person here with
some emphasis: 'I also' [Coh, Keil; KJV, NASB], 'I in (my) turn' [JPS,
NJB, REB, TEV]. Some, however, add no emphasis, translating simply
'I' [Mer, Gla, NICOT; CEV, NIV, NLT, NRSV]. *ʾănî* is the 1st sg.
pronoun, used especially for emphasis [BDB, Hol].

d. 1st sg. Qal perf. of נתן *ntn* (BDB p. 678), (Hol p. 249), (TWOT 1443):
'to make' [BDB, Hol; Coh, Keil, Mer, Gla, WBC; JPS, KJV, NASB,
NJB, NLT, NRSV, REB, TEV], 'to cause' [NICOT; CEV, NIV]. The
verb's perfect tense denotes an action begun in the past, the effects of
which continue [NICOT]. Many translations employ the English present
perfect tense (e.g., 'I have made') [Coh, Mer, Gla, WBC; JPS, KJV,
NIV, NJB, NLT]. CEV employs the past tense: 'I caused'. Others
employ the English present tense (e.g., 'I make') [Keil; NRSV]. Still
others employ the future tense (e.g., 'I will cause') [NICOT; REB,
TEV]. Although *ntn*'s primary sense is 'to give', it is often found with a
derived sense of 'to transform, make into something else'.

e. mas. pl. Niphal part. of בזה *bzh* (BDB p. 102), (Hol p. 36), (TWOT
224): 'despised' [Hol; Keil, Mer, Gla, NICOT, WBC; NASB, NIV,
NLT], 'contemptible' [BDB, Hol; Coh; KJV, NJB], 'despicable' [BDB;
JPS, REB]. Some translations restructure the entire clause, making the
people of Israel the secondary agents and turning the passive participle
נבזים *nibzîm* 'ones-being-despised' and the adjective וּשְׁפָלִים *ûšᵉpālîm*
'and-abased' into active verbs: 'I caused everyone to hate and despise
you' [CEV]; TEV also conflates into one verb *nibzîm* and *ûšᵉpālîm*: 'I
will make the people of Israel despise you' [TEV].

f. -ו *wə-* *waw* connective (BDB p. 251), (Hol p. 84), (TWOT 519): 'and'
[all commentators and versions].

g. mas. pl. of שפל *šāpāl* (BDB p. 1050), (Hol p. 381), (TWOT 2445):
'abased' [Mer, Gla, WBC; NASB, NRSV], 'base' [Coh, Keil; KJV],
'humiliated' [NICOT; NIV, NLT], 'vile' [JPS, NJB], 'degraded' [REB],
'humble' [Hol], 'lowly' [BDB]. CEV translates this adjective as a verb,
with the people of Israel as the agents: 'I caused everyone to despise
you'.

h. -ל *lə-* (BDB p. 510), (Hol p. 167), (TWOT 1063): 'before' [Coh, Mer,
Gla, WBC; KJV, NASB, NIV, NRSV], 'with' [Keil], 'by' [NICOT],
'to']NJB], 'in the eyes of' [JPS, NLT, REB]. CEV and TEV
restructure the clause so as to make the people of Israel the agents. The
proclitic *lə-* here introduces a dative of advantage or disadvantage.

i. constr. of כל *kōl* (BDB p. 481), (Hol p. 156), (TWOT 985a): 'all'
[BDB; all commentators and versions except the following], 'whole'

(modifying 'people') [NJB]. CEV translates 'everyone', and TEV translates 'the people of Israel'. Properly a noun, *kōl* denotes 'entirety' [Hol].

j. עַם *ʿam* (BDB p. 766), (Hol p. 275), (TWOT 1640a): 'people' [BDB, Hol; Coh, Keil, Mer, Gla, NICOT, WBC; JPS, KJV, NASB, NIV, NJB, NLT, NRSV, REB], 'everyone' [CEV]. TEV translates 'the people of Israel', making explicit which people are meant. *ʿam* denotes 'a whole people (emphasis on internal ethnic solidarity)' [Hol].

k. כְּפִי אֲשֶׁר *kəpî ʾăšer* (BDB p. 805), (Hol p. 289): 'inasmuch as' [Keil, WBC; NRSV, REB], 'to the degree that' [Mer], 'according as' [BDB; Coh; KJV], 'inasmuch as' [Hol], 'because' [Gla, NICOT; CEV, JPS, NIV, TEV], 'for' [NJB, NLT], 'just as' [NASB]. *Kəpî ʾăšer* is a compound conjunction.

l. constr. of אַיִן *ʾayin* (BDB p. 34), (Hol p. 13), (TWOT 81). *ʾayin* is properly a noun signifying 'absence', but it functions here in its construct state to negate the following participle.

m. mas. pl. Qal part. of שָׁמַר *šmr* (BDB p. 1036), (Hol p. 377), (TWOT 2414): 'to keep' [BDB, Hol; Coh, Keil, Mer, WBC; KJV, NASB, NJB, NRSV], 'to follow' [NICOT; NIV], 'to obey' [NLT, TEV], 'to keep and do' [BDB], 'to guard' [Gla], 'to observe' [Hol]. The following render the sense of the negation in one word: 'to disregard' [JPS, REB], 'to disobey' [CEV]. The English present perfect tense is used (e.g., 'you have not kept') [Coh, NICOT, WBC; KJV, NIV, NJB, NLT, NRSV]; the past tense is used ('you disobeyed') [CEV]; the present (habitual) tense is used (e.g., 'you do not keep') [Keil, Gla; JPS, NLT, REB, TEV]; the present progressive tense is used ('you are not keeping') [Mer].

n. pl. constr. of דֶּרֶךְ *derek* (BDB p. 202), (Hol p. 74), (TWOT 453a): 'way' [BDB; all commentators and versions except the following], 'will' [TEV]. The phrase is also restructured using the renderings 'you disobeyed me' [CEV] and 'you have not obeyed me' [NLT]. *Derek* denotes in its primary sense 'way, path'; a secondary sense denotes conduct or habitual pattern of living [Hol].

o. -וְ *wə-* *waw* connective (BDB p. 251), (Hol p. 84), (TWOT 519). Most commentators and versions appear to treat this connective as indicating amplification of the preceding phrase 'you(pl)-(are)-not keeping my-ways', i.e., the addressees are charged with unacceptable behavior in that they are showing partiality to others: 'and' [Keil, Mer; CEV, JPS, REB], 'but' [Coh; KJV, NASB, NIV, NLT, NRSV]. Others consider the *waw* connective to indicate an additive relation, i.e., to introduce a second charge against the addressees: 'nor' [Gla], 'and' [WBC; NJB, TEV].

p. mas. pl. Qal part. of נָשָׂא *nśʾ* (BDB p. 669), (Hol p. 246), (TWOT 1421). *Nśʾ* in its primary sense denotes 'to lift, to carry, to take'; here, however, it forms with פָּנִים *pānîm* 'faces' an idiom (see below).

q. pl. of פָּנִים *pānîm* (BDB p. 815), (Hol p. 293), (TWOT 1782a). The primary sense of *pānîm* is 'face'. *Pānîm* here, however, functions with נָשָׂא *nś*' (see above) as an idiom [Hol p. 246], [BDB p. 670]. If the syntax of the idiom is construed as positive (see SYNTAX above), then the idiom signifies 'to show partiality' [Hol; Mer, NICOT, WBC; JPS, NASB, NIV, NLT, NRSV, REB], 'to be partial' [KJV, NJB], 'to respect person' [Keil], 'to have respect of persons' [Coh], 'to fail to treat all people alike' [CEV], 'to not treat everyone alike' [TEV]. Some translations employ the English present perfect tense (e.g., 'but have shown partiality') [Coh, NICOT, WBC; KJV, NIV, NLT, NRSV]; CEV employs the past tense ('failed to treat'); Mer and NASB employ the present progressive ('are showing partiality'); some employ the present (habitual) tense (e.g., 'but show partiality') [Keil; JPS, REB, TEV]. If, on the other hand, the syntax of the idiom is construed as negative (see SYNTAX above), then the idiom signifies 'not to have consideration', and the complete thought is 'you do not have consideration with regard to the law' (similar to Prov. 6:35, where one takes no consideration of a bribe) [Gla].

r. -בְּ *bə-* (BDB p. 88), (Hol p. 32), (TWOT 193): 'in' [all commentators and versions except the following], 'with regard to' [Gla]. The proclitic is translated circumstantially 'when' [TEV]; not explicit [CEV]. The proclitic *bə-* denotes here abstract locality, e.g., 'in' [BDB, Hol].

s. תּוֹרָה *tôrâ* (BDB p. 435), (Hol p. 388), (TWOT 910d): 'instruction' [BDB, Hol; Mer, Gla; NASB, NRSV], 'law' [BDB, Hol; Coh, Keil; KJV], 'teaching' [WBC], 'rulings' [JPS], 'direction' [BDB]. Other translations employ a phrase or clause to specify the action which God finds unacceptable or the kind of instruction which is referred to: 'the instruction of the law' [NICOT], 'your interpretation of the law' [NLT, REB], 'applying the law' [NJB], 'matters of the law' [NIV], 'when you teach my people' [TEV]. The primary sense of *tôrâ* is 'instruction'; 'law' is a derived secondary sense [BDB, Hol].

QUESTION—What is to be the fate of the covenant which is under discussion? It will survive, according to Jer. 33:17–18 and ultimately according to Zech. 6:12–13 and Ps. 110, although the individual guilty priests will have to suffer the penalties threatened in the covenant and in this verse [Mer, NICOT].

QUESTION—To what refers the passage אֵינְכֶם...בַּתּוֹרָה *'ênəkem . . . battôrâ* 'you are not keeping my way, and you are showing partiality in the instruction/law'?

1. In this context it refers to showing partiality to some people over others, favoring them when applying the Law's requirements [most commentators], perhaps especially in the process of accepting or rejecting the suitability of sacrifices as they were brought to the Temple [Coh; JPS].

2. It refers to a failure on the priests' part to 'regard, consider' the *tôrâ* 'law' in their legal decisions. The priests are charged with judging cases

according to their own thinking and desires instead of according to precedence based upon the Law [Gla].

3. It denotes the activity of teaching the Law [Mer, NICOT]. The priests are charged with setting up obstacles, through their manner of teaching, to the people's proper understanding of God's requirements. This partiality in instruction was motivated by greed [NICOT].

DISCOURSE UNIT: 2:10–3:6 [Clen]. This is the "second movement." The topic is "Judah exhorted to faithfulness."

Comments on this discourse unit. This unit's surface structure and underlying notional structure are analyzed as follows (the change element, regarded as the naturally most prominent element of hortatory discourse, is noted within the movement's chiastic structure in bold type):

Surface Structure			Hortatory Notional Structure	Theme
1st constituent	A	2:10a–b	motivation	spiritual unity
2nd constituent	B	2:10c–15b	situation	faithlessness
3rd constituent	**C**	**2:15c–16**	**change**	**stop acting faithlessly**
4th constituent	B´	2:17	situation	complaints of YHWH's injustice
5th constituent	A´	3:1–6	motivation	coming messenger of judgment

DISCOURSE UNIT: 2:10–17 [CEV, NAB, NASB, NLT, NRSV]. The topic is "a broken agreement" [CEV], the "sins of the people" [NAB], "sin in the family" [NASB], "a call to faithfulness" [NLT], "the covenant profaned by Judah" [NRSV].

DISCOURSE UNIT: 2:10–16 [Clen (within the larger discourse unit of Mal. 2:10–3:6), Gla, Mer, NICOT, O'Brien, TOTC, WBC; NIV, NJB, TEV]. This paragraph realizes the second movement's semantic constituent A (the topic of which is "spiritual unity"), constituent B (the topic of which is "faithlessness") and constituent C (the topic of which is "stop acting faithlessly" [Clen]. The topic is "the rebellion of the people" [Mer], "God's concern with the marriage of his people" [NICOT], the second accusation [O'Brien], the importance of family life [TOTC], "a dispute about faithlessness" [WBC], Judah's unfaithfulness [NIV], "mixed marriage and divorce" [NJB], "the people's unfaithfulness to God" [TEV].

Comments on this discourse unit. As the previous unit (Mal. 1:6–2:9) treated the desecration of God's covenant with Levi (Mal. 2:8), so this unit addresses the community as a whole about violations to the covenant of the fathers [Gla; McKenzie] and to the covenant of marriage [Mckenzie].

As this discourse unit is considered by some to be the most exegetically difficult in Malachi [NICOT, WBC], it would be well to summarize here the exegetical positions on it. Scholars are divided between two great viewpoints on this passage: the literal and the figurative.*

1. The literal viewpoint: this view holds that the phrase בַּת־אֵל נֵכָר *baṯ ʾēl nēḵār* 'the daughter of a foreign god' (Mal. 2:11) means a foreign woman—one who worships a foreign god, and that אֵשֶׁת נְעוּרֶיךָ *ʾēšet naʿûrêḵā* 'the wife of your youth' (Mal. 2:14) and אֵשֶׁת בְּרִיתֶךָ *ʾēšet bǝrîteḵā* 'wife of your covenant' (i.e., marriage covenant) (Mal. 2:14) should be interpreted literally. Jews were breaking stipulations of the Sinaitic covenant by marrying foreign, pagan women [Coh, Mer, NICOT, TOTC, WBC; NIV]. The books of Ezra and Nehemiah chronicle the fact that many Jews of the early restoration had married foreign women [Mer, NICOT]. This led to bad social consequences: since Jewish society was mostly monogamous—and especially so among the less wealthy classes, which comprised most of the Jews who had returned from exile, the first (i.e., Jewish) wives were divorced in order to make room for the second, foreign wives [Gla]. This broke the marriage bond and brought about much suffering on the part of the first wives [Glazier-McDonald 1].

2. The figurative viewpoint: this view holds that the phrase 'the daughter of a foreign god' (Mal. 2:11) signifies the worship of a foreign, pagan god, and that the phrases 'the wife of your youth' (Mal. 2:14), and 'the wife of your covenant' (Mal. 2:14) should be interpreted as the Yahwistic religion of the nation Israel's 'youth', i.e., of the nation's earliest period.

3. The combined literal/figurative viewpoint: this view, proposed by Beth Glazier-McDonald, considers that Malachi in this discourse unit is attacking *both* intermarriage with concomitant divorce of Jewish wives *and* the resulting religious syncretism, which was wooing Israel away from YHWH, and that Malachi was thus attacking both social and religious ills of the covenant community. Thus, each viewpoint outlined above is incomplete without the other [Glazier-McDonald 1].

Arguments for the literal view include the following: (a) the problem of intermarriage between post-exilic Jews and foreign, pagan women certainly existed, as witness Nehemiah and Ezra; (b) Malachi argues in Mal. 2:15 that Jewish marriages were to produce godly offspring, and that this was thwarted by intermarriage; (c) the weeping upon YHWH's altar (Mal. 2:13) is that of the divorced Jewish women [Coh, Keil, and some traditional Jewish interpreters]; (d) divorce and intermarriage were related problems (see above in (1)) [Glazier-McDonald 1].

Arguments for the figurative view include the following: (a) had Malachi wished to literally refer to foreign women in 2:11, he would have used a more

---

* LXX treats וּבָעַל בַּת־אֵל נֵכָר *ûḇāʿal baṯ ʾēl nēḵār* 'and married the daughter of a foreign god' (Mal. 2:11) as a figure of speech and then translates it concretely, saying that Judah *has gone after other gods*, thus avoiding reference to mixed marriages, which were very common among the Hellenistic Jews [NICOT].

normal phrase, such as נשים נכריות *nāšîm nāḵəriyyôt* 'foreign women' as in 1
Kings 11:1, and that 'the daughter of a foreign god' must therefore signify a
goddess; (b) the word תועבה *tôʿēḇâ* 'abomination' is found most frequently in
Deuteronomy in the context of idolatry, and Malachi wishes to evoke this same
practice in Mal. 2:11 [WBC]; (c) the weeping on YHWH's altar (Mal. 2:13),
in the context of idolatry, suggests pagan weeping for the mythic death of a
foreign god (cf. Ezekiel 8:14) (proposed by F.F. Hvidberg, *Weeping and
Laughter in the Old Testament*, Leiden: Brill, 1962) [WBC; Glazier-McDonald
1]; (d) the institution of marriage in Malachi's time was not seen to embrace a
covenant [Abel Isaaksson, cited in WBC]; (e) an interpretation of this
discourse unit as a prophecy against syncretism and outright idolatry would
agree with the tenor of the rest of the book [Abel Isaaksson, cited in WBC].

Arguments against the literal view: (a) the weeping at YHWH's altar (Mal.
2:13) cannot be that of the divorced Jewish women, for women were never
allowed to approach the altar (Ahlström, *Joel and the Temple Cult of
Jerusalem* (VTSup21; Leiden: Brill, 1971) [quoted in Glazier-McDonald 1];
(b) Malachi does not show himself to be concerned primarily with marriage or
social reform, but rather with the purification of the worship of YHWH)
[Ahlström, *Joel . . .* , Abel Isaksson, *Marriage and Ministry in the New
Temple* (Lund: Gleerup, 1965 [quoted in Glazier-McDonald 1]; (c) early
interpretation did not consider that this discourse unit was against divorce—the
LXX and the Targum understood Mal. 2:16 as allowing divorce [WBC]; (d)
the meaning of the phrase שנא שלח *śānēʾ šallaḥ* 'he hates divorce" (?) (Mal.
2:16) is very unclear (Abel Isaksson, *Marriage . . .*) [quoted in WBC].

Arguments against the figurative view: (a) 'I hate divorce' is a legitimate
reading of *śānēʾ šallaḥ* (Mal. 2:16) [WBC]; (b) the figurative viewpoint would
cast YHWH as the *wife* of Israel—a comparison which one never finds in the
OT [WBC]; (c) the tears on YHWH's altar (Mal. 2:13) are of those whose
offerings have not been accepted by YHWH [WBC]; (d) the phrase 'children
of YHWH' is used to designate the Israelites, as in Deut. 14:1, and the
Moabites are referred to as sons and daughters of Chemosh (Num. 21:29), so
'daughter of a foreign god' by analogy could mean a pagan woman [Glazier-
McDonald 1].

A formal analysis of this discourse unit is:
(A) Ideal situation = unity: 'one God' + 'one Father"
General sin = 'infidelity' (10)
(B) Indictment/specific sin = intermarriage: 'daughter of a foreign god'
+ 'infidelity' (11)
(C) Verdict: exclusion, rejection of 'food offering' (12)
(C') Verdict: rejection of 'food offering' (13)
(B') Indictment/specific sin = divorce: 'wife of covenant' + 'infidelity'
(14)
(A') Ideal situation = unity: 'one . . . one"
General sin = 'infidelity' (15) [Wendland]

MALACHI 2:10

2:10

Is-there-not[a] one[b] father[c] for[d]-all(-of)[e]-us? Has-not[f] one God[g] created[h]-us?

LEXICON—a. הֲלוֹא *hălôʾ* (BDB p. 518), (Hol p. 170). This particle causes the question which it introduces to be taken as a rhetorical question, expecting an affirmative answer: 'is there not . . . ?' [WBC; NJB], 'have we not . . . ?' [Coh, Keil, Gla, NICOT; JPS, KJV, NIV, NRSV, REB], 'do we not/don't we . . . ? [Mer; NASB, TEV], 'don't you know that . . . ? [CEV], 'are we not all . . . ? [NLT]. *Hălôʾ* is a compound consisting of -הֲ *ha-* (an interrogative word) [BDB p. 209], [Hol p. 75], and לוֹא *lôʾ* (which expresses negation [BDB p. 518], [Hol p. 170],

b. אֶחָד *ʾeḥād* (BDB p. 25), (Hol p. 9), (TWOT 61): 'one' [BDB, Hol; Coh, Keil, Mer, Gla, NICOT, WBC; JPS, KJV, NASB, NIV, NJB, NRSV, REB], 'the same' [NLT, TEV]. CEV implies 'same' by translating 'our Father'. *ʾeḥād* is 'the number one', and also functions as an indefinite article [Hol].

c. אָב *ʾāb* (BDB p. 3), (Hol p. 1), (TWOT 4a): 'father' [all lexica, commentators, and versions]. In most translation, the identity of 'father' is left ambiguous; some translations, however, clearly identify 'father' with God [CEV, JPS, NJB, NLT]. The primary sense of *ʾāb* is 'father'; *ʾāb* has secondary senses of 'ancestor' and 'founder or originator of an ethnic group, etc.' [BDB, Hol]. *ʾāb* can also refer to YHWH as the founder of the nation of Israel [Hol].

d. -לְ *la-* (BDB p. 510), (Hol p. 167), (TWOT 1063): 'for' [WBC], 'of' [NJB]. NLT expresses this relationship by translating 'children of the same Father'. The other commentators and versions also express a kind of possessive relationship using the verb 'to have', e.g., 'we all have. . . .' The proclitic *la-* here expresses possession [BDB, Hol].

e. constr. of כֹּל *kōl* (BDB p. 481), (Hol p. 156), (TWOT 985a): 'all' [all lexica, commentators, and versions]. Properly a noun, *kōl* denotes 'entirety' [Hol].

f. הֲלוֹא *hălôʾ* (see above). All commentators and versions translate this new question as a second rhetorical question, expecting an affirmative answer, e.g., 'Did not one God create us?' [REB].

g. אֵל *ʾēl* (BDB p. 42), (Hol p. 15), (TWOT 93a): 'God' [all lexica, commentators, and versions].

h. 3rd pl. Qal perf. of בָּרָא *brʾ* (BDB p. 135), (Hol p. 47), (TWOT 278): 'to create' [all lexica, commentators, and versions], 'to fashion, shape' [BDB]. The use of *brʾ* here emphasizes the special origin of the people of Israel and their special relationship to God [NICOT; NIV], for *brʾ* 'to create' is used in the OT only of divine activity [Gla].

QUESTION—To whom does אָב אֶחָד *ʾāb ʾeḥād* 'one father, the same father' refer?

1. It refers to Abraham [Mckenzie].
2. It refers to the patriarch Jacob [Coh], or, if not Jacob, probably to Abraham [TOTC].

3. It refers to YHWH [Clen, Keil, Mer, Gla, NICOT, WBC; NIV]. This harks back to Mal. 1:6: Israel is one nation as distinct from all the heathen nations [Keil, Gla]. God alone is the Father of Israel in the sense of 'Creator,' (c.f. the following clause) [Gla, NICOT, WBC]. To consider Abraham to be the referent here would be to ignore the facts that the Ishmaelites and the Edomites were also descended from him [Keil]. This reference to YHWH as Israel's 'father' stands in antithesis to 'daughter of a foreign god' (Mal. 2:11) [NICOT].

QUESTION—Who is meant by 'us' in לכלנו ləkullānû 'to all of us' and elsewhere in this passage?

Malachi means himself and his fellow Jews. Other OT passages reflect the ideas of God's fatherhood of the nation of Israel (Exod. 4:22,23; Deut. 32:6 and Isa. 63:16; 64:68); these are applied in all cases exclusively to the nation Israel [Clen, Mer, NICOT, TOTC].

Why[a] are-we-faithless[b] (every-)man[c] to[d]-his-brother,[e] thus[f]-profaning[g] (the)-covenant(-of)[h] our-ancestors[i]?

LEXICON—a. מדוע maddûaᶜ (BDB p. 396), (Hol p. 183), (TWOT 848h): 'why' [Hol; Coh, Mer, WBC; JPS, KJV, NASB, NIV], 'wherefore' [BDB; Keil]. Many translations add 'then': 'why then' [Gla, NICOT; NJB, NRSV, REB], 'then why' [CEV, NLT, TEV], in order to highlight the antithetical relationship, one featuring contra-expectation, between the passage introduced by this question and the preceding questions [Clen].

b. 1st pl. Qal imperf. of בגד bḡd (BDB p. 93), (Hol p. 33), (TWOT 198): 'to be faithless' [NICOT, WBC, NLT, NRSV, REB], 'to act faithlessly' [BDB; Gla], 'to deal faithlessly' [Hol], 'to be treacherous' [Keil], 'to act treacherously' [BDB; Mer], 'to deal treacherously' [BDB; Coh; KJV, NASB], 'to cheat' [CEV], 'to break one's promises' [TEV], 'to break faith' [JPS, NIV, NJB]. Bḡd denotes human instability in contrast to the stability of God's covenants, as well as treacherousness in the context of marriage [Gla].

c. איש ᵓîš (BDB p. 35), (Hol p. 13), (TWOT 83a): 'every man' [Coh, Gla; KJV], 'each' [WBC; NASB], 'one' [Keil]. Most translations incorporate this word's idea in a prepositional phrase expressing distribution and reciprocity, e.g., 'with each other' [NLT]. The primary sense of ᵓîš is 'person, man as a human being' [BDB, Hol].

d. -ב bə- (BDB p. 88), (Hol p. 32), (TWOT 193): 'to' [[Mer, NICOT, WBC; NLT, NRSV, REB, TEV], 'toward' [Keil], 'against' [Coh, Gla; KJV, NASB], 'with' [CEV, JPS, NIV, NJB]. The proclitic bə- denotes here hostility [BDB, Hol].

e. constr. of אח ᵓāh (BDB p. 26), (Hol p. 8), (TWOT 62a): 'brother' [BDB, Hol; Coh, Gla, WBC; KJV, NASB], 'another' [BDB; Keil], 'one another' [Mer, NICOT; JPS, NIV, NJB, NRSV, REB, TEV], 'each other' [CEV, NLT], 'fellow' (in the sense of 'peer') [Hol]. The entire expression אִישׁ אֶת בְּאָחִיו *ʾîš bəʾāḥîw* denotes a reciprocal idea, e.g., 'each other' [Hol p. 14].

f. -לְ *lə-* (BDB p. 510), (Hol p. 167), (TWOT 1063). Mer regards *lə-* as introducing the result of the unfaithful state: 'thus profaning the covenant of our fathers'; NASB probably also expresses result: 'so as to profane'. Some translations express accompanying circumstance, employing an English participle to denote the specifics of the unfaithfulness, e.g., 'profaning the covenant of our fathers' [Coh; also Gla, NICOT, WBC; JPS, NJB, NLT, NRSV]. NIV also regards *lə-* as indicating result, but lends emphasis to the result by inverting the order of the clauses: 'why do we profane the covenant of our fathers by breaking faith with one another?' TEV regards *lə-* as indicating a coordinate relationship with the preceding thought: '. . . why do we break our promises . . . , and why do we despise the covenan . . . ?' The proclitic *lə-* here perhaps denotes accompanying circumstance, specifying in what way the people have been unfaithful.

g. Piel inf. of חלל *ḥll* (BDB p. 320), (Hol p. 105), (TWOT 661): 'to profane' [BDB, Hol; Coh, Mer, NICOT, WBC; JPS, KJV, NASB, NIV, NJB, NRSV], 'to desecrate' [Keil], 'to break' [CEV], 'to despise' [TEV], 'to violate' [Gla; NLT, REB], 'to defile' [BDB].

h. constr. of בְּרִית *bərît* (BDB p. 136), (Hol p. 48), (TWOT 282a): 'covenant' [BDB, Hol; Coh, Keil, Mer, Gla, NICOT, WBC; JPS, KJV, NASB, NIV, NJB, NLT, NRSV, REB, TEV], 'agreement' [Hol; CEV]. The construct state of *bərît* 'covenant' with אֲבֹתֵינוּ *ʾăḇōṯênû* 'our fathers' is translated as 'of' [all commentators and versions except the following]; it is also translated by a subordinate clause: 'the agreement/ covenant God made with . . . ancestors' [CEV, TEV].

i. constr. pl. of אָב *ʾāḇ* (see above): 'ancestor' [CEV, JPS, NJB, NLT, NRSV, TEV], 'forefather' [REB], 'father' [BDB, Hol; Coh, Gla, Keil, Mer, NICOT, WBC; KJV, NASB, NIV].

QUESTION—In the phrase נִבְגַּד אִישׁ בְּאָחִיו *niḇgad ʾîš bəʾāḥîw* 'we are faithless every man to his brother', to what does the faithlessness refer?

1. It refers to a lack of the covenant loyalty among the Jews which God required of them [NICOT]. As this discourse unit shows, the verb here indicates unfaithfulness to one's duties in the covenant, unfaithfulness to one's wife, and unfaithfulness to the worship of God, preferring the cult of idols [Gla]. Keil sees the verb as indicating here unfaithfulness to one's fellow Jewish brothers in divorcing his Jewish wife and in marrying a pagan wife.

2. It refers to general unreliability in all kinds of business and social agreements, reflecting general untruthfulness [TOTC].

QUESTION—What is meant by לְחַלֵּל בְּרִית אֲבֹתֵינוּ *ləhallēl bərît ʾăḇōṯēnû* 'to profane the covenant of our fathers'?

1. This is basically a cultic kind of expression, having to do with perverting the use of the sanctuary of YHWH (Mal. 2:11) [NICOT].

2. This refers to intermarriage of Jewish men with pagan women. The covenant which God made with the forefathers required that the community of Israel be kept pure from idolatrous influences. In intermarrying with pagan women, the Jewish men of the restoration were not only effecting the introduction of other gods into the covenant community, but were also themselves embracing these other gods [Gla].

QUESTION—What is meant by ברית אבתינו bərît ʾăbōtēnû 'the covenant of our fathers'?

1. It probably refers to the covenant which God concluded with the patriarchs, and perhaps especially with Jacob and Levi, since these two were mentioned in Mal.1:2-5 and Mal. 2:1-9 [Mckenzie]. Some scholars, like John Van Seters (*Abraham in History and Tradition*; New Haven: Yale University, 1975—cited in Gla) contend that by the time of the exile, the Jewish community focused more on the patriarchal covenant with its unconditional promise of the land and of many descendants, and less on the Sinaitic covenant, which stressed that these things could all be forfeited through disobedience to God [Gla].

2. It refers to the Sinaitic covenant [Mer, Gla, NICOT]. In focus here is the imperative, present in Exod. 34 and Deut. 7, not to marry pagan, foreign women [Mer, Gla], which Malachi must have been aware of [Gla].

2:11

Judah[a] has-been-faithless,[b] and[c]-(an-)abomination[d] has-been-committed[e] in[f]-Israel[g] and[h]-in-Jerusalem,[i] for[j] Judah[k] has-profaned[l] (the-)sanctuary (-of)[m] YWHW which[n] he-loves[o] and[p]-has-married[q] (the)-daughter(-of)[r] (a-)foreign[s] god.[t]

LEXICON—a. יהודה yəhûdâ (BDB p. 397), (Hol p. 130), (TWOT 850c): 'Judah' [all lexica, commentators, and versions except the following], 'people in Judah' [CEV], 'the people of Judah' [TEV]. The feminine noun yəhûdâ governs the feminine form of the associated verb בגדה bāḡədâ 'has been unfaithful', indicating that the nation's name is in focus [Gla]), but, later in the verse, yəhûdâ governs הלל hillēl 'has profaned' (a masculine verb form), thus indicating that the referent is the country, or the population, of Judah as a whole [Keil, NICOT], and connoting that evil in question is indeed everywhere [Gla].

b. 3rd fem. sg. Qal perf. of בגד bḡd (BDB p. 93), (Hol p. 33), (TWOT 198): 'to be faithless' [WBC; NRSV, REB], 'to act faithlessly' [BDB; Gla], 'to break faith' [NICOT; JPS, NIV, NJB], 'to be unfaithful' [CEV], 'to act treacherously' [BDB; Keil, Mer], 'to deal treacherously' [Coh; KJV, NASB], 'to deal faithlessly' [Hol], 'to break one's promise' [TEV]. This verb is also translated as a noun: 'treachery' [NLT]. CEV and TEV specify that the faithlessness has been directed to God. Some translations use the English present perfect tense [Coh, Mer, Gla,

NICOT, WBC; CEV, JPS, KJV, NIV, NJB, NRSV]. Some use the present tense [Keil; NLT].

c. -וְ *wə- waw* connective (BDB p. 251), (Hol p. 84), (TWOT 519): 'and' [Coh, Keil, Gla, WBC; KJV, NASB, NRSV, REB]. This conjunction is also translated as introducing amplification of the preceding sentence: by a colon [JPS], by a semi-colon [NICOT], by 'and' [TEV], by a new sentence or clause [CEV, NIV, NJB]; translation not explicit [NLT].

d. תוֹעֵבָה *tôʿēḇâ* (BDB p. 1072), (Hol p. 388), (TWOT 2530a): 'abomination' [BDB; Coh, Keil, Mer, Gla; KJV, NASB, NRSV], 'something detestable' [Hol]. Many translations render this noun as adjective + noun: 'abominable thing' [WBC; REB], 'detestable thing' [NICOT; NIV, NJB], 'disgusting sin' [CEV], 'horrible thing' [TEV], 'abhorrent thing' [JPS], not explicit [NLT]. The primary sense of *tôʿēḇâ* is 'something detestable in the cultic realm', i.e., in respect to what is related to Israel's worship of YHWH; secondary senses carry the idea of detestation into moral and then general senses [Hol].

e. 3rd fem. Niphal perf. of עשׂה *ʿśh* (BDB p. 793), (Hol p. 284), (TWOT 1708): 'to be committed' [Coh, Mer, Gla, NICOT; KJV, NASB, NIV, NRSV], 'to be done' [BDB, Hol; WBC; JPS, NJB, REB], 'to take place' [Keil]. Some translations employ the active voice, with the people as the subject: 'to commit' [CEV], 'to do' [TEV], not explicit [NLT].

f. -בְּ *bə-* (BDB p. 88), (Hol p. 32), (TWOT 193): 'in' [all commentators and versions except the following]. TEV renders 'in Israel and Jerusalem as 'all over the country'. The proclitic *bə-* denotes here locality [BDB, Hol].

g. יִשְׂרָאֵל *yiśrāʾēl* (BDB p. 975), (Hol p. 145), (TWOT 2287a): 'Israel' [all lexica, commentators, and versions except the following], not explicit [CEV].

h. -וְ *wə- waw* connective (BDB p. 251), (Hol p. 84), (TWOT 519): 'and' [all commentators and versions].

i. יְרוּשָׁלִַם *yərûšālāim* 'Jerusalem' (BDB p. 436), (Hol p. 144), (TWOT 912): 'Jerusalem' [all commentators and versions except the following], 'people in Jerusalem' [CEV]. Malachi creates an overwhelming indictment of all the Jews: having previously indicated that all the nation is guilty before God, he now adds for even more effect "in Israel and Jerusalem" [Gla].

j. כִּי *kî* connective (BDB p. 471), (Hol p. 155), (TWOT 976). The translations all seem to take this conjunction as expressing a generic-specific relationship: 'for' [Coh, Keil, Gla; JPS, KJV, NASB, NJB, NLT, NRSV], 'because' [WBC]. The same relationship is expressed by means of a colon (:) [NICOT; NIV]; also by means of a new sentence or clause [CEV, REB, TEV].

k. יְהוּדָה *yəhûḏâ* (see above): 'Judah' [all commentators and versions except the following]. Some specify inhabitants or perhaps the males of Judah: 'the men of Judah' [NLT], 'men' [TEV].

l. 3rd mas. sg. Piel perf. of הלל *ḥll* (BDB p. 320), (Hol p. 105), (TWOT 661): 'to profane' [BDB, Hol; Coh, Mer, Gla, WBC; JPS, KJV, NASB, NJB, NRSV], 'to desecrate' [Keil, NICOT, NIV], 'to defile' [BDB], 'to disgrace' [CEV], 'to defile' [NLT, TEV], 'to violate' [REB].

m. constr. of קֹדֶשׁ *qōḏeš* (BDB p. 871), (Hol p. 314), (TWOT 1990a). Many translations interpret *qōḏeš* as God's sanctuary, i.e., the Temple: 'sanctuary' [Keil, Gla, NICOT; NASB, NIV, NJB, NLT, NRSV], 'holy place' [WBC], 'sacred place' [REB], 'temple' [CEV, TEV]. *Qōḏeš* is taken by others to mean God's holy quality: 'holiness' [Coh; KJV]. Some translations are ambiguous: 'holy thing' [Mer], 'what is holy' [JPS]. The primary sense of *qōḏeš* is something to which the divine quality adheres and thus must be treated carefully [Hol]. A secondary sense is the quality of 'otherness' of God—that which sets him apart from anyone else [BDB, Hol]. Yet another sense is places, such as sanctuaries, which are dedicated to God and thus bear in some sense his divine quality [BDB, Hol].

n. אֲשֶׁר *ʾăšer* (BDB p. 81), (Hol p. 30), (TWOT 184): 'which' [Coh, Keil, Gla, NICOT, WBC; KJV, NASB, NRSV, TEV], 'that' [Mer; CEV], not explicit [REB]. *ʾăšer* is a relative particle.

o. 3rd mas. sg. Qal perf. of אָהֵב *ʾhḇ* (BDB p. 12), (Hol p. 5), (TWOT 29a): 'to love' [all lexica, commentators, and versions except the following], 'beloved' [NJB, NLT], 'to desire' [JPS]. Most translations employ the English present tense; KJV employs the past.

p. -ו *wə*- *waw* connective (BDB p. 251), (Hol p. 84), (TWOT 519): 'and' [all commentators and versions except the following], 'by' [NICOT; NIV, NLT]. TEV employs a new sentence with no conjunction. Some translations and commentaries clearly regard this connective as specifying a generic-specific relationship—that the profanation (חלל *hillēl* 'has profaned') referred to above is explicated further in the verse: וּבָעַל בַּת־אֵל נֵכָר *ûḇāʿal baṯ ʾēl nēḵār* 'and married the daughter of a foreign god' [Coh, Gla, NICOT; NIV, NJB, NLT, REB, TEV]. CEV appears to regard the *waw* connective as introducing a coordinate relationship: 'you have disgraced the temple . . . and you have [worshipped] other gods'. Still other translations and commentaries are ambiguous [WBC; JPS, KJV, NRSV].

q. 3rd mas. sg. Qal perf. of בָּעַל *bʿl* (BDB p. 127), (Hol p. 43), (TWOT 262): 'to marry' [all lexica, commentators, and versions except the following], 'to espouse' [JPS]. CEV specifies its understanding that *bʿl* here refers figuratively to the worship of idols: 'worshipping other gods'. All translations employ, at least by implication, the English present perfect tense, except Keil, which employs the present. The root meaning of *bʿl* is 'to become master'—used of a man when taking a wife; but the verb here may implicitly direct attention to the service of idols [Gla].

r. constr. of בַּת *baṯ* (BDB p. 123), (Hol p. 51), (TWOT 254b): 'daughter'
[all lexica, commentators, and versions except the following]. Some
translations specify their understanding that *baṯ ʾēl nēḵār* refers to
foreign women who worship pagan gods: 'women who worship' [NLT,
TEV]. CEV specifies its understanding that the text here refers to idol
worship on the part of the Jewish men: the phrase *baṯ ʾēl nēḵār* is
translated 'other gods'.

s. נֵכָר *nēḵār* (BDB p. 648), (Hol p. 238), (TWOT 1368b). This noun is
generally translated as an adjective: 'foreign' [Mer, NICOT, WBC;
NASB, NIV, NRSV, REB, TEV], 'strange' [Coh, Keil; KJV 'alien'
[JPS, NJB], not explicit [NLT]. The primary sense of *nēḵār* is 'a foreign
land' [Hol], or 'that which is foreign' [BDB].

t. constr. of אֵל *ʾēl* (BDB p. 42), (Hol p. 15), (TWOT 93a): 'god' [all
lexica, commentators, and versions except the following], 'idol' [NLT].

QUESTION—What is the force of תּוֹעֵבָה *tôʿēḇâ* in this passage?

1. This word, signifying deeds which are detestable from a religious point
of view, was employed in Deut. 18:9–13 to describe heinous practices of
the various pagan groups among whom Israel would find herself upon
entering into Canaan. Malachi's use of *tôʿēḇâ* here sends a signal that
Judah's misdeeds are bringing her into the same kind of idolatry
[NICOT].

2. This word simply denotes any rituals which do not belong to the worship
of YHWH [Gla].

QUESTION—To what does יִשְׂרָאֵל *yiśrāʾēl* 'Israel' refer?

1. 'Israel' here is synonymous with 'Judah' and refers to YHWH's covenant
people. There is no allusion here to the former northern kingdom
[NICOT, TOTC].

2. 'Israel' here refers, as it often does, to the totality of YHWH's worshippers in the Temple, i.e., the community of YHWH's covenant. Here
Malachi is saying that the people's idolatry has defiled the covenant-
stipulated and regulated worship of YHWH [Gla].

QUESTION—To what does יְרוּשָׁלַיִם *yərûšālāim* 'Jerusalem' refer?

It refers to the heart-center of God's covenant people, their religious
capital, the place of God's presence among his people [NICOT].

QUESTION—To what does קֹדֶשׁ *qōḏeš* refer?

1. It refers to the nation of Israel, which was formed by YWHW to be
cherished by himself, and which was therefore set apart for himself (cf.
Exod. 19:6; Jer. 2:3: Ezek. 9:2) [Coh, Keil, NICOT]. The Targum
translates: 'because the house of Judah desecrated themselves, who have
been sanctified by the Lord, and whom he loves' [NICOT].

2. It probably refers to the Temple [Gla, NICOT, TOTC, WBC]. By this
reference, Malachi appears to have been implying that the priests and
Levites were also engaged in the evil conduct he is describing [TOTC].
About one quarter of the 300+ references to *qōḏeš* in the OT refer to the
Temple sanctuary [Gla].

3. It refers to the covenant of YHWH with Israel, since keeping the covenant is the opposite of what the people have done in worshipping foreign gods [Mer].

QUESTION—To what does נכר בת־אל ובעל *ûḇāᶜal baṯ ᵓēl nēḵār* 'and married the daughter of a foreign god' refer?

See the discussion at the start of this discourse unit.

2:12

(a₁) May- YHWH -cut-off[a] the-man[c] who[d] does[e]-this,
*(b₁) (the-)one-awake[f-1]/calling[f-1] and[g]-(the-)one-answering,[h]

(a₂) May- YHWH -cut-off[a] to[i.e., from][b]-the-man[c] who[d] does[e]-this
*(b₂) (the-)witness[f-2] and[g]-(the-)one-answering[h]

(c) from[i]-the-tents(-of)[j] Jacob,[k]
(d) and/even-though[l]-bringing[m] (a-)gift[n] to[o]-YWHW(-of) hosts.

SYNTAX—The expression לאיש *lāᵓîš* nominally 'to the man' consists of the proclitic -ל *lə-*, the definite article -ה *ha-*, and איש *ᵓîš* 'person', where most versions and some commentators (Gla, NICOT, WBC) consider the proclitic to be introducing 'person' as a direct object of the verb כרת *krṯ* 'to cut off'. (See (a₁) above.)

Some, however, regard the proclitic *lə-* as introducing a dative of disadvantage, e.g., 'may the Lord cut off to the man (i.e., to the man's hurt) that doeth this hims that calleth and him that answereth out of the tents of Jacob' [Coh; also Keil, TOTC; NJB]. NIV admits this interpretation as an alternative. (See (a₂) above.)

NASB regards *lāᵓîš* as a focusing device: 'as for the man who does this. . . .' Unfortunately, the NASB translation of the rest of the verse is unintelligible: 'as for the man who does this, may the Lord cut off from the tents of Jacob everyone who awakes and answers. . . .'

*TEXT—Because of the difficulty of the phrase ער וענה *ᶜēr waᶜōneh*, translated above as '(the-)one-awake/calling and-(the-)one-answering', various proposed emendations of the Masoretic text have been followed by some versions:

1. עד וענה *ᶜēḏ waᶜōneh* (translated above as '(the-)one-witnessing and-(the-)one-answering') 'any to witness or answer' [NRSV], 'witness and advocate' [NJB]. These translations mean 'anyone who defends such evil-doing'.

2. שרש וענף *šereš waᶜānāp̄* 'root and branches', i.e., leaving nothing of the offender's family [Glazier-McDonald 2]. This is perhaps the approach taken by JPS 'may the Lord leave him who does this no descendants'.

3. REB follows the lead of an ancient Arabic version: 'nomad and settler' [cited in TOTC].

LEXICON—a. 3rd mas sg. Hiphil jussive—or 3rd mas. sg. Hiphil imperf.—of כרת *krṯ* (BDB p. 503), (Hol p. 165), (TWOT 1048): 'to cut off' [BDB; Coh, Keil, Mer, Gla, NICOT, WBC; KJV, NASB, NIV, NLT, NRSV], 'to remove' [TEV], 'to deprive' [NJB], 'to leave (no descendants)'

[JPS], 'to banish' [REB], 'to root out, eliminate' [Hol]. CEV employs a phrase: 'to no longer let one belong'. Most commentaries and versions express here the jussive, i.e., a wish, e.g., 'may the Lord remove' [TEV]; Keil and KJV express a simple future: 'will cut off'.

b. -לְ *lǝ-* (BDB p. 510), (Hol p. 167), (TWOT 1063): 'to' [Coh, Keil], 'from' [NASB]. This proclitic is also translated by virtue of the choice of verb: 'to deprive' (i.e., to cut off from) [NJB]. Those who adopt the first syntactic interpretation above regard this proclitic as introducing the direct object of the verb 'to cut off'. The proclitic *lǝ-* here either introduces a dative of disadvantage or functions as a particle introducing a direct object phrase [BDB, Hol].

c. אִישׁ *ʾîš* (BDB p. 35), (Hol p. 13), (TWOT 83a): 'man' [all lexica, commentators, and versions except the following]. Other versions employ a pronoun, e.g., 'those who did this' [TEV].

d. אֲשֶׁר *ʾăšer* (BDB p. 81), (Hol p. 30), (TWOT 184): 'who' [Gla, WBC; CEV, JPS, NASB, NIV, NLT, NRSV, REB, TEV], 'that' [Keil; KJV], 'anyone who' [Mer], no translation [NICOT]. *ʾăšer* is a relative particle.

e. 3rd mas. sg. Qal imperf. of עָשָׂה *ʿśh* (BDB p. 793), (Hol p. 284), (TWOT 1708): 'to do' [all lexica, commentators, and versions except the following]. 'Who does this' is also translated as 'who are guilty' [CEV] and as 'such an offender' [NJB]. This verb is translated employing the English present tense [most commentators and versions], the past tense [TEV], and the present perfect [NLT].

f-1. mas. sg. Qal part. of עוּר *ʿôr* (BDB p. 734), (Hol p. 268), (TWOT 1587): 'to be awake' [Hol; Mer, WBC], 'to awake' [NASB], 'waker' [BDB; Keil]—these translations picture the night-watchmen around the tents of Jacob [TOTC]; '(sexually) aroused one' [Gla]. Others believe the sense here to be 'to call' [Coh]; from this is derived the translation 'master' (in the sense of 'teacher'—the one who calls to the pupils) [KJV]. REB adopts the view that *ʿôr* here signifies 'to roam about' and that עָנָה *ʿnh* below signifies here 'to remain in one place'): 'nomad'.

As many contemporary authorities believe that the phrase *ʿēr wǝʿōneh*, whatever its literal meaning, signifies 'anyone at all', some versions translate the expression concretely: 'whoever he may be' [NICOT; NIV], 'every last man' [NLT]. Mer follows this interpretation also. CEV, and TEV do not explicity translate this phrase.

f-2. עֵד *ʿēd* (BDB p. 729), (Hol p. 265), (TWOT 1576b): 'witness' [BDB, Hol; NJB]. This noun is also translated as a verb: 'to witness' [NRSV].

g. -וְ *wǝ-* *waw* connective (BDB p. 251), (Hol p. 84), (TWOT 519): 'and' indicating an additive relationship [all commentators and versions except REB], 'or' [REB].

h. mas. sg. Qal part. of עָנָה *ʿnh* (BDB p. 772), (Hol p. 277), (TWOT 1650): 'to answer' [BDB, Hol; Coh, Keil, Mer, WBC; NASB, NRSV]. This verb is also translated as a noun: 'advocate' [NJB], 'scholar'

[KJV]. REB views ʿnh as here signifying 'to remain in one place: 'settler'.

i. מִן min (BDB p. 577), (Hol p. 200), (TWOT 1212): 'from' [BDB; Mer, Gla, NICOT, WBC; NASB, NIV, NLT, NRSV, REB, TEV], 'out of' [BDB, Hol; Coh, Keil; KJV]. Some express this idea by the choice of verb: 'to no longer let [the guilty] belong to . . .' [CEV], 'to leave no descendants dwelling in . . .' [JPS], 'to deprive . . . of witness and advocate in the tents of . . .' [NJB]. The preposition min expresses separation.

j. pl. constr. of אֹהֶל ʾōhel (BDB p. 13), (Hol p. 5), (TWOT 32a): 'tent' [all lexica, commentators, and versions except the following], 'tabernacle' [KJV], 'community' [TEV], 'people' [CEV], 'nation' [NLT], 'dwelling' [REB].

k. יַעֲקֹב yaʿăqōb (BDB p. 784), (Hol p. 138), (TWOT 1676f): 'Jacob' [all lexica, commentators, and versions except the following], 'Israel' [NLT, TEV]. 'The tents of Jacob' refers to the community of Israel (see Jer. 30:18) [NIV]. As such, CEV translates 'his (God's) people'.

l. -וְ wə- waw connective (BDB p. 251), (Hol p. 84), (TWOT 519). Some translations interpret this waw connective in an additive manner: 'and' [JPS (taking 'and' to introduce a second element of the description of the same person under discussion)], 'as well as' [Mer (taking the waw connective in the same way as above)], 'or' [NASB]; [Coh, WBC (ambiguous)], [Keil; KJV]. Other translations interpret the waw connective so as to introduce a concessive clause and take it to introduce a clause describing the same person: 'even though' [NICOT; NIV, REB], 'even if' [CEV], 'and yet' [NLT].

m. mas. sg. Hiphil part. of נָגַשׁ ngš (BDB p. 620), (Hol p. 227), (TWOT 1297): 'to bring' [BDB; NICOT; NIV, NLT, NRSV, REB], 'to offer' [Hol; Coh, Keil, WBC; KJV], 'to present' [Mer; JPS, NASB, NJB], 'to eagerly decide to offer' [CEV], 'to participate in' [TEV], 'to bring near' [Gla].

n. מִנְחָה minḥâ (BDB p. 585), (Hol p. 202), (TWOT 1214a): 'gift' [WBC; CEV], 'sacrifice' [Hol; Keil], 'offering' [BDB; Coh, Mer, Gla, NICOT; JPS, KJV, NASB, NIV, NJB, NLT, NRSV, REB, TEV].

o. -לְ lə- (BDB p. 510), (Hol p. 167), (TWOT 1063): 'to' [expressed implicitly or explicitly by all commentators and versions]. The proclitic lə- here introduces a dative of advantage [BDB, Hol].

QUESTION—To what does אָהֳלֵי יַעֲקֹב ʾohŏlê yaʿăqōb 'the tents of Jacob' refer?

It refers to the community of Israel; the expression looks back to the times of wandering in the wilderness, when first mention was made of the kind of punishment which figures in this verse [Mer]. "The tents of Jacob" might more precisely mean the community of YHWH's worshippers. Malachi charges Israel with having become self-serving in its worship of YHWH, and that the ones who intermarry will be excommunicated from the worshipping community [Gla].

QUESTION—The phrase וענה ער ʿēr wəʿōneh is enigmatic. What accounts for its various translations?

1. Wellhausen proposed emending the Masoretic text to וענה ער ʿēḏ wəʿōneh ('the witness and the one who answers') with the proposed meaning 'the plaintiff and the defender,' the idea being that anyone defending the evildoer described in 2:11 should be cut off from the community [Glazier-McDonald 2, Fuller]. Based on the LXX reading ἕως, which most often translates the Hebrew preposition ער ʿad, the RSV adopted Wellhausen's emendation of ער ʿēḏ. The NIV alternative translation follows this approach. NJB uses this proposed emendation to make the prophet say that he wishes such an offender to be deprived of any defenders when he stands in court. Evidence for such an emendation is cited from a Dead Sea scroll (4QXIIª), which in fact reads ʿēḏ [Fuller].

2. Accepting the above emendation, A. Van Hoonacker proposed that the two words were synonymous and meant 'the defense of such evildoing,' and that Malachi wished to see an end to all such perverted argumentation. Hoonacker made the phrase ומגיש מנחה ליהוה צבאות ûmaggîš minḥâ layhwh ṣəḇāʾôṯ 'and bringing gifts to YHWH of hosts' to refer to the defenders of the evildoing, and suggested that Malachi was wishing that such defenders be deprived of all worship privileges [Glazier-McDonald 2].

3. Torrey proposed an emendation of וענף שרש šereš wəʿānāp 'root and branches', i.e., leaving nothing of the offender's family [Glazier-McDonald 2]. This is perhaps the approach taken by JPS 'may the Lord leave him who does this no descendants'.

4. Alternative interpretations which preserve the Masoretic text ʿēr wəʿōneh include the following:
   a. ʿēr wəʿōneh is seen by many as a proverbial expression meaning 'whoever he may be' i.e., 'he who wakes and he who answers' or 'he who calls and he who answers". The KJV rendering and the NIV preferred translation follow, in one way or another, this alternative.
   b. W. Rudolph posited that ער ʿēr is a participle of עיר ʿyr 'to protect' and proposed 'to react, appeal' as a translation of ענה ʿnh, suggesting that the phrase signified that the offender should be removed from the community [cited in Gla].
   c. Keil believes that ʿēr wəʿōneh 'those who wake (others) and those who respond' signifies one's descendants, and that the prophet is wishing that YHWH will deprive the guilty of any descendants [Keil]. JPS follows this interpretation.
   d. ʿnh is interpreted as the Qal participle, not of ʿnh 'to answer", but of another ʿnh, the Piel of which is known signify 'to sexually

assault,' in which case the Qal could theoretically signify 'to have
sexual relations by mutual consent.' Admitting that עוּר *ʿôr* 'to stir
oneself up, be awake' (of which *ʿēr* is the Qal participle) can signify
any kind of arousal, not just from sleep, one arrives at a translation
'the one who is sexually aroused and the lover'—i.e., the Israelites
who went lusting after foreign women. Ultimately the Israelites who
married foreign women would be seen as having also accepted their
gods and the pagan fertility cults which had made inroads into Israel
during her history [Glazier-McDonald 2; this same argument is
incorporated in Gla of the same author].

QUESTION—To what does וּמַגִּישׁ מִנְחָה לַיהוה צְבָאוֹת *ûmaggîš minḥâ
layhwh ṣᵊbāʾôt* 'and bringing gifts to YHWH of hosts' refer?

1. This phrase is a further specification of the one whom it is hoped
   YHWH will cut off—he is guilty of the already described offense and he
   compounds his guilt by presuming to bring an offering to YHWH [Mer,
   Gla; JPS]. Other translations view this phrase in the same way, but in a
   concessive relationship to the preceding clause instead of an additive
   relationship: 'even though he bring . . .' [NICOT; CEV; NIV, NLT,
   REB].

2. The phrase stands as the second object of God's punishment so that the
   sense of the passage is: 'may God not only cut off every descendant of
   such an offender (or every defender of such an offender) from the
   community of Israel, but also any one who would presume to offer a
   sacrifice for him in expiation of his sin' [Keil; KJV].

3. The phrase expresses a privilege which the prophet hopes that YHWH
   will never again allow the guilty person: the offender is to be cut off
   from the community of Israel and not allowed to worship YHWH again
   [TEV]. JPS extends this thought to the offenders descendants.

2:13

And[a]- another[b] -thing[c] you(pl)-do:[d] (you(pl))-cover[e] (with-)tears[f] (the)-
altar(-of)[g] YHWH, weeping[h] and[i]-groaning[j] because/so-that[k] (he) still[l]
-(does-)not[m] turn(-with-favor)[n] toward[o]-the-offering[p] or[q]-accept[r] favor[s]
from[t]-your(pl)-hand.[u]

LEXICON—a. -וְ *wᵊ- waw* connective (BDB p. 251), (Hol p. 84), (TWOT
     519): 'and' [Coh, Keil, Gla, WBC; CEV, JPS, KJV, NASB, NRSV].
     Many translations do not explicitly translate this connective, but
     nevertheless express an additive relation; 'for' [Mer].

   b. fem. sg. of שֵׁנִי *šēnî* [BDB p. 1041), (Hol p. 379), (TWOT 2421b):
     'another' [NICOT; NASB, NIV, NLT, REB, TEV], 'second' [BDB,
     Hol; Keil]. This word is also translated as an adverb: 'again' [Mer;
     KJV, NJB], 'also' [WBC], 'further' [Coh], 'else' [CEV], 'as well' [JPS,
     NRSV], 'moreover' [Gla].

   c. fem. sg. of זֹה *zeh* (BDB p. 260), (Hol p. 86), (TWOT 528): '(another)
     thing' [NICOT; NIV, NLT, REB, TEV], 'this' [Coh, Keil, Mer, Gla,

WBC; JPS, KJV, NASB, NRSV], 'what else' [CEV], 'something'
[NJB]. The demonstrative pronoun *zeh* functions here anaphorically,
referring to what follows [Hol] in a neutral way, e.g., 'this' [BDB].

d. 2nd mas. pl. Qal imperf. of עשה *ʿśh* (BDB p. 793), (Hol p. 284),
(TWOT 1708): 'to do' [all lexica, commentators, and versions]. The
English present tense is employed [all commentators and versions except
the following], the present progressive [CEV], and the present perfect
[KJV].

e. Piel inf. of כסה *ksh* (BDB p. 491), (Hol p. 161), (TWOT 1008): 'to
cover' [BDB, Hol; Coh, Keil, Mer, Gla, NICOT, WBC; JPS, KJV,
NASB, NJB, NRSV], 'to flood' [CEV, NIV], 'to drown' [REB, TEV].

f. דמעה *dimʿâ* (BDB p. 199), (Hol p. 73), (TWOT 442b): 'tears' [all
lexica, commentators, and versions]. All translations add 'with',
considering it to be implied in English.

g. מזבח *mizbēaḥ* 'altar' (BDB p. 258), (Hol p. 188), (TWOT 525b): 'altar'
[all lexica, commentators, and versions].

h. בכי *bəkî* (BDB p. 113), (Hol p. 40), (TWOT 243b): 'weeping' [all
lexica, commentators, and versions except the following]. CEV conflates
this word and the following word אנקה *ʾănāqâ* 'groaning', translating
them as 'to cry noisily'.

i. -ו *wə- waw* connective (BDB p. 251), (Hol p. 84), (TWOT 519): 'and'
[all commentators and versions].

j. אנקה *ʾănāqâ* (BDB p. 60), (Hol p. 23), (TWOT 134a): 'groaning'
[BDB; NASB], 'sigh' [Keil], 'sighing' [Coh], 'groan' [Hol], 'crying'
[BDB], 'wailing' [NICOT; NJB, TEV], 'moaning' [JPS], 'crying out'
[KJV]. This noun is also translated with a verb: 'to groan' [Mer, Gla,
WBC; NLT, NRSV], 'to wail' [NIV], 'to cry noisily' [CEV], 'to moan'
[REB].

k. מן *min* (BDB p. 577), (Hol p. 200), (TWOT 1212). Most translations
express reason here: 'because' [Mer, NICOT, WBC; CEV, NASB,
NIV, NJB, NLT, NRSV, TEV], 'insomuch' [Coh; KJV]. Some
translations, however, express result: 'so that' [Keil; JPS], 'thus' [Gla].
REB expresses adversative addition: 'but he still refuses to look at . . .'
The preposition *min* here introduces cause or effect.

l. constr. of עוד *ʿôd* (BDB p. 728), (Hol p. 267), (TWOT 1576): 'still'
[BDB], '(no) longer' [Mer, Gla; NASB, NIV, NRSV], 'anymore' [Coh,
Keil, WBC; JPS, KJV]; translation not explicit [CEV, NLT]. The
primary sense of *ʿôd*, formally a noun, denotes 'permanence, constancy'
[Hol]; here *ʿôd* functions as an adverb 'again, still' [Hol].

m. constr. of אין *ʾayin* (BDB p. 34), (Hol p. 13), (TWOT 81). *ʾayin* is
properly a noun signifying 'absence', but functioning here in its
construct state to negate the following infinitive.

n. Qal inf. of פנה *pnh* (BDB p. 815), (Hol p. 293), (TWOT 1782): 'to turn
toward' [BDB], 'to turn' [Hol; Keil, WBC]. Gla translates the infinitive
literally: 'a turning (to)'. Most translations, however, express a

secondary sense of פְּנוֹת אֶל *pənôṯ ʾel* 'to turn toward': 'to regard' [Coh; KJV, JPS, NASB, NRSV], 'to consider' [NJB], 'to pay heed to' [Mer], 'to pay attention to' [NICOT; NIV, NLT], 'to be pleased' [CEV], 'to look at' [REB], 'to accept' [TEV]. The verb *pnh* is translated using the English present tense [all commentators and versions except the following], using the future tense [Gla, WBC].

o. אֶל *ʾel* (BDB p. 39), (Hol p. 16), (TWOT 91): 'toward' [Hol; WBC], 'to' [Keil, Gla]. The primary function of the preposition *ʾel* is to indicate motion or direction to or towards something [BDB, Hol].

p. מִנְחָה *minḥâ* (BDB p. 585), (Hol p. 202)), (TWOT 1214a): 'offering' [all lexica, commentators, and versions except the following], 'sacrifice' [Hol; Keil], 'oblation' [JPS]. Some translations add a possessive pronoun 'your' [CEV, NIV].

q. -וְ *wə-* *waw* connective (BDB p. 251), (Hol p. 84), (TWOT 519). All translations express an additive relation here: 'or' [Gla, NICOT, WBC; KJV, NASB, NIV, NJB, NRSV, REB], 'nor' [Mer], 'neither' [Coh], 'and' [Keil; CEV, JPS, NLT].

r. Qal inf. constr. of לָקַח *lqḥ* (BDB p. 542), (Hol p. 178), (TWOT 1124): 'to accept' [Keil, Mer, NICOT; CEV, JPS, NASB, NIV, NJB, NLT, NRSV], 'to receive' [Hol; WBC; Coh, KJV, REB], 'to take' [BDB, Hol]. Gla translates the infinitive literally: 'a taking of (favor)'.

s. רָצוֹן *rāṣôn* (BDB p. 953), (Hol p. 345), (TWOT 2207a). Some translations understand *rāṣôn* as the object of *lāqaḥaṯ* 'to receive': 'favor' [BDB, Hol; Gla], 'well-pleasing thing' [Keil]. *Rāṣôn* is understood here in its primary sense of 'something which gives pleasure', referring specifically to the sacrificial offerings [Keil, Gla]. Others also regard *rāṣôn* as the object, translating it as 'what you bring him' [TEV] or 'what you offer' [JPS]. Most translations, however, translate as if there were implied an object pronoun governed by *lāqaḥaṯ* 'to receive' and these render *rāṣôn* adverbially, e.g., 'with favor, with good will': 'favor' [WBC; NASB, NRSV], 'good will' [BDB; Coh; KJV], 'pleasure' [NICOT; NIV, NLT], 'favorably' [Mer; REB]. The entire phrase is rendered, then, as 'nor accepts it favorably', etc.

t. מִן *min* (BDB p. 577), (Hol p. 200), (TWOT 1212): 'from' [Mer, Gla, NICOT, WBC; NASB, NIV, NJB], 'at' [Coh, Keil; KJV, NRSV]. The preposition *min* indicates here perhaps spatial motion from starting point, or perhaps logical cause.

u. constr. of יָד *yāḏ* (BDB p. 388), (Hol p. 127), (TWOT 844): 'hand' [all commentators and versions except the following]; this expression is also translated concretely as 'you' [NJB, REB]. It is also translated as a subordinate clause acting as the restructured object of *lāqaḥaṯ* 'to receive': 'what you offer' [JPS], 'what you bring' [TEV]. Translation not explicit [NLT].

QUESTION—To what do בְכִי *bəkî* 'weeping' and אֲנָקָה *ʾănāqâ* 'groaning' refer?

1. They might refer to syncretistic practices among the Jews, perhaps especially to fertility rites [Gla]. A Jew married to a pagan woman (see Mal. 2:11) would be obliged to participate in her rites of weeping at the mythical death of the god-lover (בַּעַל *baʿal*) of her goddess [(F.F. Hvidberg, *Weeping and Laughter in the Old Testament* (Leiden: Brill, 1962), p. 122; quoted in Glazier-McDonald 2]. Such a syncretistic worshipper would introduce his wife's cult into the Temple itself [Gla].

2. They refer to ostentatious lamentation, probably of Jews who wanted God to come to their aid in time of drought, sickness, etc. [TOTC].

3. They refer to the sincerity of those who sought God's help and who honestly wondered why it did not come [WBC].

4. They refer to the Jews' realization that their worship and sacrifices had no effect with God. They interpreted the crop failure spoken of in Mal. 3:10–12 as evidence of God's displeasure [NICOT].

5. They refer to the lamenting of the divorced wives in YHWH's sanctuary. כַּסּוֹת *kassôt* 'to cover' is interpreted as indirect action: the husbands indirectly cover the altar with tears by causing their wives to weep on it [Coh, Keil]. The Targum and Jerome also follow this interpretation [TOTC].

QUESTION—How should מִן *min* (inherent in מֵאֵין *mēʾên*) be read?

1. It should be read as introducing a reason [Coh, Mer, NICOT, WBC; CEV, KJV, NASB, NIV, NJB, NLT, NRSV, TEV].

2. It should be read as introducing a result [Keil, Gla; JPS].

3. It should be read as expressing adversative addition: 'but he still refuses to look at . . .' [REB].

2:14

And/Yet/But[a]-you(pl)-say,[b] why[c]? Because[d] YHWH has-witnessed[e] between[f]-you(sg) and[g]-between (the-)wife(-of)[h] your(sg)-youth,[i] whom[j] you(s) have-been-faithless[k] with[l]-her, although[m]-she[n] (is/was)[o] your-companion[p] and[q]-(the-)wife(-of)[r] your(sg)-covenant.[s]

LEXICON—a. -וְ *wə- waw* connective (BDB p. 251), (Hol p. 84), (TWOT 519). This connective is often translated here in an additive manner: 'and' [Keil; CEV, NJB]. It is also translated concessively: 'yet' [Coh, Gla; KJV, NASB] and adversatively: 'but' [Mer, Gla, WBC; JPS]; not explicit [NICOT; NIV, NLT, NRSV, REB, TEV].

b. 2nd pl. Qal perf. of אמר *ʾmr* (BDB p. 55), (Hol p. 21), (TWOT 118): 'to say' [BDB, Hol; Coh, Keil, Gla, WBC; KJV, NASB], 'to ask' [Mer, NICOT; JPS, NIV, NJB, NRSV, REB, TEV], 'to cry out' [NLT], no translation [CEV, NLT, REB].

c. עַל־מָה *ʿal mâ* (BDB p. 554), (Hol p. 184). Some translations render literally just the one (compound) word of the Hebrew question: 'why' [Hol; Mer, NICOT, WBC; NIV, NJB, REB], 'wherefore' [BDB; Coh,

Keil, Gla; KJV], 'upon what basis' [Hol], 'for what reason?' [NASB].
Many others make explicit to varying degrees their understanding of the
full, implied question: 'because of what?' [JPS], 'why does he not?'
[NRSV], 'why he no longer accepts them' [TEV], 'why isn't God
pleased?' [CEV], 'why has the Lord abandoned us?' [NLT].

d. עַל־כִּי ʿal kî (BDB p. 758), (Hol p. 155): 'because' [all lexica,
   commentators, and versions].

e. 3rd mas. sg. Hiphil perf. of עוּד ʿôḏ (BDB p. 729), (Hol p. 266),
   (TWOT 1576d): 'to witness' [WBC; NLT], 'to bear witness' [BDB;
   Gla; REB], 'to be (a) witness' [Hol; Coh, Keil, Mer; JPS, KJV, NASB,
   NRSV], 'to act as (the) witness' [NICOT; NIV], 'to stand as witness'
   [NJB]. Two translations make explicit their idea of the content of the
   testimony—that the husbands have sinned against their wives: 'he knows
   you have broken your promise to the wife' [TEV], 'he knows that each
   one of you men has been unfaithful to the wife' [CEV]. NLT also makes
   explicit its idea of the content of the testimony—that God is aware of the
   vows taken by the couples at their marriage: 'the Lord witnessed the
   vows you and your wife made to each other on your wedding day'. REB
   makes explicit the dynamic of the testimony: 'against you on behalf of
   your wife' [REB]. The English present perfect tense is often used in
   translating this verb, e.g., 'The Lord has witnessed': [all commentators
   and versions except the following]; the past tense is used, e.g., 'The
   Lord acted as a witness': [NICOT; NLT, NRSV]. The present tense is
   also used, e.g., 'The Lord is witness': [CEV, JPS, NJB, TEV]; the
   present progressive tense is also used, e.g., 'The Lord is acting as
   witness': [NIV].

f. constr. of בֵּין bayin (BDB p. 107), (Hol p. 38), (TWOT 239a):
   'between' [all lexica, commentators, and versions except CEV, REB,
   TEV (see above)]. The primary sense of the noun bayin is 'interval';
   here it functions as a preposition [Hol].

g. -ו wə- waw connective (BDB p. 251), (Hol p. 84), (TWOT 519): 'and'
   [all commentators and versions except CEV, REB, TEV (see above)].

h. constr. of אִשָּׁה ʾiššâ (BDB p. 61), (Hol p. 29), (TWOT 137a): 'wife'
   [all lexica, commentators, and versions].

i. constr. of נְעוּרִים nəʿûrîm (BDB p. 655), (Hol p. 240), (TWOT 1389d):
   'youth' [all lexica, commentators, and versions except the following],
   '[the wife whom] you married when you were young' [CEV, TEV],
   'when you were young' [NLT]. The primary sense of nəʿûrîm is 'youth
   as a stage of life' [Hol].

j. אֲשֶׁר ʾăšer (BDB p. 81), (Hol p. 30), (TWOT 184): 'whom' [all
   commentators and versions except the following], 'because' [NIV].
   Some translations omit the relative and begin a new sentence [NLT,
   REB]. ʾăšer is a relative particle.

k. 2nd mas. sg. Qal perf. of בָּגַד bḡd (BDB p. 93), (Hol p. 33), (TWOT
   198): 'to be faithless' [NICOT, WBC; NRSV], 'to act treacherously'

[BDB; Keil, Mer], 'to deal treacherously' [BDB; Coh; KJV, NASB], 'to break faith' [JPS, NJB, NIV, REB], 'to break one's promise' [CEV, TEV], 'to be disloyal' [NLT], 'to deal deceitfully' [Gla].

l. -בּ *bə-* (BDB p. 88), (Hol p. 32), (TWOT 193): not explicitly translated by most commentators and versions, since such a translation would be redundant in English, 'with' [NIV], 'against' [NASB]. The proclitic *bə-* functions here as a verb complementizer [BDB, Hol].

m. -וּ *wə-* *waw* connective (BDB p. 251), (Hol p. 84), (TWOT 519). All translations translate as concession here: 'although' [Gla; TEV], 'though' [Coh, Mer, NICOT; JPS, NASB, NIV, NLT, NRSV, REB], 'even though' [NJB], 'whereas . . . nevertheless' [Keil], 'yet' [WBC; KJV].

n. הִיא *hîʾ* 3rd fem. sg. prn.: 'she' [all commentators and versions].

o. All translations read here as implied a verb: *hyh* 'to be' [all commentators and versions except NLT], 'to remain' [NLT]. Some use the English past tense [Gla, NICOT; NLT, TEV], although most employ the present tense [Coh, Keil, Mer, WBC; JPS, KJV, NASB, NIV, NRSV, REB].

p. constr. of חברת *ḥăḇeret* (BDB p. 289), (Hol p. 95), (TWOT 598d): 'companion' [Hol; Coh, Keil, Mer, Gla, WBC; KJV, NASB, NRSV], 'partner' [NICOT; CEV, JPS, NJB, NIV, REB, TEV], 'consort' [BDB]. NLT adds an adjective: 'faithful companion'. *Ḥăḇeret* denotes a female companion in marriage, i.e., wife [BDB, Hol].

q. -וּ *wə-* *waw* connective (BDB p. 251), (Hol p. 84), (TWOT 519). All commentators and versions express here an additive relationship, e.g., 'and'.

r. constr. of אשה *ʾiššâ* (see above): 'wife' [all lexica, commentators, and versions except JPS], 'spouse' [JPS].

s. constr. of ברית *bərît* (BDB p. 136), (Hol p. 48), (TWOT 282a): 'covenant' [all lexica, commentators, and versions except the following]. *Bərît* is also translated as an adjective: 'legal' [NICOT], 'covenanted' [JPS]; and as adjective/noun + noun: 'marriage covenant' [NIV], 'solemn covenant' [REB], 'marriage vows' [NLT]. The interior semantic relations of the expression *bərîtekā* 'your covenant' are made explicit by some: 'you promised before God that you would be faithful to her' [TEV], 'you promised that . . .' [CEV]. The Hebrew construct relationship between אשה *ʾiššâ* 'wife' and ברית *bərît* 'covenant' is expressed by many translations with 'of': 'wife of your covenant' [all commentators and versions except the following]. Others render 'wife by covenant', 'wife by marriage covenant', etc. [Mer; NASB, NJB, NRSV]. Many others express the relationship by means of adjective/ noun + noun (see above).

QUESTION—In what way is YHWH said to be a witness between a husband and his first, Jewish wife?

1. Although there is no evidence that ancient Jewish weddings involved religious ceremonies [NICOT], marriage was instituted as part of God's will for mankind, and he was invoked in blessings upon the marriage [Coh, Keil, NICOT, TOTC]. Prov. 2:17 speaks of a covenant of God relating to marriage [Keil, TOTC].

2. There is no evidence that a formal covenant characterized Jewish weddings of Malachi's period. Therefore the entire discourse unit should be taken figuratively: in this passage, YHWH is said to be witness to the covenant that was concluded between himself and Israel; Israel is cast as the husband, and YHWH as the wife of the young Israel [C.C. Torrey, "The Prophecy of Malachi", *Journal of Biblical Literature* 17 (1898), cited in WBC; also Abel Isaaksson, cited in WBC].

QUESTION—To what does בְּרִיתֶךָ *bərîtekā* 'your covenant' refer?

1. It refers to legal marriage contracts which were drawn up at the time of marriage among the Jews of this era [Kimchi, cited in Coh; Mer, NICOT].

2. It refers to the Sinaitic covenant "of the fathers" discussed in Mal. 2:10—the age-old ban on intermarriage with pagan women [Gla, following C.C. Torrey, "The Prophet Malachi" (*Journal of Biblical Literature* 17 (1898): 1–15], and Abel Isaksson, *Marriage and Ministry in the New Temple* (Lund: C.W.K. Gleerup, 1965)]. This second position does not necessarily rule out the possibility that marriage contracts existed at this time among the Jews. Contracts might well have accompanied the payment of bride-wealth. Moreover, many covenants were oral only, made before witnesses, although certainly as binding as written ones [Gla].

3. It refers to the Sinaitic covenant in which Israel pledged to be faithful to YWHW, as a husband pledges fidelity to his wife [Abel Isaaksson, cited in WBC]. Isaaksson argues that marriage in this era did not involve covenants, but were rather simple financial arrangements between men [Abel Isaaksson, *Marriage and Ministry in the New Temple*, Lund: C.W.K. Gleerup, 1965; cited in Gla].

QUESTION—To what does אֵשֶׁת נְעוּרֶיךָ *ʾēšet nəʿûrêkā* 'the wife of your youth' refer?

1. This phrase refers to the wives whom the Jewish young men married and to whom they promised their fidelity, it being the custom to marry at an early age [NICOT].

2. This phrase refers metaphorically to the God of Israel: the community of Israel had pledged fidelity to YWHW in the Sinaitic covenant [C.C. Torrey, "The Prophet Malachi" (*Journal of Biblical Literature* 17 (1898): 1–15; cited in WBC; Abel Isaaksson, *Marriage and Ministry in the New Temple*, Lund: C.W.K. Gleerup, 1965; cited in WBC].

2:15

This verse has proved impossible to interpret to everyone's satisfaction. Indeed, some commentators regard the Hebrew text as probably having been corrupted, perhaps deliberately so [NICOT, TOTC].

SYNTAX—The various syntactic interpretations are presented below side by side to allow easy comparison.

LEXICON—Because the syntactic interpretations vary so much, the translations of lexical items also vary. They are presented in association with the syntactic interpretations below.

(a) And^a-not^b-one^c (has-)done/does^d (this) (who has) even^e-(a-)remnant(-of)^f spirit^g to^h-himself.^{i} [Coh, Keil, Mer, Gla, NICOT; NASB]	(a) And^a(has-)(YHWH)-not^b made^d one (-being)^c, (having) even^e-(a)-remnant (-of)^f spirit^g to^h-himself^i? / (having) both^e-flesh^f (and) spirit^g to^h-himself^i? [WBC; CEV, JPS, KJV, NIV, NJB, NLT, NRSV, REB, TEV]
(b$_1$) And^j-what^k (did/does) the-one^l? [Keil, NICOT]	(b$_1$) And^j-why^k (did God make) the-one^l? [CEV, KJV, NIV, NLT, TEV]
(c$_1$) (He was) seeking^m offspring(-of)^n God.^{o} [Keil, NICOT]	(c$_1$) (Because he was) seeking^m offspring (-of)^n God.^{o} [Same]
(b$_2$) And^j-what^k (is) the-one^l seeking^m? [Coh, Gla]	(b$_2$) And^j-what^k (was) the-one^l seeking^m? [JPS, NJB, NLT, NRSV, REB]
(c$_2$) Offspring(-of)^n God ^{o}? [Same]	(c$_2$) Offspring(-of)^n God.^{o} [Same]
(b-c) And^j-what^k (did) the-one^l (when-)seeking^m offspring(-of)^n God^o? [Mer; NASB]	(b-c) And^j-why^k (was) the-one^l seeking^m offspring(-of)^n God^o? [WBC]

Syntactic Interpretation 1

(a) And^a-not^b-one^c (has-)done/does^d(this) (who has) even^e-(a-)remnant(-of)^f spirit^g to^h-him(self).^{i} [Coh, Keil, Mer, Gla, NICOT; NASB]

(b$_1$) And/For^j-what^k (did/does) the-one^l? [Keil, NICOT]
(c$_1$) (He was/is) seeking^m offspring(-of)^n God.^{o} [Keil, NICOT]

(b$_2$) And^j-what^k (is) the-one^l seeking^m? [Coh, Gla]
(c$_2$) Offspring(-of)^n God^o? [Coh, Gla]

(b-c) And^j-what^k (did) the-one^l (do) (when-)seeking^m offspring(-of)^n God^o? [Mer; NASB]

LEXICON associated with syntactic interpretation 1—a. -ן *wə- waw* connective (BDB p. 251), (Hol p. 84), (TWOT 519): 'and' [Coh, Keil, Gla], 'but' [NASB], not explicit [Mer, NICOT].

   b. לֹא *lō'* (BDB p. 518), (Hol p. 170), (TWOT 1064). *Lō'* expresses negation. See below for translation.

   c. אֶחָד *'eḥāḏ* (BDB p. 25), (Hol p. 9), (TWOT 61): 'not one' [Coh, Keil, Gla; NASB], 'no one' [Mer, NICOT]. *'eḥāḏ* is 'the number one', and also functions as an indefinite article [Hol].

d. 3rd mas. sg. Qal perf. of עשׂה ʿśh (BDB p. 793), (Hol p. 284), (TWOT 1708): 'to do' [BDB, Hol; Coh, Keil, Mer, Gla; NASB], 'to act' [NICOT]. All translations supply some kind of deictic reference to an implied action, e.g., 'no one does this' [Mer]. Keil and Gla employ the English past tense, Mer the present, and NICOT the present conditional 'would do'.

e. -ו wə- waw connective (BDB p. 251), (Hol p. 84), (TWOT 519): 'even' [Mer], 'still' [Keil], 'and' [Gla]. NICOT does not translate the waw connective explicitly, but still expresses in the passage, as do the preceding, an idea of concession. Not explicit [Coh; NASB].

f. constr. of שׁאר šəʾār (BDB p. 984), (Hol p. 357), (TWOT 2307a): 'remnant' [BDB, Hol; Keil, Mer, Gla; NASB], 'residue' [BDB; NICOT], 'exuberance' [Coh].

g. רוח rûaḥ (BDB p. 924), (Hol p. 334), (TWOT 2131a): 'spirit' [BDB, Hol; Coh, Keil, NICOT], 'the Spirit' [Mer; NASB], 'reproductive ability' [Gla].

h. -ל lə- (BDB p. 510), (Hol p. 167), (TWOT 1063): five translations render an idea of possession with 'to have' [Coh, Keil, Mer, Gla; NASB]. The same idea is also conveyed by 'with' [NICOT]. Mer reinforces 'to have' with the phrase 'in him'. The proclitic lə- here introduces a dative of possession [BDB, Hol].

i. 3rd mas. sg. prn.: 'him' [Mer].

j. -ו wə- waw connective (BDB p. 251), (Hol p. 84), (TWOT 519): 'and' [Keil, Gla; NASB]. Coh translates a reason relation: 'for'. Not explicit [Mer, NICOT].

k. מה mâ (BDB p. 552), (Hol p. 183), (TWOT 1149): 'what' [BDB, Hol; Coh, Keil, Mer, Gla, NICOT; NASB]. The interrogative particle m often functions as a pronoun, e.g., 'what?', and often as an adverb 'why?' or 'how?'

l. אחד ʾeḥāḏ (see above): with the definite article, 'the one' [Coh, Keil, NICOT], 'that one' [Mer, Gla; NASB].

m. mas. sg. Qal part. of בקשׁ bqš (BDB p. 134), (Hol p. 46), (TWOT 276): 'to seek' [BDB, Hol; Coh, Keil, Mer, Gla, NICOT; NASB].

n. constr. of זרע zeraʿ (BDB p. 282), (Hol p. 92), (TWOT 582a): 'offspring' [BDB, Hol; Mer, NICOT; NASB], 'descendants' [Hol], 'seed' [Coh, Keil, Gla].

o. אלהים ʾĕlōhîm (BDB p. 43), (Hol p. 17), (TWOT 93c): 'God' [BDB, Hol; Coh, Keil, Mer, Gla]. The noun is also translated as an adjective: 'godly' [NICOT].

Questions relating to Syntactic Interpretation 1 of Mal. 2:15a

QUESTION—To what does אחד ʾeḥāḏ 'one' refer?

It must refer to a category of mankind, since the phrase '(who has) even-(a-)remnant(-of) spirit to-himself' cannot possibly refer to God [Keil].

QUESTION—What does רוּחַ *rûaḥ* 'spirit' mean?

1. It signifies God's Spirit, which leads one to godliness. One having even a bit of inclination toward godliness would never have engaged in such divorce and remarriage [Mer]. Similarly, Keil interprets *rûaḥ* here as the God-given power to acquire virtue.

2. It signifies the insight or good sense accorded by one's desire for God. One who wants to have godly children would not divorce his Jewish wife in order to marry a pagan [NICOT].

3. It signifies generally the power, dependent upon God, to will and to execute any action; specifically, here it signifies man's ability to beget children, which Malachi sees as coming from God. God threatens, as one of the punishments of unfaithfulness, to make the offenders sterile (cf. Hosea 4:10); such a person will have absolutely none, 'not a remnant', of God's spirit left in him [Gla].

Questions relating to Syntactic Interpretation 1 of Mal. 2:15b

QUESTION—How is this syntactic interpretation explained?

1. In this syntactic interpretation, Mal. 2:15b includes in Hebrew only the following: וּמָה הָאֶחָד *ûmâ hā'eḥāḏ*, 'and what the one?' The commentators represented above supply the verb 'to do' (read by implication from the previous clause—cf. Eccl. 2:12), yielding 'And what did/does the one?' [Keil, NICOT]. Here הָאֶחָד *hā'eḥāḏ* 'the one' signifies Abraham, who is understood here as being cited approvingly: he sent away Hagar, for it is natural that his example would be invoked by those Jews who wished to defend their own divorces [Keil and most Jewish commentators, according to Coh]. On the other hand, *hā'eḥāḏ* is seen by Mer to refer to Abraham as a bad example which is not to be followed, patriarch though he was. Still a third interpretation is held by NICOT: *hā'eḥāḏ* 'the one' signifies anyone who has sound spiritual judgment.

2. In this syntactic interpretation, Mal. 2:15b includes in Hebrew the following: וּמָה הָאֶחָד מְבַקֵּשׁ *ûmâ hā'eḥāḏ məbaqqēš* 'and what was the one seeking?' Here *hā'eḥāḏ* 'the one' signifies anyone who, having taken a pagan wife, hopes that his marriage will bring forth children; the prophet is understood as telling him to give up such hope, for God will not bless his union [Gla].

Questions relating to Syntactic Interpretation 1 of Mal. 2:15c

QUESTION—How is this syntactic interpretation explained?

1. Mal. 2:15c is comprised of מְבַקֵּשׁ זֶרַע אֱלֹהִים *məbaqqēš zeraʿ 'ĕlōhîm* 'seeking seed of God'. This functions as the answer to the question in Mal. 2:15b 'And what (does/did) the one' [Keil, NICOT].

QUESTION—What is the nature of the construct relationship between זֶרַע *zeraʿ* 'offspring' and אֱלֹהִים *'ĕlōhîm* 'God'?

1. It expresses source: 'seed of God (i.e., promised by God and therefore to come from God)' [Gla, Keil, Mer]; the same

interpretation is employed by Coh but made explicit: 'a seed given
of God').
2. It expresses a quality: 'godly', i.e., of a nature which is like God
[NICOT; NASB].
QUESTION—What is the significance of *mᵊḇaqqēš zeraᶜ ᵊlōhîm*
'seeking seed of God'?
It answers the question, 'What did this one (Abraham) do?' Abraham
did indeed send away Hagar, but, unlike the motives of Malachi's
Jewish antagonists, his own motives in so doing were pure, for he was
only seeking to obey God [Keil, Mer, and most Jewish commentators,
according to Coh].
2. Mal. 2:15c is comprised of אלהים זרע *zeraᶜ ᵊlōhîm* 'seed of God'.
This functions as the answer to מבקש האחד ומה *ûmâ hāᵊeḥād
mᵊḇaqqēš* 'for what seeketh the one?' [Coh].

Questions relating to Syntactic Interpretation 1 of Mal. 2:15b-c
QUESTION—How is this syntactic interpretation explained?
Mer takes parts (b) and (c) to be linked together circumstantially: 'when
seeking'.
QUESTION—What is the significance of מבקש זרע אלהים *mᵊḇaqqēš zeraᶜ
ᵊlōhîm* 'seeking seed of God'?
It is part of a rhetorical question, 'What did this one (Abraham) do when
he sought children from God?' Abraham's unfaithfulness to Sarah in taking
Hagar as a concubine was prompted by his desire to have the offspring
which God promised him. Malachi is telling the Jews not to emulate their
ancestor's action [Mer].

Syntactic Interpretation 2
(a) And[a](has-)(YHWH)-not[b] made[d] one[c](-being), (having) yet[e]-(a)-*residue
(-of)[f-1] spirit[g] to[h]-himself[i]? / (having) both[e]-*flesh[f-2] (and) spirit[g] to[h]-
him(self)[i]? [WBC; CEV, JPS, KJV, NIV, NJB, NLT, NRSV, REB, TEV]

(b₁) And[j]-why[k] (did God make) the-one[l]? [CEV, KJV, NIV, NLT, TEV]
(c₁) (Because he was) seeking[m] offspring(-of)[n] God.[o] [Same]

(b₂) And[j]-what[k] (was) the-one[l] seeking[m]? [JPS, NJB, NLT, NRSV, REB]
(c₂) Offspring(-of)[n] God.[o] [Same]

(b-c) And[j]-why[k] (was) the-one[l] seeking[m] offspring(-of)[n] God[o]? [WBC]
*TEXT—Some scholars accept the Masoretic text, which reads שאר *šᵊᵃār*
'remainder, remnant' [WBC; JPS, KJV]. Others, however, believe that
better sense is made by a reading of שאר *šᵊᵊēr* 'flesh; body; self' [CEV,
NIV, NJB, NLT, NRSV, REB, TEV].
LEXICON associated with Syntactic Interpretation 2—a. -ו *wᵊ- waw*
connective (BDB p. 251), (Hol p. 84), (TWOT 519): 'and' [KJV], not
explicit [WBC; CEV, JPS, NIV, NJB, NLT, NRSV, REB, TEV].

b. לֹא *lōʾ* (BDB p. 518), (Hol p. 170), (TWOT 1064). The translations which follow S.I. 2 all read part (a) of this verse as a question, with *lōʾ* modifying the verb, e.g., 'has not God made . . . ?' *Lōʾ* expresses negation.

c. אֶחָד *ʾeḥād* (BDB p. 25), (Hol p. 9), (TWOT 61): 'one' (in the sense of a unity) [Hol; WBC; KJV, NIV], 'a single being' [NJB], 'all' [JPS]. CEV makes explicit its understanding of the unity: 'one person with your wife'; NLT is similar. Likewise, TEV expresses the same thought by making 'one' an adjective, saying that man and wife are made one body and spirit. NRSV and REB interpret *ʾeḥād* as qualifying God: 'one God', but also supply 'her' as the object of the verb.

d. 3ʳᵈ mas. sg. Qal perf. of עשׂה *ʿśh* (BDB p. 793), (Hol p. 284), (TWOT 1708): 'to make' [BDB; WBC; JPS, KJV, NIV, NLT, NRSV, REB, TEV], 'to create' [CEV, NJB], 'to produce' [Hol].

e. -ו *wǝ- waw* connective (BDB p. 251), (Hol p. 84), (TWOT 519): 'yet' [KJV], 'both' [NRSV, REB], 'so that' [JPS]. Not explicit [WBC; CEV, NIV, NJB, NLT, TEV].

f-1. constr. of שְׁאָר *šǝʾār* (BDB p. 984), (Hol p. 357), (TWOT 2307a): 'residue' [BDB; KJV], 'last remnant' [WBC], 'remainder' [Hol]. This noun is also translated as a verbal adjective: 'all remaining' [JPS]

f-2. שְׁאֵר *šǝʾēr* (BDB p. 984), (Hol p. 357), (TWOT 2308a): 'flesh' [BDB, Hol; NIV, NJB, NRSV, REB], 'body' [Hol; NLT, TEV], 'self' [BDB, Hol]. CEV appears to combine the ideas of 'body' and 'spirit' below: 'one person'.

g. רוּח *rûaḥ* (BDB p. 924), (Hol p. 334), (TWOT 2131a): 'spirit' [BDB, Hol; NIV, NLT, NRSV, REB, TEV], 'the Spirit' [BDB, Hol; WBC; KJV], 'breath' [BDB, Hol], 'life-breath' [JPS], 'breath of life' [NJB].

h. -ל *lǝ-* (BDB p. 510), (Hol p. 167), (TWOT 1063): 'is his', indicating possession—where 'his' refers to God [WBC, but this commentator finds the passage ambiguous]; 'his'—where the referent is God and the thing possessed is 'all remaining life-breath' [JPS], 'he has'—but the referent of 'he' is ambiguous [KJV]; 'having'—where the referent is the 'single being' and the thing possessed is flesh and the breath of life' [NJB], 'his'—the referent is God and the thing possessed is the man and woman [NIV, NLT], 'his'—where the referent is God and the thing possessed is the flesh and spirit of the woman [NRSV]. TEV translates 'with her'. No translation [CEV, REB]. The proclitic *lǝ-* here introduces a dative of possession [BDB, Hol].

i. 3ʳᵈ mas. sg. prn.

j. -ו *wǝ- waw* connective (BDB p. 251), (Hol p. 84), (TWOT 519): 'and' [WBC; CEV, JPS, KJV, NIV, NLT, NRSV], not explicit [TEV].

k. מה *mâ* (BDB p. 552), (Hol p. 183), (TWOT 1149): 'why' [Hol; WBC; CEV, NIV], 'what' [BDB, Hol; JPS, NLT, NRSV], 'wherefore' [KJV], 'what . . . purpose' [TEV]. *M*, an interrogative particle, often functions as a pronoun, e.g., 'what?', and often as an adverb 'why?' or 'how?'

1. אֶחָד *ʾeḥāḏ* (see above). Many translations interpret *ʾeḥāḏ* 'one' as referring to God: 'the One' [WBC], 'that One' [JPS], 'the one God' [NRSV, REB], 'he' [CEV, NLT]. Other translations interpret *ʾeḥāḏ* 'one' to refer to the unity of marriage created by God: 'one' [KJV, NIV], 'single being' [NJB], 'in this' [TEV].

m. mas. sg. Qal part. of בקשׁ *bqš* (BDB p. 134), (Hol p. 46), (TWOT 276): 'to seek' [BDB, Hol; WBC; JPS, KJV, NIV, NJB], 'to require' [REB], 'to desire' [NRSV], 'to want' [NLT]. God's purpose is implied in some translations: 'it was so you would have . . .' [CEV], 'it was that you should have . . .' [TEV].

n. constr. of זרע *zeraᶜ* (BDB p. 282), (Hol p. 92), (TWOT 582a): 'offspring' [BDB, Hol; NIV, NJB, NRSV], 'seed' [BDB, Hol; WBC; KJV], 'children' [CEV, NLT, REB, TEV], 'folk' [JPS].

o. אלהים *ʾĕlōhîm* (BDB p. 43), (Hol p. 17), (TWOT 93c): 'God' [BDB, Hol; CEV, TEV]. This noun is also translated as an adjective: 'godly' [WBC; JPS, KJV, NIV, NLT, NRSV, REB], 'god-given' [NJB]. The construct relationship between זרע *zeraᶜ* 'offspring' and *ʾĕlōhîm* 'God' is translated by most as a quality: 'godly' [WBC; JPS, KJV, NIV, NRSV]. The construct relationship is also translated as source: 'god-given' [NJB]. It is also translated as a kind of genitive: 'and then lead them to become God's people' [CEV], 'who are truly God's people' [TEV].

Questions relating to Syntactic Interpretation 2 of Mal. 2:15a

QUESTION—How is this syntactic interpretation of Mal. 2:15a explained?
It is most natural to assume that YHWH is the subject of the verb עשׂה *ᶜśh* 'to make' [WBC].

QUESTION—What is the significance of the direct object אֶחָד *ʾeḥāḏ* 'one'?
a. 'One' refers to all mankind, created in a unity as both male and female and by implication united in marriage [WBC].
b. 'One' refers to the God-created goal of wedded unity [CEV, NIV, NJB, NLT, TEV]
c. 'One' refers to woman, referring specifically back to the first (Jewish) wife, now sent away by her faithless husband [NRSV, REB].
d. 'One' refers to all mankind, without any reference to marriage unity [JPS].

QUESTION—What is the significance of the textual choice of שׁאָר *šəᵓār* 'remainder, remnant'?
WBC translates 'The last remnant of the Spirit belongs to him', but frankly calls the rendering ambiguous. KJV also appears ambiguous: 'Yet had he the residue of the Spirit.' JPS, in translating the phrase, 'so that all remaining life-breath is His', seems to imply that all of mankind, having been created by YHWH, is under his ownership; he has therefore the right to expect that the offspring of the human race will be godly.

QUESTION—What is the significance of the textual choice of שְׁאֵר šə'ēr 'flesh, body, self'?

1. One group of these versions (CEV, NJB, TEV) conveys an idea of the bodily and spiritual union of marriage, e.g., 'Didn't God make you one body and spirit with her?' [TEV]. TOTC also favors this approach, which signifies that God created the unity of marriage in order that there might be born and raised children who would fear him [TOTC]. Two other versions (NIV, NLT) also signal the idea of the marriage union, but add that it is to be submitted to God (these versions render render לוֹ lô in the genitive sense of 'to him' [i.e., to God—possessed by God], e.g., 'Has not the Lord made them one? In flesh and spirit they are his' [NIV].

2. Two more versions (NRSV, REB) take *(having) both-flesh (and) spirit to-him(self)* to signal, not the marriage union, but the totality of a human being, here specifically the woman, e.g., 'Did not the one God make her? Both flesh and spirit are his' [NRSV]. These versions also understand *lô* in the genitive sense of 'to him', i.e., to God.

Questions relating to Syntactic Interpretation 2 of Mal. 2:15b
QUESTION—How is Syntactic Interpretation 2 of Mal. 2:15b explained?

1. Some versions assume that Mal. 2:15b is composed of וּמֶה הָאֶחָד ûmâ hā'eḥāḏ. Unlike Interpretation 1, however, these versions understand וּמֶה ûmâ in the sense of 'and why . . . ?', yielding 'And why one (i.e., and why did God make man and wife one in marriage)?' [CEV, KJV, NIV, TEV].

2. Other versions assume that Mal. 2:15b is comprised of הָאֶחָד מְבַקֵּשׁ וּמֶה ûmâ hā'eḥāḏ məḇaqqēš 'and what does the one seek?' [JPS, NJB, NLT, NRSV, REB].

3. WBC, understanding *ûmâ* as 'why?', puts Mal. 2:15b and Mal. 2:15c belong together, yielding, e.g., 'And why does the One seek a godly seed?'. Given the exhortation which follows in Mal. 2:15d, this rendering would have to be regarded as a rhetorical question with no explicit answer provided.

Questions relating to Syntactic Interpretation 2 of Mal. 2:15c
QUESTION—How is the syntactic interpretation of Mal. 2:15c explained?

1. Some assume that Mal. 2:15c is comprised of מְבַקֵּשׁ זֶרַע אֱלֹהִים məḇaqqēš zera' 'ĕlōhîm 'seeking seed of God'. This becomes the answer to the question of Mal. 2:15b 'And why one?' [CEV, NIV, TEV]. This answers the question, 'And why one?' (Why did God make man and wife one in marriage? Because he wanted godly children to come of them) [CEV, NIV, TEV].

2. Others assume that Mal. 2:15c is comprised of *zera' 'ĕlōhîm* 'seed of God', and that it becomes the answer to מְבַקֵּשׁ וּמֶה הָאֶחָד ûmâ hā'eḥāḏ məḇaqqēš 'and what does the one seek?' [JPS, NJB, NLT, NRSV, REB]. The construction relationship in the phrase *zera' 'ĕlōhîm* 'seed of

God' signifies offspring given by God, which the union of man and wife desires [NJB]; or godly offspring or people, which God desires [JPS, NLT, NRSV, REB].

DISCOURSE UNIT: 2:15d–2:16 [Clen (within the larger discourse unit of Mal. 2:10–3:6)]. The topic is "stop acting faithlessly."

2:15d
So[a]-guard[b](-yourselves)*   for/to/in[c]-your(pl)-spirit,[d]   and[e]-to[f]-(the-)wife (-of)[g] your-youth[h] *one-should-not-be-faithless/do-not-be-faithless.[i]

*TEXT—The Masoretic text reads יבגד *yibgōd* 'let no one be faithless'. Some Hebrew manuscripts, however, read תבגד *tibgōd* 'do (pl) not be faithless', apparently judging this reading to fit better in the prophet's direct discourse. Kimchi interprets *yibgōd* to mean, 'let none of you deal treacherously' [cited in Coh]. *Yibgōd* appears to be accepted by Coh, Keil, Mer, Gla, NICOT, WBC; JPS, KJV, NASB, NRSV, REB, TEV. The following versions appear to accept *tibgōd*: CEV, NIV, NJB, NLT.

LEXICON—a. -ו *wə-* *waw* connective of the attached *waw* consecutive verb (BDB p. 251), (Hol p. 84), (TWOT 519): 'so' [NICOT, WBC; JPS, NIV, NLT, NRSV, TEV], 'therefore' [Coh, Keil, Gla; KJV], 'then' [Mer; NASB, NJB], not explicit [CEV, REB].
   b. 2nd mas. pl. Niphal perf. *waw* consecutive of שמר *šmr* (BDB p. 1036), (Hol p. 377), (TWOT 2414): 'to guard oneself' [WBC; NIV, NLT], 'to take heed' [Coh, Keil, Gla, NICOT; KJV, NASB], 'to be attentive' [Mer], 'to be on one's guard' [BDB, Hol], 'to be careful' [Hol; JPS], 'to look to oneself' [NRSV], 'to make sure' [TEV], 'to have respect for' [NJB], 'to keep watch on' [REB]. This verb is translated as an imperative, e.g., 'keep watch on . . . !', by all translations except the following: (as a command cast in the future tense) 'therefore shall ye take heed' [Keil].
   c. -ב *bə-* (BDB p. 88), (Hol p. 32), (TWOT 193): 'for' [Keil; NJB], 'to' [Coh, Mer, Gla, NICOT; KJV, NASB, NRSV], 'of' [JPS] 'on' [REB], not explicit [CEV, TEV]. These are normal complementizers for the English verbs chosen to translate שמר *šmr* 'to be one one's guard' above. In contrast, the preposition 'in' [WBC; NIV] puts the phrase into a different light. The proclitic *bə-* functions here as a verb complementizer [BDB, Hol].
   d. רוח *rûaḥ* (BDB p. 924), (Hol p. 334), (TWOT 2131a): 'spirit' [Coh, Keil, Mer, Gla, WBC; KJV, NASB, NIV, REB], 'life-breath' [JPS]. *Rûaḥ* is also translated as a phrase: 'your own life' [NJB]; and reflexively: 'yourselves' [NICOT; NLT, NRSV], 'to make sure' [TEV]. No translation [CEV].
   e. -ו *wə-* *waw* connective (BDB p. 251), (Hol p. 84), (TWOT 519): the connective is translated additively as 'and' [Coh, Keil, Gla, NICOT, WBC; JPS, KJV, NASB, NIV, NJB, NRSV, REB]. The additive

relationship is also expressed by a semi-colon [NLT]. This connective is
also translated as introducing the reason for the preceding command:
'for' [Mer].

f. -בְּ *bə-* (see above): 'to' [Keil, Mer, NICOT; CEV, NRSV, TEV], 'with'
[Gla, WBC; JPS, NIV, NJB], 'against' [Coh; KJVNASB]. The proclitic
bə- functions here as a verb complementizer [BDB, Hol].

g. constr. of אִשָּׁה *ʾiššâ* (BDB p. 61), (Hol p. 29), (TWOT 137a): 'wife'
[all lexica, commentators, and versions].

h. constr. of נְעוּרִים *nəʿûrîm* (BDB p. 655), (Hol p. 240), (TWOT 1389d):
'youth' [BDB, Hol; Coh, Gla, Keil, Mer, NICOT; JPS, KJV, NASB,
NIV, NJB, NLT, NRSV, REB], not explicit [CEV, TEV]. The primary
sense of *nəʿûrîm* is 'youth as a stage of life' [Hol].

i. 3rd mas. sg. Qal imperf. of בָּגַד *bāḡaḏ* (BDB p. 93), (Hol p. 33), (TWOT
198): 'to be faithless' [NICOT, WBC; NRSV], 'to act faithlessly' [BDB;
Gla], 'to deal faithlessly' [BDB; Keil], 'to be treacherous' [Mer], 'to
deal treacherously' [BDB; Coh; KJV, NASB], 'to break faith' [JPS,
NIV, NJB], 'to be unfaithful' [CEV], 'to break one's promise' [TEV],
'not to remain loyal' [NLT]. Coh, Keil, Mer, and NICOT, as well as
JPS, KJV, NRSV, REB, and TEV accept the Masoretic יִבְגֹּד *yiḇgōḏ* 'let
no one be faithless' (although Keil translates with an English
imperative); Gla, WBC; CEV, NIV, NJB, and NLT accept the reading
תִּבְגֹּד *tiḇgōḏ* 'do (pl) not be faithless'. Most translations employ an
imperative or a command using 'let', but WBC employs the modality
'stop': 'stop being faithless', holding that the Hebrew negation אַל *ʾal*
can indicate such a modality.

QUESTION—How should -בְּ *bə-*, a proclitic, be translated?
The translations are chosen on the basis of the interpretations given to רוּחַ
rûaḥ (see below): 'in-your(pl)-spirit' appears to equate a reflexive
interpretation of *rûaḥ*, whereas 'of/for-your(pl)-spirit' seems to be more
than merely reflexive.

QUESTION—What does רוּחַ *rûaḥ* 'spirit' denote in this context?
1. It denotes one's spiritual and moral life, which would be in danger if one
divorced his wife [Keil].
2. It denotes one's own fertility: Malachi is exhorting the Jews to safeguard
their own reproductive capabilities by obeying God and remaining
faithful to their first wives [Gla].
3. *Rûaḥ* is a reflexive device, translated in some versions as 'yourselves'
'yourselves' [NLT, NRSV; also TEV by implication].

QUESTION—What is the significance of the change from 2nd mas. pl. to 3rd
mas. sg. represented in אַל־יִבְגֹּד *ʾal yiḇgōḏ* 'he should not be faithless' at the
end of this verse?
Although some have suggested an emendation of the Hebrew text to
achieve identical persons, there is insufficient textual authority for such a
change. This kind of alternation in persons occurs elsewhere in biblical
Hebrew also. Here the 3rd person signifies 'anyone' [Keil]. Although most

ancient versions suggest אל־תבגד ʾal tibḡōḏ 'you should (not) be unfaithful', and although some modern translations read this way as well, Hebrew style does not demand the 2nd pl. suffix [Mer].

2:16

(a_1) For[a] *he-hates[b-1] **divorce,[c-1] [KJV]

(a_2) For[a] *(I) hating[b-2] **divorce,[c-1] [Coh, Keil, Mer, NICOT; JPS, NIV, NJB, NLT, NRSV, TEV]

(a_3) For[a] *I-hate[b-3] **divorce,[c-1] [WBC; NASB]

(a_4) If[a] *(anyone) hating[b-2] (his wife) **divorces,[c-2] [Gla; Jones; REB]

(b) says YHWH (the-)God(of-)[d] Israel, [all commentaries and versions]

(c_2) for[e]-he-**covers[f-2] violence[g] over[h] his-garment[i], says YHWH(-of) hosts. [KJV; NASB]

(c_2) and[e]-**covering[f-1] violence[g] over[h] one's-garment,[i] says YHWH(-of) hosts. [Coh, Keil, Mer, NICOT, WBC; JPS, NIV, NJB, NLT, NRSV,TEV]

(c_4) he-covers[f-2] violence[g] over[h] his-garment,[i] says YHWH(-of) hosts. [Gla; Jones; REB]

(d) So[j]-guard-yourselves[k] in/of[l]-your(pl)-spirit[m] and[n]-(do-)not be-faithless.[o] [all commentators and versions]

SYNTAX—KJV takes God to be the subject of שׂנא śānēʾ 'he hateth putting away' [allowed by Mer], although others hold that this interpretation conflicts with the syntactic requirements necessitated by the direct speech formula ...אמר יהוה ʾāmar yhwh 'says the Lord...' [NICOT].

*TEXT—Some scholars assume an implicit 1st sg. pronoun before the MT's שׂנא śānēʾ 'he hates divorce', the vowels of which they repoint to yield the participle śōnēʾ 'hating'. This participle, translated literally as 'hating', allows then the text to signify 'I hate' [Keil, NICOT, and most versions]. WBC arrives at a semantically similar result by assuming that the verb should be read as שׂנאתי śānēʾṯî (1st mas. sg. Qal perf.) 'I hated', with the nuance of 'and still hate'. These approaches understand the introductory conjunction כי kî to signify a logical link such as 'for'.

Gla, Jones, and REB assume the participle śōnēʾ 'hating' as above, while assuming at the same time an indefinite subject of the participle and taking the introductory conjunction kî to signify 'if'. The text then reads, 'if a man, hating. . . .' Many commentators hold that the Targum and LXX adopt this approach: 'if a man hates' [e.g., NICOT, Abel Isaaksson, *Marriage and Ministry in the New Temple*, Lund, 1965 (quoted in WBC)]. This position is supported by relying on the LXX version as commented on by Theodore of Mopsuestia and Theodoret of Cyrrhus: ἀλλὰ ἐὰν μισήσῃς ἐξαποστείλαν 'but if you hate, divorce!' This LXX version became regarded as the official Greek version of Mal. 2:16 [Jones].

**TEXT—The MT reads שלח šallah, the Piel inf. constr. of שלח šlḥ 'to dismiss, send away'. This reading is accepted by the majority of commentators and versions. Others, however, repoint the vowels of šallah so that it yields *šillēaḥ* 'he dismisses' (3rd mas sg. Piel perf.) [Gla; Jones; REB].

***TEXT—If the first person is understood in line (a) above, i.e., 'for I hate divorce', then וכסה *wakissâ* 'and he covers' in line (c) must be taken with שלח *šallaḥ* 'divorce' as a coordinate object of 'hate'. In that case, כסה *kissâ*, 3rd mas. sg. Piel perf. of כסה *ksh* 'to cover', must be repointed as a Piel infinitive, כסה *kassēh* 'to cover', the verb form analogous to the Piel infinitive *šallaḥ* 'to divorce' [Wilhelm Rudolph, *Haggai-Sacharja-Maleachi*, Kommentar zum Alten Testament, Band 3, 4. Gütersloher Verlagshaus Gerd Mohn, 1976; cited in Gla. Gla]. Others, however, do not prefer to consider כסה as an infinitive, for it creates difficulties in understanding the 3rd sg. suffix 'his' with לבושו *labûšô* 'his garment' in line (c) [NICOT].

LEXICON—a. כי *kî* connective (BDB p. 471), (Hol p. 155), (TWOT 976): 'for' [Coh, Keil, Gla; JPS, KJV, NASB, NJB, NLT, NRSV], 'because' [WBC], 'if' [REB], no translation [Mer, NICOT; CEV, NIV, REB, TEV].

b-1. 3rd mas. sg. Qal perf. of שנא *śn'* (BDB p. 971), (Hol p. 353), (TWOT 2272): 'to hate' [BDB, Hol; CEV, KJV].

b-2. mas. sg. Qal part. of שנא *śn'* (see above): 'to hate' [all lexica, commentators, and versions except the following], 'to detest' [JPS]. This form is assumed by most translations, in which they understand a 1st sg. signification, 'I hate'.

b-3. 1st mas. sg. Qal perf. of שנא *śn'* (see above): 'to hate' [BDB, Hol; WBC; NASB].

c-1. Piel inf. constr. of שלח *šlḥ* (BDB p. 1018), (Hol p. 371), (TWOT 2394): 'to divorce' [BDB; all commentators and versions except the following], 'to put away' [Coh; KJV], 'to dismiss a wife' [BDB, Holl].

c-2. 3rd mas. sg. Piel perf. of שלח *šlḥ* (see above): 'to divorce' [Gla; Jones; REB].

d. constr. of אלהים *'ĕlōhîm* (BDB p. 43), (Hol p. 17), (TWOT 93c): 'God' [all lexica, commentators, and versions].

e. -ו *wa- waw* connective (BDB p. 251), (Hol p. 84), (TWOT 519): 'and' [all commentators and versions except the following], 'even' [NICOT], 'for' [KJV], 'thereby' [Gla].

f-1. Piel infinitive absolute of כסה *ksh* (BDB p. 491), (Hol p. 161), (TWOT 1008): 'to cover' [all lexica, commentators, and versions].

f-2. 3rd mas. sg. Piel perf. of כסה *ksh* (see above): 'to cover' [Gla; Jones; KJV, NASB, REB].

g. חמס *ḥāmās* (BDB p. 329), (Hol p. 109), (TWOT 678a): 'violence' [all lexica, commentators, and versions except the following], 'wickedness' [Keil], 'cruelty' [NJB, REB], 'lawlessness' [JPS], 'marks of violence' [NICOT], 'wrong' [NASB].

h. על *'al* (BDB p. 752), (Hol p. 273), (TWOT 1624p): 'over' [Hol; Keil], 'under' [NJB], 'with' [instrumental], [Gla; KJV, NASB], 'on' [Hol], 'upon' [BDB].

i. לבוש *ləḇûš* (BDB p. 528), (Hol p. 172), (TWOT 1075a): 'garment' [BDB, Hol; Coh, Keil, Mer, Gla, NICOT, WBC; KJV, NASB, NIV, NRSV], 'cloak' [NJB], 'coat' [NLT].

f.— i. This figure of speech is translated non-literally by some: 'to cover oneself with lawlessness as with a garment' [JPS], 'to cover oneself with violence' [NIV], 'to conceal one's cruelty under a cloak' [NJB], 'to overwhelm one [i.e., one's wife] with cruelty' [REB], 'to do such a cruel thing to one's wife' [TEV]. NLT employs a comparison: 'it is as cruel as putting on a victim's bloodstained coat' [NLT].

j. -ו *wə-* *waw* connective of the attached *waw* consecutive verb (BDB p. 251), (Hol p. 84), (TWOT 519): 'so' [NICOT, WBC; CEV, JPS, NASB, NIV, NLT, NRSV], 'therefore' [Coh, Keil, Mer, Gla; KJV], 'then' [NJB], not explicit [REB, TEV].

k. 2nd mas. pl. Niphal perf. *waw* consecutive of שמר *šmr* (BDB p. 1036), (Hol p. 377), (TWOT 2414): 'to guard oneself' [NLT], 'to take heed' [Coh, Keil, Mer, Gla, NICOT; KJV, NASB, NRSV], 'to guard oneself' [WBC; NIV], 'to be on one's guard' [BDB, Hol], 'to take care' [CEV], 'to have respect' [NJB], 'to make sure' [TEV], 'to be careful of' [Hol; JPS], 'to keep watch' [REB].

l. -ב *bə-* (BDB p. 88), (Hol p. 32), (TWOT 193): 'of' [JPS], 'to' [KJV, Gla; NASB, NRSV], 'for' [Keil, NJB], 'on' [REB], not explicit [CEV, TEV]. The foregoing are normal complementizers for the English verbs chosen to translate שמר *šmr* 'to be one one's guard' above. However, the preposition 'in' [WBC; NIV] puts the phrase in a different light. The proclitic *bə-* functions here as a verb complementizer [BDB, Hol].

m. רוח *rûaḥ* (BDB p. 924), (Hol p. 334), (TWOT 2131a): 'spirit' [BDB, Hol; Gla, WBC; KJV, NASB, NIV, REB], 'life-breath' JJPS]. *Rûaḥ* is also translated as a phrase: 'for your own life' [NJB]; and reflexively: 'yourself' [NICOT; NLT, NRSV]. TEV's rendering may be said to incorporate a reflexive idea: 'make sure'. No translation [CEV].

n. -ו *wə-* *waw* connective (BDB p. 251), (Hol p. 84), (TWOT 519): 'and' [all commentators and versions except the following], 'that' (denoting purpose) [Coh; KJV NASB,]. Other translations do not employ a conjunction.

o. 2nd mas. pl. Qal imperf. of בגד *bḡḏ* (BDB p. 93), (Hol p. 33), (TWOT 198): 'to be faithless' [WBC; NRSV], 'to be unfaithful' [NICOT; CEV, REB], 'to deal treacherously' [BDB; Coh, Keil; KJV NASB], 'to act treacherously' [BDB; JPS], 'to act faithlessly' [Gla], 'to be treacherous' [Mer], 'to break faith' [NIV, NJB]. This verb is also translated with longer phrases: 'to break one's promise to be faithful to his wife' [TEV], 'not to remain loyal to one's wife' [NLT].

QUESTION—What accounts for the variety of translations of שׂנא *śānē'* 'he hated'?

1. This verb, although bearing in the MT the vowel points for 3rd mas. sg. Qal perf. 'he hated' (with the nuance of 'and still hates'), is assumed by most modern commentators and versions to signify 'I hate'. One arrives at this meaning either by allowing the repointing of the first Hebrew vowel to give the mas. sg. Qal participle *śōnē'* 'hating', assuming at the same time an implicit 1st. sg. pronoun in the phrase [Keil, NICOT, TOTC], or by assuming that the verb must have originally been שׂנאתי *śānē'tî* 'I hated' (1st mas. sg. Qal perf.) [WBC].

2. Other versions appear to assume the participle *śōnē'* 'hating' as presented above, while assuming at the same time an indefinite subject of the participle and taking the introductory conjunction כי *kî* to signal a condition: 'if': 'if one who hates [his wife] divorces' [proposed by A. van Hoonacker, *Les douze petits prophètes: traduits et commentés* (Paris: Gabalda, 1908); cited in Gla]. Many commentators hold that the Targum and LXX adopt this approach: 'if a man hates' [e.g., NICOT; Abel Isaaksson, *Marriage and Ministry in the New Temple*, Lund, 1965; cited in WBC]. This position is supported by relying on the LXX version as commented on by Theodore of Mopsuestia and Theodoret of Cyrrhus: ἀλλὰ ἐὰν μισήσῃς 'but if you hate. . . .' This LXX version became regarded as the standard Greek version of Mal. 2:16 [Jones]. An alternative LXX version, the one commented on by Cyril of Alexandria and Jerome, reads ἀλλὰ ἐὰν μισήσας 'but if hating. . . .' Thus both versions support the reading of the participle *śōnē'* 'hating' [Jones].

3. KJV takes God to be the subject of שׂנא *śānē'* 'he hateth putting away' [allowed by Mer], although others hold that this interpretation conflicts with the direct speech formula . . . אמר יהוה *'āmar yhwh* . . . 'says the Lord . . .' [NICOT].

QUESTION—What is the significance of שׁלּח *šallaḥ* 'to divorce'?

1. Most ancient Jewish commentators, the Targum, and the standard LXX version (see above) read ἀλλὰ ἐὰν μισήσῃς ἐξαποστείλαν "If you hate, divorce!', where the text suggests שׁלּח *šallaḥ*, the Piel imperative 'divorce!', thus appearing to give permission for divorce. Commentators today point out, however, that this interpretation is contrary to the spirit of Malachi's message [Coh, Jones, NICOT, TOTC].

2. This word is taken by many today as a Piel infinitive signifying 'to divorce', a sending away of the wife, as in Isa. 50:1 and Deut. 22:19 [NICOT and most other commentators and versions], although some commentators in the past have disputed this sense. There are great syntactic problems, however, with using this verb form in the expression 'I hate divorce' [Jones].

3. This word should be repointed as the 3rd mas. sg. Piel perf. *šilleaḥ* 'he dismisses' to accord with וכסה *wəkissâ* 'and he covers' [first proposed by A. van Hoonacker in his *Les douze petits prophètes: traduits et*

commentés (Paris: Gabalda, 1908) and followed by Gla. This rendering is in fact supported by the LXX version as commented on by Cyril of Alexandria and Jerome: ἀλλὰ ἐὰν μισήσας ἐξαποστείλῃς 'but if hating you divorce' [Jones]. Jones also sees conclusive manuscript evidence for the reading 'if hating you divorce' in manuscripts א, A, B, and Q[11].

QUESTION—What is the literal meaning of the phrase וכסה חמס על־ לבושׁו *wəkissâ ḥāmās ʿal ləḇûšô* ?

1. The MT reads 'and he covers over his garment with violence'. Similarly, the phrase is translated 'and who covers his garment with violence' [Peshitta and Targum, supported by NICOT]. If, however, one repoints וכסה *wkssh* as a Piel infinitive *wəkassēh* 'to cover, i.e., the act of covering', as do most commentators and versions, the phrase then reads, 'covering over his garment with violence' [Gla].

2. The phrase is translated 'and violence covers his garment' by many interpreters, following the Vulgate and LXX [NICOT]. This rendering takes 'violence' to be the subject of the verb.

QUESTION—What is the significance of the phrase וכסה חמס על־לבושׁו *wəkissâ ḥāmās ʿal ləḇûšô* ?

1. חמס *ḥāmās* 'violence' stands for overt wrong having been committed, which marks indelibly the culprit [Keil, Mer, TOTC]. The garment is therefore a symbol for one's inner life and character [Keil, Mer].

2. The entire expression might denote doing violence to the institution of marriage: if one takes spreading a garment over a woman as a figure signifying the protection of one's wife (cf. Ruth 3:9, Ezek. 16:8), then covering the garment with violence here would suggest the removal of that protection [a possibility entertained by Gla].

3. The expression might signify doing injustice to one's wife on the basis of interpreting לבושׁו *ləḇûšô* 'his garment' metaphorically as one's wife, as is done in Arabic (cf. Koran, Sur 2:183, "Wives are your attire and you are theirs". [Gla]. But *ləḇûšô* does not bear this meaning anywhere in the OT [A. Van Hoonacker, *Les douze petits prophètes*. Paris: J. Gabalda & Cie., 1908; cited in Gla; NICOT].

4. The expression might signify exposing to public view one's marriage conflict, as one exposes dirt when worn on his garment [A. Van Hoonacker, *Les douze petits prophètes*. Paris: J. Gabalda & Cie., 1908; cited in Gla].

5. The phrase harks back to Mal. 2:13 in signifying the activity of animal sacrifice in the worship of YHWH: Jewish men are sending their first wives away, but they continue to sacrifice animal victims to God, bearing on their garments the bloody marks of their activity. Malachi is here prophesying against hypocrisy [NICOT].

QUESTION—What does רוח *rûaḥ* 'spirit' signify?

See the discussion of this same question in under Mal. 2:15 above.

QUESTION—How may Malachi's strong defense of marriage conforming to God's covenant with Israel be seen to fit into the historical situation of the restoration of the Jews to their land?

It is probable that the cosmopolitan air promoted within the Persian empire led the Jews to more contact with their pagan neighbors and thus to intermarriage. As polygyny among Jews occurred usually only among royalty or the richest people, the taking of a second (pagan) wife would have generally occasioned divorce of the first wife [Gla].

Ezra the scribe insisted that the Jews who had contracted mixed marriages with neighboring pagan women renounce them immediately (Ezra 9–10). Nehemiah made no such demand, but only urged that future mixed marriages be avoided. Malachi presents God as being very much against divorce. But these positions may be harmonized by postulating that these men of God were dealing with different problems. Malachi was insisting that godly marriages, those contracted within the covenant community and at least on an implicit basis of covenant loyalty between individuals, be preserved, for God was very much against the dissolution of those marriages. Ezra, on the other hand, insisted that the mixed marriages be dissolved, as they were injuring the health of the covenant community, which was of more importance than the preservation of such marriages [Mer]. The Jewish community of the restoration appears to have been called to live in much more respect of marriage than the Jews of previous times (although intermarriage was certainly condemned in Exod. 34 and Deut. 7, as well as in Judges 3:7 and 1 Kings 11:4 [Gla]). In this way, Malachi is seen to have stood for the most ideal view of marriage in the OT. There is a NT analogue, found in 1 Cor. 7, to the dissolution of mixed marriages of the restoration. But in both situations one finds the underlying motif that God means marriage to be for life [NICOT].

It is worthwhile to insist that Malachi's overriding concern was not, however, for the institution of marriage as it was presented in the divine covenant with Israel; but rather for Israel's faithfulness to that covenant itself and to the worship practices and ethics conformable to it and thus pleasing to her God [Gla].

DISCOURSE UNIT: 2:17–4:3 (2:17–3:21) [Mer]. The topic is "resistance to YHWH."

DISCOURSE UNIT: 2:17–3:12 [Ksr; NJB]. The topic is "a call to trust an unchanging God" [Ksr], "The Day of Yahweh" [NJB].

DISCOURSE UNIT: 2:17–3:6 [Clen (within the larger discourse unit of Mal. 2:10–3:6)].

Comments on this discourse unit: this paragraph, which realizes the second movement's semantic constituent B' (Mal. 2:17, the topic of which is "complaints of YHWH's injustice") and constituent A' (Mal. 3:1–6, the topic of which is the "coming messenger of judgment"), is a reason paragraph:

constituent B' presents the reason for constituent A'. Constituent A' is composed of four elements or "buildups"; the second, Mal. 3:1b-2, is marked as the most prominent by the use of the imperfect tense, by the use of פתאם *piṯʾōm* 'suddenly', by a chiasm which spans Mal. 3:1 (see the discussion of that verse below), and by the speech margin צבאות אמר יהוה *ʾāmar yhwh ṣəḇāʾōṯ* 'says YHWH of hosts'.

DISCOURSE UNIT: 2:17–3:5 [Gla, Mer, NICOT, O'Brien, TOTC, WBC; NIV, TEV]. The topic is resistance to YHWH through self-deceit [Mer], "the day of judgment" [NICOT], the third accusation [O'Brien], the Lord's coming with justice [TOTC], "a dispute about God's justice" [WBC], "the day of judgment" [NIV], "the day of judgment is near" [TEV].
Comments on this discourse unit: this unit begins with Mal. 2:17, as indicated by the ס following Mal. 2:16 in the Masoretic text. It is equally evident that the unit ends with Mal. 3:5, from the fact that, unlike this unit, the following unit (Mal. 3:6–12) does not deal with eschatology [WBC].

The Jews who had returned from exile were in a difficult and disappointing situation. They were few in number and surrounded by pagan cultures, and still subject to Persian rule. They saw no Messianic age dawning. In these circumstances, their religious life was very nominal, and their morality had declined [NICOT], as they asked why was there no divine judgment on wrongdoing [Gla, TOTC, WBC]. When they asked of God's whereabouts, they did so, not from a spirit which was longing for him to intervene, but from cynicism [Gla, TOTC] which questioned God's justice [KEIL] and which allowed them to excuse their own misdeeds [Mer]. Malachi characterized this attitude as wearying to the Lord [Mer, WBC].

Malachi accused the people of longing for "the Day of the Lord" simply so that they might triumph over their enemies and other hardships. But he pointed out to them that when YHWH intervened, it would be not only bless the godly among them, but also to punish the evildoers, thus purifying the nation [KEIL, NICOT], beginning with the priests and other Levites [WBC].

Some commentators see successive fulfillments of the prophetic elements in this discourse unit. According to this view, there were short-lived fulfillments in the inter-testamental times and in New Testament times, a first primary fulfillment with the coming of John the Baptist and then Christ, and there will be a final fulfillment with the second coming of Christ [NICOT].

Gla sees in this unit a dynamic of YHWH on the move: he comes in Mal. 3:1 towards Israel, and by Mal. 3:5 he is even nearer. If one understands Mal. 1:11 as concerning the end times, then one progresses from a universal vision of all the earth honoring YHWH to a very particular prophecy of a renewed Israel, purified first with regard to the priesthood and then in regard to the general population.

A formal analysis of this discourse unit is:
   (A) Warning—the day of judgment is coming: "judgment" + "come" +
       says Yahweh of Hosts" (2:17–3:2a)

(B) Means—purification of the people (3:2b-3a)
(B') Result—pleasing offering (3:3b-4)
(A') Warning—the day of judgment is coming: "judgment" + "come" +
says Yahweh of Hosts" (3:5) [Wendland]

2:17

You(pl)-have-wearied[a] YHWH with[b]-your(pl)-words,[c] but[d]-you(pl)-say,[e] how[f] have-we-wearied[g] *(him)? By[h]-your(pl)-saying,[i] every[j] one-doing[k] evil[l] (is) good[m] in[n](-the)-eyes(-of)[o] YWHW, and[p]-in-them he he-takes-pleasure,[q] or,[r] where[s] (is) (the-)God(-of)[t] justice[u]?

*TEXT—The MT does not have the direct object 'him'. On the basis of some ancient versions, including LXX, which reads παρωξύναμεν αὐτόν, some scholars add the Hebrew object to the Hebrew text; but in any case, its implied sense is clear from the context [Gla].

LEXICON—a. 2nd mas pl. Hiphil perf. of יגע *ygʿ* (BDB p. 388), (Hol p. 127), (TWOT 842): 'to weary' [all lexica, commentators, and versions except the following], 'to wear out' [CEV], 'to tire out' [TEV]. Most translations employ the English present perfect tense, e.g., 'you have wearied'; Keil and NICOT employ the present tense: 'you weary'.

b. -ב *bə-* (BDB p. 88), (Hol p. 32), (TWOT 193): 'with' [BDB; all commentators and versions]. The proclitic *bə-* denotes here instrument [BDB, Hol].

c. constr. of דבר *dābār* (BDB p. 182), (Hol p. 67), (TWOT 399a): 'word' [BDB, Hol; Coh, Keil, Mer, NICOT, WBC; CEV, KJV, NASB, NIV, NLT, NRSV], 'speech' [BDB], 'talk' [JPS, NJB, REB, TEV], 'prattle' [Gla].

d. -ו *wə-* waw connective (BDB p. 251), (Hol p. 84), (TWOT 519): 'but' [Mer], 'yet' [Coh, Gla, NICOT; KJV, NASB, NRSV], 'and yet' [CEV], 'and' [Keil, WBC], 'but' [JPS, TEV], not explicit [NIV, NJB, NLT, REB],

e. 2nd pl. Qal perf. of אמר *ʾmr* (BDB p. 55), (Hol p. 21), (TWOT 118): 'to say' [BDB, Hol; Coh, Keil, Mer, Gla, WBC; KJV, NASB, NRSV], 'to ask' [NICOT; CEV, JPS, NIV, NJB, NLT, REB, TEV]. All translations employ the English present tense except WBC, which employs the present perfect.

f. במה *bammâ* (BDB p. 553), (Hol p. 184): 'how' [Hol; Mer, Gla, NICOT, WBC; CEV, NASB, NIV, NJB, NLT, NRSV, REB, TEV], 'wherein' [Coh; KJV], 'wherewith' [Keil], 'by what' [JPS], 'whereby' [BDB]. *Bammâ* here expresses skepticism or cynicism.

g. 1st pl. Hiphil perf. of יגע *ygʿ* (see above): 'to weary' [BDB, Hol; Coh, Keil, Mer, Gla, NICOT, WBC; JPS, KJV, NASB, NIV, NJB, NLT, NRSV, REB], 'to tire' [TEV].

h. -ב *bə-* (see above): 'by' [Gla, NICOT; CEV, JPS, NIV, NLT, NRSV, REB, TEV], 'in' [WBC], 'inasmuch' [Mer], 'when' [KJV, NJB], 'in that ye/you say' [Coh, Keil; NASB]. The proclitic *bə-* denotes here instrument [BDB, Hol].

i. inf. construct of אָמַר *ʾmr* (see above): 'to say' [all lexica, commentators, and versions except NLT], 'to suggest' [NLT].

j. constr. of כֹּל *kōl* (BDB p. 481), (Hol p. 156), (TWOT 985a): 'everyone' [Coh, Mer, Gla, WBC; KJV, NASB], 'all' [NICOT; JPS, NIV, NRSV, REB, TEV], 'every' [Keil], 'any' [NJB]. Properly a noun, *kōl* denotes a totality of something [BDB, Hol].

k. constr. mas. sg. Qal part. of עָשָׂה *ʿśh* (BDB p. 793), (Hol p. 284), (TWOT 1708): 'to do' [all lexica, commentators, and versions except the following]. WBC translates 'everyone doing evil' with the phrase 'everyone evil', while CEV translates simply 'evil'.

l. רַע *rāʿ* (BDB p. 948), (Hol p. 341), (TWOT 2191b): 'evil' [all lexica, commentators, and versions].

m. טוֹב *ṭôḇ* (BDB p. 373), (Hol p. 122), (TWOT 793): 'good' [all lexica, commentators, and versions except the following]. CEV and NLT translate this adjective with verb phrases: 'the Lord is pleased with . . .' [CEV], 'the Lord favors . . .' [NLT].

n. בְּ- *bə-* (see above): 'in' [Coh, Keil, Mer, Gla, NICOT, WBC; JPS, KJV, NASB, NIV, NRSV, REB]. The proclitic *bə-* denotes here abstract locality [BDB, Hol].

o. dual constr. of עַיִן *ʿayin* (BDB p. 744), (Hol p. 271), (TWOT 1612a): 'eye' [BDB, Hol; Keil, Gla, NICOT, WBC; NIV, REB], 'sight' [Coh, Mer; JPS, KJV, NASB, NRSV]. The expression בְּעֵינֵי *bəʿênê* 'in the eyes of' is a figure of speech for 'in the sight of, in the opinion of' [BDB]. The expression 'in the eyes of YHWH' is also translated with expressions of thinking: 'the Lord Almighty thinks' [TEV], 'as far as Yahweh is concerned' [NJB].

p. וְ- *wə- waw* connective (BDB p. 251), (Hol p. 84), (TWOT 519): 'and' [all commentators and versions except the following], 'in fact' [TEV], 'indeed' [NJB].

q. 3rd mas. sg. Qal perf. of חָפֵץ *ḥpṣ* (BDB p. 342), (Hol p. 112), (TWOT 712a): 'to take pleasure in' [Hol; Keil, NICOT; NIV, REB], 'to delight' [BDB; Coh, Mer, Gla, WBC; JPS, KJV, NASB, NRSV], 'to be delighted' [NJB], 'to be pleased' [CEV], 'to like' [TEV], 'to favor' [NLT].

r. אוֹ *ʾô* (BDB p. 14), (Hol p. 6), (TWOT 36): 'or' [BDB, Hol; Coh, Keil, Mer, Gla, WBC; KJV, NASB, NIV, NJB, NRSV,(REB, TEV], 'or else' [NICOT; JPS]. NLT expresses an additive relationship by employing a new sentence with no conjunction: 'You have wearied him by asking. . . .' The particle *ʾô* expresses an alternative [Hol].

s. אַיֵּה *ʾayyēh* (BDB p. 32), (Hol p. 12), (TWOT 75a): 'where' [all lexica, commentators, and versions]. The interrogative adjective *ʾayyēh* 'where' is often found in poetry or in prose of an elevated nature, introducing a rhetorical question [BDB].

t. constr. of אֱלֹהִים *ʾĕlōhîm* (BDB p. 43), (Hol p. 17), (TWOT 93c): 'God' [all lexica, commentators, and versions except CEV], 'Lord' [CEV].

u. מִשְׁפָּט *mišpāṭ* (BDB p. 1048), (Hol p. 221), (TWOT 2443c): 'justice' [BDB, Hol; Coh, Mer, Gla, NICOT, WBC; JPS, NASB, NIV, NLT, NRSV, REB], 'judgment' [Keil; KJV], 'fair judgment' [NJB], 'rectitude' [BDB]. TEV employs a relative clause to translate the construct relationship between 'God' and 'justice': 'the God who is supposed to be just'. CEV also employs a clause: 'the Lord doesn't care about justice'.

QUESTION—What is the significance of הֹוגַעְתֶּם *hôḡaʿtem* 'you have wearied'?

This verb generally means to tire out from physical exertion, but it carries a sense identical to its secondary meaning here also in Isa. 43:24, that of exasperating [Gla, WBC].

QUESTION—What is the importance of Mal. 2:17 for the book's structure?

Besides introducing the discourse unit Mal. 2:17–3:5, it also ushers in the rest of the book [Gla].

QUESTION—To whom is this passage addressed?

1. The addressees are the Jewish community as a whole [Mer, NICOT].
2. The addressees are those of the Jewish population who assume that their duties of devotion and worship to God should suffice to ensure that God will prosper them, and who are now judging God's supposed lack of compliance with fulfilling his part of the covenant [M.J. Langrange, "Notes sur les prophéties messianiques des derniers prophètes," *Revue Biblique* 15 (1906), cited in Gla]. Malachi's accusations against the people in Mal. 1:14, and in Mal. 2:10–16, would tend to support this viewpoint [Gla].
3. The addressees are those Jews who have abandoned their covenantal obligations; they are referred to in Mal. 3:7ff [Keil].
4. The addressees are those Jews who still truly fear God; they long for God's justice to be revealed against the wealthy Jews, who have inter-married, promoting pagan cults by such action, and who have reduced many of their countrymen to slavery (Neh. 5). Those who wish to remain faithful to Israel's God are reaching the end of their trust in him, but they are referred to approvingly in Mal. 3:13–21 [A. van Hoonacker, *Les douze petits prophètes*. Paris: J. Gabalda & Cie., 1908; and Ernst Sellin, *Das Zwölfprophenbuch übersetzt und erklärt* (Kommentar zum Alten Testament, Band XII, zweite Hälfte. Leipzig: A. Deichertsche Verlagsbuchhandlung, 1930), cited in Gla, which adopts this interpretation].
5. The addressees are most likely the priests [WBC].

QUESTION—To whom does the phrase כָּל־עֹשֵׂה רָע *kol ʿōśēh rāʿ* 'everyone doing evil' refer?

It refers, not to the overt covenant breakers, but rather to the pagans who live among the Jews [Keil].

QUESTION—What is the significance of אַיֵּה *ʾayyēh* 'where' ?

ʾayyēh occurs in the OT as an introductory word of mocking or cynical questions, particularly referring to one god or another (cf. Mic. 7:10, Joel 2:17, Ps. 42:4, etc.) [J. Halévy, "Le prophète Malachi," *Revue Sémitique* 17 (1909); cited in Gla, NICOT].

QUESTION—What is the meaning of the phrase, אַיֵּה אֱלֹהֵי הַמִּשְׁפָּט *ʾayyēh ʾĕlōhê hammišpāṭ* 'where is the God of justice'?

1. The question calls into doubt God's existence [TOTC].
2. The question does not doubt the existence of God, but rather calls into question his reputation for just dealing [NICOT].

QUESTION—What is the semantic role played by אוֹ *ʾô* 'or'?

1. *ʾô* marks here a syllogism composed of a major premise, a minor premise, and an inference. The complainers claim: (a) God (if indeed he exists) is good (implied major premise); (b) if it is not the case that the evildoers are prospering because of God's approval (minor premise), then (c) God must not exist (inference) [Keil; A. van Hoonacker, *Les douze petits prophètes*. Paris: J. Gabalda & Cie., 1908; cited in Gla]. Clen also views *ʾô* here as marking a syllogism, but one which infers, not God's non-existence, but his refusal to give evidence of his presence.
2. *ʾô* marks perhaps a distributive relationship: some people are saying that God approves of evildoers, and others, that there is no God, or at least no just God. If not a relationship of distribution, then it marks one of alternation: sometimes the people say one thing, and sometimes another [NICOT and apparently most other commentators and versions].

QUESTION—What historical situation gave rise to the people's complaints?

Although the early years of the post-exilic Jewish community had been happy and exciting, as time passed, the people found themselves in increasing difficulty. They were still ruled by Persia; their crops were poor (Mal. 3:11), and social oppression (the upper against the lower classes) was rampant. Religious observances had become increasingly perfunctory (Mal. 1:13; 2:13), and fewer Jews were sincerely striving to follow the ancient covenant (Mal. 2:8, 10). The promised Messiah was nowhere in sight, and the "day of the Lord," when all wrongs would be righted, seemed but a dream. The evil did well for themselves, and thus the question was raised as to whether it was in fact of any use to be faithful to the old covenant [Gla, NICOT, TOTC].

QUESTION—What is the meaning of מִשְׁפָּט *mišpāṭ* 'justice'?

Mišpāṭ denotes not merely justice or fair dealing, but all the activity of a king in the just governing of his realm, ensuring harmony and peace among his subjects and victory for his people in war [Sigmund Mowinckel, *He That Cometh*. Translated by G.W. Anderson. New York: Abingdon Press, 1954; cited in Gla].

DISCOURSE UNIT: 3:1–4:6 [NAB]. The topic is "the messenger of the covenant" [NAB].

DISCOURSE UNIT: 3:1–7 [NASB, NRSV]. The topic is "the Purifier" [NASB], "the coming Messenger" [NRSV].

DISCOURSE UNIT: 3:1–5 [NLT]. The topic is "the coming day of judgment" [NLT].

DISCOURSE UNIT: 3:1 [CEV] The topic is "the promised messenger" [CEV].

3:1
Behold[a]-me (about-to-)send[b] my-messenger;[c] and[d]-he-will-clear[e] (a-/the-)way[f] before[g]-me, and[h]-suddenly[i] he-will-come[j] to[k]-his-temple,[l] the-Lord[m] whom you(pl) (are-)seeking,[n] and[o]-(the-)messenger(-of)[p] the-covenant[q] whom[r] you(pl) (are-)desirers;[s] behold,[t] he-is-about-to-come,[u] says[v] YHWH(-of) hosts.

LEXICON—a. הִנֵּה *hinnēh* (BDB p. 243), (Hol p. 82), (TWOT 510a): 'behold' [all lexica, commentators, and versions except the following], 'look(!)' [NJB, NLT], 'see' [NIV, NRSV], no translation [Gla, CEV, REB, TEV]. *Hinnēh* is a demonstrative interjection or particle [BDB, Hol].

b. mas. sg. Qal part. of שָׁלַח *šlḥ* (BDB p. 1018), (Hol. p. 371), (TWOT 2394): 'to send' [all lexica, commentators, and versions]. The English present progressive tense is used, i.e., 'I am sending' [Coh, WBC; JPS, NLT, NRSV], the present tense is used, i.e., 'I send' [Keil], the future tense is used, e.g., 'I will send' [NICOT; CEV, KJV, NIV, NJB, TEV], and an imminent kind of future expression is used, e.g., 'I am about to send' [Mer, Gla; NASB, REB]. Imminent future is denoted by הִנֵּה *hinnēh* 'behold' plus participle in Hebrew [Mer, NICOT, WBC].

c. constr. of מַלְאָךְ *malʾāk* (BDB p. 521), (Hol p. 196), (TWOT 1068a): 'messenger' [all lexica, commentators, and versions].

d. -וְ *wǝ- waw* connective of the attached *waw* consecutive verb (BDB p. 251), (Hol p. 84), (TWOT 519): 'and' [Coh, Gla, WBC; KJV, NASB, NLT]. The additive relationship is also expressed by a new clause or sentence [NICOT]. The *waw* connective is also translated as an expression of purpose: 'that . . .' [Keil], 'to . . .' [CEV, JPS, NJB, NRSV, REB, TE`]. The *waw* connective is also translated as an introduction to a relative clause, e.g., 'who will prepare . . .' [Mer; NIV]. The clause introduced by this connective is seen as a result of the preceding clause by Clen.

e. 3rd mas. sg. Piel perf. *waw* consecutive of פָּנָה *pnh* (BDB p. 815), (Hol p. 293), (TWOT 1782): 'to clear' [Hol; Coh, Gla, WBC; JPS, NASB, NJB, REB], 'to make clear' [BDB; Mer], 'to free from obstacles'

[BDB], 'to prepare' [Keil, NICOT; CEV, KJV, NIV, NLT, NRSV, TEV].

f. דֶּרֶךְ *derek* (BDB p. 202), (Hol p. 74), (TWOT 453a): 'way' [all lexica, commentators, and versions except the following], 'path' [BDB, Hol; REB], 'road' [BDB]. The phrase 'and he shall clear the way' implies a metaphor which Malachi does not further explicate [TOTC], but which may be understood as the forerunner's task of making Israel morally ready to receive the Lord [Keil].

g. constr. of לִפְנֵי *lipnê* (BDB p. 815), (Hol p. 293), (TWOT 1782b): 'before' (spatial) [all lexica, commentators, and versions except the following], 'for' [CEV], 'in the presence of' [BDB]. *Lipnê*, which functions as a compound preposition, is formally composed of the proclitic -לְ *lə-* plus the construct of פָּנִים *pānîm* 'face'.

h. -וְ *wə-* waw connective (BDB p. 251), (Hol p. 84), (TWOT 519): 'and' [Coh, Keil, Gla, WBC; JPS, KJV, NASB, NJB, NRSV]. An additive relation is also expressed by REB with a new sentence; 'then' [NICOT; CEV, NIV, NLT, TEV], 'indeed' [Mer].

i. פִּתְאֹם *pit̠ʾôm* (BDB p. 837), (Hol p. 300), (TWOT 1859a): 'suddenly' [all lexica, commentators, and versions]. *Pit̠ʾôm* is associated with ominous conditions or imminent calamities [TOTC]. Here *pit̠ʾôm* helps mark Mal. 3:1b–2 as the most prominent element in Mal. 3:1–6 [Clen].

j. 3rd mas. sg. Qal imperf. of בּוֹא *bôʾ* (BDB p. 97), (Hol p. 34), (TWOT 212): 'to come' [BDB; all commentators and versions except the following], 'to appear' [CEV], 'to arrive' [Hol].

k. אֶל *ʾel* (BDB p. 39), (Hol p. 16), (TWOT 91): 'to' [all lexica, commentators, and versions except CEV], 'in' [CEV]. The primary function of the preposition *ʾel* is to indicate motion or direction to or towards something [BDB, Hol].

l. constr. of הֵיכָל *hêk̠āl* (BDB p. 228), (Hol p. 79), (TWOT 493): 'temple' [all lexica, commentators, and versions]. The primary sense of *hêk̠āl* is 'palace', whether earthly or divine [Hol].

m. אָדוֹן *ʾād̠ôn* (BDB p. 10), (Hol p. 4), (TWOT 27b): 'Lord' [all lexica, commentators, and versions]. The primary sense of *ʾād̠ôn* is any lord or master; the word refers very frequently in the OT to YWHW, the God of Israel [BDB, Hol].

n. mas. pl. Qal part. of בָּקַשׁ *bqš* (BDB p. 134), (Hol p. 46), (TWOT 276): 'to seek' [all lexica, commentators, and versions except the following], 'to look for' [CEV, TEV]. All translate with the English present progressive tense, e.g., 'whom you are seeking' or the present tense, e.g., 'whom you seek'.

o. -וְ *wə-* waw connective (BDB p. 251), (Hol p. 84), (TWOT 519): 'and' [Coh, Keil, Mer, Gla, WBC; NASB], 'even' [KJV]. Some translate with a new clause but no conjunction, perhaps in many cases signaling apposition, i.e., that מַלְאַךְ־הַבְּרִית *malʾak̠ habbərît* 'the messenger/ angel of the covenant' is identical to הָאָדוֹן *hāʾād̠ôn* 'the Lord' [NICOT;

MALACHI 3:1   133

CEV, NIV, NLT, NRSV, TEV. Intensified apposition is also expressed: 'yes, the angel . . . is on his way' [NJB]. On the other hand, REB translates 'the messenger . . . is here, here already', presumably signaling a difference between hā³ādôn 'the Lord' and mal³ak̲ habbərît 'the messenger/angel of the covenant'. JPS translates 'as for the angel . . . , he is already coming', signaling, much like REB, a difference between 'angel' and 'Lord'.

p. constr. of מַלְאַךְ mal³āk̲ (BDB p. 521), (Hol p. 196), (TWOT 1068a): 'messenger' [all lexica, commentators, and versions except the following], 'angel' [Keil, NICOT; JPS, NJB].

q. בְּרִית bərît (BDB p. 136), (Hol p. 48), (TWOT 282a): 'covenant' [all lexica, commentators, and versions except the following]. The construct relationship between mal³āk̲ 'messenger/angel' and habbərît 'the covenant' is translated explicitly: 'the messenger . . . will . . . proclaim my covenant' [TEV]; 'the messenger is coming with my promise' [CEV].

r. אֲשֶׁר ³ăšer (BDB p. 81), (Hol p. 30), (TWOT 184): 'whom' (referring to מַלְאַךְ mal³āk̲ 'messenger/angel' [explicit or implied by all commentators and versions]. ³ăšer is a relative particle.

s. mas. pl. of חָפֵץ ḥāpēṣ (BDB p. 343), (Hol p. 112), (TWOT 712a). This noun—or adjective—means 'one who takes pleasure in something; one who has a desire for something' [Hol]. It is also translated as a verbal adjective: 'delighting in, having pleasure in' [BDB]. Most translate it as a verb: 'to desire' [CEV, JPS, Keil; NIV], 'to delight in' [Coh, Mer, Gla, NICOT, WBC; KJV, NASB, NRSV, REB], 'to long to see' [TEV], 'to long for' [NJB], 'to look for eagerly' [NLT].

t. הִנֵּה hinnēh (see above): 'behold' [all lexica, commentators, and versions except the following], 'indeed' [NRSV], not explicit [Mer, Gla; CEV, JPS, REB, TEV].

u. mas. sg. Qal. part. of בּוֹא bô³ (see above): 'to come' [BDB; all commentators and versions except the following], 'to be on one's way' [CEV, NJB], 'to be here' [REB], 'to arrive' [Hol], not explicit [TEV]. The English present tense is employed [Coh, Keil, NICOT; CEV, NJB, REB], the present progressive [Mer, WBC; JPS, NASB, NLT, NRSV], and the future [KJV, NIV]. Some translations add intensifiers: 'surely' [NLT], 'already' [JPS].

v. 3rd mas. sg. Qal perf. of אָמַר ³mr (BDB p. 55), (Hol p. 21), (TWOT 118): 'to say' [all lexica, commentators, and versions except the following], 'to answer' [TEV], not explicit [JPS].

QUESTION—Of what passage is this verse reminiscent?

It is reminiscent of Exod. 23:20, because of the similarity in wording. Indeed, the Exodus situation was similar to that faced by Malachi: in Exodus, a covenant was prepared for YHWH's people. Malachi also speaks of a new covenant in preparation. Both passages speak of an angel/messenger (מַלְאַךְ mal³āk̲) [Gla].

QUESTION—How does this verse relate to the previous verse?

1. In this verse, the promise of divine intervention and judgment is meant to answer the people's questions expressed in the previous verse [Keil]; God's promise of action is meant to meet the people's challenge of his justice [Gla, WBC].

2. This verse does not directly answer the people's claims that the God of justice is nowhere to be found; God's answer to that challenge comes in Mal. 3:5 'I will come to you in judgment' [Mer].

QUESTION—Who is מלאכי malʾākî 'my messenger'?

1. This term, which of course is identical to the name 'Malachi', probably does not refer to the prophet himself, but rather to someone who will appear in the future (identical to the referent in Mal. 3:25) to act as a forerunner of 'the messenger of the covenant' [Gla, TOTC]. The two verses are the only places in the OT which speak of a forerunner to the "Day of the Lord", God's great day of judgment [NICOT] and rule [Gla]. This passage depends upon Isa. 40:3ff and was fulfilled in the person of John the Baptist [Keil, Mer; NIV], in addition, 'my messenger' is identical to 'Elijah the prophet' (Mal. 3:23), identified by Christ as John the Baptist (Matt. 11:10) [Mer]. The idea that a collection of forerunners (see below) is meant cannot be entertained, since (a) there was no prophet between Malachi and John the Baptist, and (b) the forerunner is to come immediately before the Lord himself appears [Keil].

2. This term refers to Elijah of Mal. 3:23 [Adne Kesef, cited in Coh]. Many modern interpreters favor this view. Others propose John the Baptist. Probably the term refers to an ensemble of forerunners, culminating in John the Baptist [NICOT].

3. This term is (probably [Mer]) identical to מלאך הברית malʾak habbərît 'the messenger/angel of the covenant' found below in this verse [Mer; David L. Petersen, *Late Israelite Prophecy: Studies in Deutero-Prophetic Literature and in Chronicles*, Society of Biblical Literature Monograph Series, 23; Missoula: Scholars, 1977; cited in Gla].

QUESTION—What is the significance of ופנה־דרך לפני ûpinnâ ḏerek ləpānāy 'and he will clear a way before me'?

The expression recalls the great roads into Babylon which were leveled and adorned for the triumphal entry of kings and gods. Unlike the pagan gods, whose only splendor resided in their images, YHWH shows his glory in that he rescues his people. The expression also recalls the celebratory worship processions in Jerusalem (cf. Ps. 84:6) [Gla].

QUESTION—Who is האדון hāʾāḏôn 'the Lord'?

1. He is the God of justice referred to in Mal. 2:17 [Rashi, cited in Coh; Keil, NICOT, WBC]. He is co-referent to the 1st person pronoun in Mal. 3:5 [NICOT]. That hāʾāḏôn is God himself is clear from the phrase 'will come to his Temple' [Keil]. He is God, YHWH—although this reference to him is not made as an answer to the people's complaints

of Mal. 2:17 [Mer]. Gla also identifies hā²ādôn 'the Lord' with YHWH (and also with 'the messenger of the covenant'—see below). The word אָדוֹן ²ādôn, when applied to YHWH, refers to his position as ruler over all [Gla].

2. He is the coming Messiah [Kimchi, cited in Coh; Mer]. In a similar passage (Isa. 40:3–5) which speaks of restoring the covenant between Israel and God, Isaiah refers to God as YHWH, a name very much associated with the Mosaic covenant; in contrast, Malachi's use of ²ādôn 'Lord' may indicate his attitude—that Israel had in essence thrown out the covenant, and that if the nation still wanted God to come, he would appear as ²ādôn 'Lord, Master'. This appellation seems better suited than YHWH to the ultimate fulfillment of this passage in Christ's coming [Mer].

QUESTION—What does וּפִתְאֹם יָבוֹא אֶל־הֵיכְלוֹ הָאָדוֹן ûpit²ōm yābô² ²el hêkālô hā²ādôn 'the Lord will suddenly come to his temple' mean?

1. We can assume by it that the people were not satisfied with the second Temple, and that God would add to its glory (cf. Ezek. 43:1–5) [TOTC].

2. This was fulfilled by Christ's appearing in the Temple (Matt. 3:1–3; 21:12–17; Luke 2:41–51) [Mer].

3. This is a characteristic feature of 'the day of the Lord' in the OT. YHWH will reveal his glory and power in his own temple. On this occasion, he will judge Israel, defeat his enemies, and renew his covenant with his people, establishing righteousness in the land [Gla, following G.W. Ahlström, *Joel and the Temple Cult of Jerusalem*, Supplements to Vetus Testamentum 21. Leiden: E.J. Brill, 1971; and following Sigmund Mowinckel, *The Psalms in Israel's Worship* (2 vols; New York: Abingdon, 1962)].

QUESTION—To what do the phrases אֲשֶׁר־אַתֶּם מְבַקְשִׁים ²ăšer ²attem məbaqšîm 'whom you seek' and אֲשֶׁר־אַתֶּם חֲפֵצִים ²ăšer ²attem ḥăpēṣîm 'in whom you delight' refer?

1. They seem to refer to the 'God of justice,' which Malachi says the people were looking for in Mal. 2:17 [WBC]. They are probably ironical, for the Lord's coming will bring judgment, not indiscriminate blessing [NICOT, TOTC].

2. In the eschatological context of this chapter, the phrase ²ăšer ²attem məbaqšîm 'whom you are seeking' concerns ultimately the Messiah, whose coming has been desired for so long [Mer].

3. The phrases refer to the ability of the Israelites to go to the Temple and in worship to ask YHWH for his direction and help (cf. Ps. 24, Hos. 5:6). Once YHWH comes to his Temple, one will again be able to meet him in worship, provided that he is first purified (cf. Mal. 3:2–5) [Gla].

QUESTION—Who is מלאך הברית *malʾak habbərît* 'the messenger/angel of the covenant'?

1. He is the titular or guardian angel of Israel [Ibn Ezra, cited in Coh]. Some modern commentators adopt this viewpoint, remarking that 'covenant' here must therefore refer more to 'the covenant community' of Israel than to the covenant itself [NICOT].

2. Some consider him to be the angel who will usher in a new covenant, as an angel under God's direction introduced the Mosaic covenant (cf. Exod. 3:2; Isa. 63:9) [TOTC].

3. He is an angel who will punish all covenant violations [Rashi, cited in Coh].

4. He is Elijah (cf. 1 Kings 19:10 for Elijah's zeal for God's covenant) [Kimchi and Metsudath David, cited in Coh].

5. He is distinct from מלאכי *malʾākî* 'my messenger', the forerunner promised earlier in this verse. Christian interpretation tends to identify him with 'the Lord;' if one rejects that view, it would appear at least that he is coming at the same time as 'the Lord' [TOTC].

6. He is the angel of the Lord, who often represents God in the OT (e.g., in Gen. 16:7–14, Exod. 3:2–22, and who in fact is only quasi-distinguished from God himself) [Gla, NICOT, WBC; NJB], who in his role is formally identical with האדון *hāʾāḏôn* 'the Lord', i.e., YHWH [Gla]. This is clear from the chiastic structure of this passage, in which the stress is put upon the one coming:

    ופתאם יבוא אל־היכלו (*ûpiṯʾōm yāḇôʾ ʾel hêḵālô*)
    and suddenly he will come to his temple
    האדון אשר־אתם מבקשים (*hāʾāḏôn ʾăšer ʾattem məḇaqšîm*)
    the Lord whom you are seeking
    ומלאך הברית אשר־אתם חפצים (*ûmalʾak habbərît ʾăšer ʾattem ḥăpēṣîm*)
    and the messenger/angel of the covenant in whom you delight
    הנה־בא (*hinnēh ḇāʾ*)
    behold, he will come

    [Keil, NICOT, S.R. Driver, *The Minor Prophets*. CB. Edinburgh: T. C. and E. J. Jack, 1906, cited in WBC]. Another statement of essentially the same position is that here we have two references to God—in the first the Lord will come to his Temple, and in the second, he will appear as the 'angel of the covenant' [Keil]. Christ's coming fulfilled this prophecy, in that the identity of YWHW was revealed (in himself, the Logos of God [Keil].

7. He is identical to *malʾākî* 'my messenger' above in this verse and different from YHWH [Mer; David L. Petersen, *Late Israelite Prophecy: Studies in Deutero-Prophetic Literature and in Chronicles*, Society of Biblical Literature Monograph Series, 23; Missoula: Scholars, 1977; cited in Gla]. This is so for the following reasons: (a) the term מלאך *malʾāk* used twice in the same passage would be expected to refer

to the same person; (b) God (YHWH or otherwise) is never called a
messenger; (c) *malʾak̲ habbərît̲* 'the messenger of the covenant' must
mean one coming to announce a covenant, not a messenger promised by
the covenant or by God; and (d) John the Baptist was the messenger
promised by this passage, as shown by his audience's reaction to his
unwelcome message and by his targeting the spiritual leaders of his day,
who could loosely be called Levites, thus fulfilling Mal. 3:3 [Mer].

Against this interpretation, Gla argues that וּפִתְאֹם *ûp̲it̲ʾōm* 'suddenly'
creates a transition in the verse, allowing 'messenger of the covenant' to
be taken as distinct from 'messenger' earlier on; and that in the OT, an
angel (*malʾak̲*) often reveals YHWH himself, from whom he becomes
indistinguishable.

QUESTION—To what does הַבְּרִית *habbərît̲* 'the covenant' refer?
1. It refers to the covenant of Sinai, which included the glorious presence
   of the Lord among his people, as well as both blessings and curses,
   depending upon whether the covenant was respected or not [Keil,
   NICOT].
2. It refers to the covenant community of Israel (this viewpoint is cited in
   Coh and NICOT—see above).
3. It refers to the covenant with Levi, mentioned in Mal. 2:10, with weight
   perhaps added to this viewpoint by the remarks about the "sons of Levi"
   in Mal. 3:3 [this viewpoint is cited in WBC].
4. It refers eschatologically to the new covenant prophesied in Jer. 31:31,
   pointing ahead to the Messiah (this viewpoint is cited in WBC) [Gla].

QUESTION—To what does אֲשֶׁר *ʾăšer* in the phrase אֲשֶׁר־אַתֶּם חֲפֵצִים *ʾăšer
ʾattem ḥăp̲ēṣîm* refer?

It refers to 'messenger/angel', not to 'the covenant' [all commentators and
versions].

DISCOURSE UNIT: 3:2–4 [CEV]. The topic is *"a day of change."*

3:2

**But[a]-who (can-)endure[b] (the-)day(-of)[c] his-coming,[d] and[e]-who (can be) the-
(one who) stands[f] at[g]-his-appearing[h]? For[i] he (is/will be) like[j]-fire(-of)[k]
(a-)refiner[l] and-as-soap(-of)[m] (a-)fuller.[n]**

LEXICON—a. -וְ *wə- waw* connective (BDB p. 251), (Hol p. 84), (TWOT
    519): 'but' [Coh, Gla, WBC; JPS, KJV, NASB, NIV, NRSV, NLT,
    TEV], 'and' [Keil]. The additive relationship is also signaled by a new
    clause or sentence [Mer, NICOT; NJB, REB].
  b. mas. sg. Pilpel part. of כּוּל *kûl* (BDB p. 465), (Hol p. 152), (TWOT
    962): 'to endure' [BDB; Gla, NICOT, WBC; JPS, NASB, NIV, NLT,
    NRSV, REB, TEV], 'to bear up' [Mer], 'to resist' [NJB], 'to abide'
    [Coh; KJV], not explicit [CEV]. Many translate with the modality of
    ability, i.e., 'can', 'to be able', 'who can resist'. The concrete sense of
    the Pilpel stem is 'to clasp, hold in, contain' [Hol].

c. יוֹם *yôm* (BDB p. 398), (Hol p. 130), (TWOT 852): 'day' [BDB, Hol; Coh, Keil, Mer, Gla, NICOT, WBC; CEV, JPS, KJV, NASB, NIV, NJB, NRSV, REB, TEV]. *Yôm* often refers to the 'eschatological day of YHWH' [Hol], that time when YHWH will defeat all his enemies and establish his divine order for all time to come.

d. Qal inf. constr. of בוֹא *bô᾿* (BDB p. 97), (Hol p. 34), (TWOT 212): 'to come' [all lexica, commentators, and versions], 'to arrive' [Hol]. All translate with a verbal noun: 'coming', except the following; 'when he comes' [NLT, TEV], '(on the day) the Lord comes' [CEV].

e. -ו *wǝ- waw* connective (BDB p. 251), (Hol p. 84), (TWOT 519): 'and' [Coh, Keil, WBC; JPS, KJV, NASB, NRSV], 'or' [Gla]. The additive relationship of this connective in this context is also expressed by a new sentence [Mer, NICOT; NIV, NJB, NLT, REB, TEV]. The two rhetorical questions linked by this connective are conflated into a single statement [CEV]: 'No one will be able to stand up to him'.

f. mas. sg. Qal part. of עָמַד *῾md* (BDB p. 763), (Hol p. 275), (TWOT 1637): 'to stand' [Hol; all commentators and versions except the following], 'to remain upright' [NICOT], 'to remain standing' [NJB], 'to stand firm' [REB], 'to hold out' [JPS], 'to be able to survive' [TEV], 'to stand and face him' [NLT], 'to endure' [BDB]. Most translate with the modality of 'can' or 'to be able'.

g. -בְּ *bǝ-* (BDB p. 88), (Hol p. 32), (TWOT 193): 'at' [Keil], 'when' [Coh, Mer, Gla, NICOT, WBC; JPS, KJV, NASB, NIV, NJB, NLT, NRSV, REB, TEV]. The proclitic *bǝ-* denotes here temporality [BDB, Hol].

h. Niphal inf. of רָאָה *r᾿h* (BDB p. 906), (Hol p. 328), (TWOT 2095): 'to appear' [all lexica, commentators, and versions except the following], 'to become visible' [Hol], not explicit [CEV]. Like the verb בוֹא *bô᾿* 'to come', הֵרָאוֹתוֹ *hērā᾿ōtô* 'his appearing' is a term associated with the "Day of the Lord" [Gla].

i. כִּי *kî* connective (BDB p. 471), (Hol p. 155), (TWOT 976): 'for' [Coh, Keil, Mer, Gla; JPS, KJV, NASB, NIV, NJB, NLT, NRSV], 'because' [WBC], 'indeed' [NICOT], not explicit [CEV, REB, TEV].

j. -כְּ *kǝ-* (BDB p. 453), (Hol p. 149), (TWOT 937): 'like' [all lexica, commentators, and versions], 'as' [BDB]. The proclitic *kǝ-* expresses comparison.

k. constr. of אֵשׁ *᾿ēš* (BDB p. 77), (Hol p. 29), (TWOT 172): 'fire' [all lexica, commentators, and versions except the following], 'furnace' [CEV]. The verbless clause in which this word appears is translated in the present tense (e.g., 'he is like . . .') [Coh, Keil, Gla, NICOT, WBC; JPS, KJV, NRSV, REB], in the future tense (e.g., 'he will be like') [Mer; CEV, NIV, NJB, NLT, TEV]. Fire is used as an image in connection with YHWH's appearances (e.g., Exod. 19:24; Deut. 4), his anger (e.g., Isa. 22, 29; Zeph. 1), and his work of purification (e.g., Zech. 13) [Gla].

l. mas sg. Piel part. of צֹרֵף ṣrp̄ (BDB p. 864), (Hol p. 311), (TWOT 1972): 'refiner' [BDB, Hol; Coh, Mer, Gla, NICOT, WBC; KJV, NASB, NIV, NJB, NRSV, REB], 'smelter' [Hol; Keil; JPS]. The work of a refiner is made explicit in some translations without reference to a human agent: 'a blazing fire that refines metal' [NLT], 'a fire that refines metal' [TEV], 'a furnace that purifies silver' [CEV]. The primary sense of ṣrp̄ is 'to smelt'; a secondary sense is 'to refine' [Hol].

m. constr. of בֹּרִית bōrît (BDB p. 141), (Hol p. 49), (TWOT 288e): 'soap' [BDB; Coh, Mer, Gla, NICOT; CEV, KJV, NASB, NIV, NLT, NRSV, REB, TEV], 'lye' [BDB; Keil; JPS], 'alkali' [BDB, Hol; WBC; NJB]. Bōrît is 'alkali, obtained from soap-bearing plants *Mesembrianthemum cristallinum* (iceplant)' [Hol], employed in washing garments, etc. [BDB].

n. mas. pl. Piel part. of כָּבַס kḇs (BDB p. 460), (Hol p. 151), (TWOT 946): 'fuller' [BDB; Coh, Gla, WBC; JPS, KJV, NASB, NJB, NRSV, REB], 'launderer' [NICOT; NIV], 'washer' [Keil], 'washerman' [Mer]. Some employ a more functional description of the soap instead of literally translating בֹּרִית מְכַבְּסִים bōrît məkabbəsîm 'fuller's soap': 'strong soap that whitens clothes' [NLT], 'strong soap' [TEV], 'strong soap in a washbasin' [CEV]. Kḇs means to wash clothes, etc., by treading upon them or beating them [BDB, Hol].

QUESTION—What is the discourse role of this verse?

It is the result of Mal. 3:1; the coming of the referent of the preceding verse will result in the inability of anyone to resist him [Clen].

QUESTION—What is the general theme of this verse?

It is that God's coming is not something to be lightly desired, for it will be painful and very momentous [NICOT], impossible for anyone to endure [WBC]. It describes the purification which will result from YHWH's arrival among his people [Gla].

QUESTION—Whom does this verse concern?

1. The Levites first and then all the covenant community, who will be purified [Coh].

2. The Levites (including the priests), who are the special objects of purification [Mer].

QUESTION—To whom do the possessive suffixes 'his' refer?

1. They refer to the Lord or Angel of 3:1 (who are the same person) [Keil, NICOT].

2. They refer to the human Messenger of the Covenant of Mal. 3:1, i.e., John the Baptist in the NT, who will do his purifying work before YHWH comes [Mer].

QUESTION—What kind of questions are the two questions in this verse?

1. They are rhetorical questions, whose answer is understood to be 'no one' [Keil, NICOT].

2. They are rhetorical questions, with the understood answer to be 'only those who revere YHWH' [Gla].

QUESTION—What is the imagery of the second rhetorical question?
1. The imagery is one of who does not fall in battle but rather who holds his own in a courtroom [TOTC].
2. The imagery is one of those who have allowed YHWH to purify themselves and who are thus able to present themselves before him in worship and prayer (cf. Pss. 15, 24) [Gla].

QUESTION—What is the point of the two similes in this verse?
Both similes indicate that God will make his covenant people morally better [NICOT]. The first simile depicts a metalworker carefully watching as his fire destroys the impurities in the silver [Gla, NICOT, WBC]. The silver is completely refined when the smelter can see his own reflection in it [TOTC; A. Robinson, "God the Refiner of Silver", *Catholic Biblical Quarterly* 11 (1949) 188–190; cited in WBC]. The second simile depicts the strong cleansing action of crude but powerful alkali or lye [Keil, Gla]. These similes depict the ministry of John the Baptist; he was to refine that part of the covenant people who would accept such a ministry, that they would become ready for the Lord's coming (Matt. 3:10–11a. In contrast to this ministry, YHWH's coming would bring judgment upon the rest of the people (Matt. 3:11b-12) [Mer].

The two similes are related in that alkali could also be applied to the smelting process to enable the metal to melt quickly. The alkali also served as a catalyst in the purifying process, helping to separate dross from silver [Gla].

3:3
And[a]-he-will-sit[b] refining[c] and-purifying[d] silver,[e] and[f]-he-will-purify[g] (the-)sons(-of)[h] Levi,[i] and[j]-he-will-refine[k] them as-gold[l] and-as-silver,[m] and[n]-they-will-be[o] to[p]-YHWH bringers(-of)[q] offering(s)[r] in[s]-righteousness.[t]

LEXICON—a. -וְ *wə- waw* connective of the attached *waw* consecutive verb (BDB p. 251), (Hol p. 84), (TWOT 519): 'and' [Coh, Keil, Gla, WBC; KJV, NASB. An additive relation is also expressed with a new clause or sentence [Mer, NICOT; CEV, JPS, NIV, NJB, NLT, NRSV, REB, TEV].

b. 3rd mas. sg. Qal perf. *waw* consecutive of יָשַׁב *yšb* (BDB p. 442), (Hol p. 146), (TWOT 922): 'to sit' [BDB, Hol; Coh, Keil, Gla, NICOT, WBC; KJV, NASB, NIV, NRSV], 'to take one's seat' [NJB, REB], 'to act like' [JPS], 'to act as' [Mer], 'to come to judge like' [TEV], 'to sit and judge' [NLT], not explicit [CEV]. All employ the future tense in English, except NICOT, which employs the present tense. The verb recalls YHWH's sitting as a judge in Ps. 99 [Gla].

c. mas sg. Piel part. of צָרַף *ṣrp* (BDB p. 864), (Hol p. 311), (TWOT 1972): 'to refine' [BDB, Hol; Coh, Mer, Gla, NICOT, WBC; KJV, NIV, NJB, NLT, NRSV, TEV], 'to smelt' [Hol; Keil; JPS, NASB], 'to test' [REB], not explicit [CEV]. The primary sense of *ṣrp* is 'to smelt'; a secondary sense is 'to refine' [Hol].

d. mas. sg. Piel part. of טֹהֵר ṭhr (BDB p. 372), (Hol p. 122), (TWOT 792): 'to purify' [BDB; Coh, Keil, Mer, Gla, NICOT, WBC; KJV, NASB, NIV, NJB, NRSV, REB, TEV], 'to purge' [JPS]. This participle is also translated by a phrase making explicit the work of a silversmith: 'watching closely as the dross is burned away' [NLT], not explicit [CEV]. The primary sense of the Piel stem of ṭhr is 'to cleanse, purify' in a physical manner [BDB], 'to sweep clean, scour' [Hol].

e. כֶּסֶף kesep̄ (BDB p. 494), (Hol p. 162), (TWOT 1015a): 'silver' (the metal) [all lexica, commentators, and versions except the following], not explicit [CEV, NJB, REB].

f. -ו wə- waw connective of the attached waw consecutive verb (BDB p. 251), (Hol p. 84), (TWOT 519): 'and' [Coh, Keil, Gla, NICOT, WBC; JPS, KJV, NASB, NRSV]. The additive relationship is also expressed by a new clause or sentence: [NICOT; NIV, NJB, NLT, REB].

g. 3rd mas. sg. Piel perf. waw consecutive of טֹהֵר ṭhr (see above): 'to purify' [BDB; all commentators and versions except the following], 'to cleanse' [Gla].

h. pl. constr. of בֵּן bēn (BDB p. 119), (Hol p. 42), (TWOT 254): 'son' [BDB, Hol; Coh, Gla, WBC; KJV, NASB, NJB], 'child' [Keil], 'descendant' [BDB; CEV, JPS, NRSV].

i. לֵוִי lēwî (BDB p. 532), (Hol p. 174), (TWOT 1093): 'Levi' [BDB, Hol; Coh, WBC; CEV, JPS, KJV, NASB, NJB, NRSV]. The phrase בְּנֵי־לֵוִי bənê lēwî 'the sons of Levi' is also translated 'the Levites' [Mer, NICOT; NIV, NLT, REB], 'the priests' [TEV].

j. -ו wə- waw connective of the attached waw consecutive verb (BDB p. 251), (Hol p. 84), (TWOT 519): 'and' [Coh, Keil, Gla, WBC; JPS, KJV, NASB, NIV, NJB, NRSV, REB]. This connective is made to introduce a new independent clause [NICOT]. This connective is also made to introduce a subordinate clause, perhaps indicating manner or means: with 'refining' [NLT], with 'as a metalworker refines' [TEV].

k. 3rd mas sg. Piel perf. waw consecutive of זָקַק zqq (BDB p. 279), (Hol p. 91), (TWOT 576): 'to refine' [all lexica, commentators, and versions except the following], 'to purge' [Coh; KJV], 'to strain' [WBC], 'to purify' [BDB], no translation [CEV]. The primary sense of the Qal stem of zqq is 'to strain out, filter'; the Piel stem denotes the smelting of metals, for the impurities remain in the crucible, while the refined metal flows away [Keil].

l. זָהָב zāhāḇ (BDB p. 263), (Hol p. 87), (TWOT 529a): 'gold' [all lexica, commentators, and versions].

m. כֶּסֶף kesep̄ (see above): 'silver' [all lexica, commentators, and versions].

n. -ו wə- waw connective of the attached waw consecutive verb (see above): 'and' [Coh, Gla, WBC]; 'until [NRSV]; 'that' (indicating purpose or result) [Keil; KJV, NLT], 'so that' [JPS, NASB, NJB, TEV]; 'then' (indicating chronology or perhaps consequence) [Mer, NICOT; CEV, NIV], 'and so' [REB].

o. 3rd pl. Qal perf. *waw* consecutive of הָיָה *hyh* (BDB p. 224), (Hol p. 78), (TWOT 491): 'to be' [Coh], 'to become' [WBC]. This verb is also translated with a modality of potential: 'they will be fit to bring' [REB]. All of these translations employ the English future tense.

p. -לְ *lə-* (BDB p. 510), (Hol p. 167), (TWOT 1063): 'to/unto' [Coh, Keil, Mer, Gla, NICOT, WBC; CEV, KJV, NASB, NJB, NLT, NRSV, REB, TEV]. This relationship is also expressed as possession: 'the Lord will have' [NIV]. The proclitic *lə-* here introduces a dative of advantage.

q. mas. pl. Hiphil part. constr. of נָגַשׁ *ngš* (BDB p. 620), (Hol p. 227), (TWOT 1297): 'to bring' [BDB; CEV, NIV, REB, TEV], 'to offer' [Hol; Coh, Keil, Mer, Gla, WBC; KJV, NLT], 'to present' [NICOT; JPS, NASB, NRSV]. NLT adds 'once again', making explicit its understanding that this new condition will not be the for the first time. WBC employs a nominal construction: 'offerer'.

r. מִנְחָה *minḥâ* (BDB p. 585), (Hol p. 202), (TWOT 1214a): 'offering' [BDB, Hol; Coh, Gla, Mer, NICOT, WBC; CEV, JPS, KJV, NASB, NIV, NRSV, REB, TEV], 'sacrifice' [Hol; Keil; NLT].

s. -בְּ *bə-* (BDB p. 88), (Hol p. 32), (TWOT 193): 'in' [Coh, Keil, Gla; JPS, KJV, NASB, NIV, NRSV], 'with' [NJB]. The proclitic *bə-* denotes here character or circumstance [BDB, Hol].

t. צְדָקָה *ṣəḏāqâ* (BDB p. 842), (Hol p. 303), (TWOT 1879b): 'righteousness' [BDB, Hol; Coh, Keil; JPS, KJV, NASB, NIV, NRSV], 'uprightness' [NJB]. This noun is also translated as an adjective qualifying 'offering' or some similar word: 'righteous' [Mer, WBC], 'right' [NICOT], 'acceptable' [NLT], 'proper' [CEV]; and as a noun phrase: 'right kind of' [TEV]. The notion of *ṣəḏāqâ* is also expressed by a modality: 'they will be fit to bring offerings' [REB]. *Ṣəḏāqâ* is related to צַדִּיק *ṣaddîq* 'a thing examined and found to be in order, right' [Hol. p. 303], 'conforming to a standard' [Gla]. Among the main semantic domains of *ṣəḏāqâ* are (a) the standard of conduct required by YHWH of the members of the covenant community among themselves; (b) the equal standing of all the members in the community's law; and (c) the obedience to YHWH which is to characterize the community [TWOT].

QUESTION—Who is the agent in the first part of this verse?

1. It is YHWH [NICOT] or at least his angel, by whom he often reveals himself in the OT [Keil].

2. It is 'the messenger of the covenant', i.e., John the Baptist [Mer].

QUESTION—Who are בְּנֵי־לֵוִי *bənê lēwî* 'the sons of Levi'?

They are the Levites, who, including the priests, are at God's service in the temple, to which YWHW will come. The purification process will begin with them [Eliezer of Beaugency, cited in Coh; Keil, Gla, NICOT, TOTC] because they serve to mediate the relationship between God and the other

Israelites. The whole people will, however, be eventually included, as made clear in Mal. 3:4 [Gla, NICOT].

The significance of the phrase 'the sons of Levi' is that YHWH will purify the priesthood so that it will once again be like the Levites of old, instead of like the actual corrupt priests [Gla].

QUESTION—Of what does the purification process consist?

It consists of both ridding the Levites and the nation as a whole of those members who refuse the ministry of God, and rendering the remainder acceptable to God [Keil]. In this second part of the process, God is at work among the Levites and priests in order to fit them for his own purposes, just as the artisan, who, after having smelted and refined the precious metal, continues on to fashion beautiful objects with it [Gla].

QUESTION—What is the discourse function of the last part of this verse וְהָיוּ לַיהוה מַגִּישֵׁי מִנְחָה בִּצְדָקָה *wəhāyû layhwy maggîšê minḥ bi ṣdāq* and-they-will-be to-YHWH offerers(-of) offering(s) in-righteousness' and all of the following verse?

It is that of result; the cause is the first part of this verse [Clen, NICOT]. This phrase has a periphrastic or indirect syntactic structure, intended to connote continuous action: the purified people will continuously offer sacrifices in the way described [Keil].

QUESTION—What are the connotations of the phrase מִנְחָה בִּצְדָקָה *minḥâ biṣdāqâ* 'offerings in righteousness'?

1. The phrase denotes sacrifices which are the same as what has always traditionally been offered since they are conformable to the what was prescribed [Coh, WBC], as in Ps. 51:19, and which are conformable to the ideal [WBC] because those who offer them are pure in character [Coh].

2. The phrase denotes only the pure character of those who offer the sacrifices in question [Keil]. Such a state would be achieved in the Jewish priests who believed in Jesus, the Messiah [Mer].

3. The phrase denotes only the right way of sacrificing, i.e., the sacrifices will be presented in the manner which the Mosaic Law had set forth [NICOT].

4. A traditional Roman Catholic interpretation is that this phrase foretells the institution of the Mass [Nicot].

3:4

And[a]- (the-)offering(-of)[b] Judah[c] and-Jerusalem -will-be-pleasing[d] to-YHWH as[e](-in-the)days[f] of-old[g] and-as(in-the)years[h] gone-past.[i]

LEXICON—a. -וְ *wə- waw* connective of the attached *waw* consecutive verb (BDB p. 251), (Hol p. 84), (TWOT 519): 'and' [Keil, Mer, NICOT, WBC], 'then' [Gla; CEV, JPS, KJV, NASB, NIV, NJB, NLT, NRSV, TEV], 'thus' [REB].

b. constr. of מנחה *minḥâ* (BDB p. 585), (Hol p. 202), (TWOT 1214a): 'offering' [all lexica, commentators, and versions except the following], 'sacrifice' [Hol; Keil].

c. יהודה *yəhûḏâ* (BDB p. 397), (Hol p. 130), (TWOT 850c): 'Judah' [all lexica, commentators, and versions]. Some make explicit the understanding that the text is referring to inhabitants of these places: 'the people of Judah and Jerusalem' [CEV, NLT, TEV].

d. 3rd fem. sg. Qal perf. *waw* consecutive of ערב *ʿrḇ* [BDB p. 787), (Hol p. 282), (TWOT 1687): 'to be pleasing' [BDB, Hol; Mer, Gla, NICOT, WBC; JPS, NASB, NRSV, REB, TEV], 'to please' [CEV], 'to be pleasant' [Keil; KJV], 'to be acceptable' [NIV, NJB]. In this verb phrase, the dative 'the Lord' is turned around to become the subject: 'the Lord will accept' [NLT]. NLT adds the adverb 'once more' to the expression.

e. -כ *kə-* (BDB p. 453), (Hol p. 149), (TWOT 937): 'as' [BDB; all commentators and versions except the following], 'just as' [CEV], 'like' [BDB, Hol]. The proclitic *kə-* expresses comparison.

f. pl. constr. of יום *yôm* (BDB p. 398), (Hol p. 130), (TWOT 852): 'day' [all lexica, commentators, and versions except the following], 'the past' [CEV, TEV]. NLT conflates the two expressions כימי עולם *kîmê ʿôlām* 'as-(in-the-)days of-old' and וכשנים קדמניות *ûḵəšānîm qaḏmōniyyôṯ* 'and-as-(in-the-)years gone-past', translating 'in former times'.

g. עולם *ʿôlām* (BDB p. 761), (Hol p. 267), (TWOT 1631a): 'of old' [Gla, WBC; KJV, NASB, NRSV], 'gone by' [NICOT; NIV], 'of yore' [JPS], 'of the olden time' [Keil], 'former' [Mer; NJB, NLT, REB], 'ancient time' [BDB], 'long time ago, the dim past' [Hol].

h. pl. of שנה *šānâ* (BDB p. 1040), (Hol p. 378), (TWOT 2419a): 'year' [all lexica, commentators, and versions].

i. fem. pl. of קדמני *qaḏmōnî* (BDB p. 870), (Hol p. 313), (TWOT 1988f): 'gone past' [REB], 'ancient' [BDB], 'former' [BDB, Hol; Gla, NICOT, WBC; KJV, NASB, NIV, NRSV], 'of the past' [Keil], 'of old' [Mer; JPS, NJB].

QUESTION—What is the main point of this verse?
The entire Jewish nation will be affected by the promised purifying in the long run. Its worship of God will become acceptable to him [NICOT], for the purified priests will now be able to ensure that the nation offer right sacrifices according to YHWH's norms [Gla]. Keil sees in this verse something of a figure of speech: it is not that the animal sacrifices will continue in the Messianic era, but that Malachi pictures acceptable worship of YHWH in the only way he knows.

QUESTION—What is meant by 'Judah and Jerusalem'?
Jerusalem is the capital of the nation, Judah; thus the whole nation is referred to in this verse [NICOT].

QUESTION—What time period is meant by כימי עולם וכשנים קדמניות *kîmê ʿôlām ûkəšānîm qadmōniyyôt* 'the days long ago and the years long past'?
1. Probably a wide expanse of past time is meant, given that Mal. 2:10 might well refer to the time of Moses, that Mal. 3:7 refers to both pre- and post-Mosaic time, and that Mal. 3:22–24 refers both to Moses' time and Elijah's time. In fact, Mal. 3:4 might refer to various periods from the patriarchs' time, the judges' time, and the period of the kingdoms [NICOT].
2. The phrase refers to "the good old days," probably during the period of the First Temple [Ibn Ezra, cited in Coh].
3. Although the phrase is not definite, it probably refers here to the Mosaic period, which was characterized by Israel's utter reliance upon YHWH [Keil]; perhaps the Davidic era and the early reign of Solomon are meant here also [Keil].

DISCOURSE UNIT: 3:5–15 [CEV]. The topic is "don't cheat God."

3:5
And[a]-I-will-draw-near[b] to-you(pl) for[c]-judgment,[d] and-I-will-be[e] (a-)witness[f] quickly[g] against[h]-the-sorcerers[i] and-against-the-adulterers[j] and-against-the-ones-swearing[k] falsely,[l] and-against-the-oppressors(-of)[m] (the-)wages(-of)[n] (the-)wage-earner,[o] (the-)widow[p] and-(the-)orphan,[q] and-(the-)turners-aside(-of)[r] (the-)alien,[s] and those-who-do-not-fear[t]-me, says YHWH(-of) hosts.
LEXICON—a. -ו *wə- waw* connective of the attached waw consecutive verb (BDB p. 251), (Hol p. 84), (TWOT 519): 'and' [Coh, Keil, Gla; KJV]. An additive relation is also expressed by a new clause or sentence [Mer, NICOT; CEV, NJB, REB, TEV]; 'then' [WBC; NASB, NRSV], 'at that time' [NLT], 'so' [NIV], 'but first' [JPS].
   b. 1st sg. Qal perf. *waw* consecutive of קרב *qrb* (BDB p. 897), (Hol. p. 324), (TWOT 2065): 'to draw near' [Hol; Keil, Gla, NICOT, WBC; NASB, NRSV], 'to come near' [BDB; Coh; KJV, NIV], 'to come' [Mer; NJB], 'to appear' [REB, TEV], 'to step forward' [JPS], 'to be on one's way' [CEV]. The phrase 'I will draw near to you for judgment' is translated as 'I will put you on trial' [NLT]. All translations employ the English future tense except NJB, which employs the present progressive ('I am coming'), and CEV, which employs a kind of present ('I'm now on my way'). No indication is given in the Hebrew text as to what time this judgment will occur [Keil].
      Since a related noun (קרב *qərāb*) denotes 'struggle, battle, approach with hostile intent', *qrb* here, while denoting 'to come' like בוא *bôʾ* of Mal. 3:1, should be recognized as carrying a nuance of coming in order to fight one's enemies [Gla].
   c. -ל *la-* (BDB p. 510), (Hol p. 167), (TWOT 1063): 'for' [Gla, NICOT, WBC; NASB, NIV, NRSV], 'to' [Coh, Keil; CEV, KJV, JPS, NJB,

NLT, TEV], 'in' [Mer; REB]. (The complements (see below) of each preposition must be considered in order to judge the semantic effect of the preposition.) The proclitic lə- here expresses purpose [BDB, Hol].

d. מִשְׁפָּט mišpāṭ (BDB p. 1048), (Hol p. 221), (TWOT 2443c): 'judgment' [BDB; Coh, Keil, Mer, Gla, NICOT, WBC; KJV, NASB, NIV, NRSV], 'in court' [REB]. This noun is also translated by verb phrases: 'to put one on trial' [NJB, NLT], 'to judge' [CEV, TEV], 'to contend against one' [JPS]. The primary sense of mišpāṭ is 'decision by arbitration, or legal decision' [Hol], i.e., 'the act of deciding a case' [BDB].

e. 1st sg. Qal perf. waw consecutive of הָיָה hyh (BDB p. 224), (Hol p. 78), (TWOT 491): 'to be' [BDB, Hol; Coh, Keil, Mer, Gla, NICOT, WBC; KJV, NASB, NIV, NJB, NLT, NRSV].

f. עֵד ʿēd (BDB p. 729), (Hol. p. 265), (TWOT 1576b): 'witness' [BDB, Hol; Coh, Keil, Mer, WBC; KJV, NASB, NJB, NLT], 'relentless accuser' [JPS]. This noun is also translated as a verb: 'to testify' [NICOT; NIV, REB, TEV], 'to condemn' [CEV], 'accuser' [Gla].

g. mas. sg. Piel part. of מַהֵר mhr (BDB p. 555), (Hol p. 184), (TWOT 1152). This verb is translated as an adverb: 'quickly' [CEV], 'at once' [TEV]; and as an adjective: 'speedy' [Mer], 'swift' [Coh, Keil, Gla, WBC; KJV, NASB, NRSV], 'quick' [NICOT; NIV, REB], 'ready' [NJB, NLT]. The primary sense of mhr is 'to hurry to somewhere'; used with another verb, it acquires the force of the adverb 'quickly' [Hol].

h. -בְּ bə- (BDB p. 88), (Hol p. 32), (TWOT 193): 'against' [BDB, Hol; Coh, Keil, Mer, NICOT, WBC; JPS, KJV, NASB, NIV, NJB, NLT, NRSV, REB, TEV]. The proclitic bə- denotes here hostility [BDB, Hol].

i. mas. pl. Piel part. of כַּשֵּׁף kšp (BDB p. 506), (Hol. p. 166), (TWOT 1051]. This verbal expression is translated by many as a noun: 'sorcerer' [Coh, Keil, Mer, Gla, NICOT; KJV, NASB, NIV, NJB, NLT, NRSV, REB]. It is also translated 'to practice sorcery' [BDB, Hol; WBC; JPS], 'to practice magic' [TEV], 'to practice witchcraft' [CEV]. The practice of sorcery was common in post-exilic Judah [Keil] because of the influence of the pagan cultures in the region [NICOT].

j. mas. pl. Piel part. of נָאַף nʾp (BDB p. 610), (Hol p. 224), (TWOT 1273). This verbal expression is translated by many as a noun: 'adulterer' [Coh, Keil, Mer, NICOT; KJV, NASB, NIV, NJB, NLT, NRSV, REB, TEV]. It is also translated 'to commit adultery' [BDB, Hol; WBC; JPS], 'to cheat in marriage' [CEV]. Adultery appears to have been frequent, if one takes into account the many divorces which the Jewish husbands committed against their Jewish wives [Keil]. It is probable that Malachi intends a second meaning also—one of figurative adultery, the worship of idols (cf. 2:11) [Gla].

k. mas. pl. Niphal part. of שָׁבַע šbʿ (BDB p. 989), (Hol p. 359), (TWOT 2319): 'to swear' [BDB, Hol; Keil, Mer, WBC; JPS, NASB, NRSV], 'to give testimony' [TEV], 'to tell lies in court' [CEV]. This verbal expression is also translated as a noun: 'swearer' [Coh; KJV], 'perjurer' [NICOT; NIV, NJB, REB], 'liar' [NLT]. The sin in question lies not simply in promoting falsehood, but in profaning the name of YHWH by associating it with a falsehood [Gla]. *šbᶜ* means to invoke God as surety for the truth of one's words, at the same time naming a penalty upon oneself in case of falsehood [Hol].

l. לַשֶּׁקֶר *laššāqer* (BDB p. 1055), (Hol p. 383): 'falsely' [Mer; JPS, NASB, NRSV], 'in vain' [Hol]. This expression is also translated as an adjective: 'false' [Coh, Gla; KJV, TEV], and as a phrase: 'to a lie' [WBC; CEV]. *Laššāqer* consists of the proclitic -לְ *lə-* 'to' plus the noun שֶׁקֶר *šeqer* [TWOT 2461a] 'deceit, fraud, wrong' [BDB], 'lie, falsehood, deception' [Hol].

m. mas. pl. Qal part. constr. of עָשַׁק *ᶜšq* (BDB p. 798), (Hol p. 287), (TWOT 1713): 'to oppress' [Hol; Coh, WBC; KJV, NASB, NJB, NRSV], 'to extort' [Gla], 'to take by extortion' [BDB], 'to defraud' [NICOT; NIV], 'to press down' [Keil], 'to cheat' [Mer; NLT, JPS, REB, TEV], 'to rob' [CEV], 'to wrong' [Hol]. The participle governs three expressions in Hebrew: 'the wages of the hired man', 'the widow', 'and the orphan'. Some versions, however, supply in translation one verb to govern 'hire man' and another verb to govern 'widow' and 'orphan', and in some cases, 'stranger' as well: 'to subvert' ('the cause of the widow, orphan') [JPS], 'to mistreat' ('widows or orphans') [CEV], 'to oppress' ('widows and the fatherless/orphans') [NIV, NLT], 'to take advantage of' ('widows, orphans, and foreigners') [TEV], 'to wrong' ('the widow and the fatherless') [REB]. Cf. Lev. 19:13 and Deut. 24:14, 15 [Keil].

n. constr. of שָׂכָר *śākār* 'wages' (BDB p. 969), (Hol p. 352), (TWOT 2264.1b): 'wages' [all lexica, commentators, and versions except the following], 'pay' [CEV], 'hire' [JPS].

o. שָׂכִיר *śākîr* (BDB p. 969), (Hol p. 351), (TWOT 2264.1c): 'wage-earner' [Hol; Mer; NASB, NJB], 'hireling' [BDB; Coh, Keil, Gla, WBC; KJV], 'laborer' [NICOT; JPS, NIV], 'hired worker' [CEV, NRSV], 'hired labourer' [BDB, Hol; REB], 'employee' [NLT, TEV].

p. אַלְמָנָה *ʾalmānâ* (BDB p. 48), (Hol p. 18), (TWOT 105): 'widow' [all lexica, commentators, and versions].

q. יָתוֹם *yāṯôm* [BDB p. 450], [Hol p. 148], [TWOT 934a]: 'orphan' [BDB, Hol;l Keil, Mer, Gla; CEV, JPS, NASB, NJB, NLT, NRSV, TEV], 'fatherless' [Coh, NICOT, WBC; KJV, NIV, REB].

r. mas. pl. Hiphil part. constr. of נָטָה *nṭh* (BDB p. 639), (Hol p. 235), (TWOT 1352): 'to turn aside' [Hol; Mer, WBC; NASB], 'to thrust aside' [BDB; Gla, NICOT; NRSV, REB], 'to bow down' [Keil], 'to take advantage of' [TEV]. Some versions add in translation what they consider to be further implicit objects to the phrase: 'to turn aside one from his right' [Coh; KJV], 'to rob one of his rights' [NJB], 'to deprive

one of justice' [NIV, NLT], 'to steal the property of one' [CEV], 'to
subvert the cause of one' [JPS].

s. גֵּר *gēr* (BDB p. 158), (Hol p. 64), (TWOT 330a): 'alien' [Hol; Mer;
NASB, NIV, NRSV, REB], 'stranger' [Coh; JPS, KJV], 'sojourner'
[BDB, Hol; NICOT, WBC], 'foreigner' [Keil; CEV, NJB, TEV]. NLT
adds some specifics: 'the foreigners living among you'. גֵּרִים *gērîm*
usually referred to the class of immigrant residents in Israel, who were
to enjoy within the covenant community certain rights, although not full
rights as Israelites [BDB].

t. 3rd pl. Qal perf. of יָרֵא *yr³* (BDB p. 431), (Hol p. 142), (TWOT 907):
'to fear' [Hol; Coh, Keil, Mer, Gla, NICOT, WBC; KJV, NASB, NIV,
NLT, NRSV, REB], 'to respect' [CEV, NJB, TEV], 'to have fear'
[JPS], 'to be in awe of' [Hol].

QUESTION—What is the theme of this verse?

1. Although the Jews cried out for divine justice so that God would aid
them as the prophets Ezekiel and Haggai had promised, it is rather God
who will sit in judgment of the wrongs committed by the Jews [Keil,
NICOT, WBC]. Thus v. 5 is another part of God's answer to the plaints
recorded in Mal. 2:17; however, the action referred to here will take
place before the fulfillment of Mal. 3:1-4. For this reason, the *waw*
connective introducing this verse should be translated in such a way so
as to allow this verse to understood by itself, not as being attached to the
four previous verses [NICOT].

2. YHWH will purify the general population, after having purified the
priesthood. This verse, then, stands in logical sequence to the ones just
before, and also shows that Malachi is just as much concerned about the
nation's interior, spiritual health as he is about its God-ordained exterior
rituals. As indicated by the militaristic nuance of קָרֵב *qrb* 'to come
against', YHWH comes to defeat his enemies, those listed in this verse,
and to re-establish right order [Gla].

3. A comparison with NT theology strongly suggests that this verse refers
to Christ's second coming, whereas the first four verses of this chapter
refer to his first coming [Mer].

QUESTION—What is the nature of the catalogue of sins in this verse?

They are mainly infractions of the Ten Commandments or of God's covenant with Israel [WBC]. One notes also that these infractions are all
expressed with participles, thus denoting habitual actions [WBC]. TOTC
notes that Malachi had already preached against some of these sins, viz.,
false oath taking and adulterers, when he preached against unfaithfulness.
Mer, however, sees no particular connection between this list of sins and
the content of Malachi's preaching; here, Malachi seems intent on
characterizing any group of people who have left the true, spiritual worship
of God [Mer]. YHWH showed special care for the widows, orphans, wage-
earners, and aliens (cf. Lev. 19:13, Deut. 24:14, 15, Zech. 7:10) [TOTC].

QUESTION—How should ממהר mǝmahēr 'quickly' be understood?

1. It should be understood as 'expert', in the sense of an expert witness (cf. Ezra 7:6, in which the translation 'skilled' has the same root as this word) [TOTC].

2. It should be understood as denoting swift action on God's part, not only in prosecuting the wrong-doers, but also in witnessing against them, in passing sentence on them, and in executing the sentence [Gla, NICOT].

QUESTION—What was the significance of oppressing widows and orphans?

It was recognized, not only in Israel, but also in much of the rest of the Near East, that widows and orphans needed divine and governmental protection. To mistreat widows and orphans was to flout YHWH's will (cf. Exod. 22:22-24; Zech. 7:10) [Gla].

QUESTION—What is the significance of oppressing aliens in the land?

It is that they were similar to widows and orphans: they were vulnerable to being mistreated by the general population, among whom they lived. The Israelites were to take good care of the aliens among themselves, because they also had once been foreigners in Egypt (Deut. 10:19 [Gla, NICOT, TOTC].

QUESTION—How is ומטי־גר ûmaṭṭê gēr 'and the oppressors of the alien' to be understood?

1. Some versions (NJB, NLT, NIV, and perhaps also JPS) appear to supply the word משפט mišpāṭ 'justice' as the object of the participle 'oppressors', in the manner of Deut. 24:17; 27:19. Indeed, mišpāṭ is perhaps implied in the text, as in Amos 2:7, where נטה דרך nṭh ḏerek 'to turn aside the path' is short for 'to turn aside the paths of justice' [Gla].

2. One should take גר gēr 'alien' as the object of the participle, as in Amos 5:12 [Keil].

3. Other versions and commentators (e.g., NICOT, WBC; REB) adopt for the participle a sense of 'those who turn aside someone from his rights' [NICOT].

QUESTION—How is the phrase ולא יראוני wǝlōʾ yǝrēʾûnî 'and those who do not fear me' understood?

It is seen as the sum of, or the source of, all the other sins listed in this verse [Keil, Mer, Gla, NICOT; JPS, NLT]. This is so, because the fear of YHWH denotes a reverence for him which obligates one to follow his covenant and to adopt YHWH's concerns as his own, including YHWH's social concerns, which are in focus in this verse [Gla].

DISCOURSE UNIT: 3:6-18 [NIV] The topic is "robbing God."

DISCOURSE UNIT: 3:6-15 [NLT]. The topic is "a call to repentance."

DISCOURSE UNIT: 3:6-12 [Gla, Mer, NICOT, O'Brien, TOTC, WBC; TEV]. The topic is "Resistance through Selfishness" [Mer]. The topic is "robbing God" [NICOT]. The topic is the fourth accusation [O'Brien]. The topic is God's desire to bless his people [TOTC]. The topic is "a dispute about repentance" [WBC]. The topic is "the payment of tithes" [TEV].

Comments on this discourse unit: this discourse unit functions parenthetically between two announcements that God will judge, i.e., between Mal. 2:17–3:5 and Mal. 3:13–21 [NICOT, TOTC]. Its role is to tell why God's promised blessings have not yet come [WBC]; it continues the Day of the Lord theme [Gla].

A formal analysis of the unit is:
    (A) Introduction: a divine premise (v. 6)
      (B) Appeal: 'repent!' (v. 7)
        (C) Indictment: 'you have robbed me' (v. 8)
          (D) Verdict: CURSE! (v. 9a)
        (C') Indictment: 'you are robbing me' (v. 9b)
      (B') Promise—blessings upon those who repent (vv. 10–11)
    (A') Conclusion: a Messianic vision (v. 12) [Wendland]

3:6
(a₁) For/Since/Truly[a] I, YHWH,* I-have- not -changed [Coh, Keil, Mer, Gla, NICOT; NASB, NIV, NRSV, REB]
(a₂) Because/For[a] I (am) YHWH,* I-have- not -changed,[b] [WBC; CEV, JPS, KJV, NLT, TEV]

(b₁) and/therefore[c]-you(pl), the-sons(-of)[d] Jacob, you(pl)-have- not -perished.[e]** [Coh, Keil, Mer, Gla, NICOT, WBC; KJV, NASB, NLT, NRSV, TEV]
(b₂) and[c]-you(pl),** you(pl)-have- not -ceased[e] (to be) the-sons(-of)[d] Jacob.

*SYNTAX—Most commentators and many versions treat אֲנִי יהוה *ʾănî yhwh* 'I YHWH' as a complex subject of the following verbal expression לֹא שָׁנִיתִי *lōʾ šānîtî:* 'I, YHWH, have not changed' (see a1 above). Others make a predicate of *ʾănî yhwh*, e.g., 'I am YHWH . . .' (see a₂ above).
**SYNTAX—Most commentators and versions place the pronoun אַתֶּם *ʾattem* 'you(pl)' in apposition with the following בְּנֵי־יַעֲקֹב *bǝnê yaʿăqōb* 'sons of Jacob'; this complex becomes the subject of לֹא כְלִיתֶם *lōʾ kǝlîtem* 'you have not perished' (see b₁ above). REB, however, makes a kind of equative clause out of *ʾattem* 'you' and the following words: 'you have not ceased to be the sons of Jacob' (see b₂ above).
LEXICON—a. כִּי *kî* connective (BDB p. 471), (Hol p. 155), (TWOT 976): 'for' [Coh, Keil, Gla; JPS, KJV, NASB, NRSV], 'since' [Mer], 'truly' [NICOT], 'because' [WBC], not explicit [CEV, NIV, NLT, REB, TEV].
    b. 1st sg. Qal perf. of שָׁנָה *šnh* (BDB p. 1039), (Hol p. 378), (TWOT 2419): 'to change' [all lexica, commentators, and versions except Gla], 'to go back on one's word' [Gla, following Waldman (see below)]. The English present tense is employed , e.g., 'I do not change' [BDB; all commentators and versions except the following]; CEV adds an

intensive: 'I never change'. The present perfect is also employed, e.g. 'I have not changed' [NICOT; JPS; Waldman].

c. -וְ *wə- waw* connective (BDB p. 251), (Hol p. 84), (TWOT 519): 'and' [Coh, Keil; NLT, REB]; 'therefore' [NICOT; KJV, NASB, NRSV], 'that is why' [NLT], 'so' [NIV], 'and so' [TEV]. Gla translates this connective as a topicalizer: 'but as for'. Translation not explicit [Mer].

d. pl. constr. of בֵּן *bēn* (BDB p. 119), (Hol p. 42), (TWOT 254): 'son' [BDB, Hol; Coh, Keil, Mer, Gla, WBC; KJV, NASB], 'descendant' [NICOT; CEV, NIV, NLT, TEV], 'child' [NLT, NRSV, REB].

e. 2nd mas. pl. Qal perf. of כלה *klh* (BDB p. 477), (Hol p. 158), (TWOT 982): 'to perish' [BDB; Mer; NRSV], 'to come to an end' [BDB; WBC], 'to be consumed' [Coh, Keil; KJV, NASB], 'to be destroyed' [BDB, Hol; Gla, NICOT; NIV, NLT], 'to be wiped out' [CEV], 'to be completely lost' [TEV]. REB employs a kind of equative expression, 'to cease to be'. Hol renders *klh* in this passage as 'to remain the same'.

QUESTION—What relationship does this verse have to what precedes and follows it?

1. It concludes what goes before [Clen, Keil (who sees it as explaining the theme of judgment in the preceding verse), also several other authorities cited in NICOT].

2. It begins the discourse unit 3:6–12 [Mer, NICOT], but gives at the same time the reason for Mal. 3:5 [Gla].

QUESTION—How should the introductory כִּי *kî* be understood?

1. It should be understood as a marker of emphasis, e.g., 'truly', because this verse begins a new discourse unit [NICOT]. Against this interpretation, it is argued that the *waw* connective in וְאַתֶּם *wə'attem* 'and you(pl)' probably does not function as a purely emphasizing particle, since it is attached to the emphatic pronoun [Mer].

2. It should be understood as causal, e.g., 'because, for', and as concluding the previous discourse unit [Keil, other authorities cited in NICOT].

3. It should be understood as causal, e.g., 'because, since', and as introducing the discourse unit 3:6–12 [Gla]: YHWH's character remains constant, which explains why he will deal with the present generation as he dealt with its ancestors. Thus one understands a coordination in this verse of כִּי . . . וְ- *kî* . . . *wə-* 'since . . . therefore' [Mer].

4. It should be understood as causal, e.g., 'because, since', and as attached in some way to the preceding discourse unit [WBC].

5. Some versions do not translate it, perhaps because it is seen as an editor's addition [NICOT].

QUESTION—How is the syntax of part (a) of the verse to be understood?

1. It is understood as consisting of two predications: אֲנִי יהוה *'ănî yhwh* 'I am the Lord' and לֹא שָׁנִיתִי *lō' šānîtî* 'I have not changed' [WBC; CEV, JPS, KJV, NLT, TEV, Vulgate].

2. It is better understood as one complex predication, where יהוה *yhwh* 'Lord' stands in apposition to the first sg. pronoun: 'I, the Lord, have

not changed', because this predication balances the following one: 'you,
the sons of Jacob, have not perished' [Keil, NICOT, TOTC; NASB].
That is, the two main predications concern the identities of God and the
Jews, where the verbs are adverbial circumstantial phrases:
    'I am Yahweh, unchanging,
    and you are the sons of Jacob, unceasing' [A.S.Van der Woude,
Haggai, Maleachi. POT. Nijkerk: Callenbach, 1982; cited in NICOT].

QUESTION—What is the significance of the statement, 'I am YHWH'?
It is YHWH's self-assertion at the opening of a revelation of himself or of
his will or judgment (e.g., Exod. 20:2; Lev. 19; Ezek. 7:9, 27) [Gla].

QUESTION—How is the perfect tense of לֹא שָׁנִיתִי *lōʾ šānîtî* 'I have not
changed' understood, and what is the meaning of the phrase?

  1. The verb should be understood as being in a true perfect tense, thus
     relating to past time, but also as currently relevant: God has not changed
     in his faithfulness toward Israel; he still remains loyal to her, for here
     the theme is not his unchanging abstract nature, but rather his unceasing
     fidelity to his covenant with Israel [Keil, NICOT, WBC; NIV], as is
     suggested by the language about statutes and curses in the coming verses
     [Mer]. Similarly, the Targum translates: 'I have not changed my eternal
     promise' [cited in Waldman].

  2. The verb is understood as saying that God does not change his mind
     [Rashi, cited in Waldman]. *šnh* is semantically similar to the Akkadian
     verb *ēnû* 'change', which occurs sometimes in an intransitive
     construction and signifies 'to go back on one's word, renege'. Given that
     the wider context of this passage speaks much of those who violate their
     loyalties, the phrase *lōʾ šānîtî* should be translated 'I have not gone back
     on my word', where this is understood in regard to his sentence upon the
     evildoers pronounced in Mal. 3:5 [Waldman].

QUESTION—How should one understand the phrase בְּנֵי־יַעֲקֹב *bənê yaʿăqōḇ*
'sons of Jacob'?

  1. This phrase is a poetic way of saying 'sons of Israel', i.e., Israelites.
     This phrase receives emphasis in this context, denoting the "true"
     Israelites, i.e., those who have remained faithful to God. For this reason
     they have not perished [Keil].

  2. This phrase denotes the Jews in general [implied by most other
     commentators].

QUESTION—How should one understand the phrase וְאַתֶּם בְּנֵי־יַעֲקֹב לֹא
כְלִיתֶם *wəʾattem bənê yaʿăqōḇ lōʾ kəlîtem*?

  1. By considering the context provided by the following verse, it is
     understood to mean that the Jewish nation continues to exist, in spite of
     the current generation's continuing in their ancestors' rebellion against
     God: 'and you(pl), the-sons(-of) Jacob, you(pl)-have- not -perished'. The
     Jews 'have not perished' only because of God's faithfulness to his
     covenant with them; this refutes the charge of faithlessness brought
     against him [Clen]: he will filter out the evil-doers and thus purify the

nation for his own purposes [Rashi and Kimchi, cited in Coh; Keil, NICOT, WBC]. Similarly, Gla considers that YHWH here is giving the Jews one more chance to repent; he has not changed his mind about the sentence imposed in Mal. 3:5, but has only postponed the punishment: 'you have not perished yet'. That the Jews continue to exist in spite of their sins is the justification for translating the *waw* connective as 'but' [WBC].

2. It is understood to mean 'and-you(pl), you(pl)-have-not-ceased (to be) the-sons(-of) Jacob'. One reads here by implication 'the- rebellious - sons(-of) Jacob'. In contrast to God, the Jews have not ceased to follow the rebellious ways of their ancestors [REB].

3. Similarly to (a), it is understood to mean 'and-you(pl), the-sons(-of) Jacob, you(pl)-have-not-ceased (from your fathers' unrighteousness)' [LXX (καὶ ὑμεῖς υἱοὶ Ιακωβ οὐκ ἀπέχεσθε τῶν ἀδικιῶν τῶν πατέρων ὑμῶν), where LXX combines this verse with part of Mal. 3:7].

4. It is understood to mean 'but-you(pl), the-sons(-of) Jacob, you(pl)-have-not-stood firm' [Wilhelm Rudolph, *Haggai—Sacharja 1–8—Sacharja 9–14—Maleachi*, KAT (Gütersloh: Verlaghaus Gerd Mohn, 1976; cited in Mer]. Against this view, it is held that the verb כלה *klh* probably cannot be shown to have this meaning [Mer].

DISCOURSE UNIT: 3:7–4:6 (3:7–3:24) [Clen]. This is the "third movement." The topic is "Judah exhorted to return to YHWH."

Comments on this discourse unit: this unit's surface structure and underlying notional structure are analyzed as follows (the change element, regarded as the naturally prominent element of hortatory discourse, is noted within the movement's chiastic structure in bold type):

	Surface Structure		Hortatory Notional Structure	Theme
1st constituent	A	3:7–10b	change	**return to YHWH with tithes**
2nd constituent	B	3:10c–12	motivation	future blessing
3rd constituent	C	3:13–15	situation	complacency toward serving YHWH
4th constituent	B'	3:16–4:3	motivation	the coming day
5th constituent	A'	4:4–6	change	**remember the Law**

DISCOURSE UNIT: 3:7–3:12 [Clen (within the larger discourse unit of Mal. 3:7–4:6 (3:7–3:24)].

3:7

From-(the-)days(-of)[a] your(pl)-fathers[b] you(pl)-have-turned-aside[c] from-my-statutes,[d] and- you(pl)-have- -not -kept[e] (them). Return[f] to-me, and-I-will-return[g] to-you(pl), says YHWH(-of) hosts, but[h]-you-say,[i] how[j] shall-we-return[k]?

LEXICON—a. constr. pl. of יוֹם *yôm* (BDB p. 398), (Hol p. 130), (TWOT 852): 'day' [all lexica, commentators, and versions except the following], 'time' [NICOT; CEV, NIV]. The phrase 'from the days of your fathers' is also translated 'like your ancestors before you' [TEV].

b. constr. pl. of אָב *ʾāḇ* (BDB p. 3), (Hol p. 1), (TWOT 4a): 'father' [Keil, Mer, Gla, WBC; JPS, KJV, NASB], 'forefather' [Hol; NICOT; NIV, REB], 'ancestor' [BDB, Hol; CEV, NJB, NLT, NRSV, TEV].

c. 2nd mas. pl. Qal perf. of סוּר *sûr* (BDB p. 693), (Hol p. 254), (TWOT 1480): 'to turn aside' [BDB, Hol; Mer, Gla, WBC; NASB, NRSV], 'to turn away' [NICOT; JPS, NIV, TEV], 'to depart' [Keil], 'to evade' [NJB], 'to scorn' [NLT], 'to go far away' [KJV], 'to be wayward' [REB].

d. constr. pl. of חֹק *ḥōq* (BDB p. 349), (Hol p. 114), (TWOT 728a): 'statute' [BDB; Mer, Gla, WBC; NASB, NJB, NRSV], 'ordinance' [Keil; KJV], 'decree' [NICOT; NIV], 'law' [CEV, JPS, NLT, REB, TEV], 'prescription' [Hol]. *Ḥōq* comes from חקק *ḥqq* 'to cut, inscribe' and thus suggests permanence of decrees [Gla].

e. 2nd mas. pl. Qal perf. of שׁמר *šmr* (BDB p. 1036), (Hol p. 377), (TWOT 2414): 'to keep' [BDB, Hol; Keil, Mer, Gla, NICOT, WBC; KJV, NASB, NIV, NRSV, REB, TEV], 'to observe' [Hol; JPS, NJB], 'to obey' [NLT].

f. mas. pl. Qal imv. of שׁוּב *šûḇ* (BDB p. 996), (Hol p. 362), (TWOT 2340): 'to return' [all lexica, commentators, and versions except the following], 'to turn back' [JPS, TEV]. This imperative is also translated as a condition: 'if you return' [CEV, REB].

g. 1st sg. Qal cohortative of שׁוּב *šûḇ* (see above). The sequence of an imperative followed by a cohortative introduced by a *waw* connective expresses consequence or purpose: 'then I will return to you' or 'that I may return to you' [NICOT].

h. -וְ *wə-* *waw* connective (BDB p. 251), (Hol p. 84), (TWOT 519): 'but' [Mer, Gla, NICOT, WBC; JPS, KJV, NASB, NIV, NLT, NRSV, TEV], 'and yet' [Coh]; not explicit [NJB, REB].

i. 2nd mas. pl. Qal perf. of אמר *ʾmr* (BDB p. 55), (Hol p. 21), (TWOT 118): 'to say' [BDB, Hol; Keil, Mer, Gla, WBC; KJV, NASB, NRSV], 'to ask' [NICOT; CEV, JPS, NIV, NJB, NLT, REB, TEV].

j. בַּמֶּה *bammeh* (BDB p. 553), (Hol p. 184): 'how' [Hol; Keil, Mer, WBC; JPS, NASB, NIV, NJB, NLT, NRSV, REB], 'why' [NICOT], 'wherein' [BDB; KJV], 'in respect of what' [Gla]. This interrogative word is also translated as a verb phrase: 'what must we do?' [TEV], 'in respect of what [sins]' [Gla].

k. 1st pl. Qal imperf. of שׁוּב *šûḇ* (see above): 'to return' [all lexica, commentators, and versions except the following], 'to turn back' [JPS, TEV]. Most translations employ a modality indicating obligation: 'should return' [Mer], 'shall return' [Gla; JPS, KJV, NASB], 'to have to return' [NICOT], 'are to return' [NIV, NJB, NRSV]. Other translations employ a modality of ability: 'to be able to return' [CEV, NLT, REB]. NLT makes explicit its understanding that by implication the people are protesting their innocence: 'how can we return when we have never gone away?' The phrase בַּמֶּה נָשׁוּב *bammeh nāšûḇ* is also rendered 'what must we do?' [TEV].

QUESTION—To what historical period does the phrase לְמִימֵי אֲבֹתֵיכֶם *ləmîmê ʾăḇōṯêkem* 'since the days of your fathers' refer?

It refers to the entire existence of Israel as the nation of God's covenant [Keil, Mer, Gla, NICOT, TOTC]. The Jews' ancestors who received the covenant at Sinai were immediately unfaithful to it. This fact increases the guilt of Malachi's generation, for it should have been very easy to take warning from the nation's history [Gla].

QUESTION—Where is the phrase שׁוּבוּ אֵלַי וְאָשׁוּבָה אֲלֵיכֶם *šûḇû ʾēlay wəʾāšûḇâ ʾălêkem* 'return to me and I will return to you' drawn from?

It is drawn from Zech. 1:3: שׁוּבוּ אֵלַי . . . וְאָשׁוּב אֲלֵיכֶם *šûḇû ʾēlay . . . wəʾāšûḇ ʾălêkem* 'return to me . . . and I will return to you' [TOTC, WBC]. The use of *šûḇ* 'to return' is a classic expression of repentance used by the OT prophets, e.g., Joel 2:12–14; Zeph. 2:3; Jer. 3:22 [Gla].

QUESTION—What is the meaning of the question בַּמֶּה נָשׁוּב *bammeh nāšûḇ* 'how shall we return'?

1. It means 'in what manner . . . ; i.e., how should we show that we have truly repented?' [cited in Coh].
2. It means 'how have we offended you that we need to return to you?' [Coh, Keil, Mer, NICOT, WBC; this interpretation is made explicit in NLT: 'how can we return when we have never gone away?'].

QUESTION—What is the implication of the phrase וְאָשׁוּבָה אֲלֵיכֶם *wəʾāšûḇâ ʾălêkem* 'and I will return to you'?

The phrase implies that if the people repent of their wrongdoing, God will renew the covenant relationship with Israel [Gla], forgive the people [Mer, WBC], and bring his glory back to the Temple [WBC].

3:8

(Can) (a-)person[a] *rob[b-1]/cheat[b-2] God[c]? Yet[d] you(pl) are-robbing/deceiving[e] me. But[f]-you(pl)-say,[g] how[h] have-we-robbed/deceived[i]-you(s)? The-tithe(s)[j] and-the-contribution(s).[k]

*TEXT—The MT reads קָבַע *qḇʿ*, which some take to be the original reading; *qḇʿ* is used elsewhere in the OT only in Prov. 23:23, where it should be translated 'to rob' [Mer, Gla], as there it is clearly parallel to גָּזַל *gzl* 'to plunder' [Mer]. Its meaning 'to rob' is, moreover, well established, especially if one compares Talmudic literature and various ancient versions

[Coh, Gla, NICOT, TOTC]. ('To defraud', essentially a kind of robbery, is preferred as a translation by Keil.) Moreover, the idea of robbery would seem to suit the subject of tithes and offerings much more than a theme of cheating or deceiving [Mer]. Some prefer 'to rob' rather than 'to cheat', as the former is stronger [NICOT, TOTC, WBC]. The Vulgate reads 'to rob' also [NICOT].

On the other hand, LXX reads πτερνιεῖ 'to cheat', which corresponds to the Hebrew עקב ʿqb 'to cheat', which in turn is perhaps a pun on the name Jacob. NJB and NLT follow this reading. Some feel that ʿqb was the original verb in the MT, and that, as it constituted a wordplay on 'Jacob', the scribes, out of respect for the patriarch, changed the consonants around to arrive at qbᶜ 'to rob' [NJB].

LEXICON—a. אדם ʾādām (BDB p. 9), (Hol p. 4), (TWOT 25a): 'person' [TEV], 'human being' [NJB, REB], 'anyone' [NRSV], 'a man' [BDB; Coh, Keil, Mer, Gla, NICOT; KJV, NASB, NIV], 'man' [WBC; JPS], 'people' [Hol; NLT], no translation [CEV].

b-1. 3rd mas. sg. Qal imperf. of קבע qbᶜ (BDB p. 867), (Hol p. 311), (TWOT 1981): 'to rob' [Coh, Mer, Gla, NICOT, WBC; KJV, NASB, NIV, NRSV], 'to cheat' [Mer], 'to defraud' [Keil; JPS, REB]. Some translations employ a modality: of ability, e.g., 'can one cheat God' [Mer, NJB, REB]; of propriety, e.g., 'ought one defraud God' [JPS, NLT, TEV]; of volition, e.g., 'dare one defraud God' [Keil]; and presumably of willingness, e.g., 'will one defraud God' [Coh, Gla, NICOT, WBC; KJV, NIV, NRSV]; not explicit [CEV]. BDB and Hol consider the sense of qbᶜ to be uncertain: it is perhaps 'to rob', if indeed qbᶜ is an authentic word and not just the reversal of עקב ʿqb 'to cheat'.

b-2. 3rd mas. sg. Qal imperf. of עקב ʿqb (BDB p. 784), (Hol p. 281), (TWOT 1676): 'to cheat' [Hol; NJB, NLT, TEV], 'to assail insidiously' [BDB].

c. אלהים ʾělōhîm (BDB p. 43), (Hol p. 16), (TWOT 93c): 'God' [all lexica, commentators, and versions except the following]; not explicit [CEV].

d. כי kî connective (BDB p. 471), (Hol p. 155), (TWOT 976): 'yet' [all commentators and versions except the following], 'indeed' [Mer], no translation [CEV]. Keil seems to regard kî as introducing a phrase which expresses circumstance in the mind of the prophet: 'Dare a man indeed defraud God, that (kî) ye have defrauded me?'

e. mas. pl. Qal part. of קבע qbᶜ or of עקב ʿqb (see above): 'to rob' [Coh, Mer, Gla, NICOT, WBC; CEV, KJV, NASB, NIV, NRSV], 'to deceive' [NJB], 'to defraud' [Keil; JPS, REB], 'to cheat' [NLT, TEV]. NJB employs the modality of attempt: 'you try to deceive me'. Some translations employ the English present perfect tense, e.g., 'you have robbed me' [Keil; KJV, NLT]; many employ the present progressive, e.g., 'you are robbing me' [Mer, Gla, WBC; CEV, JPS, NASB, NRSV,

TEV]; and some employ the present (habitual) tense, e.g., 'you rob me'
[Coh, NICOT; NIV, REB].

f. -וְ wə- waw connective (BDB p. 251), (Hol p. 84), (TWOT 519): 'but'
[Coh, Mer, Gla, NICOT, WBC; KJV, NASB, NIV, NLT, NRSV]. A
formal additive relationship, perhaps providing sarcasm here, is
expressed: 'and' [Keil; JPS]; an additive relationship, intensified with
sarcastic force, is expressed: 'and here you are, asking' [CEV].

g. 2nd pl. Qal perf. of אָמַר ʾmr (BDB p. 55), (Hol p. 21), (TWOT 118):
'to say' [BDB, Hol; Coh, Keil, Mer, Gla, WBC; KJV, NASB, NRSV],
'to ask' [NICOT; CEV, JPS, NIV, NJB, NLT, REB, TEV].

h. בַּמֶּה bammeh (BDB p. 553), (Hol p. 184): 'how' [Hol; all
commentators and versions except the following] 'wherein' [BDB; Coh;
KJV, Gla], 'in what' [Keil]. NLT expresses explicit surprise: 'What do
you mean? When did we ever cheat you?'.

i. 1st pl. Qal perf. of קבע qbʿ or of עקב ʿqb (see above).

j. מַעֲשֵׂר maʿăśēr (BDB p. 798), (Hol p. 208), (TWOT 1711h): 'tithe'
[BDB, Hol; Coh, Keil, Mer, Gla, NICOT, WBC; JPS, KJV, NASB,
NIV, NJB, NLT, NRSV, REB, TEV]. This noun is also translated by a
clause: 'the ten percent that belongs to me' [CEV].

k. תְּרוּמָה tərûmâ (BDB p. 929), (Hol p. 395), (TWOT 2133i):
'contribution' [BDB, Hol; Mer; JPS, NJB, REB], 'offering' [BDB;
NICOT, WBC; CEV, KJV, NASB, NIV, NLT, NRSV, TEV], 'heave-
offering' [Coh, Keil], 'levy' [Gla], 'tribute' [Hol].

QUESTION—How is the phrase הַמַּעֲשֵׂר וְהַתְּרוּמָה hammaʿăśēr wəhattərûmâ
'the tithes and the contributions' to be understood?

1. One should read with LXX the additional phrase μεθ᾽ ὑμῶν εἰσιν to read
'the tithes and contributions are with you', i.e., the people were
retaining their tithes and contributions instead of giving them to God
[WBC]. LXX added this phrase to fill out the ellipsis of the MT
[NICOT].

2. The BHS proposes inserting the Hebrew proclitic -בְּ bə- in front of both
'tithes' and 'contributions', that an instrumental function may be served:
'by the tithes and the contributions'. This proposal follows the Vulgate
and several ancient versions [cited in Mer].

3. The phrase is to be understood as a short answer to the people's
preceding question, deriving much of its force from its terseness [Mer].
The definite articles refer to the funds, crops, etc., which the people
knew they were withholding [NICOT].

QUESTION—What is meant by מַעֲשֵׂר maʿăśēr 'tithe'?

This refers to the donation of a tenth of all produce to God [Mer, NICOT].

QUESTION—What was the historical situation of tithing among the Jews?

Tithing was widely practiced in ancient mid-eastern cultures [NICOT,
TOTC, WBC], but for the Jews it became obligatory under the Mosaic
Law. The tithes were meant for the Levites' use (Num. 8:28) (the Levites
were to tithe for the priests' support (see Num. 18:28) [TOTC]), but in fact

the people also benefited directly if they ate with the priests or Levites at
the place of worship [Mer] (see Deut. 12:4–9 [NICOT], Deut 14:23 [Gla]).
Two kinds of tithes were mandated, the yearly tithe (see Deut. 14:22–27)
and the triennial tithe, which was to be given to orphans, widows, and
foreigners (Deut. 14:28f), and from which a feast was made (Deut. 14:28–
29) [NICOT, TOTC].

This does not mean that tithing was faithfully practiced throughout
Israel's pre-exilic history. In fact, it seems that the relevant stipulations of
the Law were enthusiastically carried out only fitfully, and that often tithing
almost completely lapsed [WBC]. The post-exilic experience was equally
unstable: Nehemiah instituted a full program of tithing among the returned
Jews in Jerusalem, only to find it in ruins on his second visit [Gla, WBC].

QUESTION—What is meant by תרומה tərûmâ 'tribute, offering,
contribution'?

Tərûmâ signifies the people's contributions to the priests from their grain
and other produce (cf. Num. 18:12) [JPS], as well as contributions from
other goods or money gained by whatever means [Gla], and the portions of
the sacrifices which were reserved for the priests' use [TOTC]. Unlike the
tithe, the contributions were voluntary and were apparently destined solely
for the priests [Mer].

3:9

**With[a]-the-curse[b] you(pl) (are) cursed,[c] because/yet[d]-(it is)me you(pl) (are)
robbing/defrauding,[e] the-nation,[f] all(-of)[g]-it.**

LEXICON—a. -ב bə- (BDB p. 88), (Hol p. 32), (TWOT 193): 'with' [Coh,
Keil, Mer, Gla, NICOT, WBC; KJV, NASB, NRSV]. These translate
literally the idiomatic Hebrew phase 'with the curse you are cursed'.
Most other commentators and versions employ more idiomatic
expressions, given in (c) below. The proclitic bə- denotes here
instrument [BDB, Hol].

b. מארה mə'ērâ (BDB p. 76), (Hol p. 181), (TWOT 168a): 'curse' [all
lexica, commentators, and versions], 'malediction' [Hol].

c. mas. pl. Niphal part. of ארר 'rr (BDB p. 76), (Hol p. 28), (TWOT
168): 'cursed' [BDB; Coh, Keil, Mer; KJV, NASB, NRSV], 'inflicted
with a curse' [Hol]. Many translations restructure the Hebrew phrase
'you are cursed with the curse': 'to be under a curse' [CEV, NIV,
NLT], 'to suffer under a curse' [JPS], 'to be greatly cursed' [NICOT].
Some translations make 'curse' the subject, e.g., 'a curse is on you'
[NJB, REB, TEV]. Most translations express an accomplished event or
an enduring state, e.g., 'you are cursed'. WBC, however, expresses a
process: 'you are being cursed'.

d. -ו wə- waw connective (BDB p. 251), (Hol p. 84), (TWOT 519):
'because' [Mer; NIV, NJB, REB, TEV, WBC], 'yet' [Coh, Keil, Gla,
NICOT; JPS], 'for' [KJV, NASB, NLT, NRSV]. The emphasis of the
clause is on the pronoun 'me', attached to this connective [Gla].

e. mas. pl. Qal part. of קָבַע qbᶜ (BDB p. 867), (Hol p. 311), (TWOT 1981) or of עקב ʾqb (BDB p. 784), (Hol p. 281), (TWOT 1676): 'to rob' [Coh, Mer, Gla, NICOT, WBC; NASB, NIV, NRSV], 'to defraud' [JPS], 'to cheat' [Hol; NJB, NLT, TEV], 'to assail insidiously' [BDB]. Some translations employ modalities: 'to try to cheat' [NJB], 'to go on defrauding' [JPS], 'to continue to rob' [Gla]. All translations employ the English present or present progressive tenses except NLT, which employs the present perfect: 'has been cheating'. BDB and Hol consider the sense of qbᶜ to be uncertain: it is perhaps 'to rob', if indeed qbᶜ is an authentic word and not just the reversal of עקב ʾqb 'to cheat'.

f. גּוֹי gôy (BDB p. 156), (Hol p. 57), (TWOT 326e): 'nation' [all lexica, commentators, and versions]. Some translations employ the English demonstrative adjective 'this' instead of translating literally the Hebrew definite article: [Coh, Mer, WBC; KJV, NJB]; others employ 'your' or the phrase 'nation of you' [CEV, JPS, NIV, NLT, NRSV, REB]. Gôy normally refers to the peoples and ethnic groups around Israel, with emphasis upon their paganness.

g. constr. of כֹּל kōl (BDB p. 481), (Hol p. 156), (TWOT 985a). This noun is translated as an adjective: 'whole' [BDB; Coh, Keil, NICOT; CEV, JPS, KJV, NASB, NIV, NJB, NLT, NRSV, TEV], 'all' [WBC], 'entire' [Mer, Gla; REB]. The noun kōl denotes a totality of something [BDB, Hol].

QUESTION—How should בַּמְּאֵרָה bammǝʾērâ 'with-the-curse' be interpreted?

1. It should be interpreted instrumentally, but the identity of the curse is not certain [Mer].

2. It should be interpreted instrumentally, and the curse referred to is specified in Mal. 3:10–12: it called down bad harvests upon the Jews [Coh, Keil, Gla]. This is parallel to Mal. 2:2, which speaks of a ban on the crops [Gla].

3. In the surface structure of the verse's syntax, the word functions instrumentally, but there is no specific curse in mind; rather, the expression 'the curse' evokes, in fact, all attributes of curses in general. Thus, bammǝʾērâ 'with-the-curse' has adverbial force and denotes 'greatly cursed' [NICOT].

QUESTION—How should the waw connective in וְאֹתִי wǝʾōtî 'because/yet-(it is)me' be interpreted?

1. It should be interpreted as an adversative and translated as or similar to 'but' or 'yet' [Coh, Keil, Gla, NICOT; JPS].

2. It should be interpreted as signaling causation and translated as 'because' [Mer, WBC; NIV, NJB, REB, TEV]. KJV, NLT, and NRSV translate 'for', which appears here to be similar to 'because'.

QUESTION—What is the use of the Niphal participle נֵאָרִים nēʾārîm 'being-cursed'?

The participle here expresses an action begun in the past but with continuing effect in the present [NICOT].

QUESTION—How should הגוי כלו *haggôy kullô* 'the-nation all(-of)-it' be interpreted?

Here כל *kōl* is used substantively: 'all of it (i.e., all of the nation)'. Although there are in the OT certain specialized applications of the appellation *gôy* to Israel, this term is generally reserved for the pagan nations [Gla]. Here, however, the reference to Israel as *gôy* (as in Deut. 32:28, Isa. 1:4, and Judg. 2:20) suggests that God in his anger is comparing Israel to a pagan people [NICOT] and is thus rejecting her behavior [Gla].

3:10

Bring(pl)[a] all the-tithe(s)[b] into (the-)house(-of)[c] supplies,[d] and[e]-let-there-be[f] food[g] in-my-house,

LEXICON—a. mas. pl. Hiphil imv. of בוא *bô* (BDB p. 97), (Hol p. 34), (TWOT 212): 'to bring' [all lexica, commentators, and versions].

  b. מעשר *ma῾ăśēr* (BDB p. 798), (Hol p. 208), (TWOT 1711a): 'tithe' [all lexica, commentators, and versions except the following], 'ten percent' [CEV].

  c. constr. of בית *bayit* (BDB p. 108), (Hol p. 38), (TWOT 241): see below for translation. The later prophets seem to normally employ *bayit* as 'temple', which was commonly called היכל *hêkāl* in earlier times (as in Mal. 3:1) [Gla]. The primary sense of *bayit* is 'house' [BDB, Hol].

  d. אוצר *᾽ôṣār* (BDB p. 69), (Hol p. 7), (TWOT 154a). The expression *bêt hā᾽ôṣār* is translated 'storehouse' [Coh, Mer, Gla, NICOT, WBC; CEV, JPS, KJV, NASB, NLT, NIV, NRSV], 'treasure-house' [Keil], 'treasury' [NJB, REB]. NIV translates it as 'temple', presumably since the storehouse was indeed in the Temple precincts. *᾽ôṣār* denotes 'supplies' [Hol], 'treasure' [BDB, Hol], 'store' [BDB].

  e. -ו *wə*- *waw* connective (BDB p. 251), (Hol p. 84), (TWOT 519). All translations express purpose here, e.g., 'in order that there may be' except the following; 'let there be' [JPS, REB].

  f. 3rd mas. sg. Qal imperf. of היה *hyh* (BDB p. 224), (Hol p. 78), (TWOT 491): 'to be' [all lexica, commentators, and versions].

  g. טרף *ṭerep* (BDB p. 383), (Hol p. 125), (TWOT 827b): 'food' [BDB; Coh, Mer, Gla, NICOT; CEV, JPS, NASB, NIV, NJB, NLT, NRSV, REB, TEV], 'provision' [WBC], 'consumption' [Keil], 'meat' [KJV], 'nourishment' [Hol]. This noun is also translated as a phrase: 'enough food' [NLT], 'plenty of food' [TEV]. Specifically, *ṭerep* can refer to a portion of food set aside for a special use, as in Prov. 31:14–15, where the ideal wife reserves for her family a *ṭerep*, a portion of food, after having allotted some food to her servants. Similarly, *ṭerep* here is parallel to מעשר *ma῾ăśēr* 'tithe' [Gla].

QUESTION—What is meant by כל-המעשר *kol hamma῾ăśēr* 'all the tithes'?

כל *kōl* refers to the totality of something when it is in a construct relationship as here. This phrase suggests that the people in general were

keeping back part of their tithes [NICOT]. In this phrase *kōl* is emphasized
in the Hebrew word order [Keil].

QUESTION—What is meant by בֵּית־הָאוֹצָר *bêt hāʾôṣār* '(the-)house(-of)
supplies'?

It refers to the public storehouse, cf. Neh. 13:10–13 [JPS], which, certainly from the time of the later kings—at least Hezekiah [NICOT], if not
before them [Keil]—was actually a repository in the Temple complex [Gla]
for the goods tithed by the people for the priests, Levites, and the poor of
the nation. Nehemiah called the storehouse 'a great chamber' (Neh. 13:5)
and, in fact, revived the system, which had become inactive before him and
which not even Malachi's prophecy had been able to bring to life again
[Mer]. The parallelism of *bêt hāʾôṣār* with בְּבֵיתִי *bəbêtî* 'in my house'
further in the verse allows the inference that the Temple complex could
indeed store voluminous contributions [Gla].

DISCOURSE UNIT: 3:10c–3:12 [Clen (within the larger discourse unit of
Mal. 3:7–4:6 (3:7–3:24))]. The topic is "future blessing."

and[a]-test(pl)[b]-me now[c] in[d]-this,[e] says YHWH(-of) hosts, if- I-will- -not[f] -
open[g] for[h]-you(pl) (the-)windows(-of)[i] the-sky[j] and[k]-pour-out[l] to-you(pl)
blessing[m] until[n] cessation(-of)[o] sufficiency.[p]

LEXICON—a. -וְ *wə- waw* connective (BDB p. 251), (Hol p. 84), (TWOT
519): 'and' [Coh, Keil, Mer, Gla, NICOT, WBC; JPS, KJV, NASB,
NRSV]. An additive relationship is also expressed by a new clause or
sentence [CEV, NIV, NJB, NLT, REB, TEV].

   b. mas. pl. Qal imv. of בָּחַן *bḥn* (BDB p. 103), (Hol p. 37), (TWOT 230):
'to test' [BDB; Mer, Gla, NICOT, WBC; NASB, NIV], 'to prove'
[BDB; Keil; KJV], 'to put to the test' [Hol; JPS, NJB, NRSV, TEV],
'to put to the proof' [REB], 'to try' [BDB; Coh]. Some make explicit the
idea that these words constitute a challenge: 'I challenge you to put me
to the test' [CEV], 'Try it! Let me prove it to you!' [NLT].

   c. נָא *nāʾ* (BDB p. 609), (Hol p. 223), (TWOT 1269): 'now' [Coh, Keil,
Mer; KJV, NASB, NJB], 'please' [WBC]; NLT adds a clause: 'try it!';
not explicit [Gla, NICOT; CEV, JPS, NIV, NRSV, REB, TEV]. The
particle *nāʾ* expresses urgency [Hol], exhortation or pleading [BDB].

   d. -בְּ *bə-* (BDB p. 88), (Hol p. 32), (TWOT 193): 'in' [Mer, NICOT,
WBC; NASB, NIV], 'through' [Gla]. The proclitic *bə-* denotes here
abstract locality [BDB, Hol].

   e. fem. sg. of זֶה *zeh* (BDB p. 260), (Hol p. 86), (TWOT 528): 'this'
[Mer, NICOT; NASB, NIV], 'these things' [WBC]. The phrase 'in this'
is also restructured by many translations: 'herewith' [Coh, Keil; KJV],
'thus' [JPS, NRSV], 'like this' [NJB]. Translation not explicit [CEV,
NLT, REB, TEV].

   f. אִם־לֹא *ʾim lōʾ* (BDB p. 49), (Hol p. 19). Many translations employ
'if . . . not' for this conjunction, e.g., 'test me, if I will not open . . .'

[Coh, Keil, Mer, NICOT, WBC; KJV, NASB, NIV, NJB, NRSV, REB]. Some add the verb 'to see', e.g., 'see if I do not open' [NIV, NJB, NRSV, REB]. Others restructure the rhetorical conditional into a future statement, e.g., 'I will open' [Gla; CEV, JPS, NLT, TEV]. Some view *ʾim lōʾ* as introducing an apodosis (a 'then' statement), attaching it to an implied protasis (an 'if' condition). The implied protasis is inferred from the preceding commands 'bring the full tithe' and 'test me'; it, together with the apodosis, might be translated, 'if you test my promise by bringing all the tithe with devoted hearts into my treasury, then I will open the windows of heaven. . . .' [Gla]. The use of *ʾim lōʾ* with the imperfect in this context produces the format of an oath in Hebrew, most likely investing this clause with even more prominence than the following clauses which feature *waw* consecutive perfect forms [Clen]. Treated as a compound conjunction, *ʾim lōʾ* introduces indirect questions, e.g., 'whether', 'whether . . . if not' [Hol].

g. 1st sg. Qal imperf. of פתח *ptḥ* (BDB p. 834), (Hol p. 300), (TWOT 1854): 'to open' [all lexica, commentators, and versions].

h. -לְ *lǝ-* (BDB p. 510), (Hol p. 167), (TWOT 1063): 'for' [Gla, NICOT, WBC; JPS, NASB, NJB, NLT, NRSV], 'to' [Mer]. The proclitic *lǝ-* here introduces a dative of advantage [BDB, Hol].

i. constr. of אֲרֻבָּה *ʾărubbâ* (BDB p. 70), (Hol p. 26), (TWOT 156d): 'window' [Hol; Coh, Mer, NICOT, WBC; CEV, KJV, NASB, NLT, NRSV, REB, TEV], 'sluice' [BDB; Keil, Gla], 'floodgate' [JPS, NIV, NJB]. *ʾărubbâ*, although denoting in its primary sense a window, here refers to openings in the sky which were presumed to open in order for the waters above the sky to descend in the form of rain [Hol].

j. שָׁמַיִם *šāmayim* (BDB p. 1029), (Hol p. 375), (TWOT 2407a): 'sky' [BDB, Hol; JPS, REB], 'heaven' [Hol; Coh, Keil, Mer, NICOT, WBC; CEV, KJV, NASB, NIV, NJB, NLT, NRSV, TEV]. The construct relationship between אֲרֻבּוֹת *ʾărubbôt* 'windows' and הַשָּׁמַיִם *haššāmayim* 'the sky' is expressed with 'of', e.g., 'the windows of the sky' by all commentators and versions except the following; REB employs 'in': 'windows in the sky'.

k. -ו *wǝ-* *waw* connective of the attached *waw* consecutive verb (BDB p. 251), (Hol p. 84), (TWOT 519): 'and' [all commentators and versions].

l. 1st sg. Hiphil perf. *waw* consecutive of רִיק *rîq* (BDB p. 937), (Hol p. 339), (TWOT 2161): 'to pour out' [BDB, Hol; Coh, Keil, Mer, Gla, NICOT, WBC; KJV, NASB, NJB, NIV, NLT, TEV], 'to pour down' [BDB; JPS, NRSV], 'to pour' [REB], 'to flood' [CEV].

m. בְּרָכָה *bǝrākâ* (BDB p. 139), (Hol p. 50), (TWOT 285b): 'blessing' [all lexica, commentators, and versions except the following], 'good things' [TEV]. *Bǝrākâ* may denote the words of a blessing, or the blessing itself as it works good, or a gift that comes with a blessing [Hol].

n. עַד ʿaḏ (BDB p. 723), (Hol p. 264), (TWOT 1565c): 'until' [BDB, Hol; NASB].

o. constr. of בְּלִי bəlî (BDB p. 115), (Hol p. 40), (TWOT 246e). Bəlî is, properly speaking, a noun denoting 'cessation' [Hol]; here, however, it functions adverbially expressing negation [BDB, Hol].

p. דִּי ḏāy (BDB p. 191), (Hol p. 70), (TWOT 425): "sufficiency' [BDB, Hol], 'enough' [BDB, Hol]. The phrase עַד־בְּלִי־דִי ʿaḏ bəlî ḏāy is translated by adjectives: 'overflowing' [NICOT; NRSV], 'abundant' [NJB]; and by phrases: 'in abundance' [TEV], 'to superabundance' [Keil], 'until nothing is lacking' [WBC], 'that there shall be more than sufficiency' [Coh], 'until there is no room' [Mer], 'until there is no more necessity' [Hol], 'so great/so much . . . that you won't have enough room to take it in' [NIV, NLT], 'as long as there is need' [REB], 'that there shall not be room enough to receive it' [KJV], 'until there is no more need' [Gla], 'until it overflows' [NASB], not explicit [JPS]. The whole phrase means 'I will pour you out a blessing until there is not sufficiency, i.e., until my abundance can be exhausted, or, as this can never be, for ever' [BDB p. 191].

QUESTION—What is the significance of the phrase וּבְחָנוּנִי נָא בָּזֹאת ûḇəḥānûnî nāʾ bāzōʾṯ 'and test me in this'?

1. It constitutes a command to challenge God to fulfill his word. Although one finds in the OT many instances of God testing man, one finds few of the inverse [NICOT]. These few occurred almost without exception in extraordinary circumstances (Isa. 7:11–12; Judg. 6:36–40; Exod. 4:1–9), which observation raises the question as to whether this present text, so beloved of preachers, is actually intended to promise material prosperity upon all who tithe. Against the few and rather special times in which God invited people to test him stands the warning of Ps. 95:8–11 [WBC]. On the other hand, Gla, who would add to the list of references above Isa. 7:10f and Jer. 28:16f, does not find so uncommon in the OT God's invitation for his promises to be tested.

2. It constitutes more of an invitation than a command to test God, as the sequence of *waw* consecutive + imperative expresses purpose [Clen].

QUESTION—To what does בָּזֹאת bāzōʾṯ 'in this' refer?

1. It refers to the matter under consideration, i.e., the payment of tithes [NICOT; also John Merlin Powis Smith, *Malachi. The International Critical Commentary*. Edinburgh: T.& T. Clark, 1912; cited in Gla (Smith postulates that making such a 'test' contingent simply upon payment of the tithe shows that Malachi's idea of true religion contains much less ethics and spiritual dynamics than the ideas of the great prophets who preceded him)].

2. It refers to a whole-hearted repentance (see Mal. 3:7), which bears also the fruit of outward compliance with the covenant's ritual obligations [Gla].

QUESTION—What is the function of the particle נָא nāʾ?

It is probably to render the command more palatable, as in 'please' [NICOT].

QUESTION—What is meant by אֲרֻבּוֹת הַשָּׁמַיִם *ʾărubbôt haššāmayim* 'the windows/sluices of the sky/ heaven'?

This phrase, at first sight appearing to be a metaphor for God's provision, is perhaps not a figure of speech at all, since it is tied up with Israel's traditional cosmography, which featured the land and the vaulted sky (the firmament) as separating the sea below from the waters above the sky. For rain to descend, heaven's windows (*ʾărubbôt haššāmayim*) had to be opened (cf. Gen. 7:11–12) [Coh, TOTC, WBC]. Their closure was threatened by God as a penalty for disobedience to him (Deut. 11:16f) [Gla].

QUESTION—To what kind of blessing (בְּרָכָה *bərākâ*) does this verse refer?

1. This verse refers to good things in general [Keil].
2. This verse refers to probably indicates the kind of blessing which God is promising the Jews: the blessing of rain upon their fields, indicated by the reference to heaven's windows [Coh, Gla, NICOT].
3. This verse refers not only to material blessings of this life, but also to the prosperity of Israel in the end times, similar to Isa. 30:23; Joel 2:23, etc., as well as to an abundant harvest (Isa. 30:23–26; Amos 9:13) [NICOT].

3:11

And[a]-I-will-rebuke[b] for[c]-you(pl) (the-)devourer,[d] and[e]-it-will-not-ruin[f]/that[e]-it-may-not-ruin[f] for[g]-you(pl) (the-)fruit(-of)[h] the-ground,[i] and[j]- the-vine[k] in-the-field[l] will- -not -fail-to-bear[m] for[n]-you(pl), says YHWH (-of) hosts.

LEXICON—a. -וְ *wə- waw* connective of the attached *waw* consecutive verb (BDB p. 251), (Hol p. 84), (TWOT 519): 'and' [Coh, Keil, Gla, WBC; JPS, KJV], 'also' [CEV]. An additive relationship is also expressed by a new sentence [NICOT; NIV, NJB, NLT, NRSV, REB, TEV] and probably also by 'then' [Mer; NASB].

b. 1st sg. Qal perf. *waw* consecutive of גָּעַר *gʿr* (BDB p. 172), (Hol p. 63), (TWOT 370): 'to rebuke' [BDB, Hol; Coh, Keil, Mer, WBC; KJV, NASB, NRSV], 'to reproach' [Hol], 'to stop' [CEV], 'to forbid' [NJB, REB], 'to banish' [JPS], 'to not let' [TEV], 'to prevent' [NIV], 'to destroy' [NICOT], 'to restrain' [Gla]. NLT focuses on the goal of *gʿr*: 'I will guard [your crops] from insects and disease'. *Gʿr* is part of the vocabulary of cursing in the OT; it denotes the restraining of something so that it will not work as it should, or so that it will be destroyed, cf. Mal. 3:11, where the locusts are restrained by God [Gla].

c. -לְ *la-* (BDB p. 510), (Hol p. 167), (TWOT 1063): 'for' [Keil, Mer, Gla, NICOT; NASB, NRSV], 'for (your) sake(s)' [KJV, NJB], 'for your good' [Coh], 'from (you)' (complement of 'I will banish') [JPS]. Some translations omit this first dative but explicitly translate the second dative (see (g) below) in this verse [WBC; NIV, NLT, REB, TEV]. The proclitic *lə-* here introduces a dative of advantage [BDB, Hol].

d. mas. sg. Qal part. of אכל *ʾkl* (BDB p. 37), (Hol p. 14), (TWOT 85). This participle is generally translated as a noun: 'devourer' [Coh, Keil, Mer, Gla, WBC; KJV, NASB], 'locust' [CEV, JPS, NJB, NRSV], 'insect' [TEV], 'pest' [NIV, REB]. It is also translated in a very general manner: 'insects and disease' [NLT], and so as to make explicit an identification of 'devourer' with 'locust': 'devouring locust' [NICOT]. The verb *ʾkl* signifies 'to eat' [BDB, Hol].

e. -ו *wə- waw* connective (BDB p. 251), (Hol p. 84), (TWOT 519): 'and' [Coh, Gla; KJV]. Most of the translations express purpose at this point: 'that . . . may not' [Keil], 'so that . . . will/may not' [Mer, NICOT, WBC; JPS, NASB, NRSV], 'from (destroying, etc.)' [CEV, NIV].

f. 3rd mas. sg. Hiphil imperf. of שחת *šḥt* (BDB p. 1007), (Hol p. 366), (TWOT 2370): 'to ruin' [BDB, Hol; NICOT], 'to destroy' [Coh, Keil, Gla, WBC; CEV, JPS, KJV, NASB, NJB, NRSV, REB, TEV], 'to devour' [NIV], 'to corrupt' [Mer], 'to spoil' [BDB, Hol].

g. -ל *lə-* (BDB p. 510), (Hol p. 167), (TWOT 1063): 'for (you)' [WBC]. Most translations render this word as the possessive pronoun 'your' qualifying either פרי *pərî* 'fruit, crops' or אדמה *ʾăḏāmâ* 'ground'; not explicit [Mer; NASB]. The proclitic *lə-* here introduces a dative of disadvantage [BDB, Hol].

h. constr. of פרי *pərî* (BDB p. 826), (Hol p. 297), (TWOT 1809a): 'fruit' [BDB, Hol; Coh, Keil, WBC; KJV, NASB], 'produce' [Mer, Gla; NJB, NRSV, REB], 'crops' [NICOT; CEV, NIV, TEV], 'yield' [JPS]. *Pərî* can denote produce in general [BDB].

i. אדמה *ʾăḏāmâ* (BDB p. 9), (Hol p. 4), (TWOT 25b): 'ground' [BDB, Hol; Keil, Mer, WBC; KJV, NASB], 'soil' [JPS, NJB, NRSV, REB], 'land' [Coh, Gla, NICOT], not explicit [CEV, NIV, NLT, TEV]. *ʾăḏāmâ* denotes 'ground' in the sense ot tilled or tillable ground [BDB].

j. -ו *wə- waw* connective (BDB p. 251), (Hol p. 84), (TWOT 519). Most translations express an additive relationship: 'and' [all commentators and versions except the following], 'nor' [Mer; NASB], 'neither' [Coh, Gla; KJV]. An additive relationship is also expressed by a new sentence [NLT]. NJB translates 'or', making the casting of the grapes a second action which God will forbid the devourer to carry out.

k. גפן *gepen* (BDB p. 172), (Hol p. 63), (TWOT 372a): 'vine' [BDB, Hol; Coh, Keil, Mer, Gla, NICOT, WBC; JPS, KJV, NASB, NIV, NJB, NRSV, REB], 'vineyard' [CEV], 'grapevine' [TEV], 'grape' [NLT]. *Gepen* refers to a vine, generally to a grapevine [BDB].

l. שדה *śāḏeh* (BDB p. 961), (Hol p. 349), (TWOT 2236b): 'field' [BDB, Hol; Coh, Keil, Mer, Gla, NICOT, WBC; JPS, KJV, NASB, NIV, NJB, NRSV], not explicit [CEV, NLT, REB,TEV].

m. 3rd fem. sg. Piel *waw* consecutive perf. of שכל *škl* (BDB p. 1013), (Hol p. 369), (TWOT 2385): 'to fail to bear' [Hol; Gla, NICOT], 'to

cast fruit' [Coh; KJV, NIV]; 'to cast grapes' [NASB], 'to shed fruit'
[REB], 'to be barren' [NRSV], 'to miscarry' [Keil, WBC; JPS], 'to lose
fruit before harvest' [Mer], (of the grapes) 'to shrivel before they are
ripe' [NLT], (of the vines) 'to be loaded with grapes' [TEV], (of the
locusts) 'to prevent vines from bearing fruit' [NJB], (of the locusts) 'to
keep vineyards from producing' [CEV]. JPS adds 'no longer', making
explicit its reading that in fact at present the vineyards were not
producing well. The Piel stem of škl means primarily either to make
someone childless or to have a miscarriage; here, applied to a grapevine,
it means to drop fruit before it has ripened [BDB, Hol].

n. -ל lə- (BDB p. 510), (Hol p. 167), (TWOT 1063): 'for' [Gla]. This
dative is also translated as 'your', qualifying 'vine' or 'field' [Coh, Keil,
NICOT; CEV, JPS, KJV, NASB, NIV, NJB, NLT, NRSV, REB,
TEV]. This second dative of disadvantage (see (c) above) is not
explicitly translated by some [Mer, WBC]. The proclitic lə- here
introduces a dative of disadvantage [BDB, Hol].

QUESTION—What is the syntactic relation between the phrase וְגָעַרְתִּי לָכֶם
בָּאֹכֵל wəgā‘artî lākem bā’ōkēl 'and I will rebuke for you the devourer' and
the previous verse?

This phrase probably depends upon the following complex phrase in Mal.
3:10: . . . אִם־לֹא אֶפְתַּח לָכֶם אֵת אֲרֻבּוֹת הַשָּׁמַיִם ’im lō’ ’eptaḥ lākem ’et
’ărubbôt haššāmayim . . . 'if I will not open for you the windows of
heaven . . .' The whole structure, therefore, is: '[test me] if I will not
open . . . and pour out for you . . . and rebuke for you . . .' [Gla].

QUESTION—What is the common syntactic structure of the lines of text from
mid Mal. 3:10 to mid Mal. 3:11 ('if I will not open for you the windows of
heaven...and your vine will not cast for you its fruit in the field')?

The structure is verb + dative + noun. This device helps the passage's
cohesion [Gla].

QUESTION—What is the significance of גָּעַר g‘r 'I will rebuke' ?

1. In this passage, it is to thwart the attacks on the crops [Keil].
   Specifically, it is to hold back the locusts from their destructive work
   (cf. Mal. 2:3) [Gla].

2. In this passage, it is to thwart the locusts by destroying them (compare
   Mal. 2:3) [NICOT].

QUESTION—What is the significance of אֹכֵל ’ōkēl 'devourer'?

1. It is (probably [TOTC]) locusts [Coh, Gla, NICOT]. Locust eggs may
   build up in the soil during droughts and then hatch at the first rains and
   eat what they can [NICOT]. Plagues of locusts were a recurrent form of
   punishment sent by YHWH upon the Israelites (Joel 1:4; 1 Kings 8:37;
   Amos 4:9; Deut. 28:42) [Gla].

2. It is anything in general which might ruin the harvest, whether pests,
   beasts, sickness, or unfavorable weather [Keil, Mer].

QUESTION—What is the significance of the reference to גֶּפֶן *gepen* 'grapevines'?

Grapevines are the most valuable of the fruit-bearing plants and thus are mentioned as a representative of their class [NICOT, TOTC].

QUESTION—What is the sense of שׁכל *škl* 'to fail to bear' in this verse?

It is for fruit to whither and drop before ripening [Coh, Keil]. This is most likely a result of poor rainfall, a condition alluded to in Mal. 3:10 ('open for you the windows of heaven') [Gla].

3:12

And[a]- all[b] the-nations[c] -will-call- you(pl) -happy,[d] for[e] you(pl)[f] will-be (the-)land(-of)[g] delight,[h] says YHWH(-of) hosts.

LEXICON—a. -ו *wǝ- waw* connective of the attached *waw* consecutive verb (BDB p. 251), (Hol p. 84), (TWOT 519): 'and' [Coh, Keil, Gla, WBC; JPS, KJV, NASB, NJB]. An additive relationship is also expressed by a new sentence [Mer; CEV, REB]; a sequential or result relationship is also expressed: 'then' [NICOT; NIV, NLT, NRSV, TEV].

   b. constr. of כֹּל *kōl* (BDB p. 481), (Hol p. 156), (TWOT 985a): 'all' [all lexica, commentators, and versions except CEV], 'every' [CEV]. The noun *kōl* denotes a totality of something [BDB, Hol].

   c. pl. of גּוֹי *gôy* (BDB p. 156), (Hol p. 57), (TWOT 326e): 'nation' [all lexica, commentators, and versions except the following], 'the people of all nations' [TEV], 'everyone of every nation' [CEV]. *Gôy* normally refers to the peoples and ethnic groups around Israel, with emphasis upon their pagan quality.

   d. 3rd pl. Piel perf. *waw* consecutive of אשׁר *ʾšr* (BDB p. 80), (Hol p. 30), (TWOT 183): 'to call happy' [Coh, Mer; TEV], 'to bless' [WBC], 'to call blessed' [BDB; Keil, NICOT; KJV, NASB, NIV, NJB, NLT], 'to count/account happy' [JPS, NRSV, REB], 'to consider fortunate' [Gla]. CEV makes explicit its understanding of the phrase: 'everyone of every nation will talk about how I have blessed you'.

   e. כִּי *kî* connective (BDB p. 471), (Hol p. 155), (TWOT 976): 'for' [Coh, Keil, Gla, Mer, NICOT; JPS, KJV, NASB, NIV, NJB, NLT, NRSV, REB], 'because' [WBC; TEV], not explicit [CEV].

   f. אַתֶּם *ʾattem* 2nd mas. pl. prn.: 'you' [Coh, Keil, Mer, Gla, WBC; JPS, KJV, NASB, NJB, NRSV]. Some recognize the pronoun as metonymy signifying the land of Israel and translate concretely: 'yours will be' [NICOT; NIV, REB], 'your land will be' [NLT, TEV], 'your wonderful land' [CEV]. Gla translates the metonymy of the pronoun in a different way: 'you will be inhabitants of a desirable land'. *ʾattem* is the 2nd pl. pronoun 'you'.

   g. constr. of אֶרֶץ *ʾereṣ* (BDB p. 76), (Hol p. 28), (TWOT 167): 'land' [all lexica, commentators, and versions except TEV], 'place' [TEV]. *ʾereṣ* denotes 'territory, country' [BDB].

h. חפץ ḥēp̄eṣ (BDB p. 343), (Hol p. 112), (TWOT 712b): 'delight' [BDB; WBC; NJB, NLT, NRSV], 'joy' [Hol], 'good pleasure' [Keil]. This noun is translated by most versions as an adjective: 'delightsome' [Coh; KJV], 'delightful' [Mer, NICOT; NASB, NIV], 'desirable' [Gla], 'favoured' [REB], 'wonderful' [CEV]. Some employ longer phrases: 'a good place to live' [TEV], 'the most desired of lands' [JPS].

QUESTION—What is the meaning of כל־הגוים kol haggôyim 'all the nations'?

This phrase is frequently a hyperbole denoting the nations which are near to Israel—those who have been involved with her history [NICOT]. Israel is not here included with the haggôyim 'the nations' as she was in Mal. 3:9, for she has returned, at least hypothetically, to YHWH [Gla].

QUESTION—What speaker attitude is implied in אשר ʾšr 'to call happy, blessed'?

The ones making the statement 'blessed are . . .' always express envy of the fortunate party, so it is a case of the lesser praising the state of the greater [Waldemar Jenzen, "Ašrê in the Old Testament," *Harvard Theological Review* 58 (1965); cited in Gla].

QUESTION—What are the normal elements of being considered 'happy, blessed' in the Old Testament?

They are possessing offspring and descendants, having fertile fields and prolific livestock, and seeing the defeat of one's enemies, i.e., having security (cf. Ps. 144:12–15, 127–128) [Johannes Pedersen, *Israel: Its Life and Culture*. 4 vols. London: Oxford University Press, 1973; cited in Gla].

QUESTION—What is the function of the pronoun אתם ʾattem 'you'?

It is to emphasize the subject: *you*, the chosen people [NICOT].

QUESTION—What is the nature of the חפץ ḥēp̄eṣ 'pleasure' in this passage?

1. It is the fertility of the land, which make it prosperous [implied in Keil, Gla, WBC].
2. It is not only the material prosperity promised by God, but also the spiritual blessings which accompany God's favor [TOTC].

QUESTION—What is the significance of the phrase ארץ חפץ ʾereṣ ḥēp̄eṣ ?

1. Everyone, including those of other nations, will find much pleasure in the nation [Kimchi (cited in Coh), Keil, Gla].
2. God will once again take pleasure in the land, since its people have returned to him [Rashi, Ibn Ezra (cited in, and preferred by, Coh).
3. The land will be an object of pleasure, both to the nations and to God [NICOT].

DISCOURSE UNIT: 3:13–4:6 (3:13–24) [Ksr; REB]. The topic is "a call to take inventory" [Ksr], "the righteous triumphant" [REB].

DISCOURSE UNIT: 3:13–4:3 (3:13–21) [Gla, Mer, NICOT, O'Brien, TOTC, WBC; Wendland]. The topic is the Fifth Accusation [O'Brien], resistance through self-sufficiency [Mer], "the antithesis between righteous and wicked" [NICOT], God's final judgment [TOTC], "a dispute about speaking against God" [WBC].

A formal analysis of the discourse unit is:
first half of the dispute
> (A) Objection—Yahweh is unjust: "serve God" + "doers of wickedness" (13–15)
>> (B) Justice: Yahweh "hears" those who "fear" him (16)
>> (B') Blessing: Yahweh will spare his "treasure" (17)
> (A') Refutation—Yahweh is just: "serve God" + "the wicked" (18)

second half of the dispute
> (X) Fate of the wicked: "day" + "wicked" + "ablaze" + "Yahweh of Hosts" (1)
>> (Y) Future of the God-fearing: metaphors of healing and happiness (2)
> (X') Fate of the wicked: "wicked" + "ashes" + "day" + "Yahweh of Hosts" (3) [Wendland]

DISCOURSE UNIT: 3:13–4:2 (3:13–20) [NJB]. The topic is "the triumph of the upright on the Day of Yahweh."

DISCOURSE UNIT: 3:13–3:18 [TEV]. The topic is "God's promise of mercy."

DISCOURSE UNIT: 3:13–3:15 [Clen (within the larger discourse unit of Mal. 3:7–4:6 (3:7–3:24)]. The topic is "complacency toward serving YHWH."

Comments on this discourse unit: this paragraph, which realizes the third movement's constituent C, is seen as antithetical to the preceding paragraph (constituents A and B). Constituent A is an invitation for the people to renew their faithfulness to YHWH, while constituent B promises his blessings to them if they do so, in spite of the people's cynicism, which is expressed in constituent C [Clen].

3:13
Your(pl)-words[a] have-been-strong[b] against[c]-me, says YHWH, but[d]-you(pl)-say,[e] what[f] have-we-said-among-ourselves[g] against[h]-you(sg)?

LEXICON—a. pl. constr. of דָּבָר *dābār* (BDB p. 182), (Hol p. 67), (TWOT 399a): 'word' [BDB, Hol; Keil, WBC; KJV, NASB], 'speech' [BDB]. See below for other translations.

> b. 3rd pl. Qal perf. of חָזַק *ḥzq* (BDB p. 304), (Hol p. 99), (TWOT 636): 'to be strong' [WBC], 'to be all too strong' [Coh], 'to be stout' [KJV], 'to do violence' [Keil], 'to be hard' [Mer], 'to be arrogant' [NASB]. Most translations restructure the phrase 'your words have been strong': 'to use harsh words' [NICOT; REB], 'to speak harsh words' [NRSV], 'to say harsh things' [NIV, NJB], 'to speak hard words' [JPS], 'to say horrible things' [CEV], 'to say terrible things' [NLT, TEV]; 'to be too

much'—this rendering is based on Akkadian parallels [N. Waldman, "Some Notes on Malachi 3:6; 3:15 and Psalm 42:11," *Journal of Biblical Literature* 93 (1974); cited in Gla, who points out that such a rendering creates a parallelism with Mal. 2:17: there the people's words wearied YHWH, but here they become intolerable to him]. Mer thinks that the phrase concerns cynicism against YHWH. NICOT cites 2 Sam. 24:4 and 1 Chr. 21:4, where *ḥzq*, there associated with *dābār* 'word' and עַל *ᶜal* 'over against' has the sense of 'to overrule'. Most versions use the English present perfect tense, e.g., 'have been strong'; Clen analyzes the perfect tense of the verb as expressing a state which has continued to the present time, e.g., 'are strong'. The primary sense of *ḥzq* is 'to be or become strong'; associated with words or speech, the idea is given of shameless [Hol] or perverse speech [BDB].

c. עַל *ᶜal* (BDB p. 752), (Hol p. 273), (TWOT 1624p): 'against' [all lexica, commentators, and versions except the following], 'about' [CEV, NJB, NLT, REB, TEV], 'for' (complement of 'too much': 'for me') [Gla], 'to' [Keil]. The primary function of the preposition *ᶜal* is to denote location upon or over something; here it carries a hostile sense [BDB, Hol].

d. -ו *wə- waw* connective (BDB p. 251), (Hol p. 84), (TWOT 519): 'but' [Mer, WBC; JPS, NLT, TEV], 'yet' [Coh, Gla, NICOT; CEV, KJV, NASB, NIV, NJB, NRSV, REB], 'and' [Keil].

e. 2nd mas. pl. Qal perf. of אָמַר *ᵓmr* (BDB p. 55), (Hol p. 21), (TWOT 118): 'to say' [Coh, Gla, Keil, WBC; KJV, NASB, NJB, NLT, NRSV], 'to ask' [Mer, NICOT; CEV, JPS, NIV, REB, TEV].

f. מַה *mâ* (BDB p. 552), (Hol p. 183), (TWOT 1149): 'what . . . ?' [BDB, Hol; Keil, Gla, Mer, NICOT, WBC; CEV, JPS, KJV, NASB, NIV, NJB, TEV], 'how . . . ?' [NLT, NRSV, REB], 'wherein . . . ?' [Coh].

g. 1st pl. Niphal perf. of דִּבֶּר *dbr* (BDB p. 180), (Hol p. 66), (TWOT 399): 'to speak' [Coh, Gla, Mer, WBC; NASB, NLT, NRSV, REB] 'to say' [CEV, NIV, NJB, TEV], 'to speak so much' [KJV], 'to converse against' [Keil]. Some make explicit the reciprocal nuance of the Niphal: 'to speak among oneselves' [NICOT], 'to say among oneselves' [JPS]. The Niphal stem of *dbr* denotes reciprocity: 'to speak with one another' [BDB], 'to speak together' [Hol].

h. עַל *ᵓal* see above: 'against' [all commentators and versions except the following], 'about' [NIV, TEV], not explicit [CEV].

QUESTION—Who are the addressees of this and the following verses?

1. The addressees are the Jewish community as a whole, as in the previous discourse unit [Keil, NICOT]. This implies that the majority of the community are, indeed, giving up on YHWH [NICOT]. The majority of the community has been overwhelmed and carried along by the element rebellious against YHWH [WBC].

2. The addressees are the pious element of the community who are frustrated by the actions of YHWH, which they find mystifying, given

the worldview under which they have traditionally lived and which they now find threatened or even collapsed [Gla].

QUESTION—What is the significance of the people's speaking together about YHWH?

1. It is that the people are guilty of malicious gossip about YHWH [NICOT].

2. It is part of the "murmuring" motif of the OT against YHWH or the leaders of Israel whom he appointed, which denoted, not whining complaints about him or them, but instead overt revolt against their authority, with the aim of unseating them from their positions or YHWH from his position as their God [George Coats, *Rebellion in the Wilderness* (Nashville: Abingdon, 1968), cited in WBC].

QUESTION—What is the significance of the people's question, מַה־נִּדְבַּרְנוּ עָלֶיךָ *mâ niḏbarnû ʿālêkā* 'What have we said against you?'

It is that the people are defying YHWH to disprove their accusations against him of unfaithfulness and injustice—accusations which the prophet rehearses in the following two verses [Gla]. With these accusations the people are trying to reverse the tables on YHWH in order to put him on the defensive [Mer].

3:14

You(pl)-have-said,[a] (it is) futile[b] to-serve[c] God,[d] and[e]-what profit[f] (is there) that[g] we-observed[h] his-command[i] and-that we-walked[j] mournfully[k] before/because-of[l] YHWH(-of) hosts?

LEXICON—a. 2nd mas. pl. Qal perf. of אמר *ʾmr* (BDB p. 55), (Hol p. 21), (TWOT 118): 'to say' [all commentators and versions]. The English present perfect tense is used [Coh, Gla, Mer, NICOT; CEV, JPS, KJV, NASB, NIV, NJB, NLT, NRSV, REB, TEV]. The present tense is used [Keil]; the past tense is used [WBC].

b. שָׁוְא *šāwʾ* (BDB p. 996), (Hol p. 361), (TWOT 2338a): 'futile' [NICOT; NIV, REB], 'vain' [Coh, Keil, WBC; KJV, NASB, NRSV], 'in vain' [Hol], 'foolish' [CEV], 'useless' [Mer; JPS, NJB, TEV], 'worthless' [Gla]. NLT restructures the phrase with a rhetorical question: 'what's the use?' *Šāwʾ* is associated in the OT with ideas of deception and treachery [NICOT]. The noun *šāwʾ* denotes 'emptiness, nothingness, vanity' [BDB].

c. Qal inf. of עבד *ʿbd* (BDB p. 712), (Hol p. 261), (TWOT 1553): 'to serve' [Hol; all commentators and versions], 'to labor, to work' [BDB]. With an accusative, *ʿbd* denotes 'to work for a master' [Hol].

d. אֱלֹהִים *ʾĕlōhîm* (BDB p. 43), (Hol p. 16), (TWOT 93c): 'God' [all lexica, commentators, and versions except CEV], 'the Lord God All-Powerful' [CEV].

e. -ו *wa- waw* connective (BDB p. 251), (Hol p. 84), (TWOT 519): 'and' (introducing a coordinate clause) [Coh, Keil, Gla, WBC; KJV, NASB]. A relationship of amplification is expressed by means of a new sentence at this point [Mer, NICOT; CEV, JPS, NIV, NJB, NLT, NRSV, REB, TEV].

f. בצע *beṣaᶜ* (BDB p. 130), (Hol p. 45), (TWOT 267a): 'profit' [BDB, Hol; KJV, NASB], 'use' [TEV], 'good' [NJB], 'gain' [Keil], 'profit' [Coh, Gla, Mer, WBC]. The phrase 'what profit' is also translated as a clause: 'what do we profit' [NRSV], 'what do we gain/have we gained' [NICOT; JPS, NLT, REB], 'what did we gain' [NIV], 'what do we get' [CEV]. *Beṣaᶜ* frequently denotes profit arising from unjust or violent actions [BDB]. Here, however, there is no nuance of unjust gain, rather, of simple gain [Gla].

g. כי *kî* connective (BDB p. 471), (Hol p. 155), (TWOT 976)—here this connective functions as introducing a complemental clause: 'that' [Coh, Keil, Mer, Gla; KJV, NASB]; all other translations employ 'by, of, for' to introduce a verbal complement.

h. 1st pl. Qal perf. of שמר *šmr* (BDB p. 1036), (Hol p. 377), (TWOT 2414): 'to observe' [Hol; NICOT; REB], 'to keep' [BDB, Hol; Coh, Keil, Mer, Gla, WBC; JPS, KJV, NASB, NJB, NRSV], 'to obey' [CEV, NLT], 'to carry out' [NIV], 'to do' [TEV]. In translating with the English present perfect tense, e.g., 'we have kept', some apparently make explicit their understanding that the speakers are claiming to have been faithful to YHWH until the present time [Coh, Keil, Mer, Gla, WBC; KJV, NASB].

i. constr. of משמרת *mišmeret* (BDB p. 1038), (Hol p. 220), (TWOT 2414g): 'command' [NJB, NLT, NRSV], 'rule' [REB], 'charge' [BDB; Coh, Gla, Mer, NICOT, WBC; JPS, NASB], 'requirement' [NIV], 'obligation' [Hol], 'ordinance' [KJV], 'guard' [Keil]. This noun is also translated with a clause: 'what he says' [TEV]; not explicit [CEV]. Gla holds that this noun refers generally to all covenantal obligations; Coh and NICOT, on the other hand, view it as denoting mainly cultic or worship requirements which are to be fulfilled, first by the priests and Levites, but then also by the general population.

j. 1st pl. Qal perf. of הלך *hlk* (BDB p. 229), (Hol p. 79), (TWOT 498): 'to walk' [Coh, Gla, Mer, WBC; JPS, KJV, NASB, NJB], 'to go about' [Keil, NICOT; NIV, NRSV], 'to go around' [CEV], 'to behave' [REB], 'to conduct oneself' [Hol]. NLT and TEV make explicit their understanding of *hlk* here: 'to try to show'. Some have employed the English present perfect tense, e.g., 'we have walked'—see (h) above. The primary sense of *hlk* is 'to go'; here, however, it is used with a secondary sense of 'to conduct oneself' [Hol].

k. קדרנית *qᵉḏōrannît* (BDB p. 871), (Hol p. 313), (TWOT 1989b): 'mournfully' [Coh; KJV, NJB], 'as/like mourners' [BDB; Mer; NIV, NRSV], 'in deep mourning' [Keil], 'in mourning' [NICOT, WBC; NASB], 'with humble submission' [REB], 'looking sad' [CEV], 'in abject awe' [JPS], 'earnestly' [Gla], 'unkempt, dressed in mourning attire' [Hol]. Some translations make explicit the speakers' implied purpose by translating: 'that we are sorry for our sins' [NLT], 'we are sorry for what we have done' [TEV].

1. מִפְּנֵי *mippǝnê* (BDB p. 815), (Hol p. 293): 'before' [Hol; Keil, Gla, Mer, WBC; KJV, NASB, NIV, NJB, NRSV], 'because of' [BDB; Coh], 'in abject awe of the Lord of hosts' [JPS], 'on account of' [Hol; NICOT], 'for fear of' [BDB], not explicit [CEV, REB]. *Mippǝnê*, which is a compound preposition, is formally composed of the preposition מִן *min* 'away from' plus the construct of פָּנִים *pānîm* 'face'.

QUESTION—What is the significance of Mal. 3:14-15?

1. These verses signal an obstinate claim on the part of the Israelites to be self-sufficient apart from God. They soon forgot YHWH's powerful intervention on their behalf, which had allow their return and reconstruction of Jerusalem in the first place. Those who led the way in ignoring their call to covenantal living seemed to prosper, luring on many others to question God's justice or power [Mer]. This arrogance was the result of their disappointment with God and sprang from the mistaken view that God would be—or should be—satisfied with the external performances of worship rites [Keil, NICOT].

2. These verses signal a crisis which had developed in Israelites' worldview and which threatened to collapse it. This view held that the righteous would prosper because of God's blessing and that the wicked would be punished with destruction (cf. Deut. 28, 30). Such rewards and punishments might often fall, not upon the faithful or faithless individuals themselves, but upon their clans or their descendants. This worldview thus held that the collective played a pivotal role in the pattern of divine justice, for one could always suppose that, even if a wicked person did well for himself in this life, God's retribution would certainly fall upon his clan or descendants.

The crisis referred to above began with the final years of the monarchy and was deepened by the entire exile: the community of Israel felt itself to be entirely separated from its ancestors and thrown completely upon its own responsibility, unable anymore to relate either the rewards or punishments awarded by God to any generation but its own. Bearing in mind this crisis of worldview, one cannot consider the speakers of these verses to have abandoned YHWH; rather, they spoke as they did out of a tortured search for a continued relationship with him and out of fear that such a relationship was no longer possible [citing Helmer Ringgren, *Israelite Religion* (Philadelphia: Fortress, 1966, and Gerhard von Rad, *Old Testament Theology* (2 vols; New York: Harper and Row, 1962-65)].

It would be too harsh to accuse these speakers of wishing for simple profit in their religion. The fact is that Malachi speaks much of the blessings which YHWH has in store for those who fear him and of the retribution awaiting those who renounce the ancient covenant. But these are terms to which the faithful had trouble relating anymore, with the

rise of individual responsibility before God, untempered by any more
role played by the collective [Gla].

QUESTION—What is the meaning of קדרנית qədōrannît 'like mourners'?

1. It refers to hypocritical shows of piety, which consist of wearing dark-
   colored garments of mourning, for the original root קדר qdr means 'to
   be dark, dirty' and is associated with mourning over sin (cf. Ps. 35:13–
   14, Job 30:28) [Keil, Mer, NICOT].

2. It does not refer to one's physical appearance, but rather to one's
   seriousness of purpose. Qdr, the root of qədōrannît, means 'to be dark',
   not 'to be dirty'. LXX recognizes the difference, for in Pss. 35:14;
   38:7; 42:10; and 43:2, קדר qdr, the root of qədōrannît, is translated by
   σκυθρωπάζειν 'to have a sad face'. The speakers had indeed been
   serious about the ancient covenant, but they are now questioning the
   utility of their former zealousness [Gla].

3:15

**And-now[a] we call-fortunate[b] (the-)arrogant,[c] not-only/indeed[d] (the-)ones-
doing[e] evil[f] are-built-up[g]; they- even[h] -test[i] God[j] and[k]-they-escape.[l]**

LEXICON—a. ועתה wəʿattâ (BDB p. 774), (Hol p. 287): 'and now' [BDB,
     Hol; Coh, Keil, WBC; KJV], 'in fact' [NJB], 'but now' [NIV], 'now'
     [NRSV], 'from now on' [NLT], 'and so' [JPS], 'so now' [Gla; NASB],
     'henceforth' [NICOT], 'now, therefore' [Mer]. REB's 'for our part'
     probably draws its justification as much from the emphatic Hebrew 1st
     plural pronoun 'we' following (Hol p. 22) as from the initial
     conjunction; not explicit [CEV, TEV]. Wəʿattâ often introduces a new
     thought or section [Hol]; wəʿattâ often (usually [Clen]) introduces a
     conclusion drawn from what has been previously states [BDB].

  b. mas. pl. Piel part. of אשר ʾšr (BDB p. 80), (Hol p. 30), (TWOT 183):
     'to call someone fortunate' [Hol], 'to call happy' [Coh; KJV, NJB], 'to
     call blessed' [BDB; Keil, WBC; NASB, NIV], 'to count/account happy'
     [JPS, NRSV, REB], 'to deem happy' [Gla], 'to deem blessed' [NICOT],
     'to consider happy' [Mer]. Some restructure the phrase: 'as we see it,
     proud people are the ones that are happy' [TEV], 'we will say, "Blessed
     are . . .' [NLT]. Keil and NICOT regard this participle as denoting
     imminent future action: 'we are ready to call blessed. . . .', 'from now
     on we will call blessed. . . .'

  c. mas. pl. of זד zēd (BDB p. 267), (Hol p. 86), (TWOT 547a): 'arrogant'
     [Hol; Gla, Mer, NICOT, WBC; CEV, JPS, NASB, NIV, NLT, NRSV,
     REB], 'proud' [Coh, Keil; KJV, NJB, TEV], 'presumptuous [BDB,
     Hol], 'insolent' [BDB]. The adjective zēd comes from זיד zîd 'to swell
     up, inflate'; it often denotes in the OT rebellious, impious people, and
     stands in parallelism to עשי רשעה ʿōśê rišʿâ 'doers of evil' below [Gla,
     NICOT].

  d. גם gam (BDB p. 168), (Hol p. 61), (TWOT 361a). Given the double
     occurrence of gam in this verse, some employ a 'not only . . . but'

coordination, with 'not only' occurring at this point [Keil, NICOT; NASB, TEV]; 'indeed' [Mer, Gla; JPS], 'yea' [Coh; KJV], 'certainly' [NIV], 'for' [NLT], 'also' [WBC]. Translation not explicit [CEV, NJB, NRSV, REB]. *Gam* is employed to emphasize or to associate elements together [BDB, Hol]; the coordinative *gam . . . gam* associates elements in the manner of 'both . . . and' [Hol].

e. Qal mas. pl. part. constr. of עשׂה *ʿśh* (BDB p. 793), (Hol p. 284), (TWOT 1708): 'to do' [BDB, Hol; CEV, JPS, NASB, NLT], 'to work' [Coh; KJV], 'to practice' [Mer], 'to commit' [Gla].

f. רשׁעה *rišʿâ* (BDB p. 958), (Hol p. 347), (TWOT 2222c): 'evil' [Mer; JPS, NLT], 'wickedness' [BDB; Coh, Keil, Gla; KJV, NASB], 'wrong' [CEV], 'guilt' [Hol]. The phrase 'doers of evil' is also translated 'evildoers' [NICOT, WBC; NIV, NJB, NRSV, REB], 'evil people' [TEV], 'everyone who does wrong' [CEV].

g. 3rd pl. Niphal perf. of בנה *bnh* (BDB p. 124), (Hol p. 42), (TWOT 255): 'to be built up' [Coh, Keil, Mer, Gla, WBC; NASB], 'to be set up' [KJV], 'to be established' [BDB], 'prosper' [NICOT; NIV, NJB, NRSV, REB, TEV], 'to get rich' [NLT], 'to endure' [JPS], 'to be successful' [CEV].

h. גם *gam*: see above: 'even' [Gla, WBC], 'and even' [NIV] 'yea' [Coh; KJV], 'indeed' [JPS], 'in fact' [Mer], not explicit [CEV, NJB, NLT, REB]. Some employ 'but' as part of a coordinate 'not only . . . but' complex [Keil, NICOT; NASB, TEV]. This second *gam* makes the element which it introduces ('they test God and escape') more prominent than that which is introduced by the first *gam* ('the evil doers are built up') [Clen].

i. 3rd pl. Qal perf. of בחן *bḥn* (BDB p. 103), (Hol p. 37), (TWOT 230): 'to test' [Gla, Mer, WBC; NASB, TEV], 'to try' [BDB; Coh], 'to put to the test' [Hol; NICOT; CEV, NJB, NRSV], 'to tempt' [Keil; KJV], 'to challenge' [NIV], 'to dare' [JPS], 'to put to the proof' [REB]. Some make explicit their understanding of the content of this testing: 'those who dare God to punish them' [NLT], 'they test God's patience with their evil deeds' [TEV]; i.e., they flout their covenantal responsibilities and challenge God to punish them [Metsudath David, cited in Coh]. Most translations employ the English present or habitual tense, but some use the present perfect, e.g., 'they have dared' [Keil; JPS, REB].

j. אלהים *ʾĕlōhîm* (BDB p. 43), (Hol p. 16), (TWOT 93c): 'God' [all lexica, commentators, and versions].

k. -ו *wə-* waw connective attached to the following preterite verb (BDB p. 251), (Hol p. 84), (TWOT 519): 'and' [Coh, Keil, NICOT, WBC; JPS, NASB, REB, TEV], 'even' [KJV], 'yet' [NJB]. This conjunction is left untranslated by those who restructure these formally coordinative Hebrew clauses 'for they test God and they escape' into dependent + independent clauses: 'and when they put God to the test, they always get away with it' [CEV], 'yea, they that tempt God are even delivered'

[KJV], 'and even those who challenge God escape' [NIV], 'and those who dare God to punish them go free of harm' [NLT], 'but when they put God to the test they escape' [NRSV], 'in fact, those who test God escape' [Mer].

1. 3rd pl. Niphal preterite of מלט *mlṭ* (BDB p. 572), (Hol p. 197), (TWOT 1198): 'to escape' [BDB; Gla, Mer, WBC; JPS, NASB, NIV, NRSV], 'to be delivered' [Coh; KJV], 'to be saved' [Keil], 'to come to no harm' [NJB, REB], 'to get away with it' [NICOT; CEV, TEV], 'to go free of harm' [NLT], 'to get oneself to safety' [Hol].

QUESTION—Who are the זדים *zēḏîm* 'arrogant ones'?

1. They are the heathen nations; this is so because *zēḏîm* in various other OT passages refers to the heathen (e.g., Isa. 13:11). The majority of the Israelites are claiming in this passage that the heathen are better off than they themselves are [Keil].

2. They are the openly rebellious element in Israel; the element of the population which has until now tried to remain faithful to YWHW is giving up, saying that these rebellious people are better off [Gla].

3. They are either the rebellious element in Israel or the majority of Israel's population who has already turned away from YHWH and his covenant. This is so, because *zēḏîm*, although sometimes referring elsewhere to the heathen nations, is also used of the rebellious Jews. In Malachi's context, the attitude of the surrounding nations toward YHWH can hardly have been a problem for the Jews [NICOT].

QUESTION—What is the significance of the use of נבנו *niḇnû* 'they are built up' in this passage?

1. The rebellious are sincerely saying that the heathen are better off than the Israelites who traditionally have taken YHWH's covenant seriously [Keil].

2. The Israelites' worldview deterministically held that only YHWH could build up anything, and that, therefore, if evil doers were prospering (were 'built up'—cf. Job 22:23), it was his doing. Such apparent fickleness on the part of YHWH is not understood by the speakers in this passage [Gla].

QUESTION—What is the significance of the 'testing' (from בחן *bḥn* 'to put to the test') in this verse?

It is different from the testing encouraged by YHWH in Mal. 3:10. In this earlier verse, YHWH asks the Israelites to return to him with sincere hearts and full obedience to the covenantal requirements and thus to see if this will not elicit a response of blessing from him. In Mal. 3:15, the testing is done by those who have no intention of honoring him and who do not believe that he is able or willing to punish them [Mer, Gla].

DISCOURSE UNIT: 3:16–4:6 (3:16–3:24) [Clen (within the larger discourse unit of Mal. 3:7–4:6 (3:7–3:24))].

Comments on this discourse unit: this paragraph realizes the third movement's semantic constituent B' (Mal. 3:16-4:3 (3:16-3:21)), the topic of which is "the coming day," and constituent A' (Mal. 4:4-4:6 (3:22-3:24)), the topic of which is "remember the Law" [Clen].

DISCOURSE UNIT: 3:16-3:18 [CEV, NASB, NLT, NRSV]. The topic is "faithfulness is rewarded" [CEV], "the book of remembrance" [NASB], "the Lord's promise of mercy" [NLT], "the reward of the faithful" [NRSV].

3:16

Then[a] (the-)fearers(-of)[b] YHWH spoke-with-each-other,[c] each[d] with his-companion,[e] and[f]- YHWH -listened[g] and-heeded,[h] and[i]- (a-)book(-of)[j] remembrance[k] -was-written[l] before[m]-him of/concerning/for[n]-(the-)fear-ers(-of) YHWH and[o]-(the-)esteemers(-of)[p] his-name.[q]

LEXICON—a. אָז *'āz* (BDB p. 23), (Hol p. 8), (TWOT 54): 'then' [all lexica, commentators, and versions except the following],'in this vein' [JPS], not explicit [CEV]. The adverb *'āz* can refer to a time in the past, whether from a punctiliar or durative viewpoint [BDB].

  b. mas. pl. Qal part. constr. of יָרֵא *yr'* (BDB p. 431), (Hol p. 142), (TWOT 907): 'to fear' [BDB, Hol; Coh, Keil, Gla, NICOT, WBC; KJV, NASB, NIV, NJB, NLT, TEV], 'to revere' [Mer; JPS, NRSV], 'to truly respect' [CEV]. This term sums up all covenantal responsibilities [Mer, Gla], comprising as it does love for God, devotion to him, and obedience to him [Gla].

  c. 3rd pl. Niphal perf. of דָּבַר *dbr* (BDB p. 180), (Hol p. 66), (TWOT 399): 'to speak' [Coh, Mer, Gla, NICOT, WBC; NASB, NLT, NRSV, TEV], 'to converse' [Keil], 'to speak often' [KJV], 'to talk' [JPS, NJB], 'to talk' [NIV], 'to start discussing' [CEV]. Some make explicit the subject of discussion: 'these things' [CEV], 'in this vein' [JPS], 'about this' [NJB]. The perfect form following אָז *'āz* 'then' stresses that the action in question really occurred [Kautzsch, E., ed. *Gesenius' Hebrew Grammar*, 2nd revised edition. Translated by A.E. Cowley. Oxford: The Clarendon Press: 1974; cited in Gla]. The clause containing this verb is the initial clause of an embedded narrative, the point of which is that YHWH will be faithful to those who are faithful to him. The verb נִדְבְּרוּ *nidbərû* 'they spoke with each other' is in the perfect tense and is therefore low in prominence, providing the setting for the events (encoded in the preterite) which follow in the narrative [Clen]. The Niphal stem of *dbr* denotes reciprocity: 'to speak with one another' [BDB], 'to speak together' [Hol].

  d. constr. of אִישׁ *'îš* (BDB p. 35), (Hol p. 13), (TWOT 83a): see below for translation in context. *'îš* refers to anyone in general: 'each' [Hol], 'one' [BDB].

  e. constr. of רֵעַ *rēa'* (BDB p. 945), (Hol p. 342), (TWOT 2186a): 'companion' [BDB, Hol], 'friend' [BDB, Hol]. The phrase אֶת־רֵעֵהוּ

אִישׁ ʾîš ʾeṯ rēʿēhû, a common expression of reciprocity, is here translated
as 'with/to one another' [Coh, Keil, NICOT, WBC; JPS, KJV, NASB,
NJB, NRSV, TEV], 'with each other' [NIV, NLT], 'each with his
fellow' [Gla].

f. -וְ wə- waw connective attached to the following preterite (BDB p. 251),
(Hol p. 84), (TWOT 519): 'and' [Coh, Keil, Mer, Gla, WBC; NASB,
NIV, NLT, TEV]. An additive relationship is also expressed by a new
clause or sentence [NICOT].

g. 3rd mas. sg. Hiphil preterite of קשׁב qšḇ (BDB p. 904), (Hol p. 326),
(TWOT 2084): 'to listen' [NIV, NLT, TEV], 'to pay attention' [Hol;
Gla], 'to attend' [Keil], 'to give attention' [NASB], 'to heed' [NICOT],
'to take note' [NJB, NRSV], 'to hearken' [Coh, WBC; KJV], 'to hear'
[Mer; JPS], 'to see what was happening' [CEV].

h. 3rd mas. sg. Qal preterite of שׁמע šmʿ (BDB p. 1033), (Hol p. 376),
(TWOT 2412): 'to heed' [Hol; Mer], 'to listen' [BDB, Hol; NICOT;
NJB, NLT, NRSV], 'to hear' [Hol; Coh, Keil, Gla, WBC; KJV, NASB,
NIV, TEV], 'to note' [JPS], 'to hear with attention, interest' [BDB], not
explicit [CEV]. The parallelism of šmʿ with קשׁב qšḇ 'to pay attention
to' above expresses intensity: YHWH paid very close attention [Mer].

i. -וְ wə- waw connective attached to the following preterite (see (1) below)
(BDB p. 251), (Hol p. 84), (TWOT 519): 'and' [all commentators and
versions except the following]. NICOT employs a new sentence. Mer
sees the clause introduced by this waw connective as giving background
information, out of the time sequence of the main narrative, and so
translates the connective 'now'.

j. constr. of סֵפֶר sēp̄er (BDB p. 706), (Hol p. 259), (TWOT 1540a):
'book' [BDB; Coh, Keil, Mer, Gla, NICOT, WBC; KJV, NASB, NJB,
NRSV, TEV], 'scroll' [Hol; JPS, NIV, NLT]. CEV translates
functionally: 'a reminder in his book' [CEV]. Translation not explicit
[REB].

k. זִכְרוֹן zikkārôn (BDB p. 272), (Hol p. 89), (TWOT 551b):
'remembrance' [Coh, Keil, Mer, Gla, NICOT, WBC; JPS, KJV,
NASB, NIV, NJB, NLT, NRSV], 'mention, reminder' [Hol], 'record'
[REB, TEV]. The verb from which the noun zikkārôn is formed appears
below in Mal. 4:4 (3:22) as an imperative; thus, the relationship of
result—reason between Clen's constituent B' and constituent A' is
heightened: YHWH will not forget those who remember him [Clen].

l. 3rd mas. sg. Niphal preterite of כתב ktḇ (BDB p. 507), (Hol p. 166),
(TWOT 1053): 'to be written' [BDB, Hol; Coh, Keil, Mer, Gla,
NICOT, WBC; JPS, KJV, NASB, NIV, NJB, NLT, NRSV, REB], 'to
be written down' [TEV]. CEV makes explicit the initiator of this action:
'[God] had their names written'.

m. constr. of לִפְנֵי lip̄nê (BDB p. 815), (Hol p. 293), (TWOT 1782b):
'before' (in a spatial sense) [all lexica, commentators, and versions
except the following], 'in his presence' [NIV, NJB, NLT, TEV], 'at His

behest' [JPS]. *Lipnê*, which is a compound preposition, is formally composed of the proclitic -לְ *lə-* plus the construct of פָּנִים *pānîm* 'face'.

n. -לְ *lə-* (BDB p. 510), (Hol p. 167), (TWOT 1063): 'of' [NRSV, REB, TEV], 'concerning' [NICOT; JPS, NIV], 'regarding' [Gla], 'for' [Coh, Keil, Mer, WBC; KJV, NASB]. Some express a relationship of specification with a phrase: 'to record the names of those who feared him' [NLT], 'recording those who feared him' [NJB], 'he had their names written' [CEV]. Others, however, see *lə-* here as introducing a dative of advantage: the book was written for the good of those who feared YHWH and will be used as documentation on day of his judging, recording the right conduct of those concerned [Keil, NICOT]. The proclitic *lə-* here introduces either a relationship of specification (e.g., 'concerning, regarding') or a dative of advantage (e.g., 'for') [BDB, Hol].

o. -וְ *wə-* waw connective (BDB p. 251), (Hol p. 84), (TWOT 519): 'and' [all commentators and versions except the following], not explicit [CEV].

p. mas. pl. Qal part. constr. of חָשַׁב *ḥšb* (BDB p. 362), (Hol p. 118), (TWOT 767): 'to think on/upon' [Coh; KJV, NRSV], 'to honor' [CEV, NIV], 'to respect' [TEV], 'to have respect for' [REB], 'to reverence' [Keil], 'to keep in mind' [NICOT; NJB], 'to esteem' [BDB, Hol; Mer, Gla; JPS, NASB], 'to value' [BDB, Hol; WBC], 'to love to think about one' [NLT]. Although the root meaning of *ḥšb* is 'to think, plan', it is found in Isa. 13:17 and 33:8 bearing the sense of 'to esteem, value highly'. This stands as the opposite, then, of בּוֹזֵי שְׁמִי *bôzê šamî* 'despisers of my name' (Mal. 1:6) (see also Isa. 53:6 for an example of parallelism between בּוּז *bûz* 'to despise' and לֹא חָשַׁב *lōʾ ḥšb* 'not to esteem' [Gla].

q. constr. of שֵׁם *šēm* [BDB p. 1027], [Hol p. 374], [TWOT 2405]: 'name' [all lexica, commentators, and versions except the following]. 'Name' is recognized as metonymy and translated concretely: 'him' [NLT, TEV].

QUESTION—Who are the people referred to in this verse and in the following verse?

1. They are those Israelites who, in contrast to those whose thoughts are represented in Mal. 3:13–15, have remained faithful to YHWH and who have not approved of the cynical attitude of the majority of their fellow countrymen [Coh, Keil, NICOT, WBC].

2. They are those of the community who have been brought to repentance by the prophet and who have begun to encourage each other to renew their commitment to YHWH [Mer, Gla, TOTC].

QUESTION—To what time does the adverb אָז *ʾāz* 'then' refer?

1. It refers to the time or times when the faithful element of Israel heard the unfaithful disparage YHWH and his covenant [Keil] and encouraged each other to remain firm in their faithfulness [NICOT].

2. It refers to the time when some of the rebellious Israelites repented at the preaching of the prophet [Mer, Gla].

QUESTION—To what does ספר זכרון *sēper zikkārôn* 'book of remembrance' refer?

1. It refers to the heavenly book of the names of all those who have been faithful to YHWH and to whom YHWH himself is faithful, as in Exod. 32:32-33, Ps. 69:28; 87:6, Deut. 12:1) [Mer, TOTC, WBC]. Malachi (the only prophet to do so [Gla]) calls this book 'the book of remembrance', perhaps influenced by the Persian kings' custom of recording the events and incidents of their reigns (see Esther 6:1 [Gla]) [Keil, NICOT, WBC].

2. It refers to a heavenly book which records, not only the names of the faithful, but, more to the point, their deeds of love and loyalty, as well as the evil deeds of the unfaithful [Gla]. These records will move God to action on their behalf on the day of his judgment (cf. Mal. 3:17) [Gla, NICOT]. Several kinds of divine books are mentioned in the OT, but Malachi's book is similar to that of Ps. 69:28 and Isa. 4:3.

3. It refers to nothing more than a memorandum or record created for the owner and recording for his own use an administrative decision. The writing is itself not for public viewing. Other such memoranda are referred to in Ezra 4:15 and Esther 6:1 [Deuel].

QUESTION—What does לפניו *lapānāw* 'before him (YHWH)' mean?

It means 'that the book might be opened in YHWH's presence', not that the writing was actually done in his presence [Keil].

QUESTION—What relation does the reference to the ספר זכרון *sēper zikkārôn* 'book of remembrance' have to the clauses preceding it?

1. The clause which features this expression is the climax of the embedded narrative in which it appears; moreover, the passive verbal construction results in the topicalization of *sēper* 'book' [Clen].

2. This clause stands outside the event line of the narrative as background information giving an explanation about the book. This is suggested by the use of the participles and the general flavor of the verse. The book did not originate just at that point, but had always existed [Mer].

3:17

(a₁) And[a]-they-will-become[b] to[c]-me, says[d] YHWH(-of) hosts, on[e]-the-day[f] when[g] I-will-act,[h] (a-)possession[i] [Gla; NJB]
   . . . on[e]-the-day[f] which[g] I-will-make[h] [Keil]

(a₂) And[a]-they-will-become[b] mine,[c] says[d] YHWH(-of) hosts, on[e]-the-day[f] when[g] I-will-prepare[h] (my-)possession[i] [Mer, WBC; KJV, NASB, NIV]

(a₃) And[a]-they-will-become[b] mine,[c] says[d] YHWH(-of) hosts, on[e]-the-day[f] which[g] I-will-make,[h] (my-)possession[i] [Coh, NICOT; JPS, REB]
   . . . on[e]-the-day[f] when[g] I-act[h] . . . [NLT, NRSV, TEV]

(b) and[j]-I-will-have-compassion[k] on-them as a-man has-compassion on-his-son[l] the-(one who)serves[m] him. [all commentators and versions]

SYNTAX—(a₁) Here סגלה səḡull 'possession' is taken as a second complement of והיו wəhāyû 'and they will be' (along with the first complement
לי lî 'to me'). The relative particle אשר ʾăšer is understood temporally
as 'when' [Gla; NJB]. The position of səḡull 'possession' at the end of
the phrase is thought to make the word emphatic [C.C. Torrey, "The
Prophet Malachi", *Journal of Biblical Literature* 17 (1898), cited in
Gla]. Keil follows the syntactic grouping of (a₁), but interprets the
relative particle ʾăšer substantively as 'which' and עשה ʾōśê transitively
as 'to make'. Taking səḡull 'possession' as a second verbal complement
after wəhāyû accords with Ex. 19:5 (והייתם לי סגלה wəhiyîtem lî səḡull
'and you will be to me a possession'), from which the Malachi passage
is derived [Keil, TOTC]; also, interpreting səḡull as a second complement of wəhāyû leaves the words ליום אשר אני עשה layyôm ʾăšer ʾănî
ʾōśeh 'on the day when I will act' free to comprise a syntactic unit, as in
Mal. 4:3 (3:21) [Keil].

(a₂) Here לי lî 'to me' is taken as the sole complement of והיו wəhāyû
'and they will be', עשה ʾōśeh is understood transitively, e.g., as 'I will
make', and סגלה səḡull 'possession' is taken as the object of ʾōśeh. As
in (a₁) above, the relative particle אשר ʾăšer is understood temporally,
e.g., 'when' [Mer, WBC; KJV, NIV]. The position of səḡull
'possession' at the end of the phrase is thought to make it impossible for
the word to act as a complement to wəhāyû 'and they will be' [John
Merlin Powis Smith, *Malachi.* The International Critical Commentary.
Edinburgh: T.& T. Clark, 1912; cited in Gla].

(a₃) Here again לי lî 'to me, mine' is taken as the sole complement of
והיו wəhāyû 'and they will be', presumably for the reason proposed by
Smith (see above). The relative particle אשר ʾăšer is understood substantively, e.g., 'which', and is taken to be the object of עשה ʾōśeh, which
in turn is considered to be transitive, e.g., 'I will make'. Səḡull
'possession' is considered to be in explanatory apposition to lî 'to me,
mine' [Coh, NICOT; JPS, REB; also Smith (see above, cited in Gla)].
NLT, NRSV, and TEV follow (a₃), except that they treat the relative
particle and the following verb as do Gla and NJB in (a₁).

LEXICON—a. -ו wə- *waw* connective attached to the following *waw*
consecutive (BDB p. 251), (Hol p. 84), (TWOT 519): 'and' [Coh, Keil,
Gla; JPS, KJV, NASB], 'now' [WBC]. An additive relationship is also
signaled by a new sentence [Mer, NICOT; NIV, NJB, NLT, NRSV,
REB, TEV].

b. 3rd pl. Qal perf. *waw* consecutive of היה hyh (BDB p. 224), (Hol
p. 78), (TWOT 491): 'to become' [Gla], 'to be' [BDB, Hol; Coh, Keil,
Mer, NICOT, WBC; JPS, KJV, NASB, NIV, NJB, NLT, NRSV, REB,
TEV]. The English future tense is used [all commentators and versions].
Hyh, the principal verb to be in Hebrew, has a large variety of

functions; besides providing linkage, it can also denote incipient
existence, e.g., 'to become' [BDB, Hol]. Here it certainly has that force
[Clen].

c. -לְ *lə-* (BDB p. 510), (Hol p. 167), (TWOT 1063). 'To me' is rendered
as the possessive 'mine/my' [all commentators and versions except the
following], 'to me' [Keil; CEV]. *Lə-*, often associated with *hyh* 'to be',
expresses possession in Hebrew [Gla]. This possessive expression is also
translated as 'my people' [NLT, TEV]. *Lə-* is, however, understood by
some here as expressing a dative of advantage: '(precious) to me' [Keil;
CEV]. The proclitic *lə-* here introduces a dative of possession or a dative
of advantage.

d. 3rd mas. sg. Qal perf. of אמר *ʾmr* (BDB p. 55), (Hol p. 21), (TWOT
118): 'to say' [all commentators and versions].

e. -לְ *lə-* (see above): 'in' [Coh, Mer; KJV, NIV], 'on' [Keil, Gla, NICOT;
JPS, NASB, NJB, NLT, NRSV, TEV], 'for' [WBC], 'against' [REB].
The proclitic *lə-* here expresses temporality [BDB, Hol].

f. יום *yôm* (BDB p. 398), (Hol p. 130), (TWOT 852): 'day' [Coh, Keil,
Mer, Gla, NICOT, WBC; JPS, KJV, NASB, NIV, NJB, NLT, NRSV,
REB, TEV].

g. אשׁר *ʾăšer* (BDB p. 81), (Hol p. 30), (TWOT 184): 'that' [Coh, Keil,
NICOT; JPS, NASB, REB], 'when' [Mer, Gla, WBC; KJV, NIV, NJB,
NLT, NRSV, TEV]. *ʾăšer* is a relative particle.

h. mas. sg. Qal part. of עשׂה *ʿśh* (BDB p. 793), (Hol p. 284), (TWOT
1708): 'to make' [BDB; Coh, NICOT, WBC], 'to act' [Gla; NJB, NLT,
NRSV, TEV], 'to prepare' [Mer; JPS, NASB], 'to create' [Keil], 'to
do' [BDB, Hol], 'to make up' [KJV, NIV], 'to appoint' [REB]. The
phrase ליום אשׁר אני עשׂה *layyôm ʾăšer ʾănî ʿōśeh* is also translated
functionally as 'when I come to bring justice', apparently identifying this
day with the 'Day of the Lord' [CEV].

i. סגלה *səgullâ* (BDB p. 688), (Hol p. 253), (TWOT 1460a): 'possession'
[BDB; Keil, Mer; NASB, REB], 'special possession' [Gla; NRSV],
'treasure' [Coh], 'jewels' [KJV]. This noun is also translated as a
phrase: 'treasured possession' [NICOT; JPS, NIV], 'special treasure'
[WBC; NLT], 'most prized possession' [NJB]. Some translations add a
possessive expression such as 'my' to the noun or noun phrase. This
noun is also translated as an adjective: 'precious' [CEV] and as a phrase
expressing possession: 'my very own' [TEV]. *Səgullâ* denotes 'personal
property', here applied to Israel as YHWH's property [Hol]; it may
carry a nuance of especially valued possessions [BDB].

j. -ו *wə-* *waw* connective attached to the following *waw* consecutive (BDB
p. 251), (Hol p. 84), (TWOT 519): 'and' [Coh, Keil, Gla, WBC; KJV,
NASB, NJB, NRSV, REB]. An additive relationship is also expressed
by a new sentence [Mer, NICOT; CEV, JPS, NIV, NLT].

k. 1st sg. Qal perf. *waw* consecutive of חמל *ḥml* (BDB p. 328), (Hol
p. 108), (TWOT 676): 'to have compassion' [BDB; Gla], 'to spare'

[BDB; Coh, Keil, Mer, NICOT, WBC; KJV, NASB, NIV, NJB, NLT, NRSV, REB], 'to spare in compassion' [NIV], 'to protect' [CEV], 'to be tender' [JPS].

l. בֵּן *bēn* (BDB p. 119), (Hol p. 42), (TWOT 254): 'son' [all lexica, commentators, and versions except the following], 'child' [CEV, NLT, NRSV].

m. mas. sg. Qal part. of עבד *ʿbd* (BDB p. 712), (Hol p. 261), (TWOT 1553): 'to serve' [BDB, Hol; Coh, Keil, Mer, Gla, NICOT, WBC; KJV, NASB, NIV, NJB, NRSV, REB], 'to minister' [JPS], 'to work for' [Hol]. The phrase in which this verb is included is also translated as adjectives: 'obedient' [CEV], 'obedient and dutiful' [NLT].

QUESTION—What is the discourse role of this verse?

This verse begins an embedded result paragraph (Mal. 3:17–4:3 (3:17–21)), which presents the consequences of the devout actions of the fearers of YHWH described in Mal. 3:16 [Clen].

QUESTION—To what time does לְיוֹם *layyôm* 'on the day' refer?

It refers to the 'Day of the Lord', when YHWH will come in judgment and blessing to inaugurate his rule [Keil, Mer, Gla, NICOT].

QUESTION—How should the relative particle אֲשֶׁר *ʾăšer* be translated?

1. It should be translated as a temporal expression, e.g., 'when', to accord with the interpretation of עֹשֶׂה *ʿōśeh* as 'I will act' (see below) [Gla].

2. It should be translated substantively as 'which' to accord with the understanding of עֹשֶׂה *ʿōśeh* as 'I will create' (see below) [Keil].

QUESTION—What is the meaning of עֹשֶׂה *ʿōśeh* in this verse?

1. It is 'I will act', for this accords with the sense of זֶה־הַיּוֹם עָשָׂה יְהוָה *zeh hayyôm ʿāśâ yhwh* 'this is the day on which YHWH has acted' (Ps. 118:24), where YHWH's mighty acts of deliverance on the 'Day of the Lord' are celebrated, as also in Malachi [Gla].

2. It is 'I will create', this accords with an understanding of *ʿśh* in Ps. 118:24 as 'to create' [Keil].

QUESTION—What are the background and semantic range of סְגֻלָּה *sᵊgullâ* 'possession'?

Sᵊgullâ's cognate in Akkadian, *sikiltum*, denoted first a private accumulation of money or other wealth; *sᵊgullâ* is found with this same sense in 1 Chr. 29:3 and Eccl. 2:3. Then the sense of *sᵊgullâ* was extended to denote anything highly valued because of the effort in acquiring it [Gla]. The cognate in Ugaritic, *sglt*, was applied to a lord's vassal [Gla, WBC].

One concludes, then, that *sᵊgullâ* and its cognates in other languages belonged to covenantal vocabulary of the region. The nation of Israel obedient to YHWH is characterized at Mt. Sinai as his *sᵊgullâ* (Exod. 19:5) [NICOT, WBC]. Although everything is YHWH's, Israel is to be his treasured possession [WBC], his right by redemption [Mer].

Sᵊgullâ also stands parallel to the concept of Israel's being chosen by YHWH in Ps. 135:4 [NICOT].

QUESTION—What does סגלה *saḡullâ* denote in this verse?

It denotes the remnant of Israel who are faithful to YHWH, for they fulfill the covenantal obligations. They will be spared on the Day of the Lord, when YWHW comes to execute justice and begin his reign [Coh, Keil, Gla, NICOT].

QUESTION—How should חמל *ḥml* be understood in this verse?

It should be understood as 'to spare out of compassion'. YHWH will spare his beloved faithful ones on the 'Day of the Lord' from adverse judgment and punishment [Keil, Gla]. The prototypical sparing action of YHWH occurred when he spared the Israelites on the first Passover night in Egypt from the punishment which overtook the Egyptians [Mer].

QUESTION—How should עבד *ᶜbd* 'to serve' be understood in this verse?

It should be understood as 'to be dutiful toward one', for in focus here is the obedience of the faithful in contrast to the disobedience of the others. This passage answers the discouraged claim of the cynical in Mal. 3:14, responding to them that it is indeed to the obedient that God shows his compassion [Gla].

3:18

(a₁) And[a]-you(pl)-will-return[b] and-you-will-see[c]

(a₂) And[a]-you(pl)-will-again[b] see[c]

(the-difference-)between[d]   (the-)righteous-one(s)[e]   (and-)between[f]-(the-)wicked-one(s),[g] between one-serving[h] God[i] (and-)between-one-who-does-not -serve-him.

LEXICON—a. -ו *wǝ-* *waw* connective attached to the following *waw* consecutive (BDB p. 251), (Hol p. 84), (TWOT 519): 'and' [Keil, Gla, WBC; JPS, NIV]; an additive relationship is also signaled by a new sentence with no conjunction [REB, TEV]; 'then' [Coh, Mer, NICOT; CEV, KJV, NJB, NLT, NRSV].

b. 2nd pl. Qal perf. *waw* consecutive of שוב *šûḇ* (BDB p. 996), (Hol. p. 362), (TWOT 2340): 'to return' [BDB, Hol; KJV, WBC]. This verb is translated by most as an adverb: 'again' [Coh, Keil, Gla, NICOT; NIV, NLT], 'once again' [CEV, NJB, TEV], 'once more' [Mer; NRSV, REB], not explicit [JPS]. *Šûḇ* often functions modally with another verb to indicate repetition [BDB, Hol].

c. 2nd pl. Qal perf. *waw* consecutive of ראה *rʾh* (BDB p. 906), (Hol p. 328), (TWOT 2095): 'to see' [BDB, Hol; NICOT; CEV, NIV, NJB, NLT, NRSV, TEV], 'to discern' [Coh, Mer, WBC; KJV], 'to perceive' [Keil], 'to distinguish' [Gla], 'to come to see' [JPS], 'to tell' [REB].

d. constr. of בין *bayin* (BDB p. 107), (Hol p. 38), (TWOT 239a). This noun is translated as a preposition: 'between' [BDB, Hol; Coh, Mer, Gla, WBC; KJV]. It is also translated as a phrase: 'the difference between' [Keil; CEV, JPS, NJB, NLT, NRSV, TEV], 'the distinction between' [NICOT; NIV], not explicit [REB]

e. צַדִּיק ṣaddîq (BDB p. 843), (Hol p. 303), (TWOT 1879c): 'the righteous' [BDB, Hol; Coh, Keil, Mer, Gla, NICOT, WBC; JPS, KJV, NIV, NLT, NRSV, TEV], 'the just' [BDB, Hol], 'the upright person' [NJB], 'the good' [REB], 'the godly' [Hol]. This adjective is also translated as a verb phrase which conflates the idea of 'righteous' with the idea of 'he who serves' below: 'those who obey me by doing right' [CEV]. TEV makes explicit its understanding that in focus is the Israelites' questioning the ultimate destinies awaiting these two groups of people: 'the difference between what happens to the righteous and the wicked., to the person who serves me and the one who does not'. Ṣaddîq denotes adherence to a standard, in this case, that of YHWH [Gla].

f. -לְ la- (BDB p. 510), (Hol p. 167), (TWOT 1063): 'and' [Coh, Keil, Mer, Gla, NICOT, WBC; CEV, JPS, KJV, NIV, NJB, NLT, NRSV, TEV], 'from' [REB]. The proclitic la- here reinforces the previous preposition בֵּין bēn 'between'.

g. רָשָׁע rāšāᶜ (BDB p. 957), (Hol p. 347), (TWOT 2222b): 'wicked' [BDB; Coh, Keil, Mer, Gla, NICOT, WBC; JPS, KJV, NIV, NJB, NLT, NRSV, REB, TEV], 'guilty' [Hol]. This adjective is also translated as a verb phrase which conflates the idea of 'wicked' with the idea of 'he who does not serve' below: 'those who reject me by doing wrong' [CEV]. There are many ideas associated with rāšāᶜ in the OT, among which figure pride, self-sufficiency, rebellion against God, and a denial of God's capacity to punish evil [Gla].

h. mas. sg. Qal part. of עָבַד ᶜbd (BDB p. 712), (Hol p. 261), (TWOT 1553): 'to serve' [BDB, Hol; Coh, Keil, Mer, Gla, NICOT, WBC; JPS, KJV, NIV, NJB, NLT, NRSV, TEV], 'to work for' [Hol]. The English present tense, e.g. 'who serves' or present participle, e.g., 'serving' is employed by all commentators and versions except the following; the present perfect tense, i.e., 'has served' is also employed [JPS]. This verb is also translated as a noun: 'servant' [REB].

i. אֱלֹהִים ʾĕlōhîm (BDB p. 43), (Hol p. 16), (TWOT 93c): 'God' [all lexica, commentators, and versions except the following], 'Lord' [JPS]. CEV and TEV put this verse into direct speech attributed to God: 'me'.

QUESTION—What is the meaning of וְשַׁבְתֶּם wašabtem 'and you will return'?

1. It has adverbial force in this context, indicating repetition: 'and you will see again' [Coh, Keil, Gla, NICOT].

2. It indicates the future repentance of the addressees [this view was held by Jerome and Calvin; cited in NICOT]. Šûb 'to return' is one of the main words in the OT denoting repentance.

3. It indicates that the addressees will change their minds [this view was held by Wellhausen, Driver, and others; cited in NICOT].

QUESTION—What is the significance of the phrase ורְאיתם בין צדיק לרשע
ושבתם wəšabtem ûrəʔîtem bên ṣaddîq lərāšāᶜ 'and you will again see the
difference between the righteous and the wicked'?

It is that the difference between the ultimate destinies of the righteous and
the wicked will be clearly understood and appreciated in the future, unlike
at present, in which the wicked appear to do well for themselves [Methsu-
dath David, cited in Coh, Keil, Gla, NICOT; TEV]. These destinies will
be understood by all when YHWH awards justice to the righteous and
condemnation to the wicked; this will be part of his establishment of צדקה
ṣədāqâ 'right order' on the earth [Gla, NICOT].

QUESTION—What is the explanatory parallelism in this passage?

צדיק ṣaddîq 'righteous' is parallel to עבד אלהים ᶜōbēd ʔĕlōhîm 'he who
serves God'; רשע rāšāᶜ 'wicked' is parallel to לא עבדו lōʔ ᶜăbādô 'does
not serve him' [Gla, NICOT, TOTC]. 'Righteous' and 'wicked' are terms
within a judicial point of view, while 'he who serves God' and 'he does not
serve God' are expressions belonging to a religious or covenantal point of
view [NICOT]. The contrast between the righteous and the wicked is a
major theme of the OT [WBC].

QUESTION—What is the meaning of עבד ᶜbd 'to serve' in this verse?

1. It is to worship YHWH [WBC].
2. It is to live within the covenantal relationship of Israel to YHWH
   [NICOT]; it is thus to conduct oneself properly towards YHWH, being
   motivated by the "fear" of, i.e., reverence for, him [Gla].

DISCOURSE UNIT: 4:1–6 (3:19–24) [CEV, NASB, NIV, NLT, NRSV,
TEV]. The topic is "the day of judgment" [CEV], a "final admonition"
[NASB], 'the day of the Lord' [NIV], "the coming day of judgment" [NLT],
"the great day of the Lord" [NRSV], "the day of the Lord is coming" [TEV].

4:1 (3:19)
For[a] behold,[b] the-day[c] is-coming,[d] burning[e] like[f]-the-furnace,[g] and/when[h]-
all-proud-ones[i] and-every-one-doing[j] wickedness[k] -will-become[l] stubble.[m]
And[n]- the- coming[o] -day -will-burn- them -up,[p] says YHWH(-of) hosts, so-
that/and[q] it-will- not -leave[r] to-them root[s] nor[t]-branch.[u]

CHAPTER NUMBERING—The Hebrew Bible continues chapter 3 until the
     end of the book. The English Bible derives its chapter 4 from LXX and the
     Vulgate [WBC].
LEXICON—a. כי kî connective (BDB p. 471), (Hol p. 155), (TWOT 976):
     'for' [Coh, Keil, Mer, Gla, NICOT; JPS, KJV, NASB, NJB], 'because'
     [WBC], not explicit [NIV, NLT, NRSV, REB, TEV].
   b. הנה hinnēh (BDB p. 243), (Hol p. 82), (TWOT 510a): 'behold' [Coh,
     Keil, WBC; KJV, NASB], 'lo!' [JPS], 'look' [NJB], 'see' [NRSV],
     'indeed' [Mer, Gla], 'surely' [NICOT; NIV]. The intensive idea of
     hinnēh is also made explicit in by a phrase: 'to be certain to come'

[CEV]. Not explicit [NLT, REB, TEV]. *Hinnēh* is a demonstrative interjection or particle [BDB, Hol].

c. יוֹם *yôm* (BDB p. 398) (Hol p. 130), (TWOT 852): 'day' [all lexica, commentators, and versions except CEV]. CEV further specifies *yôm* with a phrase: 'day of judgment'.

d. mas. sg. Qal part. of בּוֹא *bô>* (BDB p. 97) (Hol p. 34), (TWOT 212): 'to come' [all lexica, commentators, and versions except the following], 'to arrive' [Hol], 'to be at hand' [JPS]. The use of the participle with the interjection *hinnēh* 'behold' expresses imminent future [Gla, NICOT].

e. mas. sg. Qal part. of בָּעַר *b<r* (BDB p. 129) (Hol p. 44), (TWOT 263): 'to burn' [BDB; Coh, Keil, Mer, Gla, NICOT, WBC; JPS, KJV, NASB, NIV, NLT, NRSV, REB], 'to glow' [NJB]. This verb is also translated by an adjective: 'red-hot' [CEV], not explicit [TEV].

f. -כְ *kə* (BDB p. 453) (Hol p. 149), (TWOT 937): 'like' [Keil, Mer, Gla, NICOT, WBC; CEV, JPS, NASB, NIV, NJB, NLT, NRSV, REB], 'as' [Coh; KJV], not explicit [TEV]. The proclitic *kə* here expresses comparison [BDB, Hol].

g. תַּנּוּר *tannûr* (BDB p. 1072) (Hol p. 392), (TWOT 2526): 'furnace' [Hol; Coh, Keil, Mer, NICOT; CEV, NASB, NIV, NJB, NLT], 'oven' [Hol; Gla, WBC; JPS, KJV, NRSV, REB], not explicit [TEV]. *Tannûr* denotes a small oven for baking bread [Gla], but also a kiln for the firing of pottery [James L. Kelso, *The Ceramic Vocabulary of the Old Testament, BASOR* Supp. Studies 5–6. New Haven, Conn.: American Schools of Oriental Research, 1948; cited in Mer].

h. -וְ *wə- waw* connective attached to the following *waw* consecutive (see (1) below) (BDB p. 251), (Hol p. 84), (TWOT 519): 'and' [Coh, Keil, Mer, Gla; KJV, NASB]. An item-identification relation between הַיּוֹם *hayyôm* 'the day' and וְהָיוּ כָל־זֵדִים וְכָל־עֹשֵׂה רִשְׁעָה קַשׁ *wəhāyû kol zēdîm wəkol <ōśēh riš<â qaš* 'and all the arrogant and everyone doing evil will become stubble' is apparently expressed by a new sentence [NICOT; JPS, NIV, NJB, NLT, REB]; it is also explicitly signaled by a conjunction: 'when' [WBC; NRSV]; and by a relative pronoun: 'that' [CEV]; not explicit [TEV].

i. mas. pl. of זֵד *zēd* (BDB p. 267) (Hol p. 86), (TWOT 547a): 'proud' [Coh, Keil; CEV, KJV, NJB, TEV], 'arrogant' [Hol; Mer, Gla, NICOT, WBC; JPS, NASB, NIV, NLT, NRSV, REB], 'presumptuous' [BDB, Hol].

j. mas. sg. Qal part. constr. of עשׂה *<śh* (BDB p. 793) (Hol p. 284), (TWOT 1708): 'to do' [BDB, Hol; Keil; JPS, KJV, NASB], 'to work' [Coh], 'to commit' [Gla].

k. רִשְׁעָה *riš<â* (BDB p. 958) (Hol p. 347), (TWOT 2222c): 'wickedness' [BDB; Coh, Keil, Gla], 'evil' [JPS, NASB]. The phrase 'to do wickedness' is also translated as a noun: 'evildoer' [Mer, NICOT, WBC; NIV, NJB, NRSV, REB]; by an adjective: 'sinful' [CEV], 'wicked' [NLT], 'evil' [TEV]; and by an adverb: 'wickedly' [KJV].

l. 3rd pl. Qal perf. *waw*-consecutive of הָיָה *hyh* (BDB p. 224), (Hol p. 78), (TWOT 491): 'to become' [BDB, Hol; Keil, WBC], 'to be' [BDB, Hol; Coh, Mer, Gla, NICOT; JPS, KJV, NASB, NIV, NJB, NRSV, REB]. Some make explicit the process of becoming stubble, conflating the two clauses 'and- all-proud-ones and-every-one-doing wickedness -will-become stubble. And- the- coming -day -will-burn-them -up': 'with flames that burn up proud and sinful people, as though they were straw' [CEV], 'the arrogant and the wicked will be burned up like straw on that day' [NLT], 'all the proud and evil people will burn like straw' [TEV].

m. קַשׁ *qaš* (BDB p. 905) (Hol p. 326), (TWOT 2091a): 'stubble' [BDB, Hol; Coh, Keil, Gla, NICOT, WBC; KJV, NIV, NJB, NRSV, REB], 'chaff' [BDB; Mer; NASB], 'straw' [CEV, JPS, NLT, TEV]. The metaphor associated with *qaš* is preserved [all commentators and versions except the following]; the metaphor is transformed by some into a simile in translation [NICOT; CEV, NLT, TEV].

n. -וְ *wə- waw* connective attached to the following *waw* consecutive verb (see (p) below) (BDB p. 251), (Hol p. 84), (TWOT 519): 'and' [Coh, Keil, Gla, NICOT, WBC; JPS, KJV, NASB, NIV, NJB, REB]. An additive relation is also expressed with a new sentence [Mer; CEV, NLT, NRSV].

o. mas. sg. Qal part. of בּוֹא *bôʾ* (see above): 'to come' [BDB, Hol; Coh, Keil, Mer, Gla, NICOT, WBC; JPS, KJV, NASB, NIV, NJB, REB], not explicit [CEV, NLT].

p. 3rd mas sg. Piel perf. *waw* consecutive of לְהַט *lhṭ* (BDB p. 529), (Hol p. 173), (TWOT 1081): 'to burn up [CEV, KJV, NRSV, TEV], 'to set ablaze' [BDB; Coh, Gla; NASB, NJB, REB], 'to burn' [Keil, Mer, WBC], 'to consume' [NICOT], 'to be consumed' [NLT], 'to set on fire' [NIV], 'to scorch' [Hol]. This verb is also translated with a phrase: 'to burn to ashes' [JPS]. *Lhṭ* here perhaps evokes a picture of fire surrounding its victim, from comparison with its Akkadian cognate [E. Lipínski, *La Royauté de Yahwé dans la poésie et le culte d'ancien Israël* (Brussels: Palais der Academiën, 1965); cited in Gla].

q. אֲשֶׁר *ʾăšer* (BDB p. 81), (Hol p. 30), (TWOT 184). This particle is translated by many as introducing an expression of result, e.g., 'so that' [Coh, Keil, Mer; KJV, NASB, NRSV]. Result is also expressed with a participle: 'leaving' [NJB, REB]. An additive relation of clauses is signaled by 'and' [JPS, TEV], and by a new sentence [Gla, NICOT, WBC; NIV]. Translation not explicit [NLT]. *ʾăšer* is a relative particle.

r. 3rd mas. sg. Qal imperf. of עָזַב *ʿzb* (BDB p. 737), (Hol p. 269), (TWOT 1594): 'to leave' [BDB, Hol; Coh, Keil, Mer, Gla, NICOT, WBC; CEV, KJV, NASB, NIV, NJB, NRSV, REB]. A slightly different nuance is achieved by translating 'to leave of them' [JPS]. *ʿzb* denotes here 'to leave something for someone' [BDB, Hol].

s. שרש šōreš (BDB p. 1057), (Hol p. 384), (TWOT 2471a): 'root' [BDB, Hol; Coh, Keil, Mer, Gla, NICOT, WBC; CEV, KJV, NASB, NIV, NJB, NRSV, REB], 'stock' [JPS]. Šōreš, denoting in its primary sense the root of a plant, here denotes metaphorically a permanent basis or foundation of a people [BDB, Hol].

t. -ו wǝ- waw connective (BDB p. 251) (Hol p. 84), (TWOT 519): 'nor' [Coh, Keil, Gla, NICOT; JPS, KJV, NASB, NJB, NRSV, REB], 'or' [Mer, WBC; CEV, NIV].

u. ענף ʿānāp (BDB p. 778) (Hol p. 278), (TWOT 1657a): 'branch' [BDB, Hol; Coh, Keil, Mer, Gla, NICOT, WBC; CEV, KJV, NASB, NIV, NJB, NRSV, REB], 'bough' [BDB; JPS]. The metaphor 'leaving them neither root nor branch'—which occurs also in Ps. 80:10—expresses entire destruction and is translated as a simile, together with an English idiom: 'they will be consumed like a tree—roots and all' [NLT]. The figure of speech is dispensed with entirely by others: 'there will nothing left of them' [TEV]. See Job 18:16–20 for an extended exposition of this figure of speech [A. von Bulmerincq, *Der Prophet Maleachi*. Vol. 2. Tartu: J.G. Krüger, 1926–1932; cited in Gla].

QUESTION—What is the significance of the references to fire and burning?

בער bʿr and its derivatives are found in many references to occasions on which God revealed himself (e.g., Deut. 4:11; 5:23); the idea of fire often characterizes God's judgment falling upon the wicked (e.g., Isa. 10:17), as well as God's purifying actions (e.g., Mal. 3:2–3) [Gla]. TOTC sees in the image presented by this verse a picture of intense climactic heat on the coming 'Day of the Lord', which will wither all vegetation and render it vulnerable to brush fires.

QUESTION—What is the significance of the reference to קש qaš 'stubble'?

1. The stubble, left over from the threshing of the grain, was used to kindle the firepots, the portable ovens commonly employed in baking break. Being light and dry, the stubble was quickly reduced to ashes in the fires. The same image occurs in Isa. 5:24; 47:14; Joel 2:5; Obad. 18; and Nah. 1:10 [Gla].

2. The stubble was thrown into a תנור tannûr, which in this verse must indicate an incinerator, for the goal was to get rid of the stubble [Mer].

QUESTION—What is the significance of the reference to זדים zēdîm 'arrogant' and to עשה רשעה ʿōśēh rišʿâ 'evildoer'?

It is that these same terms appear in Mal. 3:15, referring to those who have turned against God and who seem to get away with doing so [Gla, Mer].

4:2 (3:20)

But[a]- for[b]-you(pl) (the-) fearers(-of)[c] my-name,[d] (the-)sun(-of)[e] right-eousness[f] -will-arise,[g] and[h]-healing[i] (will be) in[j]-its-wings,[k] and[l]-you(pl)-will-go-forth,[m] and[n]-you(pl)-will-gambol[o] like-calves[p] (-of) (the-)stall.[q]

LEXICON—a. -ו (see (g) below) wǝ- waw connective attached to the following waw consecutive verb (g) (BDB p. 251), (Hol p. 84), (TWOT 519):

'but' [Coh, Keil, Mer, Gla, NICOT; CEV, JPS, KJV, NASB, NIV,
NJB, NLT, NRSV, REB, TEV], 'and' [WBC].

b. -לְ *lə-* (BDB p. 510), (Hol p. 167), (TWOT 1063): 'for' [Mer, NICOT,
WBC; CEV, JPS, NASB, NIV, NJB, NLT, NRSV, REB, TEV], 'as
for' [Gla] 'unto' [Coh; KJV], 'to' [Keil]. The proclitic *lə-* here expresses
perhaps dative of advantage or perhaps movement towards something
[BDB, Hol].

c. mas. pl. Qal part. constr. of יָרֵא *yr²* (BDB p. 431), (Hol p. 142),
(TWOT 907): 'to fear' [all lexica, commentators, and versions except
the following], 'to revere' [Mer, NICOT; JPS, NIV, NRSV], 'to honor'
[CEV], 'to obey' [TEV].

d. שֵׁם *šēm* (BDB p. 1027), (Hol p. 374), (TWOT 2405): 'name' [all lexica,
commentators, and versions except TEV]. TEV recognizes the
metonymy of *šēm* here, translating it concretely as 'me'.

e. constr. of שֶׁמֶשׁ *šemeš* (BDB p. 1039), (Hol p. 378), (TWOT 2417a):
'sun' [all lexica, commentators, and versions].

f. צְדָקָה *ṣədāqâ* (BDB p. 842), (Hol p. 303), (TWOT 1879b): 'righteousness' [all lexica, commentators, and versions except the following],
'victory' [JPS], 'justice' [NJB], 'saving power' [TEV]. Some translate
'sun of righteousness with a simile: 'victory will shine like the sun'
[CEV], 'my saving power will rise on you like the sun' [TEV].

g. 3ʳᵈ fem. Qal perf. *waw* consecutive of זרח *zrḥ* (BDB p. 280), (Hol
p. 92), (TWOT 580): 'to arise' [Coh, Gla; JPS, KJV], 'to rise' [BDB;
Keil, Mer, WBC; NASB, NIV, NJB, NLT, NRSV, REB, TEV], 'to
shine forth' [NICOT], 'to shine' [Hol; CEV], 'to come forth' [BDB].

h. -וְ *wə- waw* connective (BDB p. 251), (Hol p. 84), (TWOT 519): 'and'
[Keil, NICOT; TEV]; 'with' [Coh, Mer, Gla; KJV, NASB, NIV, NJB,
NLT, NRSV, REB]. An additive relation is expressed by a new sentence
[WBC]. Some preserve in translation the full implicit Hebrew predica-
tion introduced by this connective, e.g., 'and there will be healing in its
wings' [NICOT, WBC].

i. מַרְפֵּא *marpē²* (BDB p. 951), (Hol p. 216), (TWOT 2196c): 'healing' (as
a noun) [all lexica, commentators, and versions except BDB], 'health'
[BDB].

j. -בְּ *bə-* (BDB p. 88), (Hol p. 32), (TWOT 193): 'in' [all commentators
and versions]. The proclitic *bə-* denotes here abstract locality [BDB,
Hol].

k. dual constr. of כָּנָף *kānāp* (BDB p. 489), (Hol p. 160), (TWOT 1003a):
'wing' [all lexica, commentators, and versions except the following].
Some translate *kānāp* concretely: 'ray' [CEV, NJB, TEV]. The entire
phrase 'with healing in its wings' is also translated concretely: 'to bring
healing' [JPS, TEV].

l. -וְ *wə- waw* connective attached to the following *waw* consecutive verb
(BDB p. 251), (Hol p. 84), (TWOT 519): 'and' [all commentators and

versions except the following]. An additive relation is also expressed by a new sentence [JPS, NRSV, TEV].

m. 2nd mas. pl. Qal perf. *waw* consecutive of יצא *yṣ'* (BDB p. 422), (Hol p. 139), (TWOT 893): 'to go forth' [Hol; all commentators and versions except the following], 'to go out' [BDB; Keil, Gla, NICOT, WBC; NIV, NRS, NRSV], 'to come out' [BDB; NJB], 'to go free' [NLT], 'to break loose' [REB], 'to be free' [TEV], not explicit [CEV].

n. -ו *wə-* *waw* connective attached to the following *waw* consecutive verb (BDB p. 251), (Hol p. 84), (TWOT 519): 'and' [all commentators and versions except the following]. The clause introduced by this connective is also translated so as to express the manner of going out: 'leaping'. [NJB, NLT, NRSV]. Translation not explicit [REB].

o. 2nd mas. pl. Qal perf. *waw* consecutive of פוש *pûš* (BDB p. 807), (Hol p. 290), (TWOT 1751): 'to gambol' [Coh, Gla], 'to skip' [Keil], 'to skip about' [Mer; NASB], 'to leap' [NICOT; NIV, NJB, NRSV], 'to leap with joy' [NLT], 'to jump around' [CEV], 'to paw the ground' [Hol; WBC], 'to stamp' [JPS], 'to be happy' [TEV], 'to grow up' [KJV], 'to spring about' of calves at play [BDB]. There is a strong nuance of joyful play in *pûš* [NICOT]. On the other hand, Rashi and Kimchi, two medieval Jewish commentators, interpreted *pûš* to mean to grow bigger and fatter [Coh]. Translation not explicit [REB].

p. pl. constr. of עגל *ʿēgel* (BDB p. 722), (Hol p. 264), (TWOT 1560a): 'calf' [BDB; Coh, Keil, Mer, NICOT, WBC; CEV, JPS, KJV, NASB, NIV, NJB, NLT, NRSV, REB, TEV], 'cattle' [Gla], 'bull-calf' [Hol].

q. מרבק *marbēq* (BDB p. 918), (Hol p. 214), (TWOT 2110a): 'stall' [BDB; Coh, Mer, NICOT; NASB]. This noun is also translated as an adjective: 'stalled' [Keil], 'fattening' [Hol]. The construct relationship between 'calves' and 'stall' is translated by prep. phrases: 'of the stall' [Coh; KJV] and 'from the stall' [Mer; NASB, NJB, NRSV]; by participial phrases: 'stalled' [Keil], 'well-fed' [Gla], 'stall-fed' [JPS], 'fattened' [WBC]; 'released from the stall' [NICOT; NIV, REB], 'let out of a stall' [TEV]. The thought 'of the stall' is restructured: 'let out to pasture' [NLT]. Translation not explicit [CEV].

QUESTION—who are the addressees of this verse?

They are probably the same 'fearers of YHWH' as in Mal. 3:16 [NICOT].

QUESTION—In the figure of speech וזרחה לכם יראי שמי שמש צדקה ומרפא בכנפיה *wəzārəḥ lākem yir'ê šəmî šemeš ṣədāq ûmarpê biknāp̄hā* 'for/but on you will rise the sun of righteousness with healing in its wings', what is the syntactic relationship between שמש *šemeš* 'sun' and צדקה *ṣədāq* 'righteousness'?

1. *Šemeš* 'sun' is an adverbial 'accusative of condition'; thus, *ṣədāq* 'righteousness' will shine forth 'like the sun'. This interpretation accounts for the feminine gender of וזרחה *wəzārəḥ* 'and will shine', even though *šemeš* 'sun' is masculine [cited in NICOT].

2. Šemeš 'sun' is in apposition to ṣəḏāq 'righteousness', where ṣəḏāq is the formal subject and šemeš the 'nearer definition', giving the reader an image to visualize. Assuming a construct relationship between the two words (see below) would place undue emphasis on šemeš, whereas the real point of the passage concerns ṣəḏāq [Keil, NICOT]. Parallel expressions occur in Ps. 37:6 and Is. 58:8 [NICOT].

3. Various ancient versions express a Hebrew construct relationship between šemeš 'sun' and ṣəḏāq 'righteousness': ἥλιος δικαιοσύνης (LXX) and sol iustitiae 'sun of righteousness' (Vulgate). Calvin viewed this construct relation as expressing quality: 'the sun which possesses righteousness'; Cocceius thought that it expressed function: 'the sun which brings forth righteousness'. Others see the relationship as a defining one: 'the sun which is righteousness [NICOT].

QUESTION—In the same figure of speech, how should ṣəḏāq 'righteousness' be interpreted?

1. Most ancient interpreters, Church fathers, and early commentators held that ṣəḏāq is here the Messiah, whether at his first coming or his second [Keil, NICOT].

2. Ṣəḏāq is the moral quality which the chosen of God will have on the 'Day of the Lord' [NICOT], the achieved effect of all God's saving actions [Keil]. This interpretation was proposed by Theodore of Mopsuestia and is preferred [NICOT]. Ṣəḏāq has two aspects in the OT: it comprises conformity to a standard, in this case God's; and it comprises right relationships within the covenant community. In this passage, ṣəḏāq will be given by God to his faithful people on the day when he will act, bringing to them justice and victory over all evils, and punishing the ones who have make his people suffer [NICOT]. Similarly to the foregoing view, but expanding upon it, ṣəḏāq here denotes the right order of things, the absence of which was bemoaned by the fearers of YHWH in Mal. 3:14-15 when they called the arrogant happy. This condition will be put right on the 'Day of the Lord' when all rebels against God will be condemned [Gla—see also the discussion of מרפא marpēʾ 'healing; remedy' below], the faithful will be restored to right relationship with God, and the harm done to the earth itself will be put right [Gla].

3. Ṣəḏāq 'righteousness' here denotes the total effect of salvation, as in Is. 14:8; 46:13 [Keil].

4. Ṣəḏāq 'righteousness' here denotes more or less 'victory, triumph', having acquired this sense before Malachi's time [I.G. Matthews, "Malachi." An American Commentary. Philadelphia: Judson Press, 1935; cited in WBC, who finds the same sense of ṣəḏāq in Is. 41:2, 10; 45:21, 23; 46:13; 51:5,6; this viewpoint is supported by J.M.P. Smith, A Critical and Exegetical Summary on the Book of Malachi, ICC, Edinburgh: T. & T. Clark, 1912, repr. 1961; cited in Gla. JPS also translates 'victory'].

QUESTION—In the same figure of speech, what is meant by מַרְפֵּא *marpēʾ* 'healing; remedy'?

1. *Marpēʾ* here denotes the healing and healthful fertility of the fields, brought about by the restoration of the normal seasons of the year, so that the people can prosper once again; *marpēʾ* is, then, 'healing fertility' in Malachi, as in Gen. 20:17 [Gla].

2. *Marpēʾ* here carries a wide semantic range: healing, relief from suffering, the reversal of catastrophe, and peace, including spiritual peace coming from forgiven sin (see Jer. 17:14; Is. 53:5) [Keil, NICOT].

QUESTION—In the same figure of speech, what is meant here by כָּנָף *kānāp* 'wing'?

1. *Kānāp* is a metaphor for the sun's rays: as the sun radiates its light and warmth, so YHWH will radiate upon his people his healing [Coh, Keil, WBC] and *ṣəḏāq* 'righteousness', i.e., 'right order' [Gla]. Similarly, some see *kānāp* as introducing a metaphor for the dawn, as in Ps. 139:9. Thus, YHWH will bring healing as the day of his saving actions dawns [Clen].

2. *Kānāp* is a metaphor for a fold in one's garment, serving as a sort of pocket in which a Jew would keep his money, etc. (see Num. 15:38; 1 Sam. 15:27; Zech. 8:23). The sun keeps its remedy, 'healing', in its 'pocket' [C. van Gelderen, *Het Boek Hosea*, COT. Kampen: Kok, 1953; cited in NICOT].

QUESTION—Concerning the same figure of speech, what is the origin of the association of כָּנָף *kānāp* 'wing' with שֶׁמֶשׁ *šemeš* 'sun'?

1. The image of wings and disk was drawn from the representation of the Persian god Ahuramazda; Malachi's use of the image reflects the influence of the Persian period upon him [John Gray, "The Day of Yahweh in Cultic Experience and Eschatalogical Prospect," *Svensk Exegetisk Årsbok* 29 (1974); cited in Gla].

2. The image of wings was drawn from the representation of the sun as a winged disk, commonly picturing the sun god in the art of Egypt and Mesopotamia [TOTC, WBC; Ernst Sellin, *Das Zwölfprophetenbuch übersetzt und erklärt*. Kommentar zum Alten Testament, Band XII, zweite Hälfte. Leipzig: A. Deichertsche Verlagsbuchhandlung, 1930; cited in Gla, and Rex Mason, *The Books of Haggai, Zechariah and Malachi*. The Cambridge Bible Commentary. Cambridge: Cambridge University Press, 1977; cited in Gla]. One should note that instead of symbolizing means of flight, the wings represent protective covering extended over the earth—the influence of this imagery may be seen in Ps. 17:8; 36:7; 57:1; 63:7; 91:4 [Othmar Keel, *The Symbolism of the Biblical World*. Translated by T.J. Hallett. New York: The Seabury Press, 1978; cited in Gla]. If it is true that Malachi drew his image from the winged solar disks of other nations' art, it would still be the case that he then transformed the image's import: whereas the Assyrians (and

Persians as well) used the winged disk to symbolize their imperial might, for Malachi it was a sign of the saving power of God, which would be displayed on the 'Day of the Lord' [NICOT].

3. The image of wings was drawn, not directly from Persian, Egyptian, or Mesopotamian sources, but from a stock of symbolism which had for many centuries been common in all the Near East. In this imagery, the extended wings depict YHWH's protection for his people; their metaphorical association with the sun's rays invoke life-giving warmth, light, and fertility. The Near Eastern association between the sun and righteousness (i.e., right order), seen in Ps. 19:5-11, is also expressed in Mal. 4:2. This association came to involve YHWH when the Israelites identified *El Elyon*, the god of Canaan, with YHWH [G.W. Ahlström, "Some Remarks on Prophets and Cult, " *Essays in Divinity VI; Transitions in Biblical Scholarship* (Chicago: The University of Chicago, 1968); cited in Gla]. The association of YHWH with solar characteristics shows up in OT passages such as Deut. 6:25; Ps. 27:1; Ps. 56:14 [[G.W. Ahlström, *Psalm 89: Eine Liturgie aus dem Ritual des leidenden Königs* (Lund: C.W.K. Gleerup, 1959); cited in Gla].

4. There is no need to posit that Malachi borrowed this imagery from other cultures, as there are other OT passages of figurative similarity enough to inspire him [Mer], although God is rarely if ever explicitly compared to the sun [WBC].

QUESTION—What is the simile in the phrase ויצאתם ופשתם כעגלי מרבק *wîṣāʾtem ûp̄ištem kaʿeḡlê marbēq* 'and you will go out gamboling like calves of the stall'?

1. The simile is 'like calves of the stall' [Keil]. Here a further question arises for some commentators: from where are the people going out? Jerome had answered, from this world. Another answer is from the place in which the people had taken shelter during their sufferings [Keil; S.R. Driver, *The Minor Prophets*. Century Bible. 2 vols. New York: Oxford, 1906; cited in NICOT]. Other commentators ask to where are the people going? Ibn Ezra had answered, to the sun's rays [cited in NICOT]. Von Bulmerincq had answered, to meet righteousness [A. von Bulmerincq, *Der Prophet Maleachi*. Vol. 1 (Dorpat: Matthieseus, 1926; cited in NICOT].

2. The simile is '[you will be] like calves which have gone out from the stall and are gamboling'. The point of comparison is the joy of the people, not the origin or destination of the 'going out' [NICOT]. A secondary point of comparison may reside in the expression *marbēq* 'of the stall': stall-fed cattle were fat, symbolic of prosperity; God's people will become prosperous on the 'Day of the Lord' [Gla].

4:3 (3:21)

(a) And[a]**-you(pl)-will-trample-down**[b] **(the-)wicked,**[c] **for**[d] **they-will-be ashes**[e] **under**[f] **(the-)soles(-of)**[g] **your(pl)-feet**[h]

(b₁) on-the-day[i] **when**[j] **I (will-)act,**[k]
(b₂) on-the-day[i] **which**[j] **I (will-)make**[k]

(c) says YHWH(-of) hosts.

LEXICON—a. -ו *wə-* waw connective attached to the following waw
   consecutive verb (BDB p. 251), (Hol p. 84), (TWOT 519): 'and' [Coh,
   Keil, Gla, WBC; JPS, KJV, NASB, NJB, NRSV]. An additive
   relationship is also expressed by a new sentence [Mer; CEV, NLT,
   REB, TEV]. A sequential relationship is also expressed: 'then' [NICOT;
   NIV].
   b. 2nd mas. pl. Qal perf. *waw* consecutive of עסס *ʿss* (BDB p. 779), (Hol
   p. 279), (TWOT 1660): 'to trample down' [NICOT; NIV], 'to tread
   down' [BDB, Hol; Coh, Keil, Mer, Gla, WBC; KJV, NASB, NRSV,
   REB], 'to tread upon' [NLT], 'to trample' [CEV, NJB], 'to overcome'
   [TEV]. This verb is also translated with a longer phrase: 'to trample to a
   pulp' [JPS].
   c. pl. of רשע *ršʿ* (BDB p. 957), (Hol p. 347), (TWOT 2222b): 'wicked'
   [BDB; Coh, Mer, Gla, NICOT, WBC; JPS, KJV, NASB, NIV, NJB,
   NLT, NRSV, REB, TEV], 'ungodly' [Keil], 'evil' [CEV], 'guilty'
   [Hol].
   d. כי *kî* connective (BDB p. 471), (Hol p. 155), (TWOT 976): 'for' [Coh,
   Keil, Mer, Gla, NICOT, WBC; JPS, KJV, NASB, NRSV, REB], 'and'
   [TEV]. This conjunction is also translated by a relative phrase: 'who will
   be like ashes . . .' [NJB]. Translation not explicit [CEV, NIV, NLT].
   e. אפר *ʾēp̄er* (BDB p. 68), (Hol p. 25), (TWOT 150a): 'ashes' [BDB; Coh,
   Keil, Mer, Gla, NICOT, WBC; KJV, NASB, NIV, NRSV, REB],
   'dust' [JPS, NLT, TEV]. Most translations preserve the metaphor, i.e.,
   'they will be ashes'; the figure of speech is also translated as a simile,
   e.g., 'they will be as ashes' [Gla; CEV, NJB, NLT, REB, TEV]. *ʾēp̄er*
   here is figurative of ignominy [BDB]. Gla holds that the root meaning of
   ʾēp̄er is 'ash'; this meaning seems to fits the context of burning better
   than 'dust' [NICOT], i.e., loose soil, which is thought by Hol to be the
   root meaning of *ʾēp̄er*.
   f. תחת *taḥat* (BDB p. 1065), (Hol p. 389), (TWOT 2504): 'under' [BDB,
   Hol; Coh, Keil, Mer, Gla, WBC; CEV, KJV, NASB, NIV,
   NJB, NLT, NRSV, REB, TEV], 'beneath' [JPS].
   g. pl. constr. of כף *kap̄* (BDB p. 496), (Hol p. 162), (TWOT 1022a):
   'sole' [BDB, Hol; Coh, Keil, Mer, Gla, NICOT; KJV, NASB, NIV,
   NJB, NRSV, REB], not explicit [WBC; CEV, JPS, NLT, TEV].

h. pl. of רֶגֶל *reḡel* (BDB p. 919), (Hol p. 332), (TWOT 2113a): 'foot'
[BDB, Hol; Coh, Keil, Mer, Gla, NICOT, WBC; CEV, JPS, KJV,
NASB, NIV, NJB, NLT, NRSV, REB, TEV].

i. יוֹם *yôm* 'day' (BDB p. 398), (Hol p. 130), (TWOT 852): 'day' [all
lexica, commentators, and versions except CEV]. *Yôm* is also translated
as a time expression 'when' [CEV].

j. אֲשֶׁר *ʾăšer* (BDB p. 81), (Hol p. 30), (TWOT 184): 'which' [Mer;
NASB], 'that' [Coh, Keil, NICOT; JPS, KJV], 'when'—explicit or
implied [Gla, WBC; NIV, NJB, NLT, NRSV, REB, TEV]. *ʾăšer* is a
relative particle.

k. mas. sg. pl. Qal part. of עֹשֶׂה *ʿśh* (BDB p. 793), (Hol p. 284), (TWOT
1708): 'to act' [Gla, WBC; NJB, NLT, NRSV, TEV], 'to make' [BDB;
Coh, NICOT], 'to create' [Keil], 'to prepare' [Mer; JPS, NASB], 'to
take action' [REB], 'to do' [BDB, Hol]. 'On the day that I act' is made
somewhat more explicit: 'in the day that I shall do this' [KJV], 'on the
day when I do these things' [NIV]; and even more explicit: 'when I
come to bring justice' [CEV].

QUESTION—What is the theme of this verse?

It concerns one aspect of the coming 'Day of the Lord': the righteous will
be victorious over the wicked. Here the victory consists of destroying the
wicked [Gla]. Although the OT often presents this motif of the 'Day of the
Lord' as applying to the heathen nations, here the wicked are in fact the
rebellious elements of Israel [NICOT].

QUESTION—Where does the image of crushing the wicked underfoot come
from?

1. Malachi probably derived this image from that of crushing grapes in the
winepress of God, which in the OT gives rise to a number of symbolic
applications: (a) the production of wine as a symbol of Israel's prosperity (Joel 4:18, Amos 9:13); (b) the cup of wine (the punishment)
which God forces the nations to drink (to suffer) (Pss. 60:5; 75:9; Jer.
25:15; 51:7); and (c) the condemnation itself, symbolized by the
winepress's working (Joel 4:13; Isa. 63:2-6; Mal. 4:3) [Gla].

2. This image is probably derived from the triumphal gesture of the
conquering soldier putting his foot on the necks of his prostrate, defeated
enemies (see Josh. 10:24; Isa. 51:23; Ps. 110:1) [NICOT].

QUESTION—What exactly will the righteous people trample on?

They will probably trample only on the ashes of what was once the bodies
of the wicked, for Mal. 3:19 has the wicked being slain and incinerated by
God's fire. Thus the trampling action of the righteous will add only
symbolically to the God's destruction of the wicked [Gla, NICOT].

DISCOURSE UNIT: 4:4–6 (3:22–24) Gla, Mer, NICOT, TOTC; NJB]. The
topic is "restoration through YHWH" [Mer], "Moses and Elijah" [NICOT], a
concluding exhortation [TOTC], appendices [NJB].

QUESTION—What is the relationship of Mal. 4:4-6 (3:22-24) to the rest of the book?

  1. These verses were added later to the book. The form and content of these verses are quite different from that of the rest of the book [WBC, following the majority of twentieth century scholars].

  2. These verses are an integral part of the rest of the book [Clen, Gla, Mer, O'Brien]. Far from assigning the coming messenger of Mal. 3:1—identified in these verse with Elijah—a different role, this passage speaks to the cynicism expressed in Mal. 2:17 and 3:13 and offers the future remedy for it. Similarly, the final verse of this section implies the theme of repentance by giving the strongest possible negative motivation for it. As Mal. 3:1-5 are YHWH's last words to the priests, so this section is his final words to the people at large [Gla]. It is entirely reasonable that Malachi should have ended the book with an earnest appeal for obedience to the Law of Moses, for it is on that obedience that YHWH's promised restoration rests [Mer]. From a hortatory discourse perspective, these verses comprise the final element—one of the change—in the "third movement" [Clen].

QUESTION—If one believes that these verses are a later addition, who added them?

  1. Malachi added them [NICOT, TOTC]. Although written by him, these verses constitute an addendum which is fairly independent of the book's preceding material [NICOT]. They stress the importance of observing the Law of Moses, and they also point ahead to the 'Day of the Lord' [NICOT].

  2. A Jewish scribe or teacher added them in the later, Hellenistic period of Judaism [WBC; J.M.P. Smith, *A Critical and Exegetical Summary on the Book of Malachi*, ICC, Edinburgh: T. & T. Clark, 1912, repr. 1961; cited in Gla]. These verses are not integral to the rest of the book, because they are different from it in many ways: they have no thematic continuity with the preceding material, they do not employ Malachi's pseudo-dialogue style [NICOT], they employ different terminology for the 'Day of the Lord' from the rest of the book (יום יהוה *yôm yhwh* 'the day of YHWH' and יום הגדול והנורה *yôm haggāḏôl wəhannôrā* 'the great and fearsome day' instead of היום הבא *hayyôm habbā* 'the coming day' and היום אשר אני עשה *hayyôm ʾăšer ʾănî ʿōśeh* 'the day on which I will act'), they employ אנכי *ʾānōḵî* 'I' instead of אני *ʾănî* 'I' [J.M.P. Smith, *A Critical and Exegetical Summary on the Book of Malachi*, ICC, Edinburgh: T. & T. Clark, 1912, repr. 1961; cited in Gla; WBC]; in identifying 'my messenger' of Mal. 3:1 with Elijah, Mal. 4:5-6 (33:23-24) gives him a different role, that of turning the hearts of fathers and children [WBC].

QUESTION—If one believes that these verses are a later addition, then what is the relationship among the three verses of Mal. 4:4-6?

1. Mal. 4:4 (3:22) stands as the principal addition, and 4:5-6 (3:23-24) as a secondary addition. Mal. 4:4 is an exhortative summary [WBC; J.M.P. Smith, *A Critical and Exegetical Summary on the Book of Malachi*, ICC, Edinburgh: T. & T. Clark, 1912, repr. 1961; cited in Gla], while Mal. 4:5-6 is a later effort at explaining the reference to 'my messenger' of Mal. 3:1, identifying this figure with Elijah [Rex Mason, *The Books of Haggai, Zechariah and Malachi*. The Cambridge Bible Commentary. Cambridge: Cambridge University Press, 1977; cited in Gla; A. van Hoonacker, *Les douze petits prophètes*. Paris: J. Gabalda & Cie., 1908; cited in Gla; Ernst Sellin and George Fohrer, *Introduction to the Old Testament* (Nashville: Abingdon, 1968; cited in Gla]. Mal. 4:4 was meant as a conclusion to the ensemble of the Minor Prophets [WBC].

2. All three verses were added later to conclude all the prophetic books [Wilhelm Rudolph, *Haggai—Sacharja 1-8—Sacharja 9-14—Maleachi*, KAT (Gütersloh: Verlaghaus Gerd Mohn, 1976; cited in Mer].

3. All three verses were added as appendices, not of the Book of Malachi, but of the Law and the Prophets, which form the first two sections of the Hebrew Bible (the Writings comprise the third and final section), unlike in the LXX and the English versions, where the Prophets come last. The first appendix, then (Mal. 4:4 (3:22)) points the Jewish community back to the Law of Moses, which it is enjoined to follow. The second appendix (Mal. 4:5-6 (3:23-24)) directs attention into the future and emphasizes the ministry of the prophets. The dual appendices are in accord with each other: there is no rivalry between priest and prophet [B.S. Child, "The Canonical Shape of the Prophetic Literature," Int 32 (1978), *Memory and Tradition in Israel*. SBT 37. London: SCM Press, 1962; cited in WBC].

QUESTION— If one believes that these verses are a later addition, then what epoch is represented by these verses?

These verses represent the Hellenistic period among the Jews, for the conflict between older and younger generations is considered to have arisen from the influx of Greek culture, the younger embracing it and the older rejecting it [C.C. Torrey, "The Prophet Malachi", *Journal of Biblical Literature* 17 (1898), cited in Gla]. Moreover, the emphasis on Elijah at the end of the book accords with the almost mythical stature which this prophet's memory achieved in inter-Testamental times in Judaism; his fiery ascent to heaven betokened that he did not really die and was thus destined to return in the hour of need to Israel. There are a number of references to him in the Apocrypha, which are in keeping with the aura of mystery about him [WBC].

DISCOURSE UNIT: 4:4 (3:22) [O'Brien, WBC]. The topic is a final admonition [O'Brien], a first appendix [WBC].

4:4 (3:22)

Remember(pl)[a] **(the-)teaching(-of)**[b] **Moses my-servant**[c] **which/whom**[d] **I-commanded**[e] **him/it at**[f]**-Horeb concerning/in-front-of**[g] **all Israel, (the-)statutes**[h] **and-(the-)rulings.**[i]

VERSE ARRANGEMENT—in the LXX, this verse appears at the very end of Malachi, after Mal. 4:6 (3:24), probably in accordance with the Jewish custom of not ending the public reading of a biblical portion on a gloomy note (Keil); repetitions of verses are made in reading not only Malachi, but also Isaiah, Lamentations, and Ecclesiastes (Coh).

LEXICON—a. mas. pl. Qal imv. of זכר *zkr* (BDB p. 269), (Hol p. 88), (TWOT 551): 'to remember' [BDB, Hol; Coh, Keil, Mer, Gla, NICOT, WBC; KJV, NASB, NIV, NJB, NLT, NRSV, REB, TEV], 'to be mindful of' [JPS], 'to never forget' [CEV]. *Zkr* 'to remember' in the OT always implies action as well as mental activity: the sin which YHWH does not remember does not in fact exist any more (Ps. 88:8) [B.S. Child, "The Canonical Shape of the Prophetic Literature," Int 32 (1978), *Memory and Tradition in Israel*. SBT 37. London: SCM Press, 1962; cited in WBC]. Often in the OT *zkr* occurs with 'to do' or 'to keep' (NICOT); here, the command to remember the Law of Moses comes not for the sake of a mental exercise, but to revive and strengthen the covenantal bonds between Israel and YHWH [NICOT; Gla, WBC]. To remember God is to be loyal to him [Johannes Pedersen, *Israel: Its Life and Culture* (4 vols.; London: Oxford University, 1973); cited in Gla)]

b. constr. of תורה *tôrâ* (BDB p. 435), (Hol p. 388), (TWOT 910d): 'teaching' [JPS, NRSV, TEV], 'law' [BDB, Hol; Coh, Keil, Mer, Gla, NICOT; KJV, NASB, NIV, NJB, REB], 'instruction' [BDB, Hol; NLT], 'direction' [BDB]. CEV conflates *tôrâ* 'teaching', חק *ḥōq* 'decree', and משפט *mišpāṭ* 'legal specifications' into 'laws and teaching'. WBC uses the anglicized Hebrew word: 'Torah'. The primary sense of *tôrâ* is 'instruction'; 'law' is a derived secondary sense [BDB, Hol].

c. constr. of עבד *ʿebed* (BDB p. 713), (Hol p. 262), (TWOT 1553a): 'servant' [all lexica, commentators, and versions].

d. אשר *ʾăšer* (BDB p. 81), (Hol p. 30), (TWOT 184): 'which' (referring to 'law') [Coh, Keil, Mer, WBC; KJV, NASB], 'whom' (referring to Moses) [Gla], not explicit [NICOT; CEV, JPS, NIV, NJB, NLT, NRSV, REB, TEV]. *ʾăšer* is a relative particle.

e. 1st sg. Piel perf. of צוה *ṣwh* (BDB p. 845), (Hol p. 304), (TWOT 1887): 'to command' [BDB; Coh, Keil, Mer, Gla, NICOT, WBC; KJV, NASB, NRSV], 'to charge' [BDB, JPS], 'to prescribe' [NJB], 'to tell one to deliver' [REB], 'to order' [Hol], 'to give' [CEV, NIV, NLT, TEV].

f. -ב *bə-* (BDB p. 88), (Hol p. 32), (TWOT 193): 'at' [Mer, Gla, NICOT; JPS, NIV, NJB, REB, TEV], 'on' [BDB, Hol; all commentators and

versions except the following], 'in' [Coh; KJV, NASB], 'upon' [Keil].
The proclitic bə- denotes here locality [BDB, Hol].

g. עַל ʿal (BDB p. 752), (Hol p. 272), (TWOT 1624p): 'concerning' [BDB,
Hol; WBC], 'for' [Coh, Keil, Mer, Gla, NICOT; JPS, KJV, NASB,
NIV, NJB, NLT, NRSV], 'to' [REB], 'in front of' [Hol], not explicit
[CEV]. TEV makes explicit its understanding of destination: 'for all the
people of Israel to obey'.

h. pl. of חֹק ḥōq (BDB p. 349), (Hol p. 114), (TWOT 728a): 'statute'
[Coh, Keil, Mer, Gla, WBC; KJV, NASB, NRSV], 'law' [JPS, NLT,
TEV], 'decree' [BDB; NICOT; NIV, NJB], 'rule' [Hol; REB],
'enactment' (BDB). The plural, ḥuqqîm, normally refers to the
established laws in Israel (Gla).

i. pl. of מִשְׁפָּט mišpāṭ (BDB p. 1048), (Hol p. 221), (TWOT 2443c):
'ruling' [NJB], 'rule' [JPS], 'judgment' [KJV], 'ordinance' [BDB; Coh,
Mer, Gla, NICOT, WBC; NASB, NRSV], 'law' [NIV], 'regulation'
[NLT], 'precept' [REB], 'command' [TEV], 'right' [Keil], 'legal
decision' [Hol]. The plural, mišpāṭîm, normally refers to the body of
established legal precedents [TOTC]; their objective is to maintain the
covenantal order imposed by YHWH [Gla]. They often impose
obligations upon the persons concerned, doing so as a result of the more
basic ḥuqqîm 'statutes' [Johannes Pedersen, *Israel Its Life and Culture* (4
vols.; London: Oxford University, 1973); cited in Gla]. The phrase
חֻקִּים וּמִשְׁפָּטִים ḥuqqîm ûmišpāṭîm 'the statutes and ordinances' is a
general expression for the Law of Moses (see Lev. 26:46; Deut. 4:1,5;
Ezra 7:10,11) [TOTC].

QUESTION—What is the significance of this verse?

1. This verse begins the closing of the book; here, Malachi is concerned to
summarize the people's covenantal obligations, especially in the light of
the coming 'Day of the Lord'. The injunction to follow all the teachings
of Moses comes in stark contrast to Mal. 3:7, in which God plainly
states that for generations, Israel has been in rebellion against him
[Keil]. In other words, this verse is the climax of Malachi's prophecy;
here he insists on the primal importance of community loyalty to YHWH
through the Sinaitic covenant [Gla].

2. The terminology of this verse is that of the Deuteronomic documents
[WBC].

QUESTION—What is 'Horeb'?

It is another name for Mt. Sinai, where God gave the Law to Moses for
Israel [Coh].

QUESTION—What is the referent of the relative particle אֲשֶׁר ʾăšer ?

1. The referent is תּוֹרַת מֹשֶׁה tôraṯ mōšeh 'instruction/law of Moses'
[Vulgate; cited in NICOT; also J.M.P. Smith, *A Critical and Exegetical
Summary on the Book of Malachi*, ICC, Edinburgh: T. & T. Clark,
1912, repr. 1961; cited in Gla. This view is supported by Coh, Keil,
Mer, WBC; KJV]. In this perspective, the 3rd sg. pronoun concluding

the form אותו *ʾôtô* refers to Moses. The relative particle *ʾăšer* would not be expected to refer to Moses, since the focus of this passage is not upon him, but rather upon the *tôrâ* 'instruction/law' [Keil].

2. The referent is משה *mōšeh* 'Moses'. In this perspective, the 3rd sg. prn. concluding the form אותו *ʾôtô* serves as a redundant reference to 'instruction'. Other examples of צוה *ṣwh* 'to command' with a double accusative occur in the OT, e.g., in 1 Chr. 22:13 [A. von Bulmerincq, *Der Prophet Maleachi*. Vol. 2. Tartu: J.G. Krüger, 1926–1932; cited in Gla].

QUESTION—What is meant by the תורת משה *tôraṯ mōšeh* 'instruction/law of Moses' in this passage?

1. It is the Pentateuch [K. Marti, *Das Dodekapropheton*. KHC 13. Tübingen: Mohr, 1904; cited in NICOT]. *Tôraṯ mōšeh* meant at first the ensemble of obligations assumed by Israel when it received the Sinaitic covenant; later the phrase came to mean the Pentateuch [TOTC].

2. It is Deuteronomony [J. Wellhausen, *Die kleinen Propheten übersetz und erklärt*. 4th ed. Berlin: De Gruyter, 1963; cited in NICOT].

3. It is the book of law which Ezra brought when he came to Jerusalem (see Ezra 7:6) [A. von Bulmerincq, *Der Prophet Maleachi*. Vol. 2. Tartu: J.G. Krüger, 1926–1932; cited in Gla].

4. It is impossible to say all that 'law of Moses' included in this reference of Malachi, but its context is certainly the Sinaitic covenant [NICOT].

QUESTION—What is the significance of the construct relationship between תורה *tôrâ* 'instruction/law' and משה *mōšeh* 'Moses'?

It refers to Moses' mediating the law between God and the Israelites [Gla].

QUESTION—What is meant by כל־ישראל *kol yiśrāʾēl* 'all Israel'?

This phrase means the entire community of Israel, even those Israelites who might not have been present at the giving of the law in Deut. 29, and including all future descendants of the community; for the community, comprised of all its members and for all time, is bound by the covenant [Gla].

DISCOURSE UNIT: 4:5–6 (3:23–24) [O'Brien, WBC]. The topic is the final ultimatum [O'Brien], a second appendix [WBC].

4:5 (3:23)
Behold,[a] **I will-send**[b] **to-you(pl) Elijah**[c] **the-prophet**[d] **before**[e] **(the-)coming(-of)**[f] **(the-)day(-of)**[g] **YHWH, the-great**[h] **and-the-fearful**[i] **(day).**
LEXICON—a. הנה *hinnēh* (BDB p. 243), (Hol p. 82), (TWOT 510a): 'behold' [BDB, Hol; Coh, Keil, Mer, NICOT, WBC; KJV, NASB], 'lo' [JPS, NRSV], 'see' [NIV], 'look' [NJB, NLT, REB], not explicit [Gla; CEV, TEV]. *Hinnēh* is a demonstrative interjection or particle [BDB, Hol] and can emphasize the whole clause which it begins [Hol].

b. mas. sg. Qal part. of שלח *šlḥ* (BDB p. 1018), (Hol. p. 371), (TWOT 2394): 'to send' [BDB, Hol; Coh, Keil, Mer, Gla, NICOT, WBC;

CEV, JPS, KJV, NASB, NIV, NJB, NLT, NRSV, REB, TEV]. Most
translations employ the English future tense, e.g., 'I will send'; some
employ the present progressive: 'to be sending' [NLT], and some
express imminent future, e.g., 'to be about to send' [Mer, Gla; NASB].

c. אליה ʾēliyyâ (BDB p. 45), (Hol p. 17): 'Elijah' [all lexica, commentators, and versions]. ʾēliyyâ is short for אליהו ʾēliyyāhû 'Elijah'.

d. נביא nāḇîʾ (BDB p. 611), (Hol p. 225), (TWOT 1277a): 'prophet' [all
lexica, commentators, and versions].

e. לפני lip̄nê (BDB p. 815), (Hol p. 293), (TWOT 1782b): 'before'
(temporal) [all lexica, commentators, and versions]. The compound
preposition lip̄nê is formally composed of the proclitic -ל lə- plus the
construct of פנים pānîm 'face'.

f. mas. sg. Qal perf. of בוא bôʾ (BDB p. 97), (Hol p. 34), (TWOT 212):
'to come' [all lexica, commentators, and versions except NLT], 'to
arrive' [NLT].

g. const. of יום yôm 'day' (BDB p. 398), (Hol p. 130), (TWOT 852): 'day'
[all lexica, commentators, and versions]. The construct relationship
between 'day' and YHWH 'Lord' is most often expressed by the
preposition 'of'.

h. גדול gāḏôl (BDB p. 152), (Hol p. 55), (TWOT 315d): 'great' [all
lexica, commentators, and versions except JPS], 'awesome' [JPS].

i. mas sg. Niphal part. of ירא yrʾ (BDB p. 431), (Hol p. 142), (TWOT
907): 'fearful' [BDB, Hol; JPS], 'terrible' [Coh, Keil, Mer, Gla,
NICOT, WBC; CEV, NASB, NRSV, REB, TEV], 'dreadful' [BDB;
KJV, NIV, NLT], 'awesome' [NJB].

QUESTION—What is the discourse role of this verse?

This verse gives the reason for the preceding verse: the Israelites are to
remember and obey the covenant with YHWH because he will soon send
Elijah the prophet [Clen].

QUESTION—What is the 'the great and fearful day of YHWH'?

It is the same as יום בואו yôm bôʾô 'the day of his coming' (Mal. 3:2), as
יום אשר אני עשה yôm ʾăšer ʾănî ʿōśeh 'the day on which I will act' (Mal.
3:17), and as היום הבא hayyôm habbāʾ 'the coming day' (Mal. 4:1
(3:19)), i.e., the 'day of the Lord' [Gla].

QUESTION—What is the significance of the reference to Elijah?

This reference is in keeping with calling Mt. Sinai by its other name,
Horeb, for God revealed himself to Elijah on Horeb, as he did to the
Israelites at Sinai. Moreover, Elijah turned around the course of the nation;
he was an heroic figure like Moses. But his ministry has a future nuance to
it, as his mysterious departure to heaven gave rise to the idea among the
Jewish people that, not having actually died, he would one day return
(TOTC). Hence the question raised by later Jews as to whether John the
Baptist was Elijah returned to earth [Mer].

QUESTION—To whom does הנביא אליה *ʾēliyyâ hannābîʾ* 'Elijah the prophet' refer?

  1. It refers to the great prophet Elijah the Tishbite, who will actually return in the end times [LXX; Jews in the time of Christ (see Matt. 17:10 and John 1:21); Jewish commentators and Church fathers].

  2. It refers to someone similar to the prophet Elijah in purpose and in power [Keil, Mer, NICOT]. There are other connections as well between the prophetic figure of this passage and Elijah, who was prominent in his lifetime for his faithfulness to YHWH when the whole prophetic milieu was oriented toward pagan gods, and whose ministry was validated by extraordinary miracles [Gla]. The reference to Moses and Elijah in this passage, attesting to both the law and the prophets, also points out that these figures constitute two witnesses to the truth of the coming 'Day of the Lord', as required by Jewish law in a court case [Mer]. The identity of *ʾēliyyâ hannābîʾ* is made clear by Jesus, who applied it to the figure of John the Baptist (Matt. 17:10–13) [Mer, NICOT]. This identification is at face value, however, contradicted by the Baptist's own words, 'I am not Elijah' (John 1:21). To resolve this problem, J.A.T. Robinson supposes that John considered Jesus to be the man of fire, not himself [J.A.T. Robinson, *Twelve New Testament Studies* (SCM Press, 1962); cited in TOTC]. Alternatively, one might resolve the problem by assuming that in his statement, John meant to say that he was not Elijah personally returned from heaven; he did, however, certainly consider himself the forerunner of the Christ, as he quoted Isa. 40:3 with reference to himself (John 1:23) [Keil].

QUESTION—What relation does הנביא אליה *ʾēliyyâ hannābîʾ* 'Elijah the prophet' have to the word מלאכי *malʾākî* 'my messenger' and מלאך הברית *malʾāk habbərît* 'the messenger of the covenant' of Mal. 3:1?

  1. The messenger of Mal. 3:1 is John the Baptist, who will announce Jesus' first coming; 'Elijah the prophet' of Mal. 4:5 is the forerunner who will announce Christ's second coming and work to convert the Jews to Christ [most traditional Roman Catholic commentators; cited in NICOT].

  2. *ʾēliyyâ hannābîʾ* 'Elijah the prophet' is identical to *malʾākî* 'my messenger' of Mal. 3:1, but distinct from *malʾāk habbərît* 'the messenger of the covenant' [most Protestant scholars; cited in NICOT]. The descriptions and roles of *malʾākî* of Mal. 3:1 and of *ʾēliyyâ hannābîʾ* of this verse are very similar: they are sent by YHWH, they will arrive very soon, and they will prepare the people for YHWH's coming [Gla].

  3. *ʾēliyyâ hannābîʾ* is identical to both *malʾākî* 'my messenger' and *malʾāk habbərît* 'the messenger of the covenant' of Mal. 3:1. For this reason, the figure of Elijah must be seen as having a role to play in announcing not only the first coming of Christ, but also his second coming, as is suggested also by Mal. 4:5 (3:23), where Elijah is referred to just before the 'Day of the Lord' [Mer].

4:6 (3:24)
And[a]-he-will-turn[b] (the-)heart(-of)[c] (the-)fathers[d] to[e] (their-)children,[f]
and[g]-(the-)heart(-of) (the-)children to (their-)fathers, lest[h] I-come[i] and[j]-
strike[k] the-land[l] (with-a-)ban.[m]

SYNTAX—The preposition עַל *ᶜal* 'to, towards' may be interpreted in the
   sense of accompaniment, so that the phrase 'and he will turn the fathers'
   heart to that of their children and the children's hearts to that of their
   fathers' is understood by some as 'and he will turn the fathers' heart with
   that of their children (to me)' [Gla].

LEXICON—a. -וְ *wə- waw* connective attached to the following *waw* consecutive verb (BDB p. 251), (Hol p. 84), (TWOT 519): 'and' [Coh, Keil,
   Gla, WBC; KJV, NASB]. An additive relationship is also expressed with
   a new sentence [Mer, NICOT; CEV, JPS, NIV, NJB, NLT, NRSV,
   REB, TEV].

   b. 3rd mas. sg. Hiphil perf. *waw* consecutive of שׁוּב *šûḇ* (BDB p. 996),
   (Hol p. 362), (TWOT 2340): 'to turn' [Coh, Keil, Mer, Gla, NICOT,
   WBC; KJV, NIV, NLT, NRSV], 'to reconcile' [JPS, NJB, REB], 'to
   bring together' [TEV], 'to bring back' [BDB, Hol], 'to restore' [NASB].

   c. constr. of לֵב *lēḇ* (BDB p. 524), (Hol p. 171), (TWOT 1071a): 'heart'
   [BDB; Coh, Keil, Mer, Gla, NICOT, WBC; KJV, NASB, NIV, NLT,
   NRSV], 'mind' [BDB, Hol], 'loyalty' [Hol]. The phrase 'to turn the
   heart of the fathers to the children, etc.' is rendered less figuratively by
   some: 'to lead children and parents to love each other more' [CEV], 'to
   bring fathers and children together' [TEV], and using the verb 'to
   reconcile', e.g., 'to reconcile parents with children' [JPS, NJB, REB].

   d. pl. of אָב *ʾāḇ* (BDB p. 3), (Hol p. 1), (TWOT 4a): 'father' [BDB, Hol;
   Coh, Keil, Mer, Gla, NICOT, WBC; KJV, NASB, NIV, TEV],
   'parent' [CEV, JPS, NJB, NLT, NRSV, REB].

   e. עַל *ᶜal* (BDB p. 752), (Hol p. 272), (TWOT 1624p): 'to/unto' [BDB;
   Coh, Keil, NICOT, WBC; KJV, NASB, NIV, NJB, NLT, NRSV,
   REB], 'toward' [BDB; Mer]. Some translations interpret *ᶜal* as more or
   less coordinative: 'together with' (where fathers and children together
   turn in repentance to God) [Gla].

   f. pl. of בֵּן *bēn* (BDB p. 119), (Hol p. 42), (TWOT 254): 'child' [Coh,
   Mer, Gla, NICOT, WBC; CEV, KJV, NASB, NIV, NJB, NLT,
   REB, TEV], 'son' [Keil]. בָּנִים *bānîm*, the plural of *bēn*, can refer to
   both sons and daughters [BDB, Hol].

   g. -וְ *wə- waw* connective (BDB p. 251), (Hol p. 84), (TWOT 519): 'and'
   [Coh, Keil, Mer, Gla, WBC; JPS, KJV, NASB, NJB, NLT, NRSV,
   NRSV, REB].

   h. פֶּן *pen* (BDB p. 814), (Hol p. 293), (TWOT 1780): 'lest' [all lexica,
   commentators, and versions except the following], 'that . . . not' [Keil],
   'so that . . . not' [Gla; CEV, JPS, NRSV], 'or else' [NICOT; NIV],
   'otherwise' [NLT, TEV]. This conjunction is also translated with a verb

phrase: 'to forestall' [NJB]. The conjunction *pen* denotes negative purpose.

i. 1st sg. Qal imperf. of בוא *bôʾ* (BDB p. 97), (Hol p. 34), (TWOT 212): 'to come' [all lexica, commentators, and versions except NJB], not explicit [NJB].

j. -ו *wə-* *waw* connective (BDB p. 251), (Hol p. 84), (TWOT 519): 'and' [all commentators and versions except the following]. Sometimes the phrase "lest I come and strike" is rendered with a circumstantial clause, e.g., 'so that, when I come, I do not strike' [Gla; CEV, JPS]. Translation not explicit [NJB].

k. 3rd mas. sg. Hiphil *waw*-consecutive perfect of נכה *nkh* (BDB p. 644), (Hol p. 237), (TWOT 1364): 'to strike' [Hol; NICOT; JPS, NIV, NLT, NRSV], 'to smite' [BDB; all commentators and versions except the following], 'to bring' [CEV], 'to put under' [NJB, REB]. The phrase 'to strike with a ban' is translated 'to destroy' [TEV].

l. ארץ *ʾereṣ* (BDB p. 76), (Hol p. 28), (TWOT 167): 'land' [all lexica, commentators, and versions except the following], 'whole land' [JPS], 'country' [BDB; NJB, TEV], 'earth' [KJV].

m. חרם *ḥērem* (BDB p. 356), (Hol p. 117), (TWOT 744a): 'ban' [BDB, Hol; NICOT, WBC], 'curse' [Keil, Mer; KJV, NASB, NIV, NLT, NRSV], 'a ban to destroy' [REB], 'doom' [CEV]. This noun is also translated with a noun phrase: 'utter destruction' [Coh], 'ban of destruction' [Gla], 'curse of destruction' [NJB], 'utter destruction' [JPS]. *Ḥērem* refers to goods captured in warfare and reserved for YHWH or allotted for destruction [Hol]. To strike the land with a ban is to destroy it completely [BDB].

QUESTION—What is the meaning of והשיב לב־אבות על־בנים ולב בנים על־אבותם *wəhēšîb lēb ʾābôt ʿal bānîm wəlēb bānîm ʿal ʾăbôṯām* 'and he will turn the heart of the fathers to the children, and the hearts of the children to the fathers'?

1. It is that Elijah will bring reconciliation to families which were torn apart by bitterness occasioned when fathers divorced their wives in order to marry pagan women. This reconciliation will be part of the program of the renewal of society envisioned in Near Eastern eschatology [A. Jeremias, *Babylonisches im Neuen Testament* (Leipzig: Hinrichs, 1905); cited in NICOT].

2. This phrase is a metaphor for the healing of all ruptured relationships within families and within society [Mer]. Similarly, TOTC sees the family as a microcosm of society, a workshop where all that is needed to be learned about covenantal relationships can be taught.

3. It is that, as Elijah restores the covenant between YHWH and Israel, one effect will be the reconciliation of fathers and children. The emphasis of this viewpoint is on the restored covenant and the annulment of punishments arising from the fractured covenantal relationship (e.g., the isolation of the guilty ones from the community of Israel in Mal. 2:21).

This interpretation views *wəhēšîb* 'and he will turn' as part of the classic vocabulary of repentance (from *šûb* 'to turn') [NICOT].

QUESTION—What is the significance of והשׁיב *wəhēšîb* 'and he will turn'?

This verb indicates that God himself will initiate the action of repentance in his people [NICOT].

QUESTION—What was the fulfillment of the prophecy concerning the coming of Elijah?

The fulfillment of this prophecy is referred to by the angel Gabriel in announcing the impending birth of John the Baptist: 'and he will go on before the Lord, in the spirit and power of Elijah, to turn the hearts of the fathers to their children and the disobedient to the wisdom of the righteous—to make ready a people prepared for the Lord' (Luke 1:16–17). Here the phrase 'and the disobedient to the wisdom of the righteous' is added by way of explanation. Christ himself identifies John the Baptist with Elijah in Matt. 11:10ff; Luke 7:27ff; Matt. 17:11ff and Mark 9:11ff [Keil].

QUESTION—What is the relationship between the two verbs אבוא *ʾābô* 'I will come' and והכיתי *wəhikkêtî* 'I will strike'?

The coming of YHWH is sure; what is not yet certain is whether he will strike the land with a ban [NICOT, Gla]. For that reason, *ʾābô* should be translated 'when I come' [Gla].

QUESTION—What is the meaning of חרם *ḥērem* 'ban'?

Ḥērem refers to something or someone reserved either for total destruction or for use in worshipping YHWH. Here the meaning is certainly the former [Mer, NICOT]. *Ḥērem*, in the sense of something reserved for destruction, is such because it is so foreign in nature to YHWH's covenant community that it cannot be redeemed or adapted; it must be destroyed, for it cannot be made to fit into the Israelite world or mentality [Johannes Pedersen, *Israel: Its Life and Culture* (4 vols.; London: Oxford University, 1973); cited in Gla]. To be made *ḥērem* is to be cursed in the strongest possible fashion [Roland de Vaux, *Ancient Israel* (2 vols.; New York: McGraw-Hill, 1965); cited in Gla].

QUESTION—What is the significance of הארץ *hāʾāreṣ* 'the land' as the object of a ban?

Some scholars and translators (including the KJV) in the past have taken *hāʾāreṣ* here to mean the earth, but it clearly signifies the land which was given by YHWH to his covenant community of Israel. This land is seen as the context for the people to live out their covenantal relationship to him (see Deut. 4:5, 14; 5:31; 6:1; 11:31f; 12:1). If the people are faithful, the land will benefit (see Deut. 28:2–14; Pss. 65:10–14; 72:3; Joel 4:18), but in the case of unfaithfulness, the land will suffer (see Lev. 26:32f). Most likely, then, 'the land' in this passage is a figure of speech, standing not only for the land itself, but also for the people of Israel, whom it supports [A. von Bulmerincq, *Der Prophet Maleachi*. Vol. 2. Tartu: J.G. Krüger, 1926–1932; cited in Gla; NICOT].

QUESTION—What is the significance of פֶּן־אָבוֹא וְהִכֵּיתִי אֶת־הָאָרֶץ חֵרֶם
pen ʾābôʾ wəhikkêtî ʾet hāʾāreṣ ḥērem 'lest I come and strike the land with a ban'?

It is that very possibly the prophetic ministry in Israel will not attain its objective, that the community will not return to the covenantal relationship with YHWH. In that case, the land will come under a ban [NICOT]. Unlike the mass, indiscriminate destruction which is often associated with *ḥērem* 'ban' in the OT, it would seem that, in fact, the faithful element of YHWH's people will be spared, if one compares this passage with Mal. 3:1-5; 3:13-21, and 4: 5-6 (3:23-24) [Gla]. The difference between this threat and the earlier threats of destruction in Malachi is that this final threat will not be revocable on the 'Day of the Lord'—there will be no more opportunity for repentance [Gla].